EXPERTISE IN COUNSELING AND PSYCHOTHERAPY

Expertise in Counseling and Psychotherapy

MASTER THERAPIST STUDIES FROM AROUND THE WORLD

Edited by Len Jennings
and Thomas M. Skovholt

OXFORD
UNIVERSITY PRESS

OXFORD
UNIVERSITY PRESS

Oxford University Press is a department of the University of Oxford. It furthers the University's objective of excellence in research, scholarship, and education by publishing worldwide. Oxford is a registered trade mark of Oxford University Press in the UK and certain other countries.

Published in the United States of America by Oxford University Press
198 Madison Avenue, New York, NY 10016, United States of America.

CIP data is on file at the Library of Congress
ISBN 978–0–19–022250–5

To my family, Karrie, Tristan, Emma, and Keaton. You mean the world to me.

Len Jennings

To my grandparents, Anna and Julius Skovholt and Bertha and Fred Meyer, who suffered and sacrificed, bridging languages and cultures, to offer promise and hope to their children and grandchildren.

Tom Skovholt

To the 72 master therapists from around the world. Thank you for your meaningful work and willingness to share your wisdom with us as well as with practitioners and students throughout the world.

Len Jennings and Tom Skovholt

Contents

Foreword

Clara E. Hill

I AM DELIGHTED to write the foreword for this important book on master therapists. The qualitative meta-analysis of interviews in seven studies with a total of 72 master therapists from around the world provides incredibly rich data about how these therapists think about themselves and their work. In my opinion, there is a high degree of trustworthiness in the seven studies and the meta-analysis. The procedures are well documented, the writing is clear, the themes are well supported by the quotations, the results make sense, and the authors have described their biases and done a good job of bracketing them.

WHAT DID WE LEARN?

We learned that there are eight consistent themes in what therapists from around the world say about themselves and their work. These themes make sense and provide valuable stimulus for selection and training of therapists. I particularly love and have remembered since I first read the Jennings and Skovholt (1999) study the theme that therapists are voracious learners: They continually want to learn new things and apply their learning to clients. I also like the theme of humility: These therapists are not arrogant but, rather, are very aware of how much they do not know, how complicated human beings are, and how much there is to learn. I also particularly like the theme of cognitive complexity because it does seem that one of the major skills students learn as they become therapists is to be curious and think more deeply and thoughtfully about clients. In addition to listening carefully to presenting problems, they begin to observe nonverbal behaviors, think about family dynamics, ask about physical health concerns, wonder about existential issues, and include culture and social justice in their conceptualizations.

The theoretical work of placing these eight overlapping themes into three meta-domains (learning, therapy, and humility) and then postulating about the links between the themes (complexity leads to humility leads to development) provides exciting thinking about how therapists develop. I might not develop exactly the same meta-domains or links (although I cannot know this for sure without immersing myself in the data), but this theorizing leads to exciting avenues that can be tested further to determine which models can be supported, which can lead to further model development. However, having a model from which to work is crucial at this stage of development of the science of understanding master therapists.

We also learned that therapists from seven different countries share much common thinking. Hence, despite differences in culture, training, and theoretical orientation, a good therapist may be remarkably similar in different countries. It would be interesting to extend these findings to determine whether therapists use similar interventions in sessions with clients and whether clients have comparable outcomes.

In addition, we learned that not everything was the same across samples, suggesting the influence of culture. Having a mentor was stressed in Japan and Korea; subtlety of communication in Japan; and spirituality, diversity, and self-doubt in Singapore. These cultural differences are fascinating and leave me wanting to know more about the meanings of psychotherapy in different countries.

Furthermore, the ability to synthesize results across seven qualitative studies is exciting and an advancement in qualitative research. Rarely have researchers replicated results using similar interview protocols and careful analysis. Given our previous findings (Ladany, Thompson, & Hill, 2012) about differences found when two similarly trained teams of judges analyzed the same data set, it is impressive that such consistency was found, perhaps because of the robustness of the phenomenon and the use of similar interview protocols across countries.

WHAT ARE THE LIMITATIONS THAT NEED TO BE CONSIDERED IN INTERPRETING THE RESULTS?

No research is perfect. All research is conducted by human beings, who are inherently flawed and biased. Also, all research methods have positive and negative aspects. To understand the results of any given study or body of research, we need to think carefully about the constraints that our assumptions and methods place on what we have learned. Therefore, in this space I try to place this work in some context so that readers can have a perspective on the constraints of this analysis and the take-home messages of what we learned. It is hoped that such an analysis will help in planning future research on this important topic.

The data represent conscious thoughts that the therapists were aware of and willing to share with interviewers. The participants may not have been consciously aware of other factors (e.g., darker, neurotic reasons for being a therapist), and they might have been influenced by social desirability in terms of wanting to present themselves in a positive way (it is flattering yet demanding to think of oneself as a master therapist).

We can assume that the nomination procedure yielded therapists who were highly reputed. However, it is less clear that these therapists were necessarily expert or master therapists. There is much controversy in the field about how to define and identify expertise (Tracey, Wampold, Lichtenberg, & Goodyear, 2014), with some (Shanteau, 1992; Tracey et al., 2014) claiming that there is no evidence of the development of expertise in psychotherapy because it is not possible to define expertise due to the lack of predictability of outcomes and the lack of availability of adequate feedback. In terms of criteria, reputation is generally considered to be a relatively weak criterion of expertise because of the lack of evidence of what reputation is based on (Tracey, Wampold, Goodyear, & Lichtenberg, 2015). At a minimum, it seems like we need evidence that these master therapists differed from bad therapists at the same level of experience to claim that they were expert or competent.

We also have no evidence that these therapists differed from novice therapists. Most definitions of expertise include the notion of increased quality of performance with experience (Shanteau, 1992; Tracey et al., 2014). I certainly know many novice therapists who are voracious learners, spend a great deal of time and effort in pursuing deep self-knowledge, are relationally oriented, have distinct clinical abilities, believe in the therapeutic alliance, and are humble. I would venture a guess that what distinguishes novice and expert therapists is performance (relational expertise and interventions expertise), cognitive complexity, reputation, personality, and experience. So it seems important to distinguish characteristics that are specific to experts from traits that apply to all therapists of all levels of experience.

These comments are not meant to diminish the findings but, rather, to frame them so that readers are aware of what exactly we have learned and what remains to be learned. This meta-analysis is a major contribution and yields exciting data to build upon.

WHAT IS MISSING OR SURPRISING?

I was surprised that there were not more differences across cultures. When I have traveled to different countries to give talks and when I have worked with students from other countries, I have learned much about how psychotherapy differs. For example, being directive takes on very different aspects in Asia than in the United States (Duan et al., 2012, 2015). In the United States, we tend to think of giving homework and following up in a cognitive behavioral therapy way to make sure clients have done the homework. In China, by contrast, therapists have more of a teacher and wise mentor role; they may give philosophical suggestions but would not necessarily assign specific homework or follow up to determine if homework was done.

I was also surprised that master therapists did not report themselves to be mindful, centered, present, or more peaceful. It seems to me that all the deep reflection and time spent working with clients would give therapists a sense of calmness. Perhaps they were not aware of or did not value this characteristic?

I wondered why Singaporean therapists were the only ones who expressed self-doubt. Self-doubt is certainly something I feel a lot as a therapist, given the complicated therapeutic process. Are therapists of other cultures calling this by a different term? Is this something specific to Singaporean therapists or to Asian culture? If it is Asian culture, why did Japanese therapists not endorse it?

FUTURE RESEARCH

We very much need to develop other ways for identifying competent, expert, master therapists other than just by nomination or reputation. This need is discussed in the Future Research section in Chapter 8.

In Chapter 8, the authors also discuss implications for training. From my perspective, however, it might be premature to provide implications for training. I think we need far more work differentiating novice and master therapists, and examining longitudinal changes as a result of training (Hill et al., 2015; Hilsenroth, Kivlighan, & Slavin-Mulford, 2015), before we derive such implications. Again, we need to know that expert, master therapists differ from novice therapists and that training makes a difference before we assert implications for training. Otherwise, it might be that people with natural therapeutic ability (Stahl & Hill, 2008) just are the best therapists from the start, and that it is a matter of selection rather than training.

CONCLUSIONS

At a recent conference, researchers lamented about how we generally have a lack of replication of findings in psychology. This body of work thus represents an excellent example of replicated findings and it serves as a basis for additional research about therapist competence and expertise. We can build on these findings to develop new research projects to learn more about how therapists grow and develop and how that facilitates them in helping clients. I applaud the authors for this ambitious and thoughtful project.

REFERENCES

Duan, C., Hill, C. E., Jiang, G., Hu, B., Chui, H., Hui, K., . . . Yu, L. (2012). Therapist directives: Use and outcomes in China. *Psychotherapy Research*, *22*, 442–457.

Duan, C., Hill, C. E., Jiang, G., Hu, B., Lei, Y., Chen, J., & Yu, L. (2015). The counselor perspective on the use of directives in counseling in China: Are directives different in China as in the United States? *Counselling Psychology Quarterly*, *28*, 55–77.

Hill, C. E., Baumann, E., Shafran, N., Gupta, S., Morrison, A., Peres Rojas, A., . . . Gelso, C. J. (2015). Is training effective? A study of counseling psychology doctoral trainees in a psychodynamic/interpersonal training clinic. *Journal of Counseling Psychology, 62*, 184–201.

Hilsenroth, M. J., Kivlighan, D. M., Jr., & Slavin-Mulford, J. (2015). Structured supervision of graduate clinicians in psychodynamic psychotherapy: Alliance and technique. *Journal of Counseling Psychology, 62*, 173–183.

Jennings, L., & Skovholt, T. M. (1999). The cognitive, emotional, and relational characteristics of master therapists. *Journal of Counseling Psychology, 46*, 3–11.

Ladany, N., Thompson, B. J., & Hill, C. E. (2012). Cross analysis. In C. E. Hill (Ed.), *Consensual qualitative research: A practical resource for investigating social science phenomena* (pp. 117–134). Washington, DC: American Psychological Association.

Shanteau, J. (1992). Competence in experts: The role of task characteristics. *Organizational Behavior and Human Decision Processes, 53*, 252-266. DOI: 10.1037/a0037874

Stahl, J., & Hill, C. E. (2008). A comparison of four methods for assessing natural helpers. *Journal of Community Psychology, 64*, 289–298.

Tracey, T. J. G., Wampold, B. E., Goodyear, R. K., & Lichtenberg, J. W. (2015). Improving expertise in psychotherapy. Psychotherapy Bulletin, 50(1), 7–13.

Tracy, T. J. G., Wampold, B. E., Lichtenberg, J. W., & Goodyear, R. K. (2014). Expertise in psychotherapy: An elusive goal? *American Psychologist, 3*, 218–339.

Free Access to *Master Therapists*

IN THE AWARD-WINNING BOOK, *Master Therapists: Exploring Expertise in Therapy and Counseling*, Tom Skovholt and Len Jennings were the first to apply qualitative methodology to the study of validly selected expert therapists. During the ensuing 15 years, they (and many others) have continued to expand on this research base and have explored other facets of expertise in the context of counseling and psychotherapy.

Master Therapists contains extensive qualitative research from three doctoral dissertations and an additional research study conducted on the same 10 master therapists. This intensive research project on master therapists, based on nearly 60 in-depth interviews with those considered the "best of the best" by their colleagues, is still considered the most extensive research on high-level functioning of mental health professionals ever done. The following are comments from leaders in the field of psychotherapy and counseling:

> *Master Therapists* concludes the elusive pursuit and characterization of therapeutic expertise. A sensitive, inspiring, and captivating portrait of how effective psychotherapists conduct their lives and therapy.
>
> John Norcross, PhD, *University of Scranton*

> This fascinating book addresses the intriguing question of how one moves from being a person who wants to help others to becoming a professional who effectively can. The insights contained here will not only be of interest to beginning therapists involved in clinical training, but also to therapists who have evolved professionally over the course of their careers.
>
> Marvin Goldfried, PhD, *Stony Brook University—State University of New York*

This book provides food for thought that will undoubtedly stimulate debates about the ingredients that make up psychotherapeutic excellence.

Arnold Lazarus, PhD, *Emeritus, Rutgers University*

Skovholt and Jennings and colleagues begin to unravel the mysteries of how master therapists think about and practice psychotherapy. Their interviews with ten master therapists provide the grist for the mill. This book provides trainees as well as practitioners with a vision of where they might venture.

Bruce Wampold, PhD, *University of Wisconsin–Madison*

A very important book. This book takes the mystery out of mastery. Skovholt and Jennings delineate the core conditions of the master therapist practitioners. This book doesn't just talk about therapy and counseling but rather offers an insider's view.

Jon Carlson, PhD, *Governors State University*

Preface

COUNSELING AND PSYCHOTHERAPY are two of the great inventions of the last half of the 20th century. In one innovative comparative study, aspirin used for heart attack prevention had a mean effect size of .03, whereas psychotherapy had a mean effect size of .80 (Hubble, Duncan, Miller, & Wampold, 2009, p. 27–28).

With counseling and psychotherapy, we have a way that helps individuals transform their lives. Conditions with derogatory labels once considered immutable—lazy, drunk, stupid, and angry—can now be understood as changeable when a professional counselor or therapist is intensively and positively present for the other. Sometimes, but not always, lazy is better understood as depression and despair, drunk becomes chemical dependency, stupid becomes learning disabilities, and anger is uncovered shame. All these conditions can be slowly transformed for the suffering person by a very skilled and highly ethical professional counselor or psychotherapist who is intensively dedicated to the welfare of the other person.

In the excitement to develop the counseling and therapy professions during the past half century, three paths have been taken. One path has used the epistemology of working with clients to learn about human suffering—where it comes from and how to reduce it while increasing joy and satisfaction. The great example here is, of course, Sigmund Freud. The basic formula is that the practitioner develops a method and then prescribes it to others as the way to proceed. There are hundreds of examples here. Two other examples are Michael White and narrative therapy and Jean Baker Miller and feminist therapy. For some, the development of the method has included insights about oneself that are then generalized into a method. Harry Stack Sullivan fit this description in years past with his emphasis on interpersonal anxiety, and Francine Shapiro fits this description in more recent years with her eye moment desensitization and reprocessing approach to trauma, as does Marsha Linehan and dialectical behavioral therapy.

A second path is based on empirical research as the epistemology. The book *Bringing Psychotherapy Research to Life* (Castonguay et al., 2010) is just this—a celebration of empirical research methods as the path to expertise and mastery. This book offers a remarkable tour of this path to mastery as the reader visits the life work of 28 eminent psychotherapy researchers such as Aaron Beck and cognitive therapy, Leslie Greenberg and emotionally focused therapy, and Lorna Smith Benjamin and interpersonal reconstructive therapy for intimate attachments that have gone awry.

Carl Rogers walked both of these paths—the practitioner who learned from practice (e.g., his early work in Rochester, New York, and later at the University of Chicago) while also being a dedicated researcher. For example, Rogers introduced the idea of recording one's sessions and learning from them, a method now used throughout the world in counselor and psychotherapist training programs.

For both of these paths, using one's experience and using the empirical research, expertise, and mastery was described as following the prescribed method–approach–technique, sometimes with a strict manual to be followed. As part of going down Path One or Path Two, *the person of the counselor or therapist is considered the vessel that delivered the method.* The person of the counselor or therapist was secondary to the method. As part of this intense focus on method as the ultimate objective, great competition between methods went on for decades. There are so many examples: Directive approach advocates battled against non-directive approach advocates, Adlerians competed against Jungians, cognitive therapists expressed that changing cognition was key while emotionally focused practitioners said the key to the cure was affect, and so on. Like grass fires that seem to be extinguished, only to start smoldering and then igniting again, these method wars continue now, although with less intensity. Why less intensity?

The major reason is because the outcome research keeps finding equivalence across approaches. This is stated in the concluding chapter of *Bringing Psychotherapy Research to Life* by Angus et al. (2010) when they write of "the equivalence of positive outcome findings achieved across different therapy approaches" (p. 354) and "outcomes among different therapy approaches were found to be equivocal and could not be explained" (p. 359). This is actually an old song, sung first by Rosenzweig (1936), later by Jerome Frank in *Persuasion and Healing* (1973), and then relatively recently by Wampold (2001). For example, investigator bias seems to be central when differences are found between methods (Angus et al., 2010).

Path Three

With equivalent results across methods, the focus has shifted to factors that transcend one particular method. What are they? One common factor with all approaches is the impact of the counselor or therapist. This is Path Three to expertise and mastery in counseling and therapy. With Path Three, *the method is the vessel delivering the counselor or therapist.*

With this perspective, the person of the counselor or therapist became more important. The first major exploration of the development of the counselor or therapist was an intensive study of 100 practitioners captured in *The Evolving Professional Self* (Skovholt & Rønnestad, 1992). Other major research books on the development of the counselor or therapist include *How Therapists Develop: A Study of Therapeutic Work and Professional Growth* by Orlinsky and Rønnestad (2005), which is based on survey data from a large international sample, and *The Developing Practitioner: Growth and Stagnation of Therapists and Counselors* by Rønnestad and Skovholt (2013), which contains data from a variety of research methods. At the same time as the normative development of counselors and therapists became a focus as described in these three books, the exploration of expertise took on more importance.

The larger stage is the general exploration of expertise, and the smaller stage is the exploration of counselor and therapist expertise. Examples from the larger stage include academic research books such as Chi, Glaser, and Farr's (1988) *The Nature of Expertise*. Other notable books in expertise are the popularized Gladwell (2008) *Outliers: The Story of Success* and the scholarship version in Ericsson, Charness, Hoffman, and Feltovich's (2006) *Cambridge Handbook of Expertise and Expert Performance*.

Merging the two trends of studying the development of the counselor or therapist and studying the nature of expertise led to the study of master therapists. This was an exciting change of direction. If we can know about experts and then emulate them, then the complexity of the work of counseling and therapy can drain away and the therapist can proceed and feel empowered as a helper of others. If the Path One and Path Two approaches do not lead to better outcomes in counseling and therapy, will the pursuit of actual experts do it? A key is to ask, How does one validly find experts? A first approach in finding experts was to find American Board of Professional Psychology (ABPP) board-certified psychologists. ABPP began in 1947. The ABPP exam requires work samples (session videotape, report, etc.), and therefore ABPP psychologists are certified to have advanced competencies in their specialty areas. (In the past, the level for passing was considered expertise; beginning in 2013, the level, reflecting the standards in medicine, is competence). The second author has been an examiner for 53 oral exams for ABPP and is thus familiar with this method of assessing advanced competence. Harrington (1988) studied ABPP board-certified psychologists as a first Path Three attempt to find and study actual counseling/therapy experts by giving them a variety of objective instruments. The study was well done, but the results were not very helpful in really understanding expert counselors and therapists.

A third method to find experts was the way most often used by people in general. Aside from using computerized search and referral tools such as "Yelp" or "Angie's List," many of us ask a friend or relative for a reference to an expert or master dentist, house remodeler, physician, babysitter, car mechanic, or attorney. The criterion is mastery or expertise in one's small world of effort or what in the expertise literature is called the domain. The expert may not be famous like a writer of notable books or be a distinguished research professor at an elite university. This same approach has been used with this third method of finding therapy expertise. In 1996, Jennings was one of the first researchers to use this nomination method to find master therapists. It was a combination of peer nomination, snowball sampling, and extreme case sampling. Individuals who were repeatedly named by a variety of informants constituted the core participant pool for the Jennings study. Those nominees who received more than a certain number or the highest percentage of nominations were considered "master therapists." The use of peer nomination procedures has shown to have good psychometric support. Anastasi and Urbina (1997) state, "When checked against a variety of practical criteria dependent on interpersonal relations, such ratings usually have been found to have good concurrent and predictive validity" (p. 468). This method has been used in other fields such as business. The classic Peters and Waterman's (1982) book, *In Search of Excellence*, utilized an informed group of observers to identify the most innovative and excellent US companies. Most of the existing master therapist studies used this sampling method (Carvalho & Matos, 2011a, 2011b; Goh, Starkey, Skovholt, & Jennings, 2007; Hirai, 2010; Jennings & Skovholt, 1999; Jennings et al., 2004, 2008, 2012; Kwon & Kim, 2007; Mullenbach & Skovholt, 2004; Řiháček, Kahancová, Jennings, Roubal, & Vybíral, 2015; Smith, 2008; Sullivan, Skovholt, & Jennings, 2004).

The current book consists of studies that have used Path Three to counseling and therapy expertise. In the years since the 1996 Jennings study, this method of finding counseling and therapy experts, in order to learn from them, has grown in influence and popularity. This is documented by the use of the Path Three studies in the book by Sperry and Carlson (2013) titled *How Master Therapists Work: Effecting Change from the First Through the Last Session and Beyond*. In addition, there have been a number of spin-off and extension studies of master practitioners, such as the Miranda (2012) study of genetic master counselors. Prior to this book, there have been three summary chapters bringing together the work on master therapists. First, there was a chapter titled "Portrait of the Master Therapist: The Highly Functioning Self" (Skovholt, Jennings, & Mullenbach, 2004). That was followed by "Practitioner Mastery and Expertise" (Skovholt, Vaughan, & Jennings, 2012) and then "Master Therapists: Exploration of Expertise" (Jennings, Skovholt, Goh, & Lian, 2013). Chapter 8 of this book offers an even more comprehensive summary model, with a focus on qualitative data representing 72 master therapists from around the world.

Now we briefly mention some of the original master therapist research in this Path Three approach to counseling and therapy expertise—research that is the foundation of the current book. The 1996 Jennings dissertation was published in the *Journal of Counseling Psychology* (Jennings & Skovholt, 1999), in which the cognitive, emotional, and relational model of master therapists was first introduced to a broader audience. From the qualitative research process, we found that the master therapists sample of 10, as a composite, possessed highly desirable cognitive, emotional, and relational characteristics, and we put forth that these three areas need to be present and well-developed in order to perform at the expert level in the counseling and therapy field. Using the same sample of master therapists from the original Jennings 1996 study, three more studies explored various characteristics of these experts, including self-care practices (Mullenbach & Skovholt, 2004), ethical values (Jennings, Sovereign, Bottorff, Mussell, & Vye, 2005), and the working alliance (Sullivan, Skovholt, & Jennings, 2004). In Skovholt and Jennings' (2004) *Master Therapists: Exploring Expertise in Therapy and Counseling*, we compiled and synthesized these four studies to offer an elaborate portrait of the characteristics of master therapists in the chapter titled "Portrait of the Master Therapist: Developmental Model of the Highly Functioning Self" (Skovholt et al., 2004). (This chapter is available for free at http://www.oxfordclinicalpsych.com/mastertherapists.)

We have include the original Jennings and Skovholt (1999) study in the Appendix because it was the starting point for the six international studies that followed in that each international study used similar purposeful sampling strategies, similar research and interview questions, and essentially replicated our 1999 study in each of the chapter authors' home countries. Moreover, the Jennings and Skovholt study was included in the qualitative meta-analysis, resulting in a total of seven master therapists' studies that make up our concluding chapter.

In addition to building on this foundation of research, we are also responding to a call for the internationalization of research on counseling and psychotherapy (Gerstein, Heppner, Ægisdóttir, Leung, & Norsworthy, 2009). Studies from around the world offer a more global perspective of psychotherapy expertise and can increase our knowledge of cultural competency by providing rich examples of how counseling and psychotherapy is conducted in a variety of countries. In contrast to most US psychological research in which samples comprise less than 5% of the world's population (Arnett, 2008), our study is composed of mostly non-US therapists. For the US audience, we agree with Christopher, Wendt, Marecek, and Goodman (2014) when they urge US psychologists to consider not just "learning *about* other psychologies . . . [but] be open to learning *from* them—that is, to reassessing or even revising their own ways of thinking" (p. 652). We were certainly enriched and challenged by the lessons and stories these 72 master therapists offered. Our hope is that this book will contribute to both the understanding of culturally specific elements of counseling and psychotherapy and a more global understanding of the master therapist construct. This second goal fits with Path Three as part of the many decades-long search for ways to be of most help to those who suffer emotionally.

Expertise in Counseling and Psychotherapy: Master Therapist Studies from Around the World captures the Path Three of research on master therapists. It is exciting that a number of researchers from various regions of the world have answered the call to study master therapists in their home countries. In this book, researchers from seven countries share their findings on master therapists. An integration of these research studies, via qualitative meta-analysis, follows. Briefly, a qualitative meta-analysis (QMA) approach is interpretive, instead of aggregative, and creates a product that goes beyond isolated qualitative studies and pursues the incremental accumulation of knowledge (Finfgeld,

2003). QMA provides the opportunity for "stock-taking" once there is a critical mass of qualitative studies on the same topic.

Fortunately, we now have a critical mass of qualitative studies on the topic of master therapists in which a substantial amount of data can be pooled, analyzed, and synthesized. A team of researchers (authors of Chapter 8) did just that and asked a few basic questions to frame their investigation. What can we learn from these highly regarded therapists from around the world? What do these therapists have in common? How do they differ? What unique challenges do they encounter in their home country? In this book, 72 master therapists from seven countries, representing hundreds of hours of interviews, help tell the story of the master therapist from a global perspective.

Preview of Chapters

In Chapter 1, Len and Tom, along with Heather Hessel, Sharada Lakhan, and Michael Goh, examine the current state of therapist variables and master therapists research, describe the validity of the peer nomination process for selecting master therapists, and make the case for compiling and synthesizing international qualitative research to further our understanding of the master therapist construct. In the next six chapters, qualitative findings on master therapists from around the world are presented. The chapter authors provide the reader with a fascinating description of the context of counseling and culture related to their home countries. Chapters 2–4 highlight research conducted from a Western perspective. In Chapter 2, Len, Tomáš Řiháček, Mária Kahancová, Jan Roubal, and Zbyněk Vybíral explore the characteristics of Czech master therapists. In Chapter 3, Allyson Smith and William Whelton share their study on Canadian master couple therapists. Chapter 4 showcases Helena Moura de Carvalho and Paula Mena Matos' qualitative research on Portuguese master therapists. In the next section, Chapters 5–7 highlight master therapist research from an Eastern perspective. In Chapter 5, Len and colleagues explore the characteristics of Singaporean master therapists. This study also included a qualitative meta-analysis comparing Singaporean and US master therapists and was the starting point for the major QMA we feature in the final chapter. Tatsuya Hirai and Michael Goh present Japanese master therapists in Chapter 6 and also provide comparisons between Japanese and US master therapists. In Chapter 7, Kyoung-In Kwon and Chang-Dae Kim present their study on Korean master group therapists.

In the final, integrative chapter (Chapter 8), Len and Tom, along with Ashley Sovereign, Salina Renninger, Michael Goh, Sharada Lakhan, and Heather Hessel, share their qualitative meta-analysis research in which they analyzed the findings from the studies presented in the previous chapters and offer the Synthesis Model of Master Therapists from Around the World. To tie it all together, the authors offer suggestions for training and research based on their extensive findings. Finally, in the Appendix, readers will find the first master therapist research study, "The Cognitive, Emotional, and Relational

Characteristics of Master Therapists," originally published in the *Journal of Counseling Psychology*, in its original form.

In all, this book represents more than 10,000 hours of effort by the 20 researchers and 72 master therapists from seven countries. We now invite you into the exciting and inspiring world of the master therapist and hope it informs your professional journey.

References

Anastasi, A., & Urbina, S. (1997). *Psychological testing* (7th ed.). Englewood Cliffs, NJ: Prentice Hall.

Angus, L., Hayes, J. A., Anderson, T., Ladany, N., Castonguay, L. G., & Muran, C. (2010). Future directions: Emerging opportunities and challenges in psychotherapy research. In L. G. Castonguay, J. Christopher Muran, L. Angus, J. A. Hayes, N. Ladany, & T. Anderson (Eds.), *Bringing psychotherapy research to life* (pp. 353–362). Washington, DC: American Psychological Association.

Arnett, J. J. (2008). The neglected 95%: Why American psychology needs to be less American. *American Psychologist, 63*, 602–614.

Carvalho, H. M., & Matos, P. M. (2011a). Ser e tornar-se psicoterapeuta parte I: Diálogo entre experiências pessoais e profissionais [Being and becoming a psychotherapist: Part I. Dialogue between personal and professional experiences]. *Psicologia: Ciência e Profissâo, 31*(1), 80–95.

Carvalho, H. M., & Matos, P. M. (2011b). Ser e tornar-se psicoterapeuta parte II: Diálogo entre mudanças pessoais e profissionais [Being and becoming a psychotherapist: Part II. Dialogue between personal and professional changes]. *Psicologia: Ciência e Profissâo, 31*(4), 778–799.

Castonguay, L. G., Muran, J. C., Angus, L., Hayes, J. A., Ladany, N., & Anderson, T. (Eds.). (2010). *Bringing psychotherapy research to life*. Washington, DC: American Psychological Association.

Chi, M. T. H., Glaser, R., & Farr, M. J. (Eds.). (1988). *The nature of expertise*. Hillsdale, NJ: Erlbaum.

Christopher, J. C., Wendt, D. C., Marecek, J., & Goodman, D. M. (2014). Critical cultural awareness: Contributions to a globalizing psychology. *American Psychologist, 69*(7), 645–655.

Ericsson, K. A., Charness, N., Hoffman, R. R., & Feltovich, P. J. (2006). *The Cambridge handbook of expertise and expert performance*. New York, NY: Cambridge University Press.

Finfgeld, D. L. (2003). Metasynthesis: The state of the art—So far. *Qualitative Health Research, 13*, 893–904.

Frank, J. (1973). *Persuasion and healing: A comparative study of psychotherapy*. Baltimore, MD: Johns Hopkins University Press.

Gerstein, L. H., Heppner, P. P., Ægisdóttir, S., Leung, A. S., & Norsworthy, K. L. (Eds.). (2009). *International handbook of cross-cultural counseling: Cultural assumptions and practices worldwide*. Thousand Oaks, CA: Sage.

Gladwell, M. (2008). *Outliers: The story of success*. Boston, MA: Little Brown.

Goh, M., Starkey, M. T., Skovholt, T. M., & Jennings, L. (2007). *In search of cultural competence in mental health: A study of expert multicultural counselors and therapists*. Unpublished manuscript, University of Minnesota, Minneapolis, MN.

Harrington, K. M. (1988). *Personal characteristics of diplomats defined as master therapists*. Unpublished doctoral dissertation, University of Minnesota, Minneapolis, MN.

Hirai, T. (2010). *Personal and professional characteristics of Japanese master therapists: A qualitative investigation on expertise in psychotherapy and counseling in Japan*. Unpublished doctoral dissertation, University of Minnesota, Minneapolis, MN.

Hubble, M. A., Duncan, B. L., Miller, S. D., & Wampold, B. E. (2009). Introduction. In B. L. Duncan, S. D. Miller, B. E. Wampold, & M. A. Hubble (Eds.), *The heart and soul of change: Delivering what works in therapy* (pp. 23–46). Washington, DC: American Psychological Association.

Jennings, L. (1996). *Personal characteristics of master therapists*. Unpublished doctoral dissertation, University of Minnesota, Minneapolis, MN.

Jennings, L., D'Rozario, V., Goh, M., Sovereign, A., Brogger, M., & Skovholt, T. (2008). Psychotherapy expertise in Singapore: A qualitative investigation. *Psychotherapy Research, 18*(5), 508–522.

Jennings, L., Gulden, A., Oien, M., D'Rozario, V., Goh, M., & Skovholt, T. M. (2012). Multicultural knowledge and skills of Singaporean master therapists. *Journal of Asia Pacific Counseling, 2*(2), 133–146.

Jennings, L., & Skovholt, T. M. (1999). The cognitive, emotional, and relational characteristics of master therapists. *Journal of Counseling Psychology, 46*, 3–11.

Jennings, L., Skovholt, T. M., Goh, M., & Lian, F. (2013). Master therapists: Exploration of expertise. In M. H. Rønnestad & T. M. Skovholt (Eds.), *The developing practitioner: Growth and stagnation of therapists and counselors* (pp. 213–246). New York, NY: Wiley.

Jennings, L., Sovereign, A., Bottorff, N., Mussell, M. P., & Vye, C. (2005). Nine ethical values of master therapists. *Journal of Mental Health Counseling, 27*(1), 32–48.

Kwon, K., & Kim, C. (2007). Analysis of the characteristics of Korean master group counselors. *Korean Journal of Counseling, 8*(3), 979–1010.

Miranda, C. J. C. (2012). *Portrait of the master genetic counselor: A qualitative investigation of expertise in genetic counseling*. Unpublished doctoral dissertation, University of Minnesota, Minneapolis, MN.

Mullenbach, M., & Skovholt, T. M. (2004). Emotional wellness and professional resiliency of master therapists. In T. M. Skovholt & L. Jennings (Eds.), *Master therapists: Exploring expertise in therapy and counseling* (pp. 77–106). Boston, MA: Allyn & Bacon.

Orlinsky, D. E., & Rønnestad, M. H. (2005). *How psychotherapists develop: A study of therapeutic work and professional growth*. Washington, DC: American Psychological Association.

Peters, T. J., & Waterman, R. H. (1982). *In search of excellence: Lessons from America's best-run companies*. New York, NY: Harper & Row.

Řiháček, T., Kahancová, M., Jennings, L., Roubal, J., & Vybíral, Z. (2015). *Czech master therapists*. Unpublished manuscript. Masaryk University, Brno, Czech Republic.

Rønnestad, M. H., & Skovholt, T. M. (2013). The developing practitioner: Growth and stagnation of therapists and counselors (pp. 213–246). New York, NY: Wiley.

Rosenzweig, S. (1936). Some implicit common factors in diverse methods of psychotherapy: "At last the Dodo said, 'Everybody has won and all must have prizes.'" *American Journal of Orthopsychiatry, 6*, 412–415.

Skovholt, T. M., & Jennings, L. (2004). *Master therapists: Exploring expertise in therapy and counseling*. Boston, MA: Allyn & Bacon.

Skovholt, T. M., Jennings, L., & Mullenbach, M. (2004). Portrait of the master therapist: The highly-functioning self. In T. M. Skovholt & L. Jennings (Eds.), *Master therapists: Exploring expertise in therapy and counseling* (pp. 125–146). Boston, MA: Allyn & Bacon.

Skovholt, T. M., & Rønnestad, M. H. (1992). *The evolving professional self: Stages and themes in therapist and counselor development*. New York, NY: Wiley.

Skovholt, T. M., Vaughan, M., & Jennings, L. (2012). Practitioner mastery and expertise. In T. M. Skovholt (Ed.), *Becoming a therapist: On the path to mastery* (pp. 203–242). New York, NY: Wiley.

Smith, A. (2008). *Personal characteristics of master couple therapists*. Unpublished doctoral dissertation thesis, University of Alberta, Edmonton, Alberta, Canada

Sperry, L., & Carlson, J. (2013). *How master therapists work: Effecting change from the first through the last session and beyond*. New York, NY: Routledge.

Sullivan, M., Skovholt, T. M., & Jennings, L. (2004). Master therapists' construction of the therapy relationship. In T. M. Skovholt & L. Jennings (Eds.), *Master therapists: Exploring expertise in therapy and counseling*. Boston, MA: Allyn & Bacon.

Wampold, B. E. (2001). *The great psychotherapy debate: Models, methods and findings*. Mahwah, NJ: Erlbaum.

Acknowledgments

FIRST AND FOREMOST, I thank my wife Karrie for her love, patience, and support throughout this multiyear project. To my friend, mentor and co-author, thank you Tom Skovholt for being the inspiration for this line of research two decades ago. You continue to amaze me with your generosity and willingness to give so much of yourself to students, graduates, colleagues, clients, family, and friends. You have definitely mastered the cognitive, emotional, and relational domains of life! A special thanks to Ashley Sovereign, who as a first-year doctoral student in 1999 maybe did not realize what she was getting into when she joined our research team. Thank you Ashley for your energy and expertise on the many CQR teams of which you have been a part since 1999. Thank you Michael Goh for your cultural sensibilities and willingness to audit several master therapist projects. Thank you Zbyněk Vybíral for supporting the Czech master therapist research project during my visit to Masaryk University. Special thanks to Tomáš Řiháček and Mária Kahancová, who, with good humor and incredible energy, labored with me for two intensive weeks to consensually code and analyze the Czech master therapist data. I thank the University of St. Thomas for supporting my work through a sabbatical and several research grants. Thank you Chris Vye for your leadership as chair and continuous support of my projects. In addition, I acknowledge all of the University of St. Thomas researchers involved with this project. Thank you to Salina Renninger, Sharada Lakhan, and Heather Hessel for several years of dedicated work on this project.

Len Jennings

I HAVE HAD the great blessing of being able to work with doctoral students as their advisor—specifically for this book, those advisees who, as researchers, have searched for higher level therapist and counseling performance. My most sustaining and rewarding work in this area has been with Len Jennings. He was an amazing doctoral student who has turned into a trusted and valuable colleague and coauthor. I got lucky when he chose the University of Minnesota for his PhD.

Other advisees and students have made valuable contributions to practitioner mastery. Thank you Mary Mullenbach, Michael Sullivan, Kevin Harrington, Fengqin Lian, Yoonhee Sung, and Jian-Ming Hou for your research work.

For this book on practitioner mastery around the world, I note the richness I have received by living and working in other countries. The most sustained times have been as a Fulbright Lecturer in Turkey, university lecturer in Singapore, and researcher in Norway. I appreciate the kindness I have received in these and other countries and the inspiration of therapists and counselors all over the world intensively working to help others live richer, deeper, and more satisfying lives.

Tom Skovholt

WE APPRECIATE THE editorial wisdom Dana Bliss provided as this book advanced from an idea to a reality.

Len Jennings and Tom Skovholt

About the Contributors

Megan Brogger, PsyD, LP, is a partner and co-owner of Lumin Advantage Consulting. She works with clients throughout the country to promote and sustain organizational and leadership excellence. By applying her experience and background in behavioral, social, and systems science, she helps individuals, teams, and organizations turn off autopilot and approach work, leadership, or changes intentionally and strategically. She received her doctorate from the University of St. Thomas in Counseling Psychology, where she worked with Dr. Len Jennings on the master therapist project.

Helena Moura de Carvalho, PhD, earned her PhD in Psychology from the Faculty of Psychology and Educational Sciences at the University of Porto, Portugal. She is an assistant professor in psychology in the School of Education at the Polytechnic Institute of Porto and a researcher in the nongovernmental organization APDES. She has been developing research in attachment theory and psychotherapeutic relationship, HIV/AIDS counseling, drugs, social exclusion, and human rights. As a professor, she has been lecturing classes in SSH methods, Social and Communitarian Interventions and Mental Health. She is a member of the Center for Psychology at the University of Porto and a member of Research of Education and Community Intervention research units.

Vilma D'Rozario, PhD, is an associate professor with the Psychological Studies Academic Group at the National Institute of Education (NIE), Nanyang Technological University. She teaches pre-service counseling and graduate group counseling courses. Her research interests are in master therapists, service learning, and the benefits of nature and the outdoors on well-being. She is actively involved in student life on campus as adviser to the NIE Service Learning Club. She volunteers extensively in environmental and wildlife conservation projects in Singapore. She is cofounder of Cicada Tree Eco-Place, which promotes nature, culture, and eco-living and aims to provide environmental education for all. Also, she is on the board of the Jane Goodall Institute (Singapore), another local organization involved in environmental education.

Michael Goh, PhD, is a professor of comparative and international development education, associate vice provost for equity and diversity, and affiliated faculty with the Interdisciplinary Center for the Study of Global Change at the University of Minnesota. A counseling psychologist by training, he studies cultural competence in counseling, teaching, and intercultural education and training. He has received numerous awards for excellence in teaching in Singapore and the United States, and he is nationally recognized for his leadership on equity and diversity issues. In 2010, he was named the inaugural recipient of the College of Education and Human Development Marty and Jack Rossman Faculty Development Award for his creativity and innovation in scholarship, teaching, and service.

Heather Hessel, MA, is a doctoral student in the Couple and Family Therapy program in Family Social Science at the University of Minnesota, Twin Cities. She holds an MA in Counseling Psychology from the University of St. Thomas and an MLIS from the Information Studies department at the University of California, Los Angeles. She has published and presented research on parent–child relationships and on the use of information and communication technologies in families. She is also interested in how emerging technologies can be used by clinicians to provide effective therapy.

Tatsuya Hirai, PhD, is an associate professor at Asia Pacific University, Japan. He holds a PhD in Counseling Psychology from the University of Minnesota. He has also worked as an international student counselor and career counselor in both the United States and Japan. His major interests in research and practice include the development of career education, multicultural counseling, positive psychology, and global leadership.

Mária Kahancová, MA, received her master's degree in psychology and psychotherapy at Masaryk University in the Czech Republic. As a doctoral researcher in the area of psychotherapy, she focuses on therapist effects. She also works as a therapist in a residential aftercare center for clients with alcohol addiction.

Chang-Dai Kim, EdD, is a professor of counseling at Seoul National University. He is the current president of the Korean Counseling Association, which is one of the largest counseling professional organizations in Korea. His research interests include the effect of various counseling interventions on emotion regulation, the application of neuroimaging technique on counseling research, and the development of counseling models for exiles from North Korea. He is coauthor of *Introduction of Counseling, Lessons from Korean Master Group Psychotherapists*, and *Disintegration and Re-integration of Exiles from North Korea.*

Kyoung-In Kwon, PhD, is a professor of counseling at the Kwangwoon University in Korea. As a researcher and counselor, she has great interest in group counseling and counselor factors. She has conducted research on the development of Korean master group counselors, ethics in group counseling, and supervision of group work. She also has been actively involved in providing training for group counselors.

Sharada Lakhan, MA, is a doctoral student in the counseling psychology program at the University of St. Thomas, and she worked with Len Jennings as a graduate assistant from 2012 through 2015. Currently, her predoctoral internship is with the Indian Health Board of Minneapolis. Her interests include social justice approaches to counseling, multicultural counseling, trauma work, and dual diagnosis.

Paula Mena Matos, PhD, earned her PhD in psychology from the Faculty of Psychology and Educational Sciences of the University of Porto, Portugal, where she teaches in the fields of clinical, health, and developmental psychology. She has been coordinating several scientific research projects and is a member of the direction board of the Center for Psychology at the University of Porto, where she is responsible for the research group on relationships, processes of change, and well-being. She also practices as a psychotherapist at the Psychology Counseling Centre and has supervised clinical psychologists for the past 20 years.

Salina Renninger, PhD, LP, is the director of training and an assistant professor of counseling psychology at the University of St. Thomas, and she maintains a private practice. Having also been a director of training at a predoctoral internship, a significant part of her career has focused on training students to become practitioners of counseling psychology. The international master therapist project has deepened her understanding of how to train students for work in a global society.

Tomáš Řiháček, PhD, is a psychologist and psychotherapist. He is an assistant professor at the Department of Psychology, Faculty of Social Studies, Masaryk University in Brno, Czech Republic, where he teaches courses on qualitative methods and psychotherapy research. His research interests include psychotherapist development, psychotherapy integration, and other topics in psychotherapy research. He also operates a part-time private practice.

Jan Roubal, MD, PhD, is an assistant professor of psychotherapy at Masaryk University in Brno, Czech Republic. He also works as a psychotherapist, psychiatrist, supervisor, and psychotherapy trainer. He publishes texts mostly on psychotherapy in clinical practice and has coedited a Czech publication, *Current Psychotherapy*, and an international publication, *Gestalt Therapy in Clinical Practice: From Psychopathology to the Aesthetics of Contact*.

Allyson Smith, PhD, is a psychologist who works with individual adults and couples. She graduated from the University of Alberta in 2008, where she completed her dissertation under the supervision of Dr. William Whelton. She has worked in a variety of settings, including hospitals, a university counseling clinic, a trauma center, and private practice. She currently works in private practice in Ottawa, Ontario, Canada.

Ashley Sovereign, PsyD, LP, is an associate professor and director of clinical training for the counseling psychology doctoral program at Saint Mary's University of Minnesota. She writes qualitative research items for the research and statistics domain of the Examination for the Professional Practice of Psychology (EPPP) and has a part-time private clinical psychotherapy practice. She teaches graduate-level courses in qualitative research, clinical supervision, dissertation writing, group psychotherapy, counseling theory and skills, and working with LGBTQ clients.

Zbyněk Vybíral, PhD, is a professor of social psychology and psychotherapy at Masaryk University, Brno, Czech Republic. He had been editor and publisher of the Czech journal *Konfrontace* since 1990 and is currently senior editor of the Czech scientific journal *Psychoterapie.* He is author of *Psychologie Komunikace* [*Psychology of Communication*], *Psychologie Jinak* [*Psychology Otherwise*], and coeditor of *Soucasna Psychoterapie* [*Contemporary Psychotherapy*]. He has worked as a psychotherapist in private practice in the past.

William J. Whelton, PhD, is a professor of counseling psychology at the University of Alberta. His research has principally focused on such topics as emotional processes in psychotherapy, emotional aspects of self-criticism and resilience to self-criticism, and emotional processes in eating disorders and their treatment. He has been trained in and practices emotion-focused therapy and relational gestalt therapy. He has a growing interest in the history of psychology, including such figures as Otto Rank and his influence on humanistic and experiential therapies such as that of Carl Rogers.

EXPERTISE IN COUNSELING AND PSYCHOTHERAPY

1 The World of Expertise in Counseling and Psychotherapy

Len Jennings, Thomas M. Skovholt, Heather Hessel,
Sharada Lakhan, and Michael Goh

Introduction

Numerous research studies have evaluated the efficacy of counseling and psychotherapy, with initial emphasis on theory, techniques, and client variables. However, influential research performed more than 25 years ago suggested that the characteristics and attitudes of the therapist may contribute more to successful outcomes than specific therapeutic techniques or theory (Lambert, 1989). As a result, during the past two decades, researchers have sought to understand the personal qualities that therapists bring to their work. This emphasis on the therapist has only grown in these decades. For example, in a book described as perhaps the most important book on psychotherapy, *The Great Psychotherapy Debate: The Evidence for What Makes Psychotherapy Work* by Wampold and Imel (2015), the authors write, "Psychotherapy is a primarily interpersonal treatment" (p. 37). Wampold and Imel's evaluation fits with our notion that it is the therapist's personal and relational qualities rather than a specific method or technique that are key to professional effectiveness. In an exhaustive outcome research study of the work of 70 psychotherapists, Nissen-Lie et al. (2015) found just that. The best outcomes were achieved by therapists who combined professional self-doubt with personal self-love defined as self-affiliation.

One area of this research explores therapist variables by studying the general characteristics of expert practitioners. These master therapists represent the "best of the best" in the profession and are considered those capable of handling the most difficult cases and working with the broadest range of clients (Miller, 1993). They are also well-regarded by their peers and are often viewed as a "therapist's therapist" (Jennings & Skovholt, 1999, p. 4). A major goal in this line of research has been to identify the personal characteristics that might contribute to mastery in conducting psychotherapy. In this chapter, we provide an overview of research on therapist variables in general and master therapist characteristics specifically. A major part of this chapter and book describes the background and findings of qualitative studies that have explored the following questions: "What is a master therapist?" and "What common personal and professional characteristics and themes resonate with this group of elite individuals?" In addition, we make a case for enhancing our perspective on master therapists by harnessing the burgeoning data from master therapist studies from around the world.

A Call to Research on Therapist Factors

Research has shown that a strong emphasis has been placed on the importance of theory and techniques in studying what works in psychotherapy and that there is an inadequate amount of research available on the therapist factors that most contribute to successful outcomes (Hubble, Duncan, Miller, & Wampold, 2009; Lambert, 1989; Miller, 1993; Miller, Hubble, Duncan, & Wampold, 2009; Wampold & Imel, 2015). Numerous studies and meta-analyses across multiple client populations have belied the promise of standard treatments that can be studied by graduate students and applied by practitioners in a manualized fashion to fit specific mental health problems (Albert, 1997; Luborsky, McLellan, Diguer, Woody, & Seligman, 1997). Both of these statements apply as well to couple and family counseling, in addition to individual therapy (Miller et al., 2009). Some research has instead shown that the best therapists diverge from the established procedures, with the suggestion that strict adherence to manualized process can interfere with the working relationship at times and can result in less successful outcomes (Castonguay, Goldfried, Wiser, Raue, & Hayes, 1996; Henry, Schact, Strupp, Butler, & Binder, 1993; Strupp & Anderson, 1997). In the largest qualitative study of therapist development ($N = 100$), Skovholt and Rønnestad (1992) found this divergence from the conventional and ordinary. One experienced practitioner stated,

> I learned all the rules and so I came to a point—after lots of effort—where I knew the rules very well. Gradually, I modified the rules. Then I began to use the rules to let me go where I wanted to go. Lately, I haven't been talking so much in terms of rules. (pp. 66–67)

Instead of producing a clear path toward standardization, what has emerged from the long-standing debate concerning the effectiveness of particular theoretical orientations is an understanding that successful psychotherapy arises from a complex interplay of therapeutic factors. The common factors approach has called for a foundational change in the way that therapy is conceptualized, seeking to identify those global factors that contribute to successful therapy and how those elements interact with each other (Hubble et al., 2009; Wampold & Imel, 2015). One of those critical factors is the person of the therapist. Research on the outcome variance attributable to therapists shows that therapists do contribute to successful therapy (Beutler et al., 2004). Repeatedly, researchers have called for additional work to be done to explore what qualities the most effective therapists possess that contribute to successful outcomes, in part to understand how to assist in the development of new therapists both in the United States and in countries and cultures around the world.

Research findings have varied regarding the importance of the therapist on outcome in psychotherapy. Wampold and Brown (2005) found that variability in therapist effectiveness in clinical practice was approximately 5% above the sampling error. This percentage can be compared to results from research studies that found variability of 1–18% (Wampold & Brown, 2005). One hypothesis for these differences is distinctions between the methodologies used in more rigidly effected clinical trials versus those used in more naturalistic studies (Wampold & Brown, 2005). In their exploratory study, Wampold and Brown also found that therapist performance increases medication effectiveness. In 2007, Baldwin, Wampold, and Imel cited evidence that "between 5% and 10% of the variance in outcomes is due to therapists—that is, 5%–10% of the total variability in outcomes is attributable to between-therapist differences" (p. 843). The variability between therapists was particularly apparent in the area of building a therapeutic alliance, which has previously been viewed as more attributable to patient variability than to therapist variability. Given these findings, understanding what makes psychotherapy successful surely involves understanding the person of the therapist.

The previously mentioned findings dovetail with the common factors approach. Hubble et al. (2009) call for the profession to focus research and training on other factors besides theories and their espoused techniques. Instead, proponents of the common factors model have also directed attention to the therapist, recognizing that therapeutic change is not something that can be standardized like a recipe, where therapists just mix together the right ingredients in the right amount and produce change at an expert level (Hubble et al., 2009). Rather, the therapeutic factors that produce successful results in therapy are more interdependent and reciprocal and less static and reductive (Hubble et al., 2009). Lindgren, Folkesson, and Almqvist (2010) also call for additional research and understanding of the contributions of the individual therapist, and they argue for exploration of a "g factor" in the person of the therapist, who embodies the competencies required for successful therapeutic intervention.

The Therapist's Contribution to Successful Psychotherapy

Given the relative importance of the therapist in determining outcome, researchers have studied a wide variety of different qualities of the therapist, although with little clear indication of what qualities account for the variability in outcome. Lambert (1989) describes significant research on therapist characteristics, divided between "static traits" and "process variables." Among others, these factors have included demographics, personality traits, attitudes/values, training, orientation and techniques, experience, and style. In the 1994 edition of Bergin and Garfield's *Handbook of Psychotherapy and Behavior Change*, Beutler, Machado, and Neufeldt began classifying therapist variables into four different quadrants along two dimensions: extratherapy traits versus therapy-specific states and observable versus inferred characteristics (reworded in the 2004 edition). The first dimension runs on a spectrum from specific experiences and sense of presence during therapy to those more enduring characteristics that are apparent even in nontherapeutic settings. The second dimension illustrates the spectrum from those factors that can be observed to those that are only suggested by behavior or self-report.

In attempting to better understand the factors associated with variability among therapists, research has identified a number of characteristics that are not correlated with effectiveness, including age, sex, race, religion, marital status, and level of clinical experience (Blatt, Sanislow, Zuroff, & Pilkonis, 1996). Huppert et al. (2001) found similar results using cognitive–behavioral therapy for age, gender match, and experience, although there was an acknowledgment that perhaps general experience conducting therapy was found to be a factor. Hubble et al. (2009) state that research shows that the following factors do not account for variability (in efficacy) among therapists: "age, gender, years of experience, professional discipline, degree, training, licensure, theoretical orientation, amount of supervision, personal therapy, specific or general competence, use of evidence-based methods" (p. 38). With respect to factors that fall in the observable traits quadrant, Beutler et al. (2004) are in agreement with previous conclusions about the sex, age, and race of the therapist in viewing them as inadequate predictors of therapeutic results. In addition, Beutler et al. found little support for training (amount and professional discipline) or experience as good predictors of outcome. Years of experience, in particular, is often put forth as an important factor in correlation with therapeutic expertise, and Beutler et al. distinguish between the value of clinical contact in and of itself and the development of expertise in particular techniques, suggesting that there is some support for general contact. However, as Betan and Binder (2010) remind the profession, "Twenty years of experience is not the same as one year of experience repeated twenty times" (p. 142), meaning that experience by itself is not synonymous with professional growth and development.

Orlinsky et al. (2001) analyzed quantitative results from a large international study of therapists to better understand influences on professional development and how training could facilitate therapeutic expertise. Their findings point to early career client contact as a key component in growth, along with long-standing supervision and having positive results in the therapist's own personal therapy. These points reinforce other findings on the importance of "experiential and interpersonal learning" in development (Orlinsky et al., 2001, p. 140). Similarly, Lindgren et al. (2010) point to the integration of professional influences and a personal translation of those influences, citing Sandell's (1983) idea of "private theory" and "official theory." The emphasis here is on the facility and persistence of the therapist to take standard professional theories and techniques, and clinical experiences, and create both personal meaning and professional learning from them. Thus, although experience on its own may not be a causal factor in therapy outcome, the richness with which a therapist continues to integrate her personal self with her professional experience impacts the way she provides service to clients.

It may be that our way of understanding therapist development within theories is the wrong model. Practitioners are often asked what theories they use or what "they are," as in "I use interpersonal, CBT, and narrative" or "I am an existential therapist." As discussed previously, long-term therapist development involves an integration of personal identity and professional identity—and professional functioning is influenced by a three-legged stool based on learning from clients, research, and personal life. Mix all of this together and we have unique development of a therapist moving toward expertise. The better metaphor is that of artist: Georgia O'Keeffe is Georgia O'Keeffe, not just an American modernist. Another example is senior-level college teachers: Each has a unique style by then. Therapist expertise at the senior level is a unique expression of style.

Lindgren et al.'s (2010) work moves the discussion from Beutler et al.'s (2004) observed traits (e.g., experience) to observable and inferred states (i.e., in-session ways of being). Using Leary's circumplex model of communication charting the two dimensions of friendly-to-unfriendly and dominant-to-submissive, researchers found strong support for high "friendly" therapist ratings and some effect of the similarities between therapist and client in the dominant-to-submissive scale (Beutler et al., 2004). Research has also shown the role of reciprocity in topic agreement and verbal patterns (Beutler et al., 2004). Some inferred therapist states are repeatedly correlated with results, although a predictive relationship has not been established. One example is attitudes concerning development of a therapeutic relationship, which has shown great durability as a correlative factor (Beutler et al., 2004). In a meta-analysis of 28 studies, Beutler et al. found a moderate relationship between therapeutic relationship and outcomes. Further exploration of the therapeutic alliance could help the profession develop a better understanding of how the inferred state of some therapists contributes more successfully to building an alliance and scoping and refining this concept.

Beutler et al.'s (2004) analysis shows promise in the exploration of other inferred traits of psychotherapists and laments the lack of funding available for this kind of research. Among others, these traits may include well-being, values, attitudes, and beliefs—both as an aspect of the therapist herself and also in relationship with corresponding traits in the client whom she is treating. In particular, therapist emotional well-being and cultural attitudes have been found to be positively correlated with outcome, although not specifically in a causal relationship (Beutler et al., 2004). Wampold and Brown (2005) acknowledge that their work focused on how much the therapists contributed to successful change and not on how they did it or what they might possess that facilitated it. Further research into inferred traits will help fill a void in our understanding of what more successful therapists are bringing to their work.

In Search of the Expertise in Counseling and Psychotherapy

Research in the field of expertise suggests best methods for studying the inferred traits of particularly effective therapists. Chi (2006) identifies two methods to use when studying expertise. The first method is to identify experts in a particular domain and attempt to develop an understanding of how they perform. The second method is to study relative expertise, involving comparisons between practitioners to observe and identify what is similar between them. This second method, emphasized in this book, allows researchers to define psychotherapy expertise more broadly.

The goal of understanding *performance* in a particular professional domain underpins Chi's (2006) first method of inquiry. Some researchers emphasize that therapy outcomes are the key measure of therapy expertise (Orlinsky, 1999; Tracy, Wampold, Lichtenberg, & Goodyear, 2014). We argue that outcome measures alone do not capture the complexity of the master therapist. First, these outcome measures usually measure short-term symptom change, an important goal but limited in its scope. Moreover, the person of the psychotherapist is considered a primary tool in the therapy process. As such, we believe it is reasonable to conclude that outcomes facilitated by a therapist will encompass not only those actions that are observable in the therapy room but also those qualities that are embodied in the person of the therapist. Although their observable therapeutic performance may occur in the therapy room, the way that therapists choose to live, the values they hold, the relationships they have cultivated, how they have changed through personal and professional development, and their views on what therapy is about are all inextricably linked to how they are with their clients and ultimately perform in the professional domain. As cited in Miller (1993), Kottler (1991) asserts that "therapists should not use their skills as plumbers or electricians use their tools; rather, in the best cases, through training, practice, and dedication, therapeutic skills become part of the therapist's very being" (p. 9).

We recognize the importance of many paths to understanding psychotherapy expertise. Of course, therapist outcome data should be part of the equation, but we do not agree that it is the key determinate of excellence in psychotherapy. As Hill, Spiegel, Hoffman, Kivlighan, and Gelso (2015) suggest, multiple criteria can be used to assess expertise, including "performance as assessed by relationship expertise and interventions expertise, cognitive processing, client outcomes, experience, reputation, and the person of the therapist" (p. 2).

Chi (2006) uses the term "master" to signify those experts who have achieved the highest level of proficiency. Some of the qualities that have traditionally been attributed to a "master" include the ability and qualifications to teach others and membership in an elite group whose opinions form the rules and standards around performance. At the same time, however, Chi distinguishes between an expert who may have achieved some level of public prominence and one who performs at an expert level without attracting widespread attention. In the field of psychotherapy, some research on prominent, well-known therapists has been undertaken (Kottler & Carlson, 2003; Sperry & Carlson, 2014). However, not as much information is available about the experts who operate with less celebrity. It is reasonable to think that researching "everyday" master therapists would be more relevant to the field of psychotherapy.

The field has not yet developed a definitive understanding of the personal and professional qualities of the most successful therapists (Hubble, Duncan, Miller, & Wampold, 2009). Chi (2006) highlighted one characteristic of experts as having extensive tacit knowledge, a kind of knowledge that is often more challenging to articulate. This idea supports the study of more general characteristics, attitudes, and values rather than attempting to elicit specific procedural information from expert therapists. Lambert (1989) also argues against more research that breaks down the therapist contribution into discrete parts, and he favors a more holistic approach. Betan and Binder (2010) examined the literature that focuses on cognitive skills that expert therapists use when conceptualizing client problems, acknowledging the difficulties in studying psychotherapy expertise because so much of the work cannot be compartmentalized into discrete skills. In addition, they described how outcomes can change over time. An example is a person's experience with a teacher: A student may view a teacher's effectiveness one way immediately after a class and quite differently on reflection 5, 10, or 20 years later. These complexities suggest the use of qualitative research methods that emphasize exploration and integration.

Selection of Master Therapists

The peer nomination process is an intuitive selection method used by people thousands of times every day throughout the world—for example, "Can you recommend a good dentist [doctor, car mechanic, plumber, therapist, or teacher]?" Psychometrically, peer nomination methods have demonstrated effectiveness in identifying excellence in various vocational arenas such as the military and insurance, secretarial, and management fields, as well as for medical students and factory workers (Norton, 1992). Student peer evaluation in the medical field has long been noted as a better predictor of performance during residency training than faculty evaluations or grades (Korman & Stubblefield, 1971; Kubany, 1957; Lurie, Nofziger, Meldrum, Mooney, & Epstein, 2006). In elementary school settings, Cole and White (1993) found that peer ratings of behavioral conduct, attractiveness, social acceptance, and athletic and academic competence were significantly correlated with teachers' ratings and their peers' self-reports. Sonnentag (1998) found that peer nominations are not affected by likeability, and measurement expert Anne Anastasi stated the following about peer nomination: "When checked against a variety of practical criteria dependent on interpersonal relations, such ratings usually have been found to have good concurrent and predictive validity" (Anastasi & Urbina, 1997, p. 468).

For most of the master therapists studies in this book, only those receiving a certain number of nominations based on a few criteria were selected to be participants and considered as master therapists. In addition, as the nomination process "snowballed" (i.e., snowball sampling; Patton, 2002), many of the participants received multiple nominations by other therapists also considered "master therapists." This selection process is consistent with Chi's (2006) definition of masters, which states that "a master can be that expert who is regarded by the other experts as being 'the' expert, or the 'real' expert, especially with regard to subdomain knowledge" (p. 22). Another example of peer nomination is the classic Peters and Waterman (1982) study in which the authors used this method to identify the most innovative and excellent US corporations.

Master Therapists Research

One line of research emerging during approximately the past 20 years has utilized qualitative methods to develop some understanding of those characteristics common to expert therapists. Beginning in the United States and focusing on personal characteristics, these studies have grown to incorporate international perspectives and have spawned similar work that explores more specific qualities of master therapists. By using personal reflection as a research tool, the master therapist studies have focused on what Beutler et al. (2004) referred to as inferred qualities, with the focus of the questions varying along the extratherapy and therapy-specific spectrum.

Goldberg (1992) interviewed 12 psychiatrists recommended by colleagues and found that they had the common characteristics of being caring, sensitive, and dedicated to their clients' welfare and their own professional and personal growth. In 1997, Albert conducted a qualitative study of 12 psychiatrists identified through the process of peer nomination. Albert asked an initial group of psychiatrists to nominate other practitioners who they trusted to provide therapy for their own friends and family, and then Albert repeated this nomination process. The focus of Albert's inquiry was on uncovering what these exceptional practitioners actually did during therapy, asking about how they related to their clients and how they chose and conducted their therapeutic interventions.

A series of master therapists studies began at the University of Minnesota as dissertation research with Thomas Skovholt as advisor. With a base of the large $N = 100$ study of normative counselor/therapist development (Rønnestad & Skovholt, 2013; Skovholt & Rønnestad, 1992), the idea was to explore expertise rather than just normative professional development. First, Harrington (1988) reported findings from a quantitative study that researched psychologists who had achieved Diplomate status with the American Board of Professional Psychology (ABPP). This occurred during the years when success at ABPP board certification was pegged at the expert level and there was a significant failure rate. Currently, success at ABPP board certification is, as with medicine, pegged at the competent level. This study asked the participants to self-identify with words from the Adjective Check List. The results showed that Diplomates associated themselves with such a wide variety of descriptors that no clear picture of an expert therapist emerged (Jennings & Skovholt, 1999).

As a next dissertation project, Jennings (1996) moved from the quantitative methods used by Harrington (1988) to the qualitative methods used by Skovholt and Rønnestad (1992) in their study of normative counselor/therapist development. The Jennings' dissertation was later published in the *Journal of Counseling Psychology* (Jennings & Skovholt, 1999). Jennings explored broader characteristics of expert or "master" therapists. Using an open interview process with 10 practitioners identified through multiple rounds of peer nomination, Jennings acquired rich data that illustrated the characteristics of these experts, particularly in regard to the practice of therapy and development as a therapist. The findings from this research led to the development of a model of nine categories under three domains of abilities: cognitive, emotional, and relational (CER model of master therapists). The original Jennings CER model was further developed with the addition of three more qualitative projects studying the same 10 master therapists. One study was Mullenbach's (2000) dissertation on expert's self-care and resiliency patterns and the second was Sullivan's (2001) dissertation on the working alliance. For the third study, transcriptions from the Jennings and Skovholt (1999) study were qualitatively re-analyzed to identify ethical values of master therapists (Jennings, Sovereign, Bottorff, & Mussell, 2004).

These series of studies became known as the Minnesota Master Therapist Research Project, and the studies were featured in the book, *Master Therapists: Exploring Expertise in Therapy and Counseling* (Skovholt & Jennings, 2004). The book included a joint qualitative project by Skovholt, Jennings, and Mullenbach (2004), who worked together to develop a portrait of the master therapist. The researchers combined the data of the three dissertation projects and from the secondary qualitative analysis examining ethical values. The integrated findings in the book's final chapter were based on 10 master therapists who were interviewed an average of six times totaling more than 100 hours of interview data (Skovholt et al., 2004). From their joint work together as qualitative researchers, four descriptions of characteristics emerged: eight sets of paradoxical characteristics, 16 identifying characteristics, 21 word characteristics, and the central characteristics of the CER model of master therapists, first described by Jennings (1996). The authors of the final portrait chapter went on to describe the implications of this portrait of the master therapist via nine themes (Skovholt et al., 2004).

The Minnesota Master Therapist Research Project was followed by similar qualitative studies of master therapists that focused on specific therapist characteristics, including cultural competence (Goh, Starkey, Skovholt, & Jennings, 2007; Jennings et al., 2012), spirituality (Menigat, 2007); and the use of career interventions (Shy, 2008). In addition, six qualitative studies have followed the general format and methodology of the Jennings and Skovholt (1999) study to learn about master therapists in countries other than the United States. These six international studies are presented in chapters 2–7 and represent master therapists from the Czech Republic, Canada, Portugal, Singapore, Japan, and Korea. In addition, we have included the entire Jennings and Skovholt (1999) *Journal of Counseling Psychology* article in the Appendix. We highly recommend that the reader begin with this article because it sets the stage for the six international master therapists studies that are featured in this book.

Emergence of Qualitative Meta-Analysis in the Study of Master Therapists

In 2008, Jennings et al. utilized a set of questions largely derived from the original 1999 study to interview expert therapists practicing in Singapore. The results were analyzed and organized into 16 themes within four categories: personal characteristics, developmental influences, approach to practice, and ongoing professional growth. In conducting a qualitative meta-analysis (QMA) between the findings from Jennings and Skovholt (1999) and Jennings et al. (2008), the researchers found that 20 of the 25 themes were either "strongly" or "moderately" related between the two studies. Only 5 themes were considered divergent. The results from this initial QMA imply a set of master therapist core characteristics that extend beyond geographic and cultural boundaries (see Chapter 5 for a full account of the results). The final chapter of this book expands on the 2008 QMA by using qualitative methods to create a meta-synthesis of seven master therapist studies from around the world: Jennings and Skovholt (1999); Kwon and Kim (2007); Jennings et al. (2008); Smith (2008); Hirai (2010); Carvalho and Matos (2011a, 2011b); and Řiháček, Kahancová, Jennings, Roubal, and Vybíral (2015).

Individual qualitative studies are rich with information but capture only a fraction of the broader phenomena. However, as qualitative methodology expands in the field of counseling psychology, there are an increasing number of related studies that may be analyzed through QMA. By combining studies through qualitative meta-analysis, a broader and more nuanced perspective can be developed (Finfgeld, 2003).

Finfgeld (2003) argues that the QMA (or meta-synthesis) approach is interpretive rather than merely aggregative and creates a product that goes beyond "one-shot" studies and pursues the incremental accumulation of knowledge. By bringing together multiple related studies, the essential elements within them may be uncovered and the original individual results may be a transformed into a new conceptualization (Schreiber, Crooks, & Noerager Stern, 1997). The interpretive nature of QMA creates a space in which information across studies may be synthesized and relationships between categories discovered.

Timulak (2009) describes this method of analysis as being accomplished by treating the findings (categories, abstracted descriptions, and rich narratives) of primary studies as data for further analysis and attempts to conduct a rigorous secondary qualitative analysis. The goal of QMA is similar to that of quantitative meta-analysis in that it "seeks to create a systematic logic within which findings from distinct studies in a field can be rigorously integrated into stronger and more generalizable knowledge claims" (Thorne,

2009, p. 571). QMA has the potential to strengthen the findings of individual qualitative studies as triangulation occurs within the process, adding to the generalizability of the findings. In this process, categories across multiple qualitative studies are examined in a way that allows for increasing richness in definitions and the ability to conceptualize and understand the data in a more nuanced way (Finfgeld, 2003).

The Importance of a Global Perspective on Master Therapists

In this book, we are also interested in the practice of therapy and particularly expert therapists around the world. What are the characteristics of master therapists in different countries? Will we find more similarities or differences? What are cultural nuances in therapeutic practices?

Globalization, a term used to describe our increasing interconnectedness around the world, is an extremely familiar term for many disciplines. In the area of counseling and psychotherapy, this term has heightened applicability because ours is a discipline that involves human-to-human contact. Sources of help and types of help take on new shapes and meaning through customs, traditions, and cultural taboos that make it difficult to transfer and apply skills. Goh (2005) argued for both the expected and inextricable relationship between cultural competence and master therapists. Specifically, one can easily imagine the optimal kind of empathy that is often required when therapists have to cross or navigate cultural complexities in the therapeutic relationship.

Marsella (1998), as quoted by Kogan (2000), notes,

> We need a new psychology. It's no longer sufficient to train our students in isolation of other disciplines from students across the world, from contact with different cultures. We need a psychology attuned to the changing times, a psychology that is alert to ethnocentric biases inherent in the Western academia psychology and one that values the diverse psychologies of the world. (p. 53)

Since Marsella's clarion call, scholarly efforts to capture what we know about counseling practices around the world have grown (Gerstein & Ægisdóttir, 2005; Gerstein, Heppner, Ægisdóttir, Leung, & Norsworthy, 2009; Kwan & Gerstein, 2008;). The Minnesota International Counseling Institute (Skovholt, Hansen, Goh, Romano, & Thomas, 2005) was convened in the 1980s to bring together international scholars and practitioners, mostly trained in the United States, to discuss challenges in applying mostly Western or US-centric theories and techniques outside the United States.

Heppner, Leong, and Chiao (2008) remind us that counseling psychology as a field grew out of international sociopolitical and economic events that impacted the United States (e.g., world wars and natural disasters) and also that in many instances counseling psychologists have been invited to contribute to international and educational development around the world. However, Heppner et al. summarize nine challenges in the internationalization of counseling practices:

1. Overcoming our ethnocentrism
2. Enhancing cross-cultural competence
3. Cultural sensitivity versus imposed etics in theory development
4. Supporting and extending indigenous psychologies
5. Promoting the integration of multicultural and cross-cultural foci
6. Promoting cross-national research collaborations
7. Promoting culturally valid practice around the world
8. Enhancing and promoting international education
9. Collaboration among counseling organizations

The authors also describe internationalizing as referring to "the inclusion of cross-national and cross-cultural perspectives in the predominant Western perspectives of counseling practice and research as traditionally operationalized in the United States" (p. 68).

By including international studies in our compilation, we hope to add to the field's internationalization efforts by exploring the practices of expert therapists in several countries. In doing so, we hope to address some of the challenges raised by Heppner et al. (2008). In particular, qualitative studies about the practices of expert therapists in different countries offer rich descriptive narratives for how optimal therapy works in different country and cultural contexts. Sue (1999) noted the need for more qualitative studies to understand old and new constructs from different cultural perspectives. An inductive analysis allows the researcher to understand the data without imposing preexisting expectations on the topic of study within cross-cultural contexts. In addition, Christopher, Wendt, Marecek, and Goodman (2014) recommend that

> psychologists who wish to study people in culture would do best to incorporate methods that move outside traditional laboratory experiments and quantitative methods. . . . The urgent need for critical cultural awareness among psychologists suggests the time is ripe for qualitative inquiry to have a much more prominent and visible role in US psychology, alongside quantitative methods. (p. 653)

The international studies in this book also invite readers to consider a more ethno relative or intercultural view toward expertise in therapy rather than an ethnocentric or monocultural view. Marsella (1998) and Sue (1999) claim that one of the reasons why cross-cultural research has not been as conclusive or useful is the bias and value-laden assumptions and hypotheses of previous research methodologies and viewing results from Western lenses. Sue (1999) recommends "a variety of research methods, including qualitative and ethnographic strategies . . . to create a more substantial knowledge base" (p. 1076). Marsella (1998) states that the "increased use of qualitative research orientations and methods will enhance psychology's knowledge of context, meaning, and power asymmetries [and] will reduce Western psychology's ethnocentric biases" (p. 1287).

In some of the international studies, readers will discover indigenous practices from local, cultural, and religious traditions and also read about how some therapists constantly negotiate theories and techniques they learned from a different country (frequently the United States) to apply and be relevant to their country contexts. In the case of Singapore, multiculturalism also has to be viewed from a very distinct historical, sociopolitical lens different from the multicultural counseling paradigm in most psychotherapy training programs in the United States. These studies therefore offer a glimpse into how multicultural and cross-cultural foci integrate. In addition, many of the studies represent cross-national collaborations of researchers from multiple countries.

Clearly, this volume is far from exhaustive and does not attempt to represent the vast expanse of expert practice around the world or even regions of the world. We also caution against attempts to overgeneralize or essentialize cultures and countries. Given increasing global connectedness, Hermans and Kempen (1998) aptly compare trying to do research in this globalizing context with trying to study "moving cultures" (p. 1111). Rather than traditional East versus West dichotomies, the influence of knowledge and cultures in multilateral geographical directions has created "hybridized" multicultural societies difficult to categorize. Instead, we emphasize reading each international study with what Christopher et al. (2014) recommend: (1) critical cultural awareness that acknowledges our own theoretical groundings and biases and (2) hermeneutics—cultural interpretation and meaning-making that most closely originates from the country of study.

References

Albert, G. (1997). What are the characteristics of effective psychotherapists? The experts speak. *Journal of Practical Psychology and Behavioral Health, 3*(1), 36–44.

Anastasi, A., & Urbina, S. (1997). *Psychological testing* (7th ed.). Englewood Cliffs, NJ: Prentice Hall.

Baldwin, S. A., Wampold, B. E., & Imel, Z. E. (2007). Untangling the alliance–outcome correlation: Exploring the relative importance of therapist and patient variability in the alliance. *Journal of Consulting and Clinical Psychology, 75*(6), 842–852.

Betan, E. J., & Binder, J. L. (2010). Clinical expertise in psychotherapy: How expert therapists use theory in generating case conceptualizations and interventions. *Journal of Contemporary Psychotherapy, 40*(3), 141–152.

Beutler, L., Machado, P., & Neufeldt, S. (1994). Therapist variables. In A. Bergin & S. Garfield (Eds.), *Handbook of psychotherapy and behavior change* (4th ed.). New York, NY: Wiley.

Beutler, L. E., Malik, M., Alimohamed, S., Harwood, T. M., Talebi, H., Noble, S., & Wong, E. (2004). Therapist variables. In M. J. Lambert, A. Bergin, & S. Garfield (Eds.), *Handbook of psychotherapy and behavior change* (pp. 227–306). New York, NY: Wiley.

Blatt, S. J., Sanislow, C. A., Zuroff, D. C., & Pilkonis, P. A. (1996). Characteristics of effective therapists: Further analyses of data from the National Institute of Mental Health treatment of depression collaborative research program. *Journal of Consulting and Clinical Psychology, 64*, 1276–1284.

Carvalho, H. M., & Matos, P. M. (2011a). Ser e Tornar-se Psicoterapeuta Parte I: Diálogo entre Experiências Pessoais e Profissionais/Being and becoming a psychotherapist Part I: Dialogue between personal and professional experiences. *Psicologia: Ciência e Profissâo, 31*(1), 80–95.

Carvalho, H. M., & Matos, P. M. (2011b). Ser e tornar-se psicoterapeuta parte II: Diálogo entre mudanças pessoais e profissionais/Being and becoming a psychotherapist Part II: Dialogue between personal and professional changes. *Psicologia: Ciência e Profissâo, 31*(4), 778–799.

Castonguay, L. G., Goldfried, M. R., Wiser, S., Raue, P. J., & Hayes, A. M. (1996). Predicting the effect of cognitive therapy for depression: A study of unique and common factors. *Journal of Consulting and Clinical Psychology, 64*(3), 497–504.

Chi, M. (2006). Two approaches to the study of experts' characteristics. In K. A. Ericsson (Ed.), *The Cambridge handbook of expertise and expert performance* (pp. 21–30). New York, NY: Cambridge University Press.

Christopher, J. C., Wendt, D. C., Marecek, J., & Goodman, D. M. (2014). Critical cultural awareness: Contributions to a globalizing psychology. *American Psychologist, 69*(7), 645–655.

Cole, D. A., & White, K. (1993). Structure of peer impressions of children's competence: Validation of the peer nomination of multiple competencies. *Psychological Assessment, 5*, 449–456.

Finfgeld, D. (2003). Metasynthesis: The state of the art—So far. *Qualitative Health Research, 13*(7), 893–904.

Gerstein, L. H., Heppner, P. P., Ægisdóttir, S., Leung, S. A., & Norsworthy, K. L. (2009). *International handbook of cross-cultural counseling: Cultural assumptions and practices worldwide.* Thousand Oaks, CA: Sage.

Gerstein, L. H., & Ægisdóttir, S. (2005). Guest editors of special issue: Counseling around the world. *Journal of Mental Health Counseling, 27*, 95–184.

Goh, M. (2005). Cultural competence and master therapists: An inextricable relationship. *Journal of Mental Health Counseling, 27*, 71–81.

Goh, M., Starkey, M., Skovholt, T. M., & Jennings, L. (2007). *A qualitative study of culturally competent psychotherapists*. Unpublished manuscript, University of Minnesota, Minneapolis, MN.

Goldberg, C. (1992). *The seasoned psychotherapist*. New York, NY: Norton.

Henry, W. P., Schact, T. E., Strupp, H. H., Butler, S. F., & Binder, J. L. (1993). Effects of training in time-limited dynamic psychotherapy: Mediators of therapists' responses to training. *Journal of Consulting and Clinical Psychology, 61*, 441–447.

Heppner, P. P., Leong, F. T. L., & Chiao, H. (2008). The growing internationalization of counseling psychology. In S. D. Brown & R. W. Lent (Eds.), *Handbook of counseling psychology* (4th ed., pp. 68–85). New York, NY: Wiley.

Hermans, H. J. M., & Kempen, H. J. G. (1998). Moving cultures: The perilous problems of cultural dichotomies in a globalizing society. *American Psychologist, 53*, 1111–1120.

Hill, C. E., Spiegel, S. B., Hoffman, M. A., Kivlighan, D., & Gelso, C. J. (2015, June). *Expertise in psychotherapy revisited.* Paper presented at the 46th International Annual Meeting of Society for Psychotherapy Research, Philadelphia, PA.

Hirai, T. (2010). *Personal and professional characteristics of Japanese master therapists: A qualitative investigation on expertise in psychotherapy and counseling in Japan.* Unpublished doctoral dissertation, University of Minnesota, Minneapolis, MN.

Hubble, M. A., Duncan, B. L., Miller, S. D., & Wampold, B. E. (2009). Introduction. In B. L. Duncan, S. D. Miller, B. E. Wampold, & M. A. Hubble (Eds.), *The heart and soul of change: Delivering what works in therapy* (pp. 23–46). Washington, DC: American Psychological Association.

Huppert, J. D., Bufka, L. F., Barlow, D. H., Gorman, J. M., Shear, M. K., & Woods, S. W. (2001). Therapists, therapist variables, and cognitive–behavioral therapy outcomes in a multicenter trial for panic disorder. *Journal of Consulting and Clinical Psychology, 69*, 747–755.

Jennings, L. (1996). *The personal characteristics of master therapists*. Unpublished doctoral dissertation, University of Minnesota, Minneapolis, MN.

Jennings, L., D'Rozario, V., Goh, M., Sovereign, A., Brogger, M., & Skovholt, T. (2008). Psychotherapy expertise in Singapore: A qualitative investigation. *Psychotherapy Research, 18*(5), 508–522.

Jennings, L., Gulden, A., Oien, M., D'Rozario, V., Goh, M., & Skovholt, T. M. (2012). Multicultural knowledge and skills of Singaporean master therapists. *Journal of Asia Pacific Counseling, 2*(2), 133–146.

Jennings, L., & Skovholt, T. M. (1999). The cognitive, emotional, and relational characteristics of master therapists. *Journal of Counseling Psychology, 46*(1), 3–11.

Jennings, L., Sovereign, A., Bottorff, N., & Mussell, M. P. (2004). Ethical values of master therapists. In T. M. Skovholt & L. Jennings (Eds.), *Master therapists: Exploring expertise in therapy and counseling* (pp. 107–124). Boston, MA: Allyn & Bacon.

Kogan, M. J. (2000). Internationalizing psychology's curriculum. *Monitor on Psychology, 31*(9), 53.

Korman, M., & Stubblefield, R. L. (1971). Medical school evaluation and internship performance. *Journal of Medical Education, 46*, 670–673.

Kottler, J. A. (1991). *The compleat therapist*. San Francisco, CA: Jossey-Bass.

Kottler, J. A., & Carlson, J. (2003). *Bad therapy: Master therapists share their worst failures*. New York, NY: Brunner-Routledge.

Kubany, A. (1957). Use of sociometric peer nominations in medical education research. *Journal of Applied Psychology, 41*, 389–394.

Kwan, K. K., & Gerstein, L. H. (2008). Envisioning a counseling psychology of the world: The mission of the International Forum. *The Counseling Psychologist, 36*, 182–187.

Kwon, K., & Kim, C. (2007). Analysis of the characteristics of Korean master group counselors. *Korean Journal of Counseling, 8*(3), 979–1010.

Lambert, M. (1989). The individual therapist's contribution to psychotherapy process and outcome. *Clinical Psychology Review, 9*(4), 469–485.

Lindgren, O., Folkesson, P., & Almqvist, K. (2010). On the importance of the therapist in psychotherapy: A summary of current research. *International Forum of Psychoanalysis, 19*, 224–229.

Luborsky, L., McLellan, A. T., Diguer, L., Woody, G., & Seligman, D. A. (1997). The psychotherapist matters: Comparison of outcomes across twenty-two therapists and seven patient samples. *Clinical Psychology: Science and Practice, 4*(1), 53–65.

Lurie, S. J., Nofziger, A. C., Meldrum, S., Mooney, C., & Epstein, R. M. (2006). Temporal and group-related trends in peer assessment amongst medical students. *Medical Education, 40*, 840–847.

Marsella, A. (1998). Toward a "global-community psychology": Meeting the needs of a changing world. *American Psychologist, 53*(12), 1282–1291.

Menigat, D. J. O. (2007). *Exploring expert counselors spiritual development and how it contributes to their counseling work*. Unpublished doctoral dissertation, Ohio University, Athens, OH.

Miller, L. (1993). Who are the best psychotherapists? Qualities of the effective practitioner. *Psychotherapy in Private Practice, 12*(1), 1–18.

Miller, S. D., Hubble, M. A., Duncan, B. L., & Wampold, B. E. (2009). Delivering what works. In B. L. Duncan, S. D. Miller, B. E. Wampold, & M. A. Hubble (Eds.), *The heart and soul of change: Delivering what works in therapy* (pp. 421–429). Washington, DC: American Psychological Association.

Mullenbach, M. (2000). *Master therapists: A study of professional resiliency and emotional wellness.* Unpublished doctoral dissertation, University of Minnesota, Minneapolis, MN.

Nissen-Lie, H. A., Rønnestad, M. H., Høglend, P. A., Havik, O. E., Solbakken, O. A., Stiles, T. C., & Monsen, J. T. (2015). Love yourself as a person, doubt yourself as a therapist? *Clinical Psychology and Psychotherapy, 22*, 317–327.

Norton, S. M. (1992). Peer assessments of performance and ability: An exploratory meta-analysis of statistical artifacts and contextual moderators. *Journal of Business and Psychology, 6*, 387–399.

Orlinsky, D. E. (1999). The master therapist: Ideal character or clinical fiction? *Journal of Counseling Psychology, 46*(1), 12–15.

Orlinsky, D. E., Botermans, J., Rønnestad, M. H., & The SPR Collaborative Research Network. (2001). Towards an empirically grounded model of psychotherapy training: Four thousand therapists rate influences on their development. *Australian Psychologist, 36*(2), 139–148.

Peters, T. J., & Waterman, R. H. (1982). *In search of excellence—Lessons from America's best-run companies.* London, England: HarperCollins.

Řiháček, T., Kahancová, M., Jennings, L., Roubal, J., & Vybíral, Z. (2015). *Czech master therapists.* Unpublished manuscript. Masaryk University, Brno, Czech Republic.

Rønnestad, M. H. & Skovholt, T. M. (2013). *The developing practitioner: Growth and stagnation of therapists and counselors.* New York: Routledge.

Schreiber, R., Crooks, D., & Noerager Stern, P. (1997). Qualitative meta-analysis. In J. M. Morse (Ed.), *Completing a qualitative project: Details and dialogue* (pp. 311–328). Thousand Oaks, CA: Sage.

Shy, J. D. (2008). *Expert and novice practitioner use of the computer-based test interpretation for the self-directed search: A qualitative analysis.* Unpublished doctoral dissertation, Florida State University, Tallahassee, FL.

Skovholt, T. M., Hansen, S. S., Goh, M., Romano, J. L., & Thomas, K. A. (2005). The Minnesota International Counseling Institute (MICI) 1989–present: History, joyful moments, and lessons learned. *International Journal for the Advancement of Counseling, 27*, 17–33.

Skovholt, T. M., & Jennings, L. (Eds.). (2004). *Master therapists: Exploring expertise in therapy and counseling.* Boston, MA: Allyn & Bacon.

Skovholt, T. M., Jennings, L., & Mullenbach, M. (2004). Portrait of the master therapist; Developmental model of the highly functioning self. In T. M. Skovholt & L. Jennings (Eds.), *Master therapists: Exploring expertise in therapy and counseling* (pp. 125–146). Boston, MA: Allyn & Bacon.

Skovholt, T. M., & Rønnestad, M. H. (1992). Themes in therapist and counselor development. *Journal of Counseling and Development, 70*(4), 505–515.

Sonnentag, S. (1998). Identifying high performers: Do peer nominations suffer from a likeability bias? *European Journal of Work and Organizational Psychology, 7*(4), 501–515.

Smith, A. (2008). *Personal characteristics of master couple therapists.* Unpublished doctoral dissertation thesis, University of Alberta, Edmonton, Alberta, Canada.

Sperry, L., & Carlson, J. (2014). *How master therapists work: Effecting change from the first through the last session and beyond*. New York, NY: Routledge.

Strupp, H. H., & Anderson, T. A. (1997). On the limitations of therapy manuals. *Clinical Psychology: Science and Practice, 4*(1), 76–82.

Sue, S. (1999). Science, ethnicity, and bias: Where did we go wrong? *American Psychologist, 54*(12), 1070–1077.

Sullivan, M. F. (2001). *Master therapists' construction of the therapy relationship*. Unpublished doctoral dissertation, University of Minnesota, Minneapolis, MN.

Thorne, S. (2009). The role of qualitative research within an evidence-based context: Can metasynthesis be the answer? *International Journal of Nursing Studies, 46*, 569–575.

Timulak, L. (2009). Meta-analysis of qualitative studies: A tool for reviewing qualitative research findings in psychotherapy. *Psychotherapy Research, 19*(4–5), 591–600.

Tracy, T. J. G., Wampold, B. E., Lichtenberg, J. W., & Goodyear, R. K. (2014). Expertise in psychotherapy: An elusive goal? *American Psychologist, 3*, 218–339.

Wampold, B. E., & Brown, G. S. (2005). Estimating variability in outcomes attributable to therapists: A naturalistic study of outcomes in managed care. *Journal of Consulting and Clinical Psychology, 73*(5), 914–923.

Wampold, B. E., & Imel, Z. E. (2015). *The great psychotherapy debate: The evidence for what makes psychotherapy work*. New York, NY: Routledge.

2 Czech Master Therapists

Tomáš Řiháček, Mária Kahancová, Len Jennings, Jan Roubal, and Zbyněk Vybíral

Introduction

Traditionally, psychotherapy research has focused more on the study of *psychotherapies*, rather than *psychotherapists*, "as if therapists, when properly trained, [were] more or less interchangeable" (Orlinsky & Ronnestad, 2005a, p. 5). However, research on the effectiveness of psychotherapy has shown that the proportion of variance attributable to therapists is much higher than the proportion explainable by a treatment (Wampold, 2001). For instance, Kim, Wampold, and Bolt (2006) analyzed the data from the National Institute of Mental Health Treatment of Depression Collaborative Research Program and found approximately 8% of the variance in outcomes to be attributable to therapists, whereas they found 0% to be due to the particular treatment delivered. The existence of a therapist effect has been confirmed also in naturalistic studies (Lutz, Leon, Martinovich, Lyons, & Stiles, 2007; Okiishi et al., 2006; Okiishi, Lambert, Nielsen, & Ogles, 2003). In Lutz et al.'s (2007) study, as much as 17% of the variance in estimated rates of patient improvement was explained by therapist differences.

Several studies discovered a relationship between various therapists' personal characteristics and their ability to create, maintain, and repair the working alliance. In their review, Ackerman and Hilsenroth (2003) found that therapists' personal attributes, such as being flexible, honest, respectful, trustworthy, confident, warm, interested, and open, contributed positively to the alliance. The results of Anderson, Ogles, Patterson,

Lambert, and Vermeersch's (2009) study suggest that a portion of the variance in outcome between therapists is due to their ability to handle interpersonally challenging encounters with clients. Furthermore, a meta-analysis indicates that the quality of the therapeutic alliance is more a result of therapist actions or characteristics and, therefore, that the therapists' role is the most important for achieving beneficial outcomes (Del Re, Flückiger, Horvath, Symonds, & Wampold, 2012). All these studies provide further support for a previous conclusion by Wampold (2001) that the person of the therapist has to be viewed as a critical factor in the success of therapy.

According to Sandell (as cited in Lindgren, Folkesson, & Almqvist, 2010), therapists' efficacy can be explained by "a general factor" associated with therapists' personality rather than specific techniques and orientations. Research focused on outstanding therapists promises to be a fruitful path to answer the question of what comprises this "general factor" (Saxon & Barkham, 2012). Several studies have explored various characteristics of master (expert, eminent) therapists, such as therapeutic focus of master therapists of different orientations (Goldfried, Raue, & Castonguay, 1998), interventions associated with emotional experiencing (Wiser & Goldfried, 1998), principles of the facilitation of client change (Levitt & Williams, 2010), the concept of clinical wisdom (Levitt & Piazza-Bonin, 2016), construction of the therapeutic relationship (Sullivan, Skovholt, & Jennings, 2005), ethical values (Jennings, Sovereign, Bottorff, Mussell, & Vye, 2005), and psychotherapy integration (Hickman, Arnkoff, Glass, & Schottenbauer, 2009). The Czech study, however, follows a series of studies focusing on a more general description of master therapists' characteristics (Carvalho & Matos, 2011a, 2011b; Hirai, 2010; Jennings & Skovholt, 1999; Jennings et al., 2008; Kwon & Kim, 2007; Smith, 2008). Although a qualitative meta-analysis (QMA) of these six studies (Jennings et al., 2015) shows that many of master therapists' characteristics are interculturally valid, each of the studies reported some specific themes, suggesting that at least some of these characteristics are culturally bound. For instance, in contrast to US therapists, Singaporean therapists tended to speak more about their work than about their personal selves, and they tended to avoid answering such questions even when directly asked. These reactions may be attributed to Singaporean cultural values, such as humility (Jennings et al., 2008). Hirai's (2010) study on Japanese therapists found a higher emphasis on the nonverbal aspect of communication and looser personal boundaries between therapists and their clients (compared to US milieu), which corresponds to the collectivistic nature of the Japanese culture. In the Korean study, master group counselors' openness and comfort for self-disclosure, as well as their willingness to demonstrate their group work in front of others for a training purpose, was emphasized (Kwon & Kim, 2007). Given these differences, we may expect that a study conducted in the Czech cultural context may contribute another unique perspective on what it means to be a master therapist. To provide a basis for interpretation of the results, we first provide a brief overview of the historical and political situation in the Czech Republic during the past several decades.

THE HISTORICAL AND POLITICAL CONDITIONS OF THE CZECH PSYCHOTHERAPEUTIC SCENE

Despite the fact that Sigmund Freud was born in Příbor, a town situated in the Czech region (a part of the Austro-Hungarian Empire at that time), it was not until the early 1930s that the psychoanalytic movement began to develop here. Psychoanalytic ideas were brought to Czechoslovakia[1] by immigrant Jewish psychoanalysts and Russian scholars. A group of psychoanalysts established in Prague finished its existence in 1939 after the Nazi occupation of Czechoslovakia. After having survived the interwar period, a new psychoanalytic group was established in 1946. However, it had quite a short life and had to be dissolved in 1952 under the ideological pressure of the communist regime (Hoskovcová et al., 2010).

After World War II, the development of psychotherapy in the Czech Republic was deeply affected by the communist regime, in both negative and positive ways. As Kratochvíl (2012) explains, the impact of the political situation was strongest during the consolidation of communist power in the 1950s and during the so-called "normalization" after the occupation by the Soviet army in the 1970s. In the 1950s, when the political pressure was most apparent, Czech psychology was fully conformed to Stalin's view that psychology was an obedient servant of ideology. Dialectical materialism and Pavlov's theory of higher nervous activity became the official doctrine of Czechoslovak psychology, and all scholarly works had to reference I. P. Pavlov at that time. Other approaches, such as psychoanalysis, were pejoratively called "bourgeois" and "reactionary." Professionals who advocated these approaches publicly put themselves in danger of persecution.

At that time, psychotherapy was mostly developed as a part of inpatient psychiatric service and alcohol abuse treatment. Several psychiatrists were influenced by an early behaviorism, as well as Maxwell Jones' concept of community psychotherapy (Rubeš & Vybíral, 1991). A unique form of behavioral psychotherapy was also developed based on the involvement of patients in the management of a community treatment, sport activities, or writing diaries and songs. Another original treatment approach, influenced by Moreno's psychodrama, was called "psycho-gymnastics" (Junová & Vybíral, 1990).

According to Kratochvíl (2012), in the second half of the 1960s, the political pressure became less intensive and psychotherapy began to develop more freely. During 1968 and 1969, the psychotherapeutic scene was practically free of any political ideology. This allowed the community of Czech and Slovak therapists to develop a cohesion needed to survive the new onset of communist power during the period of "normalization" in the 1970s. Dynamically oriented trainings and trainings in family therapy were organized, as well as workshops and conferences, the contents of which reflected psychotherapy trends in the Western world, including officially prohibited actions (e.g., a weekend training with Virginia Satir).

In times when the political influence was more restrictive, psychotherapy became an underground activity. One of the most famous Czech psychoanalysts recollects that he practiced psychoanalysis secretly, in early morning or late evening hours, and wrote about it so that psychoanalytic thoughts could be spread further (V. Mikota, personal communication, September 9, 2015). Translations of important Western publications were distributed in typed samizdat[2] copies until 1989. Even under these unfavorable circumstances, many remarkable studies appeared (Hoskovcová et al., 2010). The lack of choice in literature and trainings (with several exceptions, such as psychodynamic therapy and family therapy) often motivated therapists to attend various courses and workshops irrespective of their theoretical orientation. Theoretical purity was not an issue for many of them (S. Dudová, personal communication, September, 2010).

ORIGINAL PSYCHOTHERAPEUTIC APPROACHES

Restricted opportunities to travel to Western countries and to access international literature formed a state of relative isolation, which led to the unique and creative development of psychotherapy in Czechoslovakia and, later, the Czech Republic (Wigfall, 2001). Several original therapeutic approaches were formed, some of which are widespread in the Czech therapeutic scene even today. The most distinct are discussed here.

Community-Based Group Psychodynamic Therapy

An original version of a psychodynamic training was developed by Jaroslav Skála, Eduard Urban, and Jaromír Rubeš, and it is known as "SUR" (the acronym represents the initial letters of the three founders' surnames). The lack of information about developments throughout the world led the founders toward creativity and natural eclecticism, combining thoughts from various therapeutic approaches (psychodynamic, expressive, and behavioral), as well as creating their own conceptions. The training lasts 5 years, during which trainees complete more than 500 hours of group-based personal therapy. It is based on a community format: Several trainee groups form a community, which becomes a trainee's "tertiary family" (Zlámaný, 2013). Each group is led by two trainers of various theoretical orientations, typically a man and a woman. In his empirical reflection, Zlámaný described three pillars of the training: ego strengthening, saturation of a trainee's privation, and inductive education.

During the period of totalitarism, SUR was a predominant form of systematic psychotherapy training, tolerated by the regime, and it was completed by a large number of Czech therapists. The emphasis on a group format made the training partially compatible with the communist ideology, which emphasized a positive influence of a collective. Therefore, therapeutic communities for the treatment of psychiatric patients were founded already in the 1950s (Andrlová, 2005; Kalina, 2005).

Integrated Psychotherapy

One of the pioneers of Czech psychotherapy and a founder of therapeutic sanatorium, Ferdinand Knobloch proceeded from the psychodynamic tradition. After his emigration to Canada, he created his own integrative approach called "integrated psychotherapy" (Knobloch, 2003; Knobloch & Knobloch, 1999). Utilizing the principle of therapeutic group as a diagnostic tool, he integrated the intrapsychic and interpersonal dimensions by conceptualizing an individual's mental life as a group process. Integrated psychotherapy is a synthesis of many lines of thought, including the principle of therapeutic community. According to Prochaska and Norcross (1999), integrated psychotherapy was ahead of its time and outlined several contemporary therapeutic principles.

Boš and Špitz's Eclectic Family Therapy

In the early 1970s, a modern family therapy approach was developed in the field of child inpatient psychiatry. The treatment was based on systemic ideas and techniques. A narrow circle of leading family therapy-oriented psychiatrists influenced the style of child psychiatric care in the Czech Republic, providing education, translations of articles, and contacts with leading experts in the field.

Family Therapy of Psychosomatic Disorders

Beginning in 1989, following the ideas of Boš and Špitz, Chvála and Trapková combined systemic family treatment with psychoanalytic theoretical ideas of child development (Trapková & Chvála, 2004). Influenced by the German tradition of psychosomatic clinics, they have developed a unique integrative psychosomatic approach in the Czech family- and narrative-oriented psychotherapy.

Sati-therapy

In the 1990s, a distinctive therapeutic approach based on Eastern philosophy was founded by a psychologist and Buddhist monk, Mirko Frýba. The word "sati" is the Pali word for mindfulness, and sati-therapy is thus "a treatment through mindfulness." It is based on an integration of the Buddhist ethical–psychological system of abhidhamma, the aim of which is the liberation from suffering in its various forms, person-centered therapy, Gendlin's focusing, and psychodrama (Frýba, 2008, 2013).

After the Velvet Revolution in 1989, Czechoslovakia became a democratic country, and the Czech and Slovak psychotherapy scenes began to develop in an unrestricted contact with the Euro-American psychotherapeutic tradition. Individual therapists or professional groups began to establish long-term contacts with foreign experts and institutions, translated further literature, and organized workshops and trainings. Currently, all major therapeutic traditions are represented, including psychoanalysis; psychoanalytic psychotherapy; Jungian, Adlerian, and psychodynamic psychotherapy; person-centered therapy; cognitive–behavioral therapy; Gestalt therapy; Daseinsanalysis; logotherapy and existential analysis; transpersonal therapy and holotropic breathwork; biosynthesis; Ericksonian therapy; classical hypnotherapy; autogenic training; katathym imaginative psychotherapy; transaction analysis; family and systemic therapy; Satirian therapy;

Pesso–Boyden System Psychomotor; as well as postmodern and integrative/eclectic approaches (Kratochvíl, 2012; Vybíral & Roubal, 2010).

CZECH PSYCHOTHERAPY SCENE TODAY

Psychotherapy is not a formally recognized independent profession in the Czech Republic. Institutionally, it is practiced within the purview of health care (psychiatry hospitals/departments, day clinics, addiction centers, pediatric departments, child and adolescents psychiatry departments, and less often at other somatic departments such as oncology or rehabilitation centers), social services (marriage and family counseling, child welfare, drug users' contact centers, crisis intervention centers, communities for drug addicts, services for victims of domestic violence, counseling for immigrants, etc.), and in private practice. With the exception of health care services, it is not regulated by the state. Regarding therapists' primary profession, psychotherapy is most often conducted by psychologists, psychiatrists, and social workers (Skorunka & Vybíral, n.d.). Sometimes, it is also provided by people of other primary professions, some of whom have received high recognition in the professional community, including several master therapists in our sample. Relatively recently, there has been a debate concerning whether psychotherapy should become an independent profession or whether it should be limited to health services. These two perspectives are represented by two professional organizations.

Like psychotherapy, counseling (in the sense usually denoted by this term in the Western world) is also not a formally established profession in the Czech Republic, and it is often not strictly distinguished from psychotherapy. It is most often provided by psychologists or other professionals possessing psychotherapeutic education (Simons, Hutchison, & Baštecká, 2012).

A full-fledged psychotherapy training typically takes 5 years of part-time study and consists of personal therapy, theory, therapeutic methods, and supervision (although the proportions of these components may differ training to training). Trainees are required to have completed at least a bachelor's degree in psychology, medicine, social work, pedagogy, or other related field before admittance to a training program. Psychotherapy trainings are most often provided by independent private institutes with little or no association with the academic world. Trainees are usually neither required to perform nor supported in research activities, even though they may conduct research focused on psychotherapy in fulfillment of the requirements of their academic study. Trainees typically attend their training parallel to their practice, and the training is quite expensive.

GOAL OF THE STUDY

Given the specific historical circumstances, as well as cultural differences, we were interested in an exploration of self-reported qualities of Czech master therapists and their own representations of therapeutic mastery. For the sake of compatibility with previous studies, we adopted the method of thematic analysis (Braun & Clarke, 2006) as a general means for clustering meanings into themes, combined with elements of consensual qualitative research (Hill, 2012).

Methods

PARTICIPANTS

Therapists

Nine therapists (7 male and 2 female) participated in the study. Their ages ranged from 43 to 72 years ($M = 57.56$, $SD = 10.92$), and their length of therapeutic practice varied from 14 to 46 years ($M = 29.56$, $SD = 10.15$). In terms of primary profession, three of the therapists were social workers, two were psychologists (in combination with social work, in one case), two were psychiatrists, and two represented other humanistic professions. From the perspective of theoretical orientation, the participants represented psychoanalytical psychotherapy ($n = 3$); psychodynamic psychotherapy ($n = 2$); Daseinsanalysis, a form of existential therapy ($n = 2$); psychoanalysis ($n = 1$); and integrative psychotherapy ($n = 1$). Their number of nominations ranged from 4 to 11.

Researchers

The researchers' team was composed of three analysts (M.K., T.R., and L.J.) and two auditors (J.R. and Z.V.). M.K. is Slovak, a graduate student of psychology and psychotherapeutic studies, with no therapeutic practice. As the primary researcher in this study, M.K. made great effort to reflect on her own biases and assumptions concerning the subject of the study. Prior to the study, she was interviewed by a colleague to help clarify her initial position. During this interview, she explored topics such as the importance of relational skills, awareness and self-reflection, humbleness, openness, and tolerance for ambiguity, personal integration, self-care, and desire for continuous development. This procedure helped her keep these assumptions and biases from interfering in the analysis. As a safeguard against imposing categories created in previous master therapists studies, she deliberately chose to postpone reading the results sections of the articles (Carvalho & Matos, 2011a, 2011b; Hirai, 2010; Jennings & Skovholt, 1999; Jennings et al., 2008; Kwon & Kim, 2007; Smith, 2008) until the final stages of the research process (Glaser, 1992).

The other four authors have an academic background, as well as practical experience in psychotherapy and counseling. Their respective roles in the process of analysis are described later. The heterogeneity of the research team provided an opportunity to combine the perspectives of Czech, Slovak, and US analysts, as well as the perspectives of members with different amounts of practical therapeutic experience, ranging from seasoned practitioners and supervisors to a novice trainee equipped with mostly theoretical knowledge about psychotherapy. Another source of the variability of perspectives was brought into the study by engaging both researchers who were knowledgeable of the previous work on the topic and those who deliberately postponed reading the previous research until the analysis was finished. This multiplicity of voices served as a source of triangulation, protecting the team from a one-sided view of the phenomenon under study. T.R. served as M.K.'s supervisor and was responsible for writing the chapter.

PROCEDURE

Recruitment

Following previous studies on master therapists (e.g., Jennings & Skovholt, 1999; Jennings et al., 2008), Czech master therapists were identified using a combination of a peer-nomination process and snowball sampling (Patton, 2002). We intended to address a wide network of professionals, balanced from the standpoint of theoretical orientation and inclusive of even marginal approaches on the Czech therapeutic scene. To reach this goal, all approved training institutes in the Czech Republic ($n = 37$) were included, and a total of 49 representatives of these institutes (senior therapists in the role of training guarantors) were asked to nominate 3 or more master therapists. The criteria for nomination were adopted from Jennings and Skovholt (1999). Eighteen of these therapists responded, providing the first wave of nominations. All nominees were again asked to provide their nominations and, in this way, six waves of peer-nomination took place, yielding 165 nominees who received a total of 236 nominations. Based on the distribution of nominations, we decided to include in the sample only those who received at least 4 nominations. Using this criterion, we obtained 16 nominees (who together received 39% of all nominations). Nine of the 16 agreed to participate in the study, and they comprised the final sample (together they achieved 25.9% of all nominations).

Data Creation

A semistructured interview with each participant was conducted by M.K. The interviews followed the structure outlined in Jennings and Skovholt (1999) with one modification: One question was added at the beginning, mapping the meanings of "mastery" ascribed to the term by the participants. This strategy proved to be useful because the term was found to be problematic by many of them. This observation is commented on in the Discussion section. The interviews lasted 45–120 minutes. Afterwards, audiotaped interviews were transcribed and translated into English.

Analysis

Thematic analysis (Braun & Clarke, 2006) was chosen as the method for data analysis. This choice was substantiated by the facts that (1) we intended to proceed in the inductive direction of analysis (rather than to fit the data into any sort of preconceived categories) and (2) we expected the results to be in a form of a list of themes or qualities. This method was combined with some aspects of the consensual qualitative research approach (Hill, 2012), such as consensual decision-making, to enhance the validity of the findings. The analysis proceeded in several steps described next.

First, the whole data set was analyzed by M.K. Initial codes were assigned to parts of data that were found relevant to the research question. Then, M.K., T.R., and L.J. met and discussed the first version of analysis in detail. Together, the team of analysts conducted a line-by-line analysis of each transcript and preliminary code. A consensual version of coding was sought, aiming at an even more elaborated and comprehensible set of codes.

Second, M.K. organized the set of codes into 40 working themes. Based on their similarities, as well as hierarchical relationships, these working themes were further combined by M.K. and T.R. into 16 themes, falling within six categories.

Third, following Hill's (2012) recommendation, two auditors were engaged in the study. First, Z.V. read the analyzed transcripts and provided a detailed report on the process of analysis, suggesting changes or additions in coding. The suggestions were processed by M.K., and the resulting formulation of themes was sent to the second auditor, J.R., whose task was to check for correspondence between the data and the set of themes. His suggestions were again discussed by the team and integrated in the final set of themes.

Results

The analysis yielded 16 themes organized into six categories (or superordinate themes). Table 2.1 provides the list of themes, as well as the numbers of therapists represented by each theme. Note that the characteristics are based on the participants' self-reflection and their representations of a master therapist.

HUMBLE ATTITUDE TOWARD MASTERY, CLIENTS, AND COLLEAGUES

This category captures a fundamental attitude of deep respect evinced by the participants in many aspects of their professional lives. The category covers three themes: striving for "good enough," mastery is in-between the therapist and the client, and humility and humanity.

Striving for "Good Enough"

Several participants explicitly rejected the idea that they could be called "master therapists," and others doubted whether mastery in psychotherapy exists at all. They tended to perceive mastery as an unreachable ideal and preferred to speak about striving for being

TABLE 2.1

Czech Master Therapist Themes Within Categories

Category	Theme	Frequency[a]
Humble attitude toward mastery, clients, and colleagues	Striving for "good enough"	7
	Mastery is in-between the therapist and the client	7
	Humility and humanity	7
Relationship	Relationship is healing	6
	Secure relationship	4
Awareness of one's needs, limits, and resources	Self-nurturing	6
	Keeping a boundary between one's personal and professional lives	5
	Awareness of one's weaknesses and limits	7
Continuous development	Years of practice	7
	Appreciation of diversity of life experiences	4
	Personal therapy, education, and supervision	5
Engagement	Therapists' care and curiosity	6
	Providing an encouraging perspective	5
	Judicious use of self-disclosure	4
Awareness of the complexity of psychotherapeutic work	Complex thinking about therapeutic change	6
	Creative work with information	7

[a]Numbers denote how many of the nine participants mentioned the theme.

good enough therapists. This, however, by no means indicates that the participants were content with the status quo and ceased striving for improvement. Rather, striving for being "good enough" required hard work, as well as doubting one's accomplishments, as illustrated by one participant:

> To say that I'm a good therapist is enough for me. But I still keep thinking about it. If I do this or that, will it be good? Or if I react like this or understand the client's problem that way—is it really good enough or could I perceive it another way? What would be better for the client? . . . Well, I think that it is the gist of the work to constantly think about it. Not to let it go, not to have a feeling of satisfaction that it is fine the way I do it and that it doesn't need any change or alteration. . . . I think that I am a good enough therapist but I still need to take care of it somehow. (P2)

Some participants thought that striving for "mastery" could be even a danger for the therapeutic process because it would more likely stem from a therapist's narcissistic needs rather than from his or her interest in a client's welfare. In the words of P1,

> [Therapists'] need to relate to people competes with their need for confirmation that they are excellent. So a therapist who aspires for being an excellent therapist hasn't resolved enough his or her narcissistic balance. . . . Well I think that if a therapist has a need to show off and become a famous expert, there is something wrong with it.

Other participants rejected the notion of a master therapist as associated with a personality cult (P2), competition placed in a discipline that itself "is not very competitive" (P9), or a myth creating unrealistic expectations from therapists and psychotherapy that "should be an ordinary job" (P7).

Mastery Is In-between the Therapist and the Client

For the participants, mastery was not a quality of a therapist alone. Rather, they thought about it as an interactional quality that was co-created by both what the client needs and what the therapist offers: "Maybe for somebody it is important to meet an older and experienced [therapist] and for someone else it can be important to meet a young and enthusiastic [therapist]" (P9). Different therapists can meet diverse needs of different clients, and this matching seems to be largely based on subjective criteria, such as feelings and needs. This is why one participant found it useless to search for a universal recipe for a master therapist that would suite everybody because he was afraid that therapists would be tempted to apply such a model to every patient, irrespective of their uniqueness (P1).

The interactional nature of mastery may also include an element of chance or *"favorable circumstances"* on the sides of both the therapist and the client: "When, taken from the subjective perspective of a client, something extraordinary happens, something by which the therapist really inspires the client or by which the therapist really helps the client, then the client might perceive the therapist as outstanding" (P2).

The same therapist further described how an impression of mastery can be based on a deeply unique personal experience with a particular therapist. For her, a master therapist was "a therapist, with whom I can feel that my feelings and thoughts resonate with what he is saying and with whom I really enjoy being in that state of connection" (P2).

The previous quotations show that, for our participants, a client participates in the co-created phenomenon of "mastery" to a great extent and, to use another participant's words, "It's important whether [the therapist] is outstanding from the client's perspective; he can't be outstanding just for himself alone" (P9).

Humility and Humanity

The participants believed that therapists should like people. Therapists should approach them "with regard, respect, and in a friendly mood" (P7); they should "be calm, kind, respectful, patient, and humble" and should possess "kindness, nonjudgmental [attitude], . . . consideration, tactfulness, and respect" (P4). A similar attitude of respect was expressed by another therapist: "I don't force my patients to do anything, I don't stop them from anything—at least I'm trying not to do so" (P1).

The participants tended to emphasize the basic human quality of the therapeutic activity rather than its technical aspects: "I think that master therapists don't have to use any techniques. One simply accompanies the [client] step by step, word by word, according to the client's needs" (P4). According to this participant, therapists who are inexperienced or unwilling to accommodate to a client may try to impose a technique on him or her.

In this sense, the participants tended to express an opinion that therapeutic mastery itself does not require any extraordinary qualities. Rather, it may, at least partially, consist of a willingness to give up some of their expertise in favor of a more human contact, even though it is "technical humanity" (P7)—humanity embedded in a goal-oriented therapeutic relationship. Rejecting a hierarchical and superior role of an expert, the participants spoke about their willingness to doubt. One described this willingness as having "some space left for not knowing everything and to find the answer step by step" (P9), as well as to learn from their own mistakes. This attitude of openness and humility, however, goes hand in hand with the participants' sense of confidence in their competency gained over years, as illustrated by P5: "I am able to believe that I can somehow help [my clients], that it will somehow makes sense. . . . I believe it will go well if we try together. . . . Some is some basal optimism."

The respectful attitude manifests itself in relation to not only the participants' clients but also their colleagues. A master therapist "doesn't overestimate himself or his method, and he doesn't need to define himself against his colleagues or clients at any price" (P5).

RELATIONSHIP

This category captures the role that participants ascribed to the therapeutic relationship. It covers two themes: Relationship is healing and secure relationship.

Relationship Is Healing

Many participants shared a belief that a relationship, meaningful to both the client and the therapist, is a basic healing element in psychotherapy. Psychotherapy is an encounter of two human beings: "I heal through the relationship, which happens through a living presence of two people" (P2). The difference between the two, a therapist and a client, becomes relative:

> Psychotherapy is something like a meeting of two people, one of whom is more in need and the other one is less in need. And the latter tries to help the first one somehow and tries to make a meaningful contact possible. I like it very much and I hope I'm the one less in need than people who see me, but maybe I'm not. (P7)

Some participants appreciated explicitly the mutuality of this relationship. Therapy does not serve merely the client; therapists also profit from psychotherapy and they get some of their needs satisfied:

> [Psychotherapy is] a kind of contact between two people, which gives both parties an opportunity to understand something, to achieve an insight and also to experience something positive. Both sides can actually acquire something important for themselves. I wouldn't take the therapist out of it completely. (P2)

The emphasis put on relationship evolved during the participants' careers. As beginning therapists, they used to follow rules more strictly. After they gained some experience, however, they started to give priority to the relationship: Adhering to rules became less important and their therapy became more dialogical. For instance, the participants began to allow themselves to be more authentic and daring: "Maybe it is courage to say something stronger to someone if there isn't another way. I wouldn't do it before" (P5). With increasing years of practice, the actual relationship was also perceived as a more important source of information: "I think that I more count on and actually draw from real relationships and real incidents in psychotherapy than from theory" (P6).

Secure Relationship

The participants stressed the importance of establishing and maintaining a safe environment for their clients, even though they differed in the aspects they accented in building the therapeutic alliance. One participant described how, throughout the years of practice, he himself began to feel more secure and thus was able to build trust and safety with his clients:

> I was afraid to talk about some tough themes. I told myself: "If the clients get too deep into their issues what would I do?" I felt insecure and the clients could feel it probably so they tried to protect me, I think. They protected me from their anxiety, pain and suffering. . . . And step by step, I felt securer, so we could talk and

solve tough issues. Now it is different. I really trust we can handle anything that happens. (P8)

In fostering safety, one therapist emphasized the importance of being honest, clear, and thorough with a client:

> I explain a lot the whole process . . . I also do 2–3 sessions to find out whether we are compatible as personalities or whether they like my way of working. And only then the real therapy begins. . . . I think that it is truth, precision, and maybe the thing that the whole process of [working alliance] creation is longer and it means that patients know what they can expect and they feel freedom. . . . And then, even when problems and troubles come, anything can happen between us, including misunderstanding, but once safety is created, we can talk about anything. (P4)

Among further means of creating safety, one of the participants mentioned being aware of transference and countertransference phenomena and clarifying what is on the therapist's mind to show how a client is in reality perceived by the therapist and thus to prevent the client from maintaining a distorted picture of the therapist (P3). Another participant stressed the role of adherence to ethical standards and avoiding client abuse in any form. She also added a necessity to "distinguish interpretations which are beneficial for a client from those which are not" (P2).

AWARENESS OF ONE'S NEEDS, LIMITS, AND RESOURCES

This category describes how master therapists use their self-knowledge and how they take care of themselves. It includes the following themes: self-nurturing, keeping a boundary between one's personal and professional lives, and awareness of one's weaknesses and limits.

Self-Nurturing

The participants were skilled at self-nurturing. They emphasized that psychotherapy should be a source of a therapist's joy and satisfaction but, at the same time, it should not be the *only* source. Enjoying one's job and finding it enriching (P9), along with feeling enthusiasm and passion for the work (P2), was an important aspect that helped the participants invest their energy in their therapeutic endeavors. However, they realized that there is an inherent danger they could be "parasites on their clients a little bit" (P9) if they had no other resource from which to draw their satisfaction. Therefore, having a rich personal life and background (P1) and other resources such as hobbies (P8) were viewed as a crucial aspect of maintaining one's mental health and preventing a burnout.

The participants also believed that their internal resources, such as optimism and trust in the process, help them overcome tough moments in therapy:

> I think the greatest thing I am gifted with is that I am an optimist, that I believe in happy endings, that it all ends well with people. And this is reflected in my therapies, where I can bear the burden with [my clients]. I know that it is difficult now, but when they find new life opportunities and find their freedom, they will be good. And I think this is the strongest point. (P4)

Keeping a Boundary Between One's Personal and Professional Lives

Being aware of their own needs and personal as well as professional limits, the participants were skillful in protecting themselves. They described how they delineated a boundary between their personal and professional lives. One participant, for instance, spoke about the conditions under which she could provide therapy:

> I am very strict with my friends, that means, I don't provide any therapy for them. Lots of people ask me to do so. . . . When somebody tells me: "I have a problem," I answer: "You should visit a great colleague of mine." I am a contact provider. Well, I do listen to them, but when it's always the same song, I say stop. (P4)

Another participant (P8) made it clear he does not bring his work home. It was very natural for him to stop thinking about his clients once he closed his office's door because then his mind was occupied with his hobbies and his family.

Several therapists mentioned that when reaching a point at which they believed their professional work would be hampered by their emotional state, they did not hesitate to cancel sessions for a few days (P4) or even a couple of months (P1). They were aware of how much their personal distress can influence the therapeutic process, although some of them thought this influence does not necessarily have to be detrimental. Two participants described their tentative observations that in periods of high well-being they tended to lose their therapeutic sensitivity (P5 and P6).

Awareness of One's Weaknesses and Limits

The participants did not consider themselves to be free of personal problems. They were aware of and open about their personal limits and weaknesses. One participant explained:

> An unpleasant disposition of mine is that when I don't feel close to people I don't let them know that they are important for me. Especially in a long-term therapy, it is necessary [to show this importance] because there we talk about personal things. . . . This could be a problem because people can have a feeling that I don't consider them to be interesting enough. That is my trap I would say. (P5)

Another therapist (P4) also reflected on her emotionality, describing that sometimes she displays intense emotions that are misunderstood by her clients. To handle this, she tried not to show her emotions, both positive and negative, so openly.

Some participants also mentioned that they were aware of certain types of clients or problems with which they cannot work. These limitations were formulated either on the basis of a diagnosis ("I can't work with alcoholics and drug addicts, because in these cases you have to be very strict," P4) or on the basis of a subjective sense of fitting ("Simply, when I understand or sympathize with them, I can be helpful. And then there are some clients that I can understand worse," P1).

CONTINUOUS DEVELOPMENT

This category serves as an umbrella for various sources of master therapists' development, mentioned in the interviews. It consists of the following themes: years of practice; appreciation of diversity of life experiences; and personal therapy, education, and supervision.

Years of Practice

Immersion in practice was found to be essential for the participants to develop their skills and to turn their knowledge into competence: "To learn a method is not enough; one must get it under the skin" (P8). As another participant explained, theoretical knowledge has to be connected with practice:

> There are people who read all of the Freud's book. But if you sit [a client] next to them to have a conversation with, they wouldn't know how to do it. . . . Without personal experience, even if you read many books about therapy technique, you still won't have the skill when sitting face-to-face with a client. (P2)

With ongoing practice, the participants gained therapeutic sensitivity and certain intuitive knowledge that helped them to understand and decide what needs to be done in the course of therapy with a particular client: "[The therapist] extracts something inexplicable . . . and then he feels 'this is important because of this' and 'this has to happen, so that the patient can change.' He begins to feel which things are important" (P3).

Appreciation of the Diversity of Life Experiences

The participants were appreciative of the diversity of life, both personal and professional. In their opinion, a wealth of experience of various kinds was necessary for the development of a therapist's sensitivity and receptivity: "The ability to learn from your own experience is very important" (P3). Experiencing one's own misfortunes can help a therapist to develop an understanding for various forms of clients' suffering.

Apart from the abundance of their personal experience, the participants drew from their varied professional experiences. Some of them highlighted the usefulness of working with diverse clients in different contexts:

> A therapist should have an experience . . . with different people, different ethnic groups. I worked in a prison for a while and it was a fantastic experience for me, because these are totally different people whom I usually don't meet, who are totally different, and still they were really human, understandable, likeable. (P3)

In a similar vein, one participant explicitly acknowledged the unpredictability of the therapeutic profession:

> I think that the most beautiful thing in our profession is that you never know what comes next. Every single session is different. And people are like deep wells! Everybody is different in their pain, aggression, or in positive things. You can always learn from them. And this is what I enjoy. (P4)

Personal Therapy, Education, and Supervision

The participants considered their education, personal therapy, and supervision as a basic triad for becoming a good therapist. According to them, one's own personal therapeutic experience, either individual or group therapy, was an irreplaceable source of their professional knowledge:

> I can't imagine a therapist that wouldn't go through his own therapeutic self-experience. That seems absurd to me. . . . I think without that nobody can be a good therapist. It seemed to me so obvious, that I didn't even mention it. (P2)

ENGAGEMENT

This category captures the participants' deep personal investment in the therapeutic process. It consists of three themes: therapists' care and curiosity, providing an encouraging perspective, and judicious use of self-disclosure.

Therapists' Care and Curiosity

The participants expressed curiosity and a sincere interest in their clients. They strived to understand each client in a unique way:

> My experience is that clients are unique. Even though they may have the same diagnosis and seem to be quite similar from outside . . . I feel that when we dive into it,

> it's a completely different story. And an outstanding therapist can see this and take it as an adventure. And the client can experience his own uniqueness. (P8)

Some therapists went even further to emphasize their will to "stand behind" their clients (P6) and to make "a reasonable self-sacrifice" for the benefit of their clients (P5 and P8). One of them gave an illustrative example of what he meant by "self-sacrifice": "[A colleague] had an organic patient and she was in a bad state, she was attending therapy intensively. . . . She lived next door to him and he brought her groceries every other day" (P5).

According to some participants, however, this engagement needs to be balanced with some perspective: "The therapist must stay above all but at the same time should be engaged" (P4). Finding a distance, either mentally or together with a client, was also mentioned as an important coping strategy. For instance, one participant noted the role of humor—making little relieving jokes or exploring the situation from a perspective that reduces the emotional load (P9).

Providing an Encouraging Perspective

Several participants stressed the importance of adopting a view of a client's problem that is supportive, compassionate, and accepting. For instance, one participant spoke about neurosis as "the healthiest way" and "the only healthy choice [clients] had in the pathological environment they lived in" (P6). For another participant, a therapist's role was to help a client accept the irrational part of his or her life, to "make this world a little bit more understandable," and to "evoke in [clients] an impression that it is normal, to normalize those things that are in them and [to make them] partially explainable" (P5).

To be able to do this, they tended to perceive clients' pathology as an expression of experiences of tendencies that are generally human and that could be found in the therapist himself or herself:

> I need to be able to imagine, even if I don't like it, that something similar is in me, as well. . . . And my task is to make it more understandable, so that the patient wouldn't have to be afraid of it. People usually see it like the Gorgon Medusa's head. You know that Greek myth, right? Medusa was an ugly woman who had snakes instead of her hair and turned those who beheld her into stone. So that's how people relate to what is going on inside them. They are afraid to look at it. And a therapist should help them to look at it in such a way they wouldn't be afraid of it, they wouldn't turn into stone. It means that the therapist needs to know that it is in him as well. (P1)

Judicious Use of Self-Disclosure

According to their own words, the participants were skilled in using self-disclosure judicially. They were able to reveal their emotional reactions regarding the therapeutic process, the client, or themselves. Their use of self-disclosure, however, was reflected and rare: "You have to consider how much and to what extent you should say things about you" (P9). In the words of another participant, "Self-disclosure can be great but . . . like spice, if it's too much then it's annoying" (P3).

For some of them, being emotionally present was a necessity:

> I can't be neutral. I go into the interaction. I don't need to talk about myself. About my story. I don't do that. I don't need to contaminate the client with my story. She recognizes when I'm angry, sad, unhappy, and so on, because I interact. I am not scared to express my emotions. (P8)

AWARENESS OF THE COMPLEXITY OF PSYCHOTHERAPEUTIC WORK

This category describes the participants' ability to work with information in a creative and complex manner while practicing psychotherapy. There are two themes included in this category: complex thinking about therapeutic change and creative work with information.

Complex Thinking About Therapeutic Change

The participants were able to think about the therapeutic change in a very complex manner. One participant used a metaphor of a "broken leg" to illustrate what healing can mean in the context of psychotherapy, in contrast to a more traditional medical meaning of the word:

> It's rather rare in psychotherapy that someone comes with a problem, something like "my leg is broken" and leaves [the therapy] with the leg healed. What happens more often is that the leg is healed only partially and [the client] accepts it and also understands why he is limping. And sometimes it happens that the leg is not healed at all, but it can still be a good therapy. . . . [The clients] are satisfied and when the therapist asks them about their problem, they answer: "Oh that one, I still have it," but it's no more an issue in the therapy. (P9)

Another participant shared with us that clients differ in their ability to profit from therapy, which makes the evaluation of therapeutic change problematic:

> I think that from a long-term point of view, the quality of life really changed in about 20% [of my clients]. And those who improved, but are still in need of therapy from time to time—there could be about 50% of them. And the remaining 30% are those with whom we did not match each other or who are chronic. . . . And

> there are those who can't change too much and for whom it's essential to come for support. (P4)

One participant reflected on possible discrepancies between a therapist and a client in evaluating the change: "Well, it doesn't have to be the same. The client can think that I'm useful and I can feel that I cannot help him. So it doesn't have to match" (P5). Another one provided a long enumeration of various factors that can influence the process of therapeutic change, except the therapist himself. For instance, he mentioned the synergistic impact of the whole system of care, including the team of colleagues, pharmacotherapy, regime management, providing social-work care, and working with the family system. He concluded that it proved to be difficult to extract the role of therapist from this complex influence (P6).

Creative Work with Information

The participants used creative ways of integrating knowledge and were innovative in their thinking, interconnecting cognitive, emotional, and relational sorts of information. Much of this ability displayed in their work with metaphors and importing knowledge from other fields into psychotherapy, such as in the following example:

> A book on wolves enriched me a lot. It describes how wolves behave with each other in their pack, or which bonds and processes operate there and so on. I found it more useful than books on group therapy or family therapy. Or books on cybernetics. (P8)

Another therapist used Berthold Brecht's concept of alienation, coming from theater science, to develop a therapeutic intervention:

> [The actors] were performing the play and they suddenly stopped to discuss what they were doing. This is contrary to actors acting according to Stanislavski: They immerse into the character and they are really like King Lear, and so on. . . . So, by practicing a Brechtian alienation we can achieve a certain distance from [the client's problem]. (P9)

Metaphors were also used directly in a session to translate therapeutic concepts or a therapist's understanding of the client's problem into a more comprehensible and client-friendly language. As one participant described, "Sometimes it can look weird when we talk about some technical stuff or computers [with a client]. But I try to use metaphors that are understandable for the client and come from the client's domain" (P8).

The participants were, however, not only creative but also reflective and thorough in their thinking. They strived for a balance between intuition and a systematic work: "If you can get stuck in working or thinking rigorously, then you can get stuck in constant ad hoc thinking, as well" (P5). These two modes of functioning need to be in harmony, one supporting the other:

> At first, [psychotherapy] has to become a science, and only after that it can be an art. I must learn something in a scientific way, I need a hypothesis, a paradigm to be grounded in. Then I can step out of this paradigm and look at it from a bird eye's view. And that's art, in my opinion. An art can connect the inconnectable. . . . And in my opinion, an artist is anyone who thinks in his own way and isn't afraid to break the structure. (P8)

Discussion

In our study, we described 16 themes, grouped into six categories, capturing self-reported qualities of Czech master therapists, as well as their own representations of therapeutic mastery. First, we discuss the individual categories as they emerged from our analysis. Then we offer a tentative organizing framework for the whole set of themes.

The category of *humble attitude toward mastery, clients, and colleagues* was the most saturated category in our results. Jennings et al.'s (2015) QMA found the theme of humility to be present in all analyzed studies across countries and cultures, capturing master therapists' healthy perspective on their sense of importance and on their limits of competence. Their humility was not based on a lack of confidence, as in the case of beginning therapists (Bischoff, 1997; Bischoff, Barton, Thober, & Hawley, 2002; Duryee, Brymer, & Gold, 1996), but was grounded in an awareness of their own competency. According to Skovholt, Jennings, and Mullenbach (2004), genuine humbleness of master therapists indicates their humanness and serves as a means of resistance to arrogance and narcissism. Therapists' humbleness seems to be a prerequisite for establishing a mutually responsive therapeutic relationship, as embedded in the concept of therapeutic alliance (Bordin, 1979; Gelso, 2014). In Nissen-Lie, Monsen, and Rønnestad's (2010) study, professional self-doubt, which was interpreted as a sign of a therapist's humbleness and sensitivity, was found to be positively related to working alliance development.

The therapists in our sample tended to "push away" an idea of their therapeutic mastery in favor of a collaborative perspective on the effect of psychotherapy. This is similar to Carvalho and Matos' (2011a, 2011b) finding that Portuguese master therapists emphasized their role as coauthors in the therapeutic change, giving up their control over the therapeutic process to a certain extent. The authors view this in contrast to earlier stages of the master therapists' development, when they tended to direct the process, emphasize the need of visible progress in therapy, and assumed the authorship of change. This attitude corresponds to empirical evidence showing that clients' level of active participation in therapy is one of the strongest predictors of outcome and possibly its "most important determinant" (Orlinsky, Grawe, & Parks, 1994, p. 361) and also to Lambert's (1992; Asay & Lambert, 2006) estimation that 40% of therapeutic change can be explained by factors external to therapy (i.e., clients' pre-therapy characteristics and environmental factors). Williams and Levitt (2007) showed that eminent therapists are not only aware of the importance of client agency but also use several strategies to promote it.

The participants' reluctance to consider themselves master therapists can be partially attributed also to the cultural and historic specificity of the Czech professional milieu. Due to the historical lack of independence and oppression (being in thrall of the communistic Soviet Union from 1948 to 1989, surviving the Nazi occupation from 1939 to 1945, and, in a wider sense, searching for a national identity under the Austro-Hungarian Empire until 1918), mediocrity and inconspicuousness became a survival strategy. "Standing out," at that time, attracted unwanted attention and a risk of persecution. Thus, rejecting the label of "master therapist" can also be understood as a legacy of these historical circumstances.

The category of *relationship* captures therapeutic relationship both as a condition necessary for therapeutic change and as the very means through which a change takes place. Both of these aspects can be found in Jennings et al.'s (2015) QMA and are present in the discussion on the mechanisms of therapeutic change (e.g., Newman, 2010; Sarnat, 2010). Therapists in our sample tended to emphasize the safe and supporting nature of the therapeutic relationship. Interestingly, however, the challenging aspect of the relationship, which is also present in some studies (Jennings & Skovholt, 1999; Sullivan et al., 2005), was not articulated in our data. This can probably be explained by the prevailing psychodynamic orientation of our sample.

The emphasis our participants placed on the relationship corresponds to the acceptance and empirical support it has received as a correlate of therapeutic change (Beutler et al., 2004; Hill & Knox, 2009). There is also empirical evidence that therapists' ability to handle interpersonally challenging encounters with clients (Anderson et al., 2009) and to repair alliance ruptures (Safran, Muran, & Eubanks-Carter, 2011) is positively related to outcome. A meta-analysis has also shown that the quality of the working alliance is more a result of therapists' actions or characteristics, and therefore, the therapists' role is the most important for achieving beneficial outcomes (Del Re et al., 2012).

The category of *awareness of one's needs, limits, and resources* describes master therapists' outstanding self-knowledge and an ability to take care of their own needs. Various aspects of this category are supported by other studies. Jennings and Skovholt (1999) described master therapists' ability to attend to their own emotional well-being and to be aware of how their emotional health affects the quality of their work. Similar themes were also reported by Smith (2008). Kwon and Kim (2007) described therapists' realistic notion about their abilities and their reflexivity about their personal as well as professional limits. In Hirai's (2010) study, practicing psychotherapy was experienced as natural and personally fulfilling for the therapists, which corresponds to psychotherapy being a source of joy and satisfaction for the Czech therapists. In the study by Heinonen,

Lindfors, Laaksonen, and Knekt (2012), lower enjoyment in one's work, as well as lower confidence, predicted poorer outcome, which supports the significance of this category in a successful therapeutic practice.

Reflective practice is defined as one of the foundational competencies in psychology (Rodolfa et al., 2005) and also includes the aspects of self-assessment and self-care (Fouad et al., 2009). In psychotherapy, reflective practice has been emphasized by a number of authors as well (Boswell, Nelson, Nordberg, McAleavey, & Castonguay, 2010; Celano, Smith, & Kaslow, 2010; Farber, 2010; Sarnat, 2010), and knowledge of one's limits is embedded in the ethical standards of the American Psychological Association (American Psychological Association, 2010), as well as the European Association of Psychotherapy (European Association of Psychotherapy, 2002). Adherence to these principles not only aims to prevent clients from harm but also prevents therapists from burnout (Hardiman & Simmonds, 2013; Lee, Cho, Kissinger, & Ogle, 2010).

The participants pointed to the importance of *continuous development* in both the professional and personal spheres of a therapist's life. In this sense, the category partially overlaps with the *striving for "good enough"* theme from the first category. This closely resembles results of other studies (Hirai, 2010; Jennings & Skovholt, 1999; Smith, 2008) that also reported master therapists' eagerness and ceaselessness in learning. This enthusiasm, in combination with a high cognitive capacity, is what distinguishes master therapists' "continuous development" from a mere accumulation of years of experience. There has been a shared belief, initiated by Fiedler (1950) and questioned by later studies (e.g., Wogan & Norcross, 1985), that the work of experienced therapists tends to be more homogeneous across orientations, as compared to less experienced therapists, suggesting that years of practice help therapists discover some "essence" of therapeutic work independent of theoretical orientations. Vasco and Dryden (1997) have found, however, that this is only true for therapists with high epistemological development (i.e., the high degree of complexity and flexibility that characterizes the way therapists think about ontological and epistemological matters).

Another aspect of this category, therapists' appreciation of the diversity of their profession, as well as life in general, is also apparent across studies (e.g., Jennings et al., 2008; Kwon & Kim, 2007). Whereas master therapists in the Singaporean study (Jennings et al., 2008) explicitly emphasized the importance of cultural competency, the Czech participants, working in a much less heterogeneous environment, tended to value having an experience of working with different client populations, such as children, elderly people, and prisoners.

A notable result of our study is the emphasis put by our participants on personal therapy as a prerequisite for being a good therapist. This conclusion is partly attributable to the prevailing psychodynamic orientation of our sample and partly to a high endorsement of this requirement by most of Czech training institutes. This probably distinguishes the Czech context from the US milieu where the support for trainees' personal therapy is more equivocal (Elman & Forrest, 2004; Norcross & Halgin, 2005).

The category of *engagement*, describing therapists' positive emotional investment in the therapeutic process, is also tangentially supported by other studies on master therapists, although it did not earn a position as a stand-alone category in Jennings et al.'s (2015) QMA. In the Portuguese study, Carvalho and Matos (2011a, 2011b) focused on the importance of therapists' empathy while not getting absorbed by a client's emotion. In the Korean sample, therapists reported frequent use of self-disclosure (Kwon & Kim, 2007): Compared to that, the Czech participants emphasized a thoughtful and rare self-disclosure.

Our findings in this category are again supported by process–outcome research. According to Orlinsky, Rønnestad, and Willutzki's (2004) review, therapist role engagement and credibility is positively related to outcome. Similarly, a recent meta-analysis (Farber & Doolin, 2011) showed a moderately positive relationship between positive regard and outcome. Personal investment is also a part of the so-called healing involvement, which pertains to a positively experienced and subjectively successful practice (Orlinsky & Rønnestad, 2005b). A recent study also found a positive relationship between healing involvement and outcome, especially in short-term therapy (Heinonen et al., 2012). The beneficial impact of self-disclosure has been also demonstrated, as summarized by Cooper (2008).

The last category, *awareness of the complexity of psychotherapeutic work*, captures the aspects of complexity and creativity of psychotherapy, as provided by master therapists. In Jennings et al.'s (2015) QMA, a capacity for cognitive complexity and intricate conceptualization was one of the most saturated categories, which found various manifestations in the individual studies, such as respect for the complexity of human beings (Hirai, 2010) or a sense of acceptance of the imperfect and absurd nature of human existence (Carvalho & Matos, 2011a, 2011b). In their study on expert therapists' case conceptualizations, Betan and Binder (2010) theorized on expert therapists' capacity to use theoretical and clinical knowledge in an intuitive, flexible manner that responds and adapts to the unique and complex context of the treatment. Research suggests that experienced therapists' case formulations are more reliable and of better quality (Kuyken, Fothergill, Musa, & Chadwick, 2005), more complex (Lee & Tracey, 2008), and effective in explaining client variables (Mumma & Mooney, 2007). Novice counselors attend more to surface detail, generating formulations that are more simplistic and contain less reciprocal links between categories than those of experienced counselors (Mayfield, Kardash, & Kivlighan, 1999).

BRINGING IT ALL TOGETHER

Although all the previously mentioned characteristics seem to be valid qualities of master therapists, none of them is surprising by itself. Rather, what defines a master therapist may be the configuration of these qualities. During the analysis, we noticed that the themes allow themselves to be organized in a series of opposites. This idea did not gain enough support in the data because one of the two polarities was usually less saturated and more implicit. Therefore, we reserved this consideration for the discussion. For instance, master therapists' humility can be contrasted with their confidence and talent (the latter polarity being more "hidden" in the data). Their accent laid on relationship can be put into contrast with their technical skillfulness or craftsmanship (the latter again being in the background). Protecting their personal and professional boundaries stands against the depth of therapists' compassion. The emphasis on a continuous development may have overshadowed something that we may call "a beginner's position"—that is, an ability to see the therapeutic situation anew and remain in a state of curiosity. Master therapists' engagement, and even readiness for self-sacrifice in some cases, contrasts with their ability to "stay above" and consider the therapeutic process from a distance (which is somewhat covered by the *awareness of complexity* theme but is not fully articulated in the data). Master therapists' complex thinking itself is in contrast with their ability to act intuitively and with lightness (partially covered by the theme of *creative work with information*).

This idea of organizing master therapists' characteristics into opposites to accent their paradoxical nature has already appeared in Jennings, Skovholt, Goh, and Lian (2013), although their list of opposites differs from ours. Although an accent put by therapists on one or another pole may differ in various contexts and countries, we may hypothesize that what defines a master therapist is the ability to balance these polarities and to resolve these inherent tensions without prematurely sticking to one of the poles. This hypothesis, however, needs to be tested in future studies.

LIMITATIONS

Despite our effort to create a balanced and representative sample, our group of master therapists is substantially skewed toward a psychodynamic orientation. This fact, as well as its possible consequences, was mentioned repeatedly in the discussion. Future research on Czech master therapists should therefore more systematically include therapists of various orientations.

Another limitation of this study is an absence of a comparison group. Including a group of beginning therapists or a group of "average" (i.e., non-master) experienced therapists would allow us to conclude which of the resulting themes are really unique for master therapists (Orlinsky, 1999). This question would be better answered, however, through a correlational design. In the present study, we limit ourselves to an exploration of self-reported qualities of peer-nominated Czech master therapists and their own representations of therapeutic mastery.

The sampling strategy (i.e., peer nomination) represents only one possible approach to the identification of master therapists. Although this strategy takes into consideration the professional reputation of a therapist among his or her colleagues, it does not account for the client perspective and may possibly lead to an omission of certain characteristics important from a client's view (Tracey, Wampold, Lichtenberg, & Goodyear, 2014). We adopted this strategy for the sake of compatibility with the previous set of studies based on the seminal Jennings and Skovholt's (1999) study. Other possible approaches used in other studies include nomination by expert therapists (Goldfried et al., 1998); objective criteria such as being a founder of a therapeutic school, being a supervisor, or having published a certain number of publications on psychotherapy (Levitt & Williams, 2010); and achieving high-outcome indicators in an outcome study (Okiishi et al., 2003).

The term "master therapist" itself was viewed as problematic both by the participants and by the authors of this study and could not be easily translated. We decided to keep to a verbatim translation "mistrovský terapeut/terapeutický mistr" (a master therapist/therapeutic master). We were, however, aware of different connotations the term has in the Czech language: It is mostly used in connection with art, sport, or craft and can be perceived with negative connotations of "showing off." Therefore, we were ready to explore the participants' own meanings attributed to the term. Many of them had to reformulate it into a more suitable term, such as "a good therapist" or "a good-enough therapist." For future studies in the Czech context, we recommend using a term free from negative connotations, such as "a very experienced therapist."

A further problem may consist in the fact that interviews can provide access to explicit aspects of mastery only. Those aspects that are implicit (Oddli, Halvorsen, & Rønnestad, 2014) or embodied (Cracium, 2013) may remain undetected. These aspect are probably difficult to verbalize and to reflect on or might lose their value when verbalized (Skovholt, 2013), which may be the reason why mastery is nonteachable and so difficult to achieve.

Whereas the previous consideration was epistemological in nature, the last one is ontological: The very concept of mastery can be considered problematic in light of recent research. In Kraus, Castonguay, Boswell, Nordberg, and Hayes' (2011) study, therapist effectiveness correlated poorly across various domains, which suggests that therapist competencies may be domain or disorder specific rather than reflecting a core attribute of therapeutic mastery. Similarly, Lutz et al. (2007) concluded that therapists probably tend to achieve greater success with certain kinds of patients. These studies encourage researchers to explore beyond the concept of a generalist master therapist and consider our participants' notion that mastery is specific and co-created by a therapist and a client in their joint endeavor. Future research is needed to explore this idea of "co-created mastery" as well as mastery in psychology's many subspecialties.

Conclusion

Although we are aware that there may be aspects of mastery that are inaccessible to self-reflective exploration, we believe that the characteristics discovered in this study, as well as in other studies contained in this volume, may provide inspiration for therapists on various levels of professional development. A realistic image of a master therapist can serve as "a compass" for beginning professionals and can help them accept the paradoxical nature of the profession, as well as the inherent imperfection and deep humanity of those who are so often idealized. Despite the fact that master therapists' characteristics show fundamental similarity across countries and cultures, conducting studies in diverse environments may contribute to the formulation of a rich and culturally sensitive description of what is means to be a master therapist.

Acknowledgment

This study was supported by Czech Science Foundation grant GAP407/11/0141.

Notes

1. Czechoslovakia was formed in 1918 following the collapse of the Austro-Hungarian Empire after World War I. In 1993, it was divided into two independent states, the Czech Republic and Slovakia.

2. The word "samizdat" derives from the Russian language and means "self-published." It refers to the creation and distribution of publications that were prohibited by the communistic regime. Being a key form of dissident activity, it was repressed and punished.

References

Ackerman, S. J., & Hilsenroth, M. J. (2003). A review of therapist characteristics and techniques positively impacting the therapeutic alliance. *Clinical Psychology Review*, *23*, 1–33. doi:10.1016/S0272-7358(02)00146-0

American Psychological Association. (2010). *Ethical principles of psychologists and code of conduct*. Retrieved from http://www.apa.org/ethics/code/principles.pdf

Anderson, T., Ogles, B. M., Patterson, C. L., Lambert, M. J., & Vermeersch, D. A. (2009). Therapist effects: Facilitative interpersonal skills as a predictor of therapist success. *Journal of Clinical Psychology*, *65*(7), 755–768. doi:10.1002/jclp.20583

Andrlová, M. (2005). *Současné směry v české psychoterapii: Rozhovory s významnými psychoterapeuty* [Current approaches in Czech psychotherapy: Interviews with eminent psychotherapists]. Prague: Triton.

Asay, T. P., & Lambert, M. J. (2006). The empirical case for the common factors in therapy: Quantitative findings. In M. A. Hubble, B. L. Duncan, & S. D. Miller (Eds.), *The heart & soul of change: What works in therapy* (pp. 33–56). Washington, DC: American Psychological Association.

Betan, E. J., & Binder, J. L. (2010). Clinical expertise in psychotherapy: How expert therapists use theory in generating case conceptualizations and interventions. *Journal of Contemporary Psychotherapy*, *40*(3), 141–152. doi:10.1007/s10879-010-9138-0

Beutler, L. E., Malik, M., Alimohamed, S., Harwood, T. M., Talebi, H., Noble, S., & Wong, E. (2004). Therapist variables. In M. J. Lambert (Ed.), *Bergin and Garfield's handbook of psychotherapy and behavior change* (5th ed., pp. 227–306). New York, NY: Wiley.

Bischoff, R. J. (1997). Themes in therapist development during the first three months of clinical experience. *Contemporary Family Therapy, 19*(4), 563–580. doi:10.1111/j.1752-0606.2002.tb01193.x

Bischoff, R. J., Barton, M., Thober, J., & Hawley, R. (2002). Events and experiences impacting the development of clinical self confidence: A study of the first year of client contact. *Journal of Marital and Family Therapy, 28*(3), 371–382. doi:10.1111/j.1752-0606.2002.tb01193.x

Bordin, E. S. (1979). The generalizability of the psychoanalytic concept of the working alliance. *Psychotherapy: Theory, Research and Practice, 16*(3), 252–260.

Boswell, J. F., Nelson, D. L., Nordberg, S. S., McAleavey, A. A., & Castonguay, L. G. (2010). Competency in integrative psychotherapy: Perspectives on training and supervision. *Psychotherapy: Theory, Research, Practice, Training, 47*(1), 3–11. doi:10.1037/a0018848

Braun, V., & Clarke, V. (2006). Using thematic analysis in psychology. *Qualitative Research in Psychology, 3*(2), 77–101. doi:10.1191/1478088706qp063oa

Carvalho, H. M., & Matos, P. M. (2011a). Ser e Tornar-se Psicoterapeuta Parte I: Diálogo entre Experiências Pessoais e Profissionais [Being and becoming a psychotherapist Part I: Dialogue between personal and professional experiences]. *Psicologia: Ciência E Profissâo, 31*(1), 80–95.

Carvalho, H. M., & Matos, P. M. (2011b). Ser e tornar-se psicoterapeuta parte II: Diálogo entre mudanças pessoais e profissionais [Being and becoming a psychotherapist Part II: Dialogue between personal and professional changes]. *Psicologia: Ciência E Profissâo, 31*(4), 778–799.

Celano, M. P., Smith, C. O., & Kaslow, N. J. (2010). A competency-based approach to couple and family therapy supervision. *Psychotherapy: Theory, Research, Practice, Training, 47*(1), 35–44. doi:10.1037/a0018845

Cooper, M. (2008). *Essential research findings in counselling and psychotherapy: The facts are friendly*. Thousand Oaks, CA: Sage.

Cracium, M. (2013). *Embodied expertise: The science and affect of psychotherapy*. Unpublished doctoral dissertation, University of Michigan, Ann Arbor, MI.

Del Re, A. C., Flückiger, C., Horvath, A. O., Symonds, D., & Wampold, B. E. (2012). Therapist effects in the therapeutic alliance–outcome relationship: A restricted-maximum likelihood meta-analysis. *Clinical Psychology Review, 32*(7), 642–649. doi:10.1016/j.cpr.2012.07.002

Duryee, J., Brymer, M., & Gold, K. (1996). The supervisory needs of neophyte psychotherapy trainees. *Journal of Clinical Psychology, 52*(6):663–671.

Elman, N. S., & Forrest, L. (2004). Psychotherapy in the remediation of psychology trainees: Exploratory interviews with training directors. *Professional Psychology: Research and Practice, 35*(2), 123–130. doi:10.1037/0735-7028.35.2.123

European Association of Psychotherapy. (2002). *Statement of ethical principles*. Retrieved from http://www.europsyche.org/download/cms/100510/EAP_ethical_guidelines.pdf

Farber, B. A., & Doolin, E. M. (2011). Positive regard. *Psychotherapy, 48*(1), 58–64. doi:10.1037/a0022141

Farber, E. W. (2010). Humanistic–existential psychotherapy competencies and the supervisory process. *Psychotherapy: Theory, Research, Practice, Training, 47*(1), 28–34. doi:10.1037/a0018847

Fiedler, F. E. (1950). A comparison of therapeutic relationships in psychoanalytic, nondirective and Adlerian therapy. *Journal of Consulting Psychology, 14*, 436–445.

Fouad, N. A., Grus, C. L., Hatcher, R. L., Kaslow, N. J., Hutchings, P. S., Madson, M. B., et al. (2009). Competency benchmarks: A model for understanding and measuring competence in professional psychology across training levels. *Training and Education in Professional Psychology, 3*(4, Suppl.), S5–S26. doi:10.1037/a0015832

Frýba, M. (2008). *Psychologie zvládání života: Aplikace metody abhidhamma* [Psychology of life management: Application of the abhidhamma method]. Boskovice, Czech Republic: Albert.

Frýba, M. (2013). *Umění žít šťastně: Buddhova Abhidhamma v praxi meditace a zvládání života* [The art of living happily: Buddha's Abhidhamma in the practice of meditation and life management]. Boskovice, Czech Republic: Albert.

Gelso, C. (2014). A tripartite model of the therapeutic relationship: Theory, research, and practice. *Psychotherapy Research, 24*(2), 117–131. doi:10.1080/10503307.2013.845920

Glaser, B. G. (1992). *Emergence vs. forcing: Basics of grounded theory analysis.* Mill Valley, CA: Sociology Press.

Goldfried, M. R., Raue, P. J., & Castonguay, L. G. (1998). The therapeutic focus in significant sessions of master therapists: A comparison of cognitive–behavioral and psychodynamic–interpersonal interventions. *Journal of Consulting and Clinical Psychology, 66*(5), 803–810. doi:10.1037/0022-006X.66.5.803

Hardiman, P., & Simmonds, J. G. (2013). Spiritual well-being, burnout and trauma in counsellors and psychotherapists. *Mental Health, Religion & Culture, 16*(10), 1044–1055. doi:10.1080/13674676.2012.732560

Heinonen, E., Lindfors, O., Laaksonen, M. A., & Knekt, P. (2012). Therapists' professional and personal characteristics as predictors of outcome in short- and long-term psychotherapy. *Journal of Affective Disorders, 138*(3), 301–312. doi:10.1016/j.jad.2012.01.023

Hickman, E. E., Arnkoff, D. B., Glass, C. R., & Schottenbauer, M. A. (2009). Psychotherapy integration as practiced by experts. *Psychotherapy, 46*(4), 486–491. doi:10.1037/a0017949

Hill, C. E. (2012). *Consensual qualitative research: A practical resource for investigating social science phenomena.* Washington, DC: American Psychological Association.

Hill, C. E., & Knox, S. (2009). Processing the therapeutic relationship. *Psychotherapy Research, 19*(1), 13–29. doi:10.1080/10503300802621206

Hirai, T. (2010). *Personal and professional characteristics of Japanese master therapists: A qualitative investigation on expertise in psychotherapy and counseling in Japan.* Unpublished doctoral dissertation, University of Minnesota, Minneapolis, MN.

Hoskovcová, S., Hoskovec, J., Plháková, A., Šebek, M., Švancara, J., & Vobořil, D. (2010). Historiography of Czech psychology. *History of Psychology, 13*(3), 309–334. doi:10.1037/a0020266

Jennings, L., D'Rozario, V., Goh, M., Sovereign, A., Brogger, M., & Skovholt, T. (2008). Psychotherapy expertise in Singapore: A qualitative investigation. *Psychotherapy Research, 18*(5), 508–522. doi:10.1080/10503300802189782

Jennings, L., & Skovholt, T. M. (1999). The cognitive, emotional, and relational characteristics of master therapists. *Journal of Counseling Psychology, 46*(1), 3–11. doi:10.1037/0022-0167.46.1.3

Jennings, L., Skovholt, T. M., Goh, M., & Lian, F. (2013). Master therapists: Explorations of expertise. In M. H. Rønnestad & T. M. Skovholt (Eds.), *The developing practitioner: Growth and stagnation of therapists and counselors* (pp. 213–246). New York, NY: Routledge.

Jennings, L., Sovereign, A., Bottorff, N., Mussell, M. P., & Vye, C. (2005). Nine ethical values of master therapists. *Journal of Mental Health Counseling, 27*(1), 32–47.

Jennings, L., Sovereign, A., Renninger, S., Goh, M., Skovholt, T. M., Lakhan, S., & Hessel, H. (2015). *Qualitative meta-analysis of six international master therapists studies*. Manuscript submitted for publication.

Junová, H., & Vybíral, Z. (1990). Prázdná parketa a šťastné hvězdy [An empty parquet block and happy stars]. *Konfrontace, 1*(2), 19–33.

Kalina, K. (2005). *Co je SUR?* [What is SUR?]. Retrieved from http://www.sur.cz/downloads/co_je_sur.pdf

Kim, D.-M., Wampold, B. E., & Bolt, D. M. (2006). Therapist effects in psychotherapy: A random-effects modeling of the National Institute of Mental Health Treatment of Depression Collaborative Research Program data. *Psychotherapy Research, 16*(2), 161–172. doi:10.1080/10503300500264911

Knobloch, F. (2003). A heuristic path to psychotherapy integration: One early European development. *Journal of Psychotherapy Integration, 13*(2), 107–129. doi:10.1037/1053-0479.13.2.107

Knobloch, F., & Knobloch, J. (1999). *Integrovaná psychoterapie v akci* [Integrated psychotherapy in action]. Prague, Czech Republic: Grada.

Kratochvíl, S. (2012). *Základy psychoterapie* [The basics of psychotherapy] (6th ed.). Prague, Czech Republic: Portál.

Kraus, D. R., Castonguay, L., Boswell, J. F., Nordberg, S. S., & Hayes, J. A. (2011). Therapist effectiveness: Implications for accountability and patient care. *Psychotherapy Research, 21*(3), 267–76. doi:10.1080/10503307.2011.563249

Kuyken, W., Fothergill, C. D., Musa, M., & Chadwick, P. (2005). The reliability and quality of cognitive case formulation. *Behaviour Research and Therapy, 43*(9), 1187–1201. doi:10.1016/j.brat.2004.08.007

Kwon, K., & Kim, K. (2007). Analysis of the characteristics of Korean master group counselors. *Korean Journal of Counseling, 8*(3), 979–1010.

Lambert, M. J. (1992). Psychotherapy outcome research: Implications for integrative and eclectic therapists. In J. C. Norcross & M. R. Goldfried (Eds.), *Handbook of psychotherapy integration* (pp. 94–129). New York, NY: Oxford University Press.

Lee, D. L., & Tracey, T. J. G. (2008). General and multicultural case conceptualization skills: A cross-sectional analysis of psychotherapy trainees. *Psychotherapy: Theory, Research, Practice, Training, 45*(4), 507–522. doi:10.1037/a0014336

Lee, S. M., Cho, S. H., Kissinger, D., & Ogle, N. T. (2010). A typology of burnout in professional counselors. *Journal of Counseling & Development, 88*, 131–138. doi:10.1002/j.1556-6678.2010.tb00001.x

Levitt, H. M., & Piazza-Bonin, E. (2016). Wisdom and psychotherapy: Studying expert therapists' clinical wisdom to explicate common processes. *Psychotherapy Research, 26*(1), 31–47. doi:10.1080/10503307.2014.937470

Levitt, H. M., & Williams, D. C. (2010). Facilitating client change: Principles based upon the experience of eminent psychotherapists. *Psychotherapy Research, 20*(3), 337–352. doi:10.1080/10503300903476708

Lindgren, O., Folkesson, P., & Almqvist, K. (2010). On the importance of the therapist in psychotherapy: A summary of current research. *International Forum of Psychoanalysis, 19*, 224–229. doi:10.1080/08037060903536047

Lutz, W., Leon, S. C., Martinovich, Z., Lyons, J. S., & Stiles, W. B. (2007). Therapist effects in outpatient psychotherapy: A three-level growth curve approach. *Journal of Counseling Psychology, 54*(1), 32–39. doi:10.1037/0022-0167.54.1.32

Mayfield, W. A., Kardash, C. M., & Kivlighan, D. M. (1999). Differences in experienced and novice counselors' knowledge structures about clients: Implications for case conceptualization. *Journal of Counseling Psychology, 46*(4), 504–514. doi:10.1037//0022-0167.46.4.504

Mumma, G. H., & Mooney, S. R. (2007). Comparing the validity of alternative cognitive case formulations: A latent variable, multivariate time series approach. *Cognitive Therapy and Research, 31*(4), 451–481. doi:10.1007/s10608-006-9062-5

Newman, C. F. (2010). Competency in conducting cognitive–behavioral therapy: Foundational, functional, and supervisory aspects. *Psychotherapy: Theory, Research, Practice, Training, 47*(1), 12–19. doi:10.1037/a0018849

Nissen-Lie, H. A., Monsen, J. T., & Rønnestad, M. H. (2010, November). Therapist predictors of early patient-rated working alliance: A multilevel approach. *Psychotherapy Research, 20*, 627–646. doi:10.1080/10503307.2010.497633

Norcross, J. C., & Halgin, R. P. (2005). Training in psychotherapy integration. In J. C. Norcross & M. R. Goldfried (Eds.), *Handbook of psychotherapy integration* (2nd ed., pp. 439–458). New York, NY: Oxford University Press.

Oddli, W., Halvorsen, M. S., & Rønnestad, M. H. (2014). *Expertise demonstrated: What does it mean to be an expert psychotherapist?* Retrieved from http://societyforpsychotherapy.org/expertise-demonstrated

Okiishi, J. C., Lambert, M. J., Eggett, D., Nielsen, L., Dayton, D. D., & Vermeersch, D. A. (2006). An analysis of therapist treatment effects: Toward providing feedback to individual therapists on their clients' psychotherapy outcome. *Journal of Clinical Psychology, 62*(9), 1157–1172. doi:10.1002/jclp.20272

Okiishi, J. C., Lambert, M. J., Nielsen, S. L., & Ogles, B. M. (2003). Waiting for supershrink: An empirical analysis of therapist effects. *Clinical Psychology and Psychotherapy, 10*, 361–373. doi:10.1002/cpp.383

Orlinsky, D. E. (1999). The master therapist: Ideal character or clinical fiction? Comments and questions on Jennings and Skovholt's "The Cognitive, Emotional, and Relational Characteristics of Master Therapists." *Journal of Counseling Psychology, 46*(1), 12–15. doi:10.1037/0022-0167.46.1.12

Orlinsky, D. E., Grawe, K., & Parks, B. (1994). Process and outcome in psychotherapy: Noch einmal. In A. E. Bergin & S. L. Garfield (Eds.), *Handbook of psychotherapy and behavior change* (5th ed., pp. 270–376). New York, NY: Wiley.

Orlinsky, D. E., & Ronnestad, M. H. (2005a). *How psychotherapists develop: A study of therapeutic work and professional growth*. Washington, DC: American Psychological Association.

Orlinsky, D. E., & Rønnestad, M. H. (2005b). Dimensions of work involvement. In D. E. Orlinsky & M. H. Rønnestad (Eds.), *How therapists develop: A study of therapeutic work and professional growth* (pp. 61–80). Washington, DC: American Psychological Association.

Orlinsky, D. E., Rønnestad, M. H., & Willutzki, U. (2004). Fifty years of psychotherapy process-outcome research: Continuity and change. In M. J. Lambert (Ed.), *Bergin and Garfield's handbook of psychotherapy and behavior change2* (5th ed., pp. 307–389). New York, NY: John Wiley.

Patton, M. Q. (2002). *Qualitative research and evaluation methods* (3rd ed.). Thousand Oaks, CA: Sage.

Prochaska, J. O., & Norcross, J. C. (1999). *Systems of psychotherapy: A transtheoretical analysis.* Pacific Grove, CA: Brookes/Coles.

Rodolfa, E., Bent, R., Eisman, E., Nelson, P., Rehm, L., & Ritchie, P. (2005). A cube model for competency development: Implications for psychology educators and regulators. *Professional Psychology: Research and Practice, 36*(4), 347–354. doi:10.1037/0735-7028.36.4.347

Rubeš, J., & Vybíral, Z. (1991). Co se vám tady bude zdát divný [What will seems odd to you here]. *Konfrontace, 2*(2), 6-12.

Safran, J. D., Muran, J. C., & Eubanks-Carter, C. (2011). Repairing alliance ruptures. *Psychotherapy: Theory, Research, Practice, Training, 48*(1), 80–87. doi:10.1037/a0022140

Sarnat, J. (2010). Key competencies of the psychodynamic psychotherapist and how to teach them in supervision. *Psychotherapy: Theory, Research, Practice, Training, 47*(1), 20–27. doi:10.1037/a0018846

Saxon, D., & Barkham, M. (2012). Patterns of therapist variability: Therapist effects and the contribution of patient severity and risk. *Journal of Consulting and Clinical Psychology, 80*(4), 535–546. doi:10.1037/a0028898

Simons, J. D., Hutchison, B., & Baštecká, Z. (2012). Counseling in the Czech Republic: History, status, and future. *Journal of Counseling & Development, 90*, 233–238.

Skorunka, D., & Vybíral, Z. (n.d.). *The psychotherapeutic professions in the Czech Republic.* Retrieved from http://c.ymcdn.com/sites/www.psychotherapyresearch.org/resource/resmgr/imported/events/barcelona/reports/report_czech.pdf

Skovholt, T. M. (2013). *Becoming a therapist: On the path to mastery.* New York, NY: Wiley.

Skovholt, T. M., Jennings, L., & Mullenbach, M. (2004). Portrait of the master therapist: The highly-functioning self. In T. M. Skovholt & L. Jennings (Eds.), *Master therapists: Exploring expertise in therapy and counseling* (pp. 125–146). Boston, MA: Allyn & Bacon.

Smith, A. (2008). *Personal characteristics of master couple therapists.* Unpublished doctoral dissertation, University of Alberta, Edmonton, Alberta, Canada.

Sullivan, M. F., Skovholt, T. M., & Jennings, L. (2005). Master therapists' construction of the therapy relationship. *Journal of Mental Health Counseling, 27*(1), 48–70.

Tracey, T. J. G., Wampold, B. E., Lichtenberg, J. W., & Goodyear, R. K. (2014). Expertise in psychotherapy: An elusive goal? *The American Psychologist, 69*(3), 218–229. doi:10.1037/a0035099

Trapková, L., & Chvála, V. (2004). *Rodinná terapie psychosomatických poruch* [Family therapy of psychosomatic disorders]. Prague, Czech Republic: Portál.

Vasco, A. B., & Dryden, W. (1997). Does development do the deed? Clinical experience and epistemological development together account for similarities in therapeutic style. *Psychotherapy, 34*(3), 262–271. doi:10.1037/h0087855

Vybíral, Z., & Roubal, J. (2010). *Současná psychoterapie* [Contemporary psychotherapy]. Prague, Czech Republic: Potál.

Wampold, B. E. (2001). *The great psychotherapy debate: Models, methods, and findings.* Mahwah, NJ: Erlbaum.

Wigfall, C. (2001). *SUR a vznik české psychoterapie* [SUR and the origins of Czech psychotherapy]. Retrieved from http://www.sur.cz/downloads/wigfall.doc

Williams, D. C., & Levitt, H. M. (2007). Principles for facilitating agency in psychotherapy. *Psychotherapy Research, 17*(1), 66–82. doi:10.1080/10503300500469098

Wiser, S., & Goldfried, M. R. (1998). Therapist interventions and client emotional experiencing in expert psychodynamic–interpersonal and cognitive–behavioral therapies. *Journal of Consulting and Clinical Psychology, 66*(4), 634–640. doi:10.1037/0022-006X.66.4.634

Wogan, M., & Norcross, J. C. (1985). Dimensions of therapeutic skills and techniques: Empirical identification, therapist correlates, and predictive utility. *Psychotherapy, 22*(1), 63–74.

Zlámaný, J. J. (2013). *Teorie SUR—Výcviková komunita jako terciární rodina* [SUR theory—Training community as a tertiary family]. Unpublished doctoral dissertation, Charles University, Prague, Czech Republic.

3 Canadian Master Couple Therapists

Allyson Smith and William J. Whelton

Introduction

The high need for couple therapy has been well documented (Gurman & Fraenkel, 2002; Lebow, Chambers, Christensen, & Johnson, 2012). Currently, 50% of first marriages and 60% of remarriages end in divorce (Gurman & Fraenkel, 2002; Lebow et al., 2012). Moreover, at any given time, 20% of married couples report considerable distress (Bradbury, Fincham, & Beach, 2000). People in troubled relationships are more likely to experience a number of health-related difficulties, including anxiety, depression/suicide, and acute/chronic medical problems—impaired immune function, high blood pressure, and increased health-risk behavior, such as susceptibility to sexually transmitted diseases and accident proneness (Beach, 2001; Burman & Margolin, 1992; Kiecolt-Glaser, Malarkey, Chee, & Newton, 1993; Schmaling & Sher, 2000). Couple distress is also related to social role impairment and impaired work functioning (Uebelacker & Whisman, 2006). Children in homes with parental relationship distress are prone to anxiety, depression, conduct problems, and impaired physical health (Liddle, Santisteban, Levant, & Bray, 2002).

These indices are sobering and indicate that high-quality, effective couple therapy is absolutely essential. Two evidence-based couple therapy treatments (emotionally focused couple therapy and integrative behavioral couple therapy) have been found efficacious in rigorous trials and have consistently shown that up to 70% of couples receiving treatment report significant improvement in relationship functioning (Christensen et al., 2004; Johnson, Hunsley, Greenberg, & Schindler, 1999; Lebow et al., 2012). Much of the research in couple therapy has focused on the efficacy and effectiveness of these specific treatment orientations (Sprenkle, Blow, & Dickey, 2002), with some attention paid as well to the challenges of the therapeutic alliance in this modality (Brown & O'Leary, 2000; Friedlander, Escudero, & Heatherington, 2006; Johnson & Talitam, 1997; Symonds & Horvath, 2004). Research until approximately a decade ago had focused on the development of empirically supported therapies, isolating the factors that predict clients' responses to treatment, and determining which empirically supported treatment would work best with which particular couple (Sprenkle et al., 2002).

In the individual psychotherapy outcome literature, researchers have tended to move beyond focusing on any one theoretical orientation as exclusively the "best" in order to explore other elements that are involved in the therapeutic encounter. An area of burgeoning interest in psychotherapy research is that of therapist factors as a predictor of outcome (e.g., Wampold, 2001). There is a growing awareness that systematic differences between therapists contribute substantially to whether clients improve or worsen (Wampold, 2001), and there is increasing interest in attempting to delineate what it is that characterizes those therapists who are more effective. A recent study, for example, highlighted that therapist variability in the development of the therapeutic alliance contributes more to client outcomes than does client variability (Del Re, Fluckiger, Horvath, Symonds, & Wampold, 2012).

Individual psychotherapy researchers have examined a variety of factors that therapists bring to the therapeutic encounter. There are many therapist variables that influence the therapeutic relationship: personality/coping patterns of the therapist, therapists' emotional well-being, therapists' theoretical orientation/therapeutic styles, and so on (Beutler, Machado, & Neufeldt, 1994; Beutler et al., 2004). Furthermore, publications that present both clinical opinion (Bassman, 2000; Carter, 1995; Collard, 2004; Corey, 1991; Fox, 2000; Kottler, 1991; Miller, 1993; Pittman, 1995) and empirical studies (Blatt, Sanislow, Zuroff, & Pilkonis, 1996; Coady & Wolgien, 1996; Demos & Zuwaylife, 1966; Jackson & Thompson, 1971; Laffery, Beutler, & Crago, 1989; Luborsky, McLennan, Woody, O'Brian, & Auerbach, 1985; Pope, 1996; Wicas & Mahan, 1966; Wiggins & Moody, 1983; Wiggins & Westlander, 1979) describing the qualities that make therapists effective abound. Researchers have also provided a clear description of a master individual therapist (Albert, 1997; Goldberg, 1992; Jennings & Skovholt, 1999; Skovholt & Jennings, 2004).

An exciting development during approximately the past decade in the field of couple and family therapy is the expansion beyond the exclusive focus on theoretical orientation pointed out by Sprenkle et al. (2002). Christensen (2010), for example, described a protocol that transcends any specific approach based on five central principles: (1) Provide a contextualized, dyadic, objective conceptualization of problems; (2) modify emotion-driven dysfunctional and destructive interactional behavior; (3) elicit avoided emotion-based private behavior; (4) foster productive communication; and (5) emphasize strengths and encourage positive behavior. Sprenkle, Davis, and Lebow (2009) and Lebow (2014) have also emphasized the importance of common factors and integration in the practice of couple therapy. They point to the expanded relationship system, adapting to client stage of change, and intervention strategies that work with emotion, cognition, and behavior as being relevant treatment factors that are present across models.

A few studies in the couple therapy literature have begun to examine the couple therapist, following the lead of the individual therapist literature. One study examines novice psychotherapists and compares the impact that their own attachment organizations have on their clients' experience of their therapist, therapeutic alliance, session impact, and therapy fidelity (Wittenborn, 2012). Another study (Furrow, Edwards, Choi, & Bradley, 2012) reviewed successful and unsuccessful emotionally focused therapy softening attempts and concluded that therapist emotional presence and corresponding evocative vocal quality were more likely to predict heightened levels of client emotional experience in successful softening attempts.

Whereas the individual psychotherapy outcome research has certainly expanded to include not only research on theoretical orientation but also many other factors that influence therapy, the field of couple therapy has only begun to do so. One area that has not yet been explored is the concept of the master couple therapist. Although we do have a clear description of the master individual therapist provided by the Jennings and Skovholt research team (Jennings & Skovholt, 1999; Skovholt & Jennings, 2004), the description of the master couple therapist may be different for a number of reasons. First, compared with the individual therapist, the couple therapist tends to work from a systems perspective and often conceptualizes clients' difficulties relationally rather than conceptualizing them as residing within the person, which is more common in individual therapy. The couple therapist is also working with an expanded direct treatment system, working with two clients in the room rather than the traditional therapist–client dyad, which may change the dynamics of therapy. Related to this expanded treatment system is the expanded therapeutic alliance necessary to accommodate each member of the couple. The therapist must establish a good relationship with both members of the couple rather than just one individual client, as is generally the case in individual therapy (Sprenkle et al., 2002).

Taking these differences into account, it is plausible to expect that the skills and characteristics of a master individual therapist may be different than the skills and characteristics of the master couple therapist. No research to date has explored the master couple therapist as a person and what personal characteristics and skills make him or her particularly good at working with couples. It is hoped that the current study will address this gap in the literature and provide a rich, descriptive account of the master couple therapist.

Current Study

The goal of the present qualitative study was to inductively examine the characteristics of therapists acknowledged to be masters of couple therapy. The nine participants, three men and six women, were all practicing psychotherapists in a metropolitan city in central Canada. Seven of the nine therapists were doctoral-level psychologists, and two were registered social workers. The number of years they had practiced ranged from 16 to 38 years, with a mean of 25 years of practice. These therapists were rigorously selected by their professional peers using protocols that have been well-established in the field (Jennings & Skovholt, 1999; Orlinsky, 1999). The most fundamental criterion was that they were viewed by a minimum of five peers who were personally familiar with their work as having exceptional skills and expertise in the field of couple therapy. Such was their mastery that this peer would not hesitate to send a family member to them or to go them personally for couple therapy. Data for the study came from interviews with the nominators and from transcripts of interviews with the master couples therapists as well as from narratives that these therapists wrote outlining their experiences and expertise in couple therapy. A thematic analysis and category construction of all these data were developed based on the basic, interpretive qualitative analysis proposed by Merriam (1998).

Methods

This study involved a major metropolitan area in the province of Ontario, Canada. Membership lists were obtained from both the Ontario Provincial Registry of Psychologists and the Ontario Association of Couple and Family Therapy. These lists included therapists from a number of different training backgrounds, including psychology, social work, counseling, and pastoral counseling. Neither registry included therapists with a medical background, so the researcher contacted three individuals (two general practitioners and one psychiatrist) who were known in the therapy community to practice couple therapy. Ten names from each of the previously mentioned lists (as well as the three individuals with medical backgrounds) were the beginning points of the snowball sampling procedure. Names from each list were chosen randomly, with the only criterion being that they resided in the particular metropolitan area where the research was conducted. Each of these people was contacted and asked to nominate three individuals in the area of couple therapy who they considered to be "master therapists."

Jennings and Skovholt's (1999) selection criteria to designate master couple therapists were followed, which included the three criteria listed next. A fourth criterion was added to address Orlinsky's (1999) comment regarding objective evidence.

Therefore, each individual contacted was asked to nominate therapists based on the following criteria, which are largely derived from Jennings and Skovholt's (1999) and Sullivan, Skovholt, and Jennings' (2005) studies on master therapists:

1. This person is considered by the nominating individual to be a master therapist when working with couples in his or her practice.
2. This person is most frequently thought of when referring a close family member or a close friend to a couple therapist considered to be the "best of the best."

3. Because of this person's superior skills as a couple therapist, one would have full confidence in seeing this individual for one's own personal couple therapy. Therefore, this therapist might be considered a "therapist's therapist."
4. The nominating therapist has made a referral and heard positive feedback about the work of this therapist or has consulted with this person on a case and is therefore familiar with this therapist's work.

Upon receiving the initial nominations, the researcher contacted each of the nominated therapists and followed the same procedure. This process continued until five consecutive contacts provided no new information, suggesting that saturation had been reached. Therapists who were nominated a minimum of five times by colleagues were invited to participate in the current study. Following this process, the 11 therapists who were most frequently nominated were invited by letter to participate in the study. Nine of the therapists who were invited to participate accepted the invitation. The other two individuals indicated that their schedules were overextended and were therefore unable to participate. Following the interviews of the nine primary participants, therapists who had nominated this group of nine master couple therapists (one randomly chosen nominator for each master couple therapist) were contacted by phone for brief, 15-minute interviews to expand on their decision to nominate these particular practitioners. The findings gleaned from these brief interviews were included when they acknowledged unique information not identified by the primary participants.

The primary participants were asked to take part in a qualitative interview. This interview style collects data from each individual participant through a set of open-ended questions. Although the prepared questions served as a guide for the interview process, the primary goal was to elicit the experience and perspectives of the participants in a way that was meaningful for them. Therefore, the interview process was flexible and evolved with the direction provided by the participant. A list of the interview questions is provided in Box 3.1. Many of these questions reflected Jennings and Skovholt's (1999) interview protocol. Each participant was interviewed once, with the interviews lasting approximately 1 to 1½ hours. Transcripts were later offered to participants to allow them the opportunity to provide clarification or to share any thoughts that may have emerged following the initial interview. Nominator participants were asked to participate in brief, 15-minute phone interviews regarding their perspectives on why they nominated these particular individuals. Guidelines for these brief telephone interviews are provided in Box 3.2.

Prior to their participation in the qualitative interview, primary participants were asked to write a narrative about their experience of becoming a master couples' therapist and what it means to be a master couples' therapist. Participants were provided with broad guidelines to help them "get started." These guidelines can be found in Box 3.3. It was hoped that spending time writing about their experience prior to the interview would stimulate participants' thinking about being a master couple therapist and would subsequently allow for a heightened reflective process in the interview (Anderson, 1998).

BOX 3.1

INTERVIEW QUESTIONS FOR MASTER COUPLE THERAPIST PARTICIPANTS

- What distinguishes a good couple therapist from a great couple therapist?
- What do you think are the characteristics of a master couple therapist?
- Do you see differences between characteristics or abilities between a master couple therapist and one who works with individuals?
- What would you see as the process of becoming a master couple therapist? Does experience play a role?
- What experiences/people/events have influenced or improved your practice with couples?
- Given two equally experienced therapists, why does one become an expert whereas another may not?
- What is particularly therapeutic about you?
- Is there one distinguishing aspect of your abilities that you feel serves you well in your work with couples?
- How does the person you *are* impact the therapy you *do*?
- Are you helpful with some clients and not with others? Explain.
- What is couple therapy?
- How does couple therapy heal?
- If there were a recipe for making a master therapist, what ingredients would you include?
- Is there anything you would like to add, or you feel we have missed?

BOX 3.2

INTERVIEW QUESTIONS FOR NOMINATORS

- What was it about your experience of the therapists you nominated that prompted you to nominate them as a master couple therapist?
- Could you tell me a story that highlights these individuals as a master couple therapist?
- What is it about how these therapists approach therapy that makes them so successful when working with couples?
- Presumably when deciding to nominate these particular therapists, there were other therapists who you considered and decided would not fit in this category. Without asking for identifying information, could you tell me about the therapists you decided not to nominate and what it was about them that prompted you to refrain from nominating them?

BOX 3.3
GUIDELINES FOR PERSONAL NARRATIVES

I am interested in hearing about your ideas, experiences, and beliefs about excellent couple therapists. The following questions are intended to stimulate your thinking as you prepare this written narrative. However, do not be restricted by these questions. Please feel free to frame your response in a way that describes your personal experience.

- What do you believe are the elements of an excellent couple therapist?
- Describe the process/experiences you went through on your journey toward becoming a master couple therapist?
- Were there people who influenced your development (either positively or negatively) as a couples therapist?
- What is particularly "therapeutic" about you?
- How does the person you *are* impact the therapy you *do*?
- How do you conceptualize couple therapy? Therapeutic change in couples?

With the data collected from the master couple therapists and the nominator participants, a basic interpretive and descriptive analysis was conducted. Data consisted of the transcripts of the interviews with the master therapists as well as the written narratives they completed before the interview. The data collected from the nominator participants were included in the results when they underscored a unique perspective not captured by the master couple therapists themselves. In both the descriptions and in the findings, the nominator was cited for his or her responses.

A thematic analysis and category construction of the data was performed. During this phase of research, the researcher constructs categories and develops themes that "capture some recurring pattern that cuts across 'the preponderance' of the data" (Merriam, 2002, p. 23). These categories and themes were constructed using the "constant comparison method" as described by Merriam and originally developed in grounded theory research by Glaser and Strauss (1967). Transcripts of the interviews and written narratives were broken into "units of data" or bits of information. A unit of data can be described as any meaningful piece of data. Lincoln and Guba (1985) suggested two criteria identifying a true "unit," specifically that the piece of data should be both heuristic and distinctly able to stand on its own.

As the data were broken into units, the constant comparison began. A unit was compared to another unit, and the researcher searched for similarities or regularities that emerged in the data. Because data collection and analysis should be a simultaneous process in qualitative research (Creswell, 1998; Merriam, 1998, 2002; Patton, 2002), the category construction process began following the first interview. After the initial interview, the researcher examined the written narrative and interview transcript. The data were reviewed numerous times, and tentative notes were made, including issues that were identified as interesting or relevant. At this time, data were broken into units, and possible themes that appeared to be emerging were considered. Following the second interview, the same process of breaking the data into meaningful units and searching for themes was applied to the data. Finally, the themes from the second participant were compared to the data from the first participant to identify the commonalities and differences. This process continued until each set of data was thoroughly examined. The categories and subsequent themes that emerged were named by using terms and concepts that reflected what the researcher saw in the data.

When considering internal validity, one must consider the following question: "How congruent are one's findings with reality?"(Creswell, 1998; Lincoln & Guba, 1985; Merriam, 2002). Inherent in the constructionist stance adopted by the current inquiry is support for the notion of multiple, changing realities. Merriam (1998) states,

> Because human beings are the primary instruments of data collection and analysis in qualitative research, interpretations of reality are accessed directly through their observations and interviews. We are thus "closer" to reality than if a data collection instrument had been interjected between us and the participants. (p. 203)

This position certainly highlights internal validity as a strength of qualitative research (referred to as trustworthiness).

Merriam (1998, 2002) and others (Creswell, 1998; Patton, 2002) suggest a number of strategies that qualitative researchers can adopt in order to address the concept of trustworthiness. In the current study, these strategies were employed in an attempt to make the findings as congruent with the participants' reality as possible. One strategy employed was triangulation of the data. Matheson (1988) suggests thinking about triangulation as a "holistic understanding" of the experience to construct reasonable explanations of this experience. With this in mind, data were gathered through both written narratives and qualitative interviews with the participants. Other strategies adopted to ensure adequate internal validity included a process of "peer review" featuring a reliance on peers, colleagues, and supervisors of the researcher to comment on the findings as they emerged. Two peers with a background in qualitative research reviewed transcripts (with any identification removed) and identified themes consistent with those presented in the results section. As well, supervisors and doctoral committee members freely offered insightful comments throughout the process.

Given the stance in qualitative research regarding the legitimacy of multiple realities, Merriam (2002) suggests that

> rather than demanding that outsiders get the same results [as the researcher], a researcher wishes outsiders to concur that, given the data collected, the results make sense—they are consistent and dependable. The question then is not whether

> findings will be found again, but *whether the results are consistent with the data collected.* (p. 206)

This was the concept of reliability that was adopted in the current study. Qualitative researchers (Creswell, 1998; Merriam, 1998, 2002; Patton, 2002) suggest leaving an audit trail to allow others insight into how our results and interpretations were made and using direct quotes to allow readers access to the "voices" of participants. Both of these strategies were employed in the current investigation.

Merriam (1998, 2002) describes external validity or generalizability as the applicability that the current research findings might have in other contexts. This approach to generalizability allows the reader or general audience of the study to determine the extent to which the findings from a particular study apply to their own context. In order to allow for this transferability, Mayan (2001) and Merriam (2002) suggest that the researcher provide a substantial amount of clear and detailed information to allow the reader to determine to what extent any findings may be applicable to them. Eisner (1991) describes, "the creation of an image—a vivid portrait of excellent teaching, for example—can become a prototype that can be used in the education of teachers, or for the appraisal of teachers" (p. 199). This would allow readers of this presentation of an excellent teacher to determine what is transferable to their own context. It is hoped that in the current study, a detailed description of the master couple therapists, their perspectives, and experiences will allow readers to determine which aspects of these findings would be helpful in their own practice and growth as therapists.

In the current investigation, all ethical guidelines from the University of Alberta on research with humans were followed, including informing participants of the purpose of the study, the extent and duration of their participation, and how the information was to be used. Participants were also informed of the voluntary nature of participation and were assured that they could withdraw from the study at any time. The confidentiality and anonymity of participants have been protected through the use of pseudonyms. Participants were informed that all audiotapes, transcriptions, and all other identifying data would be destroyed following the wait period after completion of the study. Signed informed consent was obtained from each participant in the study. Participants were offered the opportunity to review the transcripts to check for accuracy and omissions. No participants reported that difficult emotional responses were evoked through participation in this study; therefore, providing supportive referrals was not necessary.

Results

The following is a presentation of the themes that emerged, both from the perspective of the master couple therapists and also from the perspective of the therapists who nominated them. Participants described a remarkable level of commitment in three main areas related to their practice: a commitment to personal development and self, a commitment to professional development, and a commitment to relationships. Within each of these areas are a number of categories that are described.

COMMITMENT TO PERSONAL DEVELOPMENT AND SELF

It was evident from the discussions with this group of therapists that they place tremendous value on pursuing personal development. These therapists were actively engaged in maintaining their emotional health and openly embraced experiences that enhanced their own growth and self-awareness. It appeared that adopting the role of couple therapist was quite a natural process for these participants. Many described a "good fit" between themselves as persons and the type of role required of the psychotherapist. This natural fit appeared to evoke a passion for their role of therapists that was unmistakable as they spoke.

Striving to Maintain Emotional Health

Participants stressed the importance of the emotional health of the couple therapist to ensure quality services. One participant made the following comment regarding his views on what constitutes an excellent couple therapist and the importance of emotional health in the practice of couple therapy:

> They have to be relatively healthy. That's important because in our field . . . there are a lot of famous couples therapists, that I would never send people to . . . because they tend to be so highly narcissistic that they'll lash out at their clients. So they have to be relatively healthy . . . people pick up on that.

Another participant discussed the importance of being emotionally grounded, both in the context of being a therapist and in her personal life: "I'm told often, you know this goes with the age, I'm 65, that I'm grounded, that I have wisdom . . . hopefully, by the time I'm at 65, I've got some wisdom." She goes on to discuss emotional health in the context of doing therapy and identifies an "internal quietness" as being important in her work as a couple therapist.

Participants also discussed the importance of actively maintaining their emotional health and appeared to consciously take steps to ensure that their own mental health remains intact. Although participants discussed this commitment as being integral to their practice, the traditions each therapist adopted were unique and personal.

One participant notes that she would pursue personal therapy if she believed that her emotional health was interfering with her work as a therapist. She is also aware that staying well rested is vital to her productivity:

> If I am ever aware that my emotional health is in the way, I would go into therapy, right? . . . is how I'd go about that . . . and I work very, very hard at not being

> tired when I work. . . . I've cut down to 4 days a week . . . and I don't work Fridays usually. And I go to bed very, very early at night. I don't do much. When I'm working, I work. I'm not out partying every night. Anyway, I'm way too old for that. [laughter]

This participant also describes a colleague's experience of having difficulty with conflict in her work with couples. She discusses her colleague's recognition of the pattern in herself and the subsequent decision to engage in personal therapy to address it. She stresses the importance of addressing any issues that one is facing and dealing with them in order to be able to engage productively in the therapeutic encounter:

> In fact, I remember working with someone who was realizing that she actually lost it when there was conflict. When she figured that out, she went off and did some therapy, actually. It was about home, when she was a kid. And she got past it and she was fine.

Another participant describes the active steps she takes to maintain her own emotional health and achieve balance in her life. Taking time off to spend time with friends and family is critical for her. Also, she cites that balancing the time she spends doing psychotherapy with other energy producing activities is essential:

> I try to keep myself emotionally healthy. That's why I'm going away for a month . . . and why I take a month off in the summer. I make sure that I don't, I'm not overloaded with clients. Although at this time of year, it's not easy. . . . And I try to respect myself . . . exercise, good diet, lots of fun in my life. Lots of time with my grandkids. . . . Lots of sleep. You know, so I think I look after my emotional health because if I'm not healthy, my clients can't be healthy.

Another participant believes that the process of becoming an effective psychotherapist requires a therapist to engage in his or her own personal psychotherapy. When he supervises psychology students, he strongly encourages them to engage in this practice:

> What I always tell psychology students is that if you want to become a therapist, go to therapy yourself . . . and I know that that's . . . the traditional requirement to become a psychoanalyst, and I think that everyone that wants to become a therapist should go in therapy themselves . . . you don't need to have outstanding problems to bring them to therapy, but just to know who you are, what belongs to you . . . and you can differentiate that with from what belongs to the other person.

One participant describes the impact of a tense family background on her own development and believes that personal therapy was instrumental in helping her to address these issues. She believes that these experiences would have likely negatively impacted her work as a therapist had she not addressed them in her own psychotherapy:

> I think it impacts what I am doing in the room. I think it does very much . . . going to therapy for me and continuing my development as a therapist. Because I come from a family background where [describes tense family background], I could imagine that if I didn't deal with that, my clients probably wouldn't fight very much. I'd make sure that they don't fight very much because I might be afraid of that. And I'd make sure that we don't go into certain kinds of feelings here because I'm afraid of those feelings, right? But because I have come to terms with these things, it's perhaps easier for me to let others now travel those waters where it can be scary to have this intense feeling just now. And I think I'm going to fall apart, I think I'm going to go crazy. Those kinds of feelings. If I had not done my own personal work, it [personal experience] would have a negative impact. But hopefully, cross your fingers, because of the kind of personal work that I have been doing, I maintain this . . .

Another participant highlights the importance of monitoring herself when doing therapy so that she can be aware of the standard of care she is providing. She places a great deal of value on maintaining a balance in her life and not getting overloaded in an attempt to provide the best therapy possible for couples:

> Even if you're physically tired, you can't be there. You know, it's like you have to really . . . keeping yourself cleared out of stuff. . . . For me, my biggest problem is I overdo things, you know. So I'm pretty intense in whatever I do, so I have to be careful with balancing that, so that I don't take on too much and therefore, you know, cut myself thin. So that, when I'm seeing someone, to be able to be, kind of monitor myself and be aware that, okay how was that session? Well, you were too tired to really listen. Or you missed that . . .

In describing someone who he would not consider a master couple therapist, one participant discussed the integral practice of working through one's own personal issues. He maintains that it is important to deal with our own "stuff" so that it does not become apparent when delivering couple therapy:

> They don't have their own act together. . . . They haven't done the work on themselves . . . and that kind of comes out in different ways, you see them, interact with them, or even supervise them. . . . They haven't looked at their own stuff. . . . They're still, you can just see it coming through in their words, in their presentation of self, and the way they present to clients and stuff. . . . You can still see too much of them coming through . . . their issues of life, you know . . . they're a little

angry, a little down. . . . I would think that's the first thing that comes to mind. . . . I think that comes across.

Embracing Personal Growth and Self-Awareness

Participants indicated that a commitment to personal growth was essential in order to become truly competent when offering psychological services to couples. One respondent reported, "Throughout my career I have always . . . wanted to develop myself." When she was asked to describe characteristics of a less effective therapist, this participant described someone who was not "willing to go the extra mile in terms of developing themselves."

Part of this personal growth appeared to involve a commitment to developing self-awareness, which participants then used in the professional realm. Participants revealed that their own previous experiences (both general life experiences and previous professional experiences) impact their current practice. One participant noted that having a wide range of knowledge and experience was integral to her work in couple therapy:

> I think you have to have a wide range of knowledge and experience. And in all honesty, there's nothing wrong with being a young therapist, but I think that my life experiences give me a different perspective, you know?

Another participant agreed with this perspective. She reported that as she gained more life experience, she found that she was able to relate to clients' experiences in the professional context on a more personal level:

> I think my life experience helps me identify, or, you know, I can take parts of myself or parts of my life experience and relate to people, right? I think when I was younger; sometimes it was hard . . . there were lots of experiences I couldn't relate to. And as you get older and live more life, it's easier to . . . relate to lots of different kinds of experiences.

One participant was clear that although her life experiences do inform her work as a couple therapist, she does not work through her own experiences with her clients. She feels fortunate that she has had a variety of life experiences, which she believes helps her relate to clients:

> And I bring my life experiences, but I don't work through my life experiences with my clients. But . . . they inform . . . and experiences inform me and give me perspective on what I'm experiencing with a couple. I'm fortunate that I've had jobs that I've gotten exposed to people from just a variety of situations.

She goes on to discuss the professional confidence that grew from her own experience as a therapist and her life experience in general. From these encounters, she felt more confident and grounded in being able to contend with whatever came into the room:

> And I don't think you get there until you're really comfortable with feeling that you know enough and are able to have some mastery over enough models, that you can say, "I've got enough here that if it really gets messy, I can swim in the session. I've got enough . . . places I can go to and that I can grab onto that or that or that." After you get enough of those under your belt, then you can let go of that nervousness, that anxiety about "Okay, what am I going to do?" You'll go wherever it takes you. And then create something to deal with that. So then, the stuff that is coming in the session doesn't scare you because you know where you can go with it.

A number of participants discussed the importance of being aware of one's own professional limitations when practicing couple therapy: "I think it's important to know what your limitations are." These participants described a stance that was characterized by openness and nondefensiveness. One manifestation of this open style appears to be the practice of consulting with trusted colleagues and asking for opinions/advice from other couples therapists. Participants described their tendency to consult with colleagues when they faced a difficult case or an unclear situation: "I think that what comes to mind is usually when I get challenged like that then I start talking to other therapists, in terms of trying to get some input." After describing a rather challenging couple with whom she was working, one participant reported that the next step she would take would be to consult with other therapists at her clinic; "So I need to go get supervision with him, yes I consult with somebody here."

Another participant highlighted the importance of acknowledging that one is "stuck" and to reach out for help when it is needed:

> And to admit that I'm stuck. I don't know what I'm doing. Help me. So I think that's really important . . . and not having kind of an ego defense around—that I have to be right, that I can't consult and so on. So I think that that gets people in trouble, they can be working for a long time and not willing to say "I don't know."

In a related vein, another master therapist discusses knowing his limitations and preferences in terms of client issues:

> It's just not my cup of tea . . . and so when somebody phones me and says "I'm a man with deep depression for a long time, or a woman with deep depression, I say, no problem, here I refer you." . . . It's not my cup of tea, you know . . . a couple in here fighting like hell, hey I like that.

A Natural Fit Evokes Passion in Their Work

Participants discussed an ease associated with adopting the role of therapist, but particularly the role of couple therapist. Being a couple therapist appeared to be a natural evolution for them. One participant reported that "I really feel very comfortable in being part of that kind of interaction [engaging with couples]." Participants described a certain authenticity with which they assumed this role and appeared to be drawn to the profession, with one stating, "You do what you are and you are what you do."

One participant described her work with couples as an extension of who she is as a person. As one who is naturally inquisitive, intuitive, and interested in relationships, the "fit" between herself and the profession of a couple therapist was very natural:

> My work as a therapist is basically an extension of me as a person. And, so basically, I care and I'm interested. And . . . I'm very intuitive, I've always been, I didn't learn that in school. So, it feels like a gift. It's very natural. Doing therapy for me is very natural.

Another master therapist explored a number of career options before pursuing training as a couple therapist. After returning to study following a number of years in another profession, she explored her options by pursuing courses in a variety of fields. She inevitably was drawn to courses that focused on therapy:

> And so I had tried business school, I tried the hard sciences, chemistry, biology. I tried some things in the school of architecture . . . and social sciences as part of my undergraduate and just kept coming back to social sciences and going into therapy.

She went on to say that for her, being a couples therapist was in alignment with her own personal qualities:

> I don't think you can make separations and go off to work and be a therapist . . . I don't think you can separate the qualities of yourself as a person and the qualities of yourself as a person in the care of a therapist. And I bring my life experiences, but I don't work through my life experiences with my clients. But they inform . . . and experiences inform me and give me perspective on what I'm experiencing with a couple.

Perhaps as a result of this "natural fit," participants reported that they enjoy their work, with most describing it as a passion or a calling. As they were speaking, they displayed a palpable energy and excitement about their work with clients. One participant described her work with couples as a real privilege and an honor:

> Yeah, it's dramatic, it's dramatic. And then your couple will come in and they're sitting close. It's all different. It's very nice . . . then I say "oh my gosh, you can't pay

> me ever. I don't need to get paid" . . . normally, you get those interactions . . . and you think it's wonderful . . . it's such a privilege to do this work.

One participant describes her work with couples as allowing her to "live out her passion" by saying, "I felt so much more passionate about it than just doing my job. So, being great was to be able to do more than, you know, just fulfill my job requirements, but to really live out my passion." She goes on to describe a previous work setting in which work with couples was not necessarily part of the mandate, but she found herself "fitting in" important couple work:

> So, when I think about the various settings that I worked in, I was always doing that, right? And always looking for opportunities to do more, right? Even in settings where . . . it wasn't the mandate because I worked in the hospital on a medical floor. And I remember trying, getting couples in after hours. [laughter] And seeing them, right? And it wasn't my job. My job was to work with getting the patient discharged, right? So, I have always tried to fit it in, no matter where I've been working. So I think that reflects my passion, right?

A number of participants made the following statements, indicating that they believe couples therapy is a true calling for them and that they truly love their work. One said, "I think it's a vocation for me and not a job. It's like a calling and not a job." Another said, "I mean the only thing that really stands out for me is that I love what I do. I absolutely love it. . . . But I always think good, a couple . . . a whole day of couples, oh great!!" The excitement that another participant describes for practice of working with couples is clear:

> I love it more and more. I mean I really, they'll have to carry me out feet first because it really is . . . that incredible engagement with people, it's just a lifesaver. It's fantastic. It's a real high. So that has always been the case. I have always loved doing couple work. From the very first time I sat with a couple, no, not quite the first time, maybe about 6 months into it.

She goes on to say that being able to work with clients in this way is truly a privilege:

> For me, on a very personal level an absolute privilege to get to know two people. . . . Sometimes, because you uncover material more deeply than they know themselves or each other. That feels extraordinary. And to be with them in that process.

Confident, Yet Modest

A clear confidence yet underlying modesty characterized these participants. Many of the therapists who participated in this study reported that they felt honored to be nominated as an excellent couple therapist by their peers. When asked how she experienced her nomination for participation in the current study by her peers, one participant responded in the following manner:

> Surprised [laughter]. . . . I don't consider myself a master couple therapist. I like doing couples therapy and I think I do a good job, but as far as I'm concerned, masters are the ones that travel around the world and give lectures.

She maintains that a part of how she measures her own success as a couple therapist is related to the joy and energy she brings to the encounter with her clients:

> It's the joy that you bring to the experience, or the energy you bring to the experience that makes you feel you're doing a good job. I feel like I'm doing a good job. Am I a great, well-known master therapist, no, but I feel like I do a good job, personally.

As evident by the previous quote, a number of the therapists who participated in this study communicated a confidence that they were competent in their work. At the same time, participants exuded a strong sense of modesty when discussing their abilities. When asked whether he considered himself a "master therapist," one participant responded in the following manner:

> I think, you know . . . the word "master" is I think a bit pretentious. . . . I would say that I'm good at what I do, that's how I'd put it. . . . I'm a good psychotherapist, I'm a good couple therapist. I know I'm good at it. There's a few things in life that I know I can do and I know I can do this.

Another participant describes the courage or "chutzpa" she feels when working with couples:

> I have a lot of courage when I work with clients. So, it doesn't matter what kind of problems they bring me. . . . Well, first of all, I have a lot more "chutzpa" I guess you could call it. And I'm not afraid of trying new things out. I'm not afraid of making mistakes.

When describing aspects of another therapist whom she considers a master, one participant believes that confidence plays a part: "I think it's their confidence, too, I guess. Yeah, their confidence in being able to help . . . that they feel good about the work that they're doing." She goes on to say that her own confidence and ease of practice appears to inspire confidence in her clients as well: "I think because I am comfortable and confident, I think that also helps people to feel safe and secure."

When describing a "master" colleague, one participant indicates that "[Name], I think has that kind of psychological courage. [Name] is not afraid of anything. . . . She's very gutsy, I think."

Summary

The quotations presented in this section highlight these therapists' outstanding commitment to their own personal growth and development. Perhaps not surprisingly, they appear to believe that these values are an important part of doing good work with couples. They strive to maintain their own emotional health and consciously develop their own understanding of self. When meeting with these participants, this attribute is clearly conveyed in their thoughtful and open interpersonal approach. The "natural fit" they describe is evident, as is the balance of confidence and modesty in their abilities. They are clearly passionate about their work to improve couples' relationships.

COMMITMENT TO PROFESSIONAL DEVELOPMENT

These participants also displayed a remarkably solid commitment to their development in the professional realm. This commitment was evident as they discussed their teaching experiences and compelling interest in human behavior. These therapists participate in an impressive amount of continuing education and clearly value the practice of ongoing learning. With a sincere tone of modesty, participants described the benefits of being able to effectively conceptualize the issues clients face, and they discussed their views on various approaches to marital psychotherapy.

Teaching Enhances Understanding

Being in the position to teach marital therapy to others appeared to be an important piece of participants' journey toward excellence. They discussed their own experience of adopting a teaching role and maintained that this significantly improved their own knowledge and understanding in this area. Most participants were involved in some form of teaching, including being a lecturer at one of the local universities, supervising practicum students, or offering workshops to the couple therapy community.

One participant described the process of teaching a course as an important part of her own development as a therapist:

> I was one of the first people to join that team from the [Name] Hospital. So really, I was plunged into couple work . . . without ever having the theoretical part. So then I read it myself, right? But then I began to teach it later on, like a couple of years later. And *that's* when I started to get good, when I started teaching it. . . . It's such an amazing experience to teach it because (a) you have to learn it and you learn it every which way and (b) it makes you think about what you're doing and (c) you

> realize that you know so much more than these other people. So that consolidates you and it really ramps up your performance.

Another master therapist mirrored this sentiment, indicating that adopting the role of "teacher" helps to keep him up to date on current issues in psychotherapy:

> I teach at [Name of Educational Institution], so a little bit of the academic, giving workshops and conferences kind of piece comes in a bit because it forces you to . . . see all those books I've got to read for January 1st . . . so that kind of helps you get up to date a little bit on some issues . . . so you're forced always to try to be one step ahead of your students.

Finally, another participant indicated that she deliberately puts herself in positions that encourage her to teach material about which she is curious, whether it is to university classes or to students she is supervising. She maintains that "if I can teach it, then I know it":

> So for me, learning is not just . . . if I can teach it, then I know it. And so, I kind of put myself into positions where I'm teaching things that I'm curious about learning better because it makes sure that I can articulate it. Then I know that I know it well. And I know it in such a deep way that it's just going to be second nature when I use it. . . . So I did the teaching with the group for the year on [Name's] model and I also ran for a number of years a supervision group at the school board, which still runs.

The Curious Student: Commitment to Ongoing Learning

Many of the participants described themselves as being strongly committed to ongoing learning in the field of couples therapy, as well as possessing a real curiosity and inquisitiveness toward romantic relationships. One master therapist reported that she had always had an interest in relationships:

> I think I've always been very interested in relationships and in my friend's relationships and my family relationships. I do think systemically . . . I'm really more interested in how, in the dynamic, and going into them individually.

Another compared the experience of doing couples therapy to going to see a play, in that she enjoys watching the dynamics of the couple unfold:

> I think you have to be able to enjoy observing people and the patterns . . . like in a sense, when I see a couple, it's kind of like going to a play. And I really want to sit back and watch. And it's fascinating. It's like the nuances and how they relate . . . it never ceases to amaze me.

She went on to identify a deep curiosity in the context of integrity of practice:

> I think it's the continued curiosity to want to understand and learn and the integrity of their practice—they really want to figure out what I'm doing. They're not in there for the money, I mean, the money helps, but they're really curious and wanting to continue to understand—what should I do here? What's going on with this person?

One respondent maintained that her general love of adventure and discovery was evident in her approach to working with couples. She describes an approach that highlights an open inquisitiveness that creates a safe atmosphere for clients to discover important information about themselves and their relationships:

> Well, I like going and traveling, I like scuba diving. I like hiking, downhill skiing, I like adventure. I also like the adventure of therapy . . . the exploration . . . it's like mystery . . . what is going on in this couple . . . you know, what has led to this situation? So, it's like going on a little exploration . . . and figuring it out as you go along together. What are the pieces of this story that are shaping the two of you in this way and each of you individually. And what's the journey that's brought you here and what are the paths that we can take that are going to stop the destructive one, the course that we're on? So I think that the person that I am is a bit of . . . I'm quite curious about new places, new things, new analogies.

One master therapist discusses his strong commitment to pursue ongoing training even after practicing for almost 20 years. He describes a relatively intensive training program in which he is currently engaged and describes the positive impact that pursuing this training has had on his practice:

> I maintain that it's [ongoing learning] really important. . . . I'm hoping that I can have a positive impact on my clients. And I know I do. I can tell . . . if I've gone to one of those 4-days of [describes an intensive training program; 4 days, four times per year for approximately 7 years]. . . . When I come back from one of those 4-days, what opens up in my therapy sessions is different. It's deeper, it's more complete. There's a lot more of this freshness and newness kind of experience that I talked about earlier, where clients are really in touch with deep things. And there's a shift in their body-felt sense. There's a shift in the way they perceive the other person and the way they perceive themselves. And you can . . . it's palpable . . . you can feel it. That, I have much more when I've just come back from one of those 4-days. So I know that it has an impact.

Developing a Strong Ability to Conceptualize

The incredible ability to conceptualize and identify the issues that clients are facing was consistently described by these participants as being an important component of the master couple therapist. The "ability to be able to . . . pick up on what the issue is right away" was cited repeatedly by participants as being an important and not necessarily common ability.

One participant described an experience with a previous supervisor that had significantly enhanced her own development as a therapist. She was amazed by this therapist's ability to conceptualize her client's issues:

> I mean that's when you say an "excellent" therapist. . . . It's like, you could go to [Name] with a little piece of something that's happened—I mean a tiny little vignette of what happened and—boom, boom, boom. [This supervisor] knows where they are, what needs to happen next, what they're going to do next, how it's going to turn out. And it's just extraordinary.

Another went on to state,

> But on top of that, she's got this razor-edge ability to hone in exactly where she needs to be. And she gets there quicker, like months quicker, than everybody else. . . . She really is quite amazing.

One master therapist indicated that part of her perception of a master couple therapist was someone who was able to reframe a situation in a way that the average therapist may not identify:

> When the master . . . is able to see something or reframe something that most people observing wouldn't get. And they're working with and they might unpeel the onion and get down to it and you think "wow" . . . there's that, there's one thing. Or make an observation to the couple in a reframing way that is, that most of us would say, "I would never have thought of that."

One participant shared stories of consulting with a colleague or a supervisor who was able to conceptualize a case in a unique way that significantly propelled their therapy forward. This therapist was amazed by this "master" therapist's ability to conceptualize a challenging case that she had discussed with a number of seasoned psychotherapists. She believed that this therapist came to a conceptualization that others would not necessarily have identified, and that this significantly propelled the therapy process forward:

> And we were really struggling because he's afraid of commitment and when he gets closer, he pulls away and creates situations that push her away. And so

> I talked to someone, a really seasoned, he's an individual therapist, he also sees couples ... seasoned therapist. And I was just mentioning to him, and he said, you know about him ... and what he said to me was ... "Have you asked him what his sexual fantasies were towards his mother?" Hum ... and I had talked about this case before with other people and seasoned people and everything, and I said well, "He had this and this in his relationship with his mother" but I never thought of that. So I go in and I ask [my client] and I almost fell off my chair. He started to share with me his sexual fantasies that he had with his mother for up until he was a teenager. And just from a little bit of what I told this therapist, what he was seeing, you know because I had told him about the patterns and stuff and how when he gets in a committed relationship, he can't be sexual and he wasn't sexually abused. And this guy picked up right away—this guy feels guilty about his sexual fantasies, probably with his mother. ... It was amazing, it was a breakthrough. In the end, he [my client] said, was embarrassed to tell me. He said, "I can't tell you this." He was ashamed, he hid his head ... and I helped him, it's really important that he be able to talk about it because it's keeping him stuck. I knew nothing about what he was going through. And then he proceeded to tell me and I thought—wow—I would have never gotten there if I hadn't talked to that therapist.

One participant discussed the importance of being able to reflect and conceptualize when delivering psychotherapy. When she describes this attribute in herself, she reports that it is part of who she is:

> I think that a person individually needs to know, needs to be able to reflect and have insight if they're going to be a good therapist. ... Well, I think it's just as important for a therapist to have a very good ability for self-reflection, insight, and just the ability to process. And I have trained a lot of people who have not had that ability. And they have a very hard time conceptualizing what's going on with [their clients]. So I'm very quick at that, I can quickly conceptualize what's happening with someone. And I think that's because that's just who I am in my head.

Another respondent noted that although it is clearly important for an excellent couple therapist to possess strong conceptual abilities, it is also important for these abilities to be congruent with his or her own personality. He describes an encounter he has with a colleague he considers "masterful" and described the sense of "flow" she exuded:

> The thing about her that I thought was so terrific was that she had a ... really a masterful grasp of what it was she wanted to do when she was doing it. And it came across in a very natural way that was clearly congruent with her ... her personality and with her, with her conceptual framework ... so that you could ... it just flowed. There was a nice sense of flow to the whole business.

One master therapist described the contrasting experience of witnessing the work of a therapist who was "missing the mark." This story was in stark contrast to the many remarkable encounters with excellent couple therapists who quickly identified the core client issues:

> And he was doing something on infidelity. And he had a man and a wife sitting there. And the wife was raging and raging and foul-mouthed and really awful. And [Name] was telling them, but one of the things she said right off the bat was "I need to understand why did this happen?" And that went completely past [Name] and all he said was "You've got to decide, are you going to be angry forever?" . . . completely, completely, even his radar didn't even pick it up . . . and you'll see learning therapists and the couples will be going on about something and people missing where they need to be. So I think it's that ability to know where you need to be and then to be able to connect with the people, be empathic, and . . . that's what you need to have.

Developing an Approach to Couple Psychotherapy

The importance of developing a model and approach to their work with couples was a dominant theme that emerged during these interviews. Participants discussed a number of different perspectives regarding the different models of psychotherapy. These perspectives included the idea of developing an approach unique to each couple, using a model of marital psychotherapy in which the therapist has confidence (specifically in terms of empirical support), and the idea that a therapist should strive to adopt an approach that is congruent with his or her person.

A number of participants discussed the importance of using an approach that they believed was a good "fit" for the couple with whom they were working. One master therapist spoke of her tendency to have an eclectic approach and to develop a unique framework that is useful for the particular couple with whom she is working:

> And, you know . . . I love workshops. I've gone to a lot of different conferences and workshops. And so, I'm very eclectic and I pull from different places. And it's exactly that. I try to do a goodness-of-fit between the model, the skills that come out of that model and the couple that's in front of me.

Another participant discussed her own personal experience with a family member who had a learning disability. From witnessing her family member's struggle in coping with a learning disability, this therapist came to believe that each client will be unique in terms of his or her learning style. Therefore, she stressed that it is necessary to have an eclectic approach to one's practice in order to accommodate those clients for whom the traditional methods may not be as effective:

> My teaching background and my research on learning disabilities, my [family member] is LD, so is my [family member]. And it made me sensitive to the need

to be multisensory. Therapy is a very talking thing. And some people do it just by talk alone. I know from learning styles that people are not necessarily auditory learners, or express themselves auditorily, even the brightest. And so I like the sand tray, which is mostly sensory. I find that even the brightest people who talk and are just so "here up" [neck up] . . . I can get into their experience much better through something that they let their inhibitions down and I just sort of get in their play . . . and spontaneously go for things that they'd never tell me if we sat and talked for five sessions.

Another therapist discusses the importance of working from an approach firmly rooted in a clear theoretical framework but that is also flexible enough to accommodate the distinct aspects of each couple:

> All of that within a relatively clear framework, or structure, that is, somewhat firm, but yet flexible enough to be able to respect the individual, and to be flexible enough so that I can adjust it for the well-being of the client . . . the underlying principle, I think is the well-being of the client.

Finally, another master therapist describes the risks a therapist takes if only drawing from one perspective when delivering psychotherapy. She highlighted the point that clients can actually have a negative experience in therapy if a therapist relies exclusively on an approach to which a client has difficulty relating:

> I have trouble with therapists who are married to one model of doing therapy. And you see it all the time. . . . And it's interesting, I think there's an idea out there that if you don't keep to your model and hold to it, then . . . it's watered down, if you integrate other ways and approaches and stuff into your model. And so there's kind of the risk of, talking about using the "catch-all" approach, or whatever. And, in the sense that well, you're trying to throw everything in, you don't really know what you're doing and you're not really being considerate about what it is that you're trying to do and really look at it . . . but the other side is being so rigid in a model that, that you can only see certain kinds of people. . . . And that person is going to feel like a failure right away when they start therapy because they're not, they can't go there.

Some participants discussed the importance of the model they were using, specifically in terms of the empirical support it had received. They emphasized the importance of using a model that has been empirically demonstrated to be effective, which gives them confidence to draw from this model when working with couples:

> I have a model that I'm using with couples that has been researched and validated and it's not just me as a person . . . it's . . . a set of interventions and skills that can

> be taught. And because I've been doing it for a long time, I feel like I have the ability, then, to teach that. So I think it's really, the model, really helps.
>
> ... and I think that it's probably one of my greatest attributes that I know [model of psychotherapy].

Some participants discussed the importance of using a model that was congruent with the therapists' own personal characteristics. One participant stated, "It's an authenticity that allows them to blend their conceptual framework, whatever it is with their own personal qualities. And in a way, that comes across."

One respondent maintains using a framework that "fits" with him as a person ensures that he does his best work:

> And I find that's when I work best, when I have a sense of what I want to do, that conceptual thing. And I can mold it into my own character some way and put it across to people.

Summary

Whether it is through teaching, supervising, pursuing further training, or considering their approach to psychotherapy, this group of therapists describes an impressive commitment to their own development as therapists. Participants recognize the understanding that teaching brings to their practice. Their curiosity for the field and human behavior in general fuels a commitment to pursue additional training and pursue ongoing learning. Developing a strong ability to conceptualize client's issues and then applying their own approach to psychotherapy appears to be an important part of these therapists' development.

COMMITMENT TO RELATIONSHIPS

The quotations presented in this section highlight the strong value these participants place on relationships, both in the therapeutic context and also with peers. These participants have a deep awareness for the unique aspects of the alliance in couple therapy and tailor their interventions accordingly. They display personal qualities that appear to facilitate the development of strong relationships. Perhaps these impeccable relational qualities allow this group of therapists to maintain such a strong connection, even in the face of conflict. These participants' approach is firmly rooted in a fervent trust for clients' ability to determine their own paths.

Belief in the Importance of a Strong Therapeutic Relationship

Each participant discussed the importance of the therapeutic alliance in the process of couple therapy. In fact, participants maintained that a strong therapeutic alliance is paramount to effective psychotherapy. One participant goes so far as to say that the alliance is the most important part of couple therapy: "Again, I think it's who you are, it impacts your therapeutic alliance. And I really believe that the therapeutic alliance is that most important part of therapy." Another master therapist agrees, indicating that if one has the ability to form a good alliance with a couple, then he or she is likely to do good work: "To me, the therapeutic alliance with your clients is the most important thing. If you have a good therapeutic alliance with your clients, you're actually going to do good work."

Another participant indicates that he always has the therapeutic relationship in "the back of his mind." He maintains that

> the things people usually pick up on, you know without a doubt has always been good therapist–client relationship. . . . It is number one . . . and it stays number one. . . . You know they come in and they see you're friendly . . . and a good rapport. . . . I'm always focusing on relationship . . . I think that's number one.

He goes on to describe a couple he had seen in therapy in which his alliance with one partner was "dubious":

> When his wife came in, who was the more defended one . . . I knew that I would . . . there's no need to go after her . . . she would put up the walls real quick . . . so we had a great session, and I just laid right back, and I went all on her side . . . come on her side . . . just see the world as she sees it . . . do not confront, do not challenge, just come on her side . . . because her rapport with me after three sessions was dubious, she didn't know whether she wanted to trust me, and it came out that she was a fairly strong feminist, it was hard to trust a man. I didn't know any of this prior, but I could just tell that she wasn't trusting me yet . . . that's the first thing, I have to build my rapport with her and the only thing I can do that through is just to take her side entirely, even if I might change my position later . . . so that's the first part, build that rapport.

Finally, one participant discussed the importance of safety within the context of the therapeutic relationship. He indicated that feeling safe and secure in this relationship was absolutely necessary if clients are to be able to access the emotions necessary to do the work:

> That means also the ability to create a safe environment so that the person feels that it's okay to go into some deep feelings . . . even those they might be ashamed of, for instance, often that's what, that's what we need to work with, I think are, are . . . feelings and thoughts that we feel are unacceptable and so we feel ashamed of them and bury them inside, so creating a safe environment so that it's okay even . . . it's even okay to go there, where I feel the most ashamed.

The Alliance in Couple Therapy

Participants reported that the alliance with couples is of great importance in facilitating therapeutic change. Of particular interest to the couple therapist is the ability to create and maintain a strong relationship in the context of working with couples. This, as participants discuss, can be quite a challenging task when both members of the couple are at odds with each other. One participant achieves a comfortable balance by helping partners see that "they can each look at the same thing and see it differently" and assures them that each of their perspectives is important: "Again I would say, if you're empathic, you can understand one partner perfectly well and equally understand the other partner and help the couple to know that you'll be validating . . . that's a skill that couple therapists have to learn."

Another participant describes the experience of building a relationship with both members of a couple and the necessity of taking into consideration both clients' positions when framing interventions. He is continually aware of this dilemma when offering service:

> And I need to make sure that I establish and maintain a working alliance, a therapeutic alliance with each one. And I always have to have that in the back of my mind . . . each intervention with each individual is always done in the context of the relationship, the system. And I know that there's another partner listening. As I'm working with one partner, going into their anger or their hurt feelings . . . and everything I say to this partner, I know that the other partner is hearing it as well. And they're hearing it from *their* position, from *their* history, from *their* needs, and *their* feelings, which could be very, very different from what I'm saying to this client here, to this partner here.

He goes on to eloquently describe his process of maintaining the alliance with both members as a process of "thinking on two channels." He describes taking both partners' experiences into account with his choice of words and demonstrates the importance of being empathic with both members of the couple:

> It's like thinking in two channels. One channel is I'm trying to talk to this partner, partner A over here, that is experiencing very, very intense feelings . . . and let's say hurt feelings. Hurt because of what the other partner just said. Partner B just said something that was very, very hurtful. And I'm trying to be very empathic to the hurt that Partner A feels. As I'm talking about the hurt that Partner A feels—Channel 1—on Channel 2, I know that Partner B could be made to feel ashamed or humiliated or accused by me right now, if I say, for instance "You know . . . I can understand why you're hurt. Anyone would be hurt after being slapped around like that. That's incredible." Of course, now, if I've said something like that, Partner

> A might appreciate that, but Partner B is going to feel like I've just judged them, that I'm accusing them. And so, because I've got this Channel B, this second channel going on, what I'll say here might be very different. So I might say something like, "I can understand how hurt you might feel just now, after hearing what you just heard." And then, I'll immediately turn to Partner B and say "And I understand that the way you said it right now may not necessarily be an accurate reflection of how you really feel underneath, but you also are struggling with your hurt and you're trying to get it across and it's difficult to get across when you don't really feel like the other person is attentive to you." And then I'll turn back to that first partner and say, you know, "I understand that you're not deliberately being inattentive, but you have some interference, you have some difficulty. That's why you have a hard time being attentive to your partner." So I'm going back and forth like this because I'm constantly on two channels. That's sort of the best way I can describe it.

Another therapist describes the sense of being aligned with both clients simultaneously. He discusses the challenge of supporting and developing a connection with one partner without undoing the support of the other partner; this is quite a challenge:

> I feel like I'm really aligned with them . . . and I'm aligned with both of them at the same time, which is a formidable task in couples therapy . . . very difficult to give support to one in a way that will not undo the support to the other person . . . especially if they're in the middle of conflict . . . if I start supporting one, the other person might perceive that I'm no longer supporting him or her . . . and so the words that I choose, the way I will frame my intervention has to take into account both partners at the same time, all the time . . . and I find that to be one hell of a challenge . . . but when it happens, that's a good moment in therapy, a really good moment in couples therapy . . . where I feel I still have the alliance with each partner and I have an alliance with their relational system as well, that's a little bit abstract, but I get a sense of it somehow.

Personal Qualities That Facilitate Strong Relationships

Participants appeared to possess personal qualities that are conducive to developing safe, secure relationships. As well, when asked to discuss excellent or master couple therapists, participants agreed that in order to be an excellent couple therapist, one must possess strong relational qualities.

Participants discussed the qualities of authenticity and genuineness as being integral to the master couple therapist. One respondent indicated that

> I don't know, if it was me, I know that I would pick up about me . . . and what I would value, but I don't know if other people would value and that is that I'm

> real . . . and rather than sort of being stuck up and hiding behind this institution or academia or whatever, I suspect that's what my clients like about me.

She continued that it is important to ask yourself, "Are you a genuine person who's able to form good alliance with your clients?" When describing someone who she considered a master couple therapist, another master therapist stated that, "And she's also very . . . real and caring." When describing himself, one participant indicated that "I probably seem fairly straightforward, fairly authentic . . . decent enough." This therapist consistently cited authenticity as a quality that would be essential to excelling as a couple therapist.

Participants raised a number of relational qualities as important. For example, one described empathy as being important: "Because I think that . . . if you are naturally empathic, and warm, and you like people . . . I think that it makes it easier for people to be in therapy."

One participant discussed the quality of acceptance in her work with couples: "And again, tries very hard to not make any moral judgments, no matter what their clients bring in. . . . And I think that who I am is a person who is extremely accepting of various client issues, problems."

Finally, one master therapist discussed a variety of qualities related to Carl Rogers:

> I also thought of Carl Rogers . . . when he talks about unconditional positive regard, genuineness, warmth, empathy, I can't see how you could do couples therapy, or any therapy for that matter without having those, those ingredients . . . that's a very good word, very much a question of attitude . . . and again, I think Carl Rogers, when he talked about genuineness and warmth and unconditional positive regard for the client . . . God, those things are really, really key, when you think about it.

When describing a colleague who he considered masterful when working with couples, one respondent indicated that this colleague is the most empathic person he has ever known: "[Name] is a very, very empathic person, very warm."

Trustworthiness and honesty were also highlighted as important qualities to possess when forging a strong therapeutic relationship:

> They had a sense of real trust and honesty. So, basically, honest with bringing forth some of the hard messages. . . . But somehow, it was received fine by the person, who was violent. Because he talked about the real sense of honesty.

Credit was also given to a good sense of humor by many therapists when taking into consideration some of the strong therapeutic relationships they have been able to develop: "And . . . I think humor and fun and playfulness has a good part in therapy" "And I have a good sense of humor. And I think that, I find couples respond to that. Because it sort of lightens up the mood" "So integrating the hard stuff with laughter and fun and helping them be more natural with each other."

Many of the participants acknowledged their ability to quickly form a healthy alliance with the couples they see in therapy. One participant stated that "if there's one attribute of my own or talent, or something that I will own, it is that I can quickly make an alliance with people." Another participant discusses "joining our clients" as a primary consideration in terms of whether or not productive couples therapy will take place:

> That's a primary . . . consideration, that they sit there and are able to really join with their clients and with any client. . . . And that the therapist is willing to join with their client. That they're not there just to get a paycheck and sit their butt in a chair, right? And that they're really willing to join in the clients' experience. . . . To me, it's a philosophy and it's an attitude also in terms of the humanistic. People that aren't humanistic are more mechanical in the way they approach people, so to me, that makes a difference. . . . So, and I'm not afraid to, kind of let myself make that kind of connection.

Importance of Peer Relationships

Participants consistently discussed their practice of consulting with other professionals and the importance that these relationships have on their practice. One participant describes her strategy when she is confronted with a difficult case: "I think that what comes to mind is usually when I get challenged like that then I start talking to other therapists, in terms of trying to get some input." In the same vein, another master therapist describes a peer group that was important to her own development as a therapist: "And so that was a really tight group, which was an important chunk." One participant discusses the role that supervisors had played during the course of his training and how this consultation had enriched his practice:

> And maybe the other piece in this, by the way, I've had good supervisors in my time, in my masters in my PhD, supervisors who are affirming, who are risking with you, try this, try that, go ahead try that.

Another master therapist agreed with the importance of consulting with colleagues and believes that this practice is integral to maintaining one's own emotional health:

> And sometimes, if we're working, for instance with borderline clients, they can be very, very intense, and they'll project a lot of things into you, and you're going to end up carrying this stuff . . . and so it's important that you have your own support group . . . that's a requirement, you have your own peer support group, to talk about your feelings, to talk about your experience, so for me, that's . . . a very, very important ingredient.

Nominators discussed the master couple therapists' ability to form strong relationships, not only in terms of the therapeutic relationship but also with colleagues and in their personal lives. One nominator indicated that one therapist's ability to relate to others, including colleagues, contributed to his decision to nominate the therapist as a master couple therapist:

> Their ability to communicate to me what was going on . . . so they can, it's not just that they can work with a client, but they can work with a peer. . . . But the willingness for a master therapist, I think is that willingness of how they interrelate with other people.

Another nominator discussed her experience of a therapist she nominated and the therapist's tendency to seek out solid relationships, both personally and professionally: "They have solid relationships. . . . You know, and they seek out solid relationships. And they base it on that . . . but I have seen several of them consciously choosing relationships."

Trusting the Clients and Following Their Lead

Participants adopted a collaborative approach when working with clients. Often, participants would describe their clients as the experts on their own experience:

> Your clients are the people who know what they're doing, believe it or not. They might get stuck, and get hooked, and get caught, and get angry, and all of that stuff, but it's the couple that are the experts, they have to listen to their couples.

One participant described a metaphor that he introduces to clients in describing the collaborative stance he takes in therapy. He describes himself as a guide and likens the therapy experience to exploring a system of unknown caves:

> Also to trust that this is something that we're going to do together, it's a collaborative effort. . . . I don't have to have all of the answers, although sometimes some clients make you feel that you should . . . and I present it that way to clients sometimes, when I feel that it's appropriate . . . tell them, you know, we're going to work at this together . . . and I don't necessarily have all of the answers . . . this is where I use the analogy of the cave and exploring the cave. . . . I don't know what the content is, the client may know, or may not know . . . they may have an inkling of what it is, but that's why they're here, they want to know more about it . . . so it's like walking into a cave, you know, it's like a system of caves, you walk into a cave and you light up a couple of candles and you sit there and you say, okay, so what's, what's over here . . . we look at the shape of the rocks . . . and see whatever's there . . . and we try to make sense of what that means and as we look around, we say "Oh, did you notice that shadow up there? Do you want to go see it?" and so we light up a couple

> of candles up there and then there's another part of the cave or another cave that opens up and after a while, we start to get a sense of the overall person, the overall system of caves . . . and that opens up choices . . . in terms of change. . . . Okay, so this is you, this is who you are . . . what do you want to do with this?

Another participant emphasized the importance of perceiving clients as experts of their own experience in order to prevent the formation of a dependent attachment on the therapist:

> And that helps them process it and puts it back to them, rather than me being the expert on their lives. Well, I totally think they're the experts; I'm just a guide. So that they don't have to end up . . . always coming back to me.

Maintaining Connection in the Face of Conflict

Most participants stressed that effectively managing conflict is an important issue in the delivery of couple therapy. As the following quotes suggest, maintaining the secure connection described in the previous sections can be a real challenge, particularly if partners are at odds with each other.

One master therapist maintained that couples therapists must be particularly "robust around" conflict. In fact, she highlighted the necessity of the couples therapist resolving any difficulties he or she might have around dealing effectively with conflict:

> I know that some therapists have a great deal of difficulty with conflict. And I think that you have to be able to have a certain robustness around that right? . . . In fact, I remember working with someone who was realizing that she actually lost it when there was conflict. She, when she figured that out, she went off and did some therapy, actually. It was about home, when she was a kid. And she got past it and she was fine. But I think you actually have to be robust with that, well I do, when there's conflict in the session, I like it. [laughter] I've found a way of liking it. Because I will sit back and I'll let them know I'm doing it. And I will go to the process, right? And they'll know that I've gone into process, too. And that sort of helps them get off it and let it go. So it's a way of protecting yourself from being upset by it.

Throughout the interview, another participant returned a number of times to the importance of tolerating strong affect and conflict when one engages in therapy with couples. She discusses the idea of not only handling conflict well but also actually seeking it out as a piece of the work with couples:

> I think I've got courage to do this work. Strong affect doesn't worry me. I love it. I really feel it's alive when [couples do the] emotional work. . . . So that may be a

> piece of it . . . I think people are often afraid of intense emotion. And conflict. And you really get people screaming at each other. And you have to do something about it . . . and a lot of people just don't want to go there . . . and the capacity to tolerate strong affect . . . beyond tolerate, actually . . . to actually encourage it, have it be a piece of the work.

This therapist goes on to discuss the importance of allowing conflict to emerge to be able to have a better understanding of the couple dynamic. She does maintain, however, that if the interaction begins to be in any way abusive, she will set clear and firm boundaries around the expectations for behavior in the session:

> I let them scream for a bit because I need to see what; usually a lot of good interesting stuff comes out. I don't jump in and stop them right away. But then I might say something like, "Do you really want to do this now? Could you do this at home just as well? Because, you know, you're paying me a lot of money, so maybe we need to look at what's happening here and what got you into that place." And I don't have . . . I can't remember having to stop anybody who I thought was being screamingly abusive . . . I might actually put my hand on somebody and say, "I think we need to stop this now. This is getting—this feels dangerous to me. You may be saying some things that you might regret. Let's slow it down and see what's going on." I think if it was getting scary for the partner, I might stop it. I'm sure I've stopped it many times, I just can't think of it right now.

One therapist described her master colleague by saying, "She's a very straight shooter, she challenges them at a very deep level, but at the same time, they feel, you know, held by her and honored by her."

Summary

As evident in the previous quotations, these therapists are acutely aware of the value of solid relationships, both in the therapeutic relationship and also with colleagues and in their lives in general. They appear, as a group, to possess strong relational qualities that facilitate the development of alliances, which was evident in their description of themselves and other excellent couple therapist but was also clearly evident to the researcher upon meeting them individually. Their approach with clients was based on a deep trust of clients' experience that they appeared to embrace in their development of therapeutic interventions.

Discussion

The results have provided a thematic description of these master couple therapists' accounts of the attitudes, practices, and characteristics they and their nominators view as helping them to excel in this area of psychotherapeutic practice. These therapists expressed a profound commitment to their own personal development, professional development, and relationships. Many of the themes that emerged in the current study were consistent with the cognitive, emotional, and relational factors described by the original master therapist research group (Jennings & Skovholt, 1999; Skovholt & Jennings, 2004). Therapists from both studies were avid learners and possessed many of the same healthy emotional attributes (i.e., self-awareness and attending to one's own emotional well-being). Strong relationship skills and the ability to form strong working alliances with clients were also evident in both groups. Although strong conceptual abilities were certainly inherent in Jennings and Skovholt (1999) findings, these abilities were considered a necessary condition by the group of master couple therapists. Perhaps this "necessary condition" emerged in response to the fast-paced, emotionally charged dynamics that are uniquely present in the couple therapy context.

When considering the master couple therapists' commitment to personal development, both self-care and therapist self-awareness were cited as integral to the effective practice of psychotherapy. This finding supports existing psychotherapy literature (Kramen-Kahn & Downing-Hansen, 1998; Norcross, 2005) and highlights the importance of integrating self-care practices and committing to personal growth and awareness in order to ensure the effective delivery of couple therapy services. Participants also maintained that the role of couple therapist came very naturally to them, and this goodness of fit evoked in them a passion for this work. These therapists appeared to strike a balance between a healthy confidence in their abilities and the modesty and humility that characterized their demeanor.

The current study supported the general consensus in the psychotherapy literature that a commitment to ongoing learning was a central determinant in professional development (Jennings & Skovholt, 1999; Rønnestad & Skovholt, 2003; Skovholt & Jennings, 2004). These participants were conceptual masters who engaged in teaching roles that fostered a deep understanding of the therapy process. Participants discussed the issue of theoretical orientation, with seven participants preferring to adopt a model or approach that complements the couple as well as their own personality and two participants pledging allegiance to a particular approach to couple therapy.

Participants described a commitment to relationships, both within the therapeutic context and also with peers, as being vital to effective practice. These participants embodied the long-standing finding that the therapeutic alliance is an integral determinant to the delivery of effective psychotherapy. However, a number of distinct qualities of the alliance in couple therapy were raised and presented the master couple therapists with unique challenges. These included the challenge of building trust with two individuals whose trust in one another has often eroded. In order to address these challenges, this group of master couple therapists made use of their exceptional relational skills, their deep respect for couples' autonomy, and their ability to maintain connection in the face of conflict, and they used a heightened awareness when framing their interventions.

Finally, participants strongly valued peer relationships, which the literature has cited as imperative for the practicing therapist.

This study followed the growing trend in the couple therapy literature of exploring factors beyond therapeutic orientation that are involved in the successful delivery of couple therapy (Lebow, 2014; Lebow et al., 2012). When considering the results of the current study, there are a number of directions investigators may choose to pursue. One consideration is the perspective from which the current study was approached. Certainly, the master couple therapists themselves provided a wonderfully rich account of what they believed was particularly therapeutic about their practice. The perspective of the therapists who nominated them added another layer of richness to the description of these therapists' excellence. Understanding what clients believe to be particularly helpful about these therapists may shed new light on the issue of excellent couple therapists. Do the clients of master couple therapists achieve more optimal outcomes than clients of the average couple therapist? Exploring excellent couple therapists from an observational perspective, rather than through self-report, may also shed light on the concept of the master couple therapist. This observation could perhaps identify important aspects of practice to which master couple therapists may not have conscious access.

Skovholt and Jennings (2004) noted that the findings that describe their group of master therapists "dovetail with earlier descriptions from humanistic psychology of ideal human characteristics" (p. 139), such as Maslow's (1970) model of the self-actualized person, Carl Rogers' (1961) "fully functioning person," Skovholt and Rønnestad's (1995) senior therapist in the integrity stage of therapist development, and Erikson's (1963) ego integrity stage of human development. They postulated that their study might have tapped into the more general concept of the highly functioning person, regardless of the person's field of practice. The findings describing the master couple therapists in our study seem to evoke this concept as well. Further research comparing "masters" across a variety of fields could yield interesting and useful information.

In considering these results, therapists may identify strategies to improve their own practice. Engaging in strategies to maintain and develop one's own emotional health and well-being would appear vital to effective practice. Self-care is certainly not a "one size fits all" concept, and each therapist will have a unique approach to maintaining his or her own well-being. In terms of professional development, therapists are encouraged to engage in lifelong learning and to consider adopting the role of teacher/mentor. Attending to relationships, both in the professional and in the personal realm, was a central tenet in the effective practice of this group of master therapists. Therapists might consider how this may apply to their own situation.

We can also consider how these results may apply to the therapist-in-training. For example, these results suggest that fostering a climate conducive to self-awareness, self-care, and ongoing learning may be important for graduate schools to consider. Graduate schools may decide to further encourage self-growth activities, either as a part of the formal training program or as a retreat or other adjunct opportunity. According to these results, it may be useful for new therapists to be acclimatized to the practice of seeking personal psychotherapy should the need arise. Graduate programs could decide to encourage students to pursue their own psychotherapy so that they have a comprehensive understanding of the process and its potency. For this group of master couple therapists, committing to developing their own personal growth, their professional growth, and their relationship stance has been imperative. This would certainly suggest that it might be useful for all therapists to consider their own growth in each of these areas.

Although the current investigation provided a rich description of the characteristics of nine master couple therapists, a number of considerations must be noted in order to contextualize the relevance and limitations of the current findings. Perhaps the most obvious limitation of the current study is the small sample of therapists accessed. However, because the purpose of a qualitative study is to understand and not to generalize, the small sample size is justified. By providing a detailed description of the participants' experience, readers are free to draw from the results what is most meaningful for their context. A second limitation that must be noted is that participants in this study reflected a relatively culturally homogeneous sample of therapists (all of the participants were Caucasian and middle class). Therefore, the findings of this study may reflect a particular cultural perspective.

References

Albert, G. (1997). What are the characteristics of effective psychotherapists? The experts speak. *Journal of Practice in Psychology and Behavioral Health*, *3*, 36–44.

Anderson, G. (1998). *Fundamentals of educational research*. Bristol, PA: Palmers Press.

Bassman, R. (2000). Agents, not objects: Our fights to be. *Journal of Clinical Psychology*, *56*(11), 1395–1411.

Beach, S. (2001). *Marital and family processes in depression: A scientific foundation for clinical practice*. Washington, DC: American Psychological Association.

Beutler, L., Machado, P., & Neufeldt, S. (1994). Therapist variables. In A. Bergin & S. Garfield (Eds.), *Handbook of psychotherapy and behavior change* (4th ed.). New York, NY: Wiley.

Beutler, L., Malik, M., Alimohamed, S., Harwood, M., Talebi, H., Noble, S., & Wong, E. (2004). Therapist variables. In M. Lambert (Ed.), *Bergin and Garfield's handbook of psychotherapy* (5th ed.). New York, NY: Wiley.

Blatt, S., Sanislow, C., Zuroff, D., & Pilkonis, P. (1996). Characteristics of effective therapists: Further analyses of data from the National Institute of Mental Health Treatment of Depression Collaborative Research Program. *Journal of Consulting & Clinical Psychology*, *64*(4), 1276–1284.

Bradbury, T. N., Fincham, F. D., & Beach, S. R. H. (2000). Research on the nature and determinants of marital satisfaction: A decade in review. *Journal of Marriage and the Family*, *62*(4), 964–980.

Brown, P. D., & O'Leary, K. D. (2000). Therapeutic alliance: Predicting continuance and success in group treatment for spouse abuse. *Journal of Consulting & Clinical Psychology*, *68*, 340–345.

Burman, B., & Margolin, G. (1992). Analysis of the association between marital relationships and health problems: An interactional perspective. *Psychological Bulletin, 112*, 39–63.

Carter, B. (1995). Focusing your wide-angle lens. *The Family Therapy Networker, 19*, 31–35.

Christensen, A. (2010). A unified protocol for couple therapy. In K. Hahlweg, M. Grawe-Gerber, & D. H. Baucom (Eds.), *Enhancing couples: The shape of couple therapy to come* (pp. 33–46). Gottingen, Germany: Hogrefe.

Christensen, A., Atkins, D. S., Berns, S., Wheeler, J., Baucom, D. H., & Simpson, L. E. (2004). Traditional versus integrative behavioral couple therapy for significantly and chronically distressed married couples. *Journal of Consulting and Clinical Psychology, 72*, 176–191.

Coady, N., & Wolgien, C. (1996). Good therapists' views of how they are helpful. *Clinical Social Work Journal, 24*(3), 311–323.

Collard, P. (2004). Interview with Jeffrey Young: Reinventing your life through schema therapy. *Counseling Psychology Quarterly, 17*(1), 1–11.

Corey, G. (1991). *Theory and practice of counseling and psychotherapy*. Pacific Grove, CA: Brooks/Cole.

Creswell, J. (1998). *Qualitative inquiry and research design: Choosing among five traditions.* Thousand Oaks, CA: Sage.

Del Re, A. C., Fluckiger, C., Horvath, A. O., Symonds, D., & Wampold, B. (2012). Therapist effects in the therapeutic alliance–outcome relationship: A restricted-maximum likelihood meta-analysis. *Clinical Psychology Review, 32*, 642–649.

Demos, G., & Zuwaylif, F. (1966). Characteristics of effective counselors. *Counselor Education and Supervision, 5*, 163–165.

Eisner, E. (1991). *The enlightened eye: Qualitative inquiry and the enhancement of educational practice*. New York, NY: Macmillan.

Erikson, E. (1963). *Childhood and society* (2nd ed.). New York, NY: Norton.

Fox, V. (2000). Empathy: The wonder quality of mental health treatment. *Psychiatric Rehabilitation Journal, 23*(3), 292–294.

Friedlander, M., Escudero, V., & Heatherington, L. (2006). *Therapeutic alliances in couple and family therapy: An empirically informed guide to practice.* Washington, DC: American Psychological Association.

Furrow, J. L., Edwards, S. A., Choi, Y., & Bradley, B. (2012). Therapist presence in emotionally focused couple therapy blamer softening events: Promoting change through emotional experience. *Journal of Marital and Family Therapy, 38*(1), 39–49.

Glaser, B. G., & Strauss, A. L. (1967). *The discovery of grounded theory: Strategies for qualitative research*. New York, NY: Aldine.

Goldberg, C. (1992). *The seasoned psychotherapist*. New York, NY: Norton.

Gurman, A., & Fraenkel, P. (2002). The history of couple therapy: A millennial review. *Family Process, 41*(2), 199–256.

Jackson, M., & Thompson, C. (1971). Effective counselor: Characteristics and attitudes. *Journal of Counseling Psychology, 18*, 249–254.

Jennings, L., & Skovholt, T. M. (1999). The cognitive, emotional and relational characteristics of master therapists. *Journal of Counseling Psychology, 46*(1), 3–11.

Johnson, S. M., Hunsley, J., Greenberg, L., & Schindler, D. (1999). Emotionally focused couples therapy: Status and challenges. *Clinical Psychology: Science and Practice, 6*(1), 67–79.

Johnson, S. M., & Talitman, E. (1997). Predictors of success in emotionally focused marital therapy. *Journal of Marital and Family Therapy, 23*(3), 135–152.

Kiecolt-Glaser, J., Malarkey, W., Chee, M., & Newton, T. (1993). Negative behavior and long-term drinking and marital outcomes in men with severe alcohol problems. *Journal of Studies on Alcohol, 59*, 591–598.

Kottler, J. (1991). *The compleat therapist*. San Francisco, CA: Jossey-Bass.

Kramen-Kahn, B., & Downing-Hansen, N. (1998). Rafting the rapids: Occupational hazards, rewards, and coping strategies of psychotherapists. *Professional Psychology: Research and Practice, 29*(2), 130–134.

Laffery, P., Beutler, L., & Crago, M. (1989). Differences between more and less effective psychotherapists: A study of select therapist variables. *Journal of Consulting & Clinical Psychology, 57*(1), 76–80.

Lebow, J. L. (2014). *Couple and family therapy: An integrative map of the territory*. Washington, DC: American Psychological Association.

Lebow J. L., Chambers, A. L., Christensen, A., & Johnson, S. M. (2012). Research on the treatment of couple distress. *Journal of Marital and Family Therapy, 38*(1), 145–168.

Liddle, H., Santisteban, D., Levant, R., & Bray, J. (2002). *Family psychology: Science-based interventions*. Washington, DC: American Psychological Association.

Lincoln, Y., & Guba, E. (1985). *Naturalistic inquiry*. Beverly Hills, CA: Sage.

Luborsky, L., McLennan, T., Woody, G., O'Brian, C., & Auerbach, A. (1985). Therapist success and its determinants. *Archives of General Psychiatry, 42*, 602–611.

Mathison, S. (1988). Why triangulation? *Educational Research, 17*, 13-17.

Maslow, A. (1970). *Motivation and personality*. New York, NY: Harper & Row.

Mayan, M. (2001). *An introduction to qualitative methods: A training module for students and professionals*. Edmonton, Alberta, Canada: International Institute for Qualitative Methodology.

Merriam, S. (1998). *Qualitative research and case study applications in education: Revised and expanded from case study research in education*. San Francisco, CA: Jossey-Bass.

Merriam, S. (2002). *Qualitative research in practice: Examples for discussion and analysis*. San Francisco, CA: Jossey-Bass.

Miller, L. (1993). Who are the best psychotherapists? Qualities of the effective practitioner. *Psychotherapy in Private Practice, 12*(1), 1–18.

Norcross, J. C. (2005). The psychotherapist's own psychotherapy: Educating and developing psychologists. *American Psychologist, 6*(8), 840–850.

Orlinsky, D. (1999). The master therapist: Ideal character or clinical fiction? Comments and questions on Jennings and Skovholt's "The Cognitive, Emotional and Relational Characteristics of Master Therapists." *Journal of Counseling Psychology, 46*(1), 12–15.

Patton, M. Q. (2002). *Qualitative research and evaluation methods* (3rd ed.). Thousand Oaks, CA: Sage.

Pittman, F. (1995). Turning tragedy into comedy. *The Family Therapy Networker, 19*, 36–41.

Pope, V. (1996). *Stable personality characteristics of effective counselors: The Counselor Characteristic Inventory*. Unpublished doctoral dissertation. Idaho State University.

Rogers, C. (1961). *On becoming a person*. Boston, MA: Houghton Mifflin.

Rønnestad, M. H., & Skovholt, T. M. (2003). The journey of the counselor and therapist: Research findings and perspectives on development. *Journal of Career Development, 30*(1), 5–44.

Schmaling, K., & Sher, T. (2000). *The psychology of couples and illness*. Washington, DC: American Psychological Association.

Skovholt, T. M., & Jennings, L. (2004). *Master therapists: Exploring expertise in therapy and counseling*. Boston, MA: Allyn & Bacon.

Skovholt, T. M., & Rønnestad, M. H. (1995). *The evolving professional self*. Chichester, England: Wiley.

Sprenkle, D., Blow, A., & Dickey, M. (2002). Common factors and other non-technique variables in marriage and family therapy. In M. Hubble, B. Duncan, & S. Miller (Eds.), *Heart and soul of change: What works in therapy*. Washington, DC: American Psychological Association.

Sprenkle, D. H., Davis, S. D., & Lebow, J. L. (2009). *Common factors in couple and family therapy: The overlooked foundation for effective practice*. New York, NY: Guildford.

Sullivan, M., Skovholt, T. M., & Jennings, L. (2005). Master therapists' construction of the therapy relationship. *Journal of Mental Health Counseling*, *27*(1), 48–70.

Symonds, D., & Horvath, A. (2004). Optimizing the alliance in couple therapy. *Family Process*, *43*(3), 443–455.

Uebelacker, L. A., & Whisman, M. A. (2006). Moderators of the association between relationship discord and depression in a national population-based sample. *Journal of Family Psychology*, *20*, 40–46.

Wampold, B. (2001). *The great psychotherapy debate: Models, methods, and findings*. Mahwah, NJ: Erlbaum.

Wicas, E., & Mahan, T. (1966). Characteristics of counselors rated effective by supervisors and peers. *Counselor Education and Supervision*, *6*, 406–415.

Wiggins, J., & Moody, A. (1983). Identifying effective counselors through client supervisor ratings and personality–environmental variables. *The Vocational Guidance Quarterly*, *31*(4), 259–269.

Wiggins, J., & Westlander, D. (1979). Personality characteristics of counselors rated as effective or ineffective. *Journal of Vocational Behavior*, *15*, 175–185.

Wittenborn, A. K. (2012). Exploring the influence of the attachment organizations of novice therapists on their delivery of emotionally focused therapy for couples. *Journal of Marital and Family Therapy*, *38*(1), 50–62.

4 Being and Becoming a Psychotherapist in Portugal

A DIALOGUE BETWEEN PERSONAL AND PROFESSIONAL EXPERIENCES[1]

Helena Moura de Carvalho and Paula Mena Matos

Introduction

> As we strive to better serve our clients, we may find that we can learn important lessons from patterns and processes in our own lives.
> Radeke and Mahoney (2000, p. 83)

Although the evolution of research in psychotherapy has proven fruitful with many methodological advances (Beutler et al., 2004; Hill & Lambert, 2004) and with a genuine concern for empirical validation of psychotherapeutic practice, studies concerning the psychotherapist as a person and implications for psychotherapy practice have been neglected. This chapter presents the results of a qualitative study conducted with 20 Portuguese psychotherapists regarding experiences and major changes in their professional development.

Despite the fact that the psychotherapist is considered an agent of paramount importance for the development of the psychotherapeutic process (Beutler et al., 2004; Norcross, 2002; Wampold, 2001, 2006) and the recognition by psychotherapists and researchers from different theoretical orientations that the psychotherapist brings more to therapy than his or her professional training (Reupert, 2006), the empirically supported treatments movement (EST) contributed to the devaluation of this component in research for several years due to studies primarily focused on therapeutic orientations

(Beutler & Castonguay, 2006; Beutler et al., 2004). This may be due to the fact that EST research focuses on the study of therapies as a set of methods, procedures, and techniques that are per se effective in the treatment of psychological and psychiatric disorders (Orlinsky, 1989), and the subjective processes of human experience and relations are understood as a source of error to be eliminated or controlled in the research (Orlinsky & Rønnestad, 2005).

Nevertheless, this line of investigation has been disputed by studies that argue that the inter-therapist variability is a determining factor in the field of differential effectiveness, including the following:

1. Investigations that demonstrate that psychotherapists with the same theoretical orientation, using the same manualized therapy and trained, monitored, and supervised in the same context, produced different results (Castonguay, Goldfried, Wiser, Raue, & Hayes, 1996; Lambert, 1989)
2. Meta-analyses that show that the variability of psychotherapeutic results was better explained by the psychotherapist than by specific components of treatment, where the variability of psychotherapists explained 6–10% of the results (Ahn & Wampold, 2001; Del Re, Flückiger, Horvath, Symonds, & Wampold, 2012; Wampold, 2001; Wampold & Bolt, 2006)
3. Studies that identify psychotherapists who have consistently positive results and psychotherapists who have consistently negative results (Orlinsky & Howard, 1986)
4. Studies that identify psychotherapy iatrogenic effects as a result of the psychotherapists' characteristics, such as lack of empathy, underestimation of the severity of the client's problem, or negative countertransference and difficulties in managing countertransference (Hayes, Riker, & Ingram, 1997; Mohr, 1995)
5. Research and meta-analyses that support the implications of psychotherapist characteristics as important contributions to psychotherapy outcome (Beutler, Machado, & Neufeldt, 1994; Beutler et al., 2004; Laska, Smith, Wislocki, Minami, & Wampold, 2013; Luborsky, McLellan, Woody, Obrien, & Auerbach, 1985)[2]

Paradoxically, although Beutler et al. (2004) emphasize the importance of considering the characteristics of the psychotherapist other than theoretical orientations, these studies remain as an isolated island in the broad spectrum of psychotherapy research (Rønnestad & Orlinsky, 2005). In addition, these studies present several limitations (Gelso & Hayes, 2002; Lambert, 1989; Rønnestad & Orlinsky, 2005; Reupert, 2006), namely (1) most studies are limited to psychotherapists from the United States; (2) the samples are composed mostly of psychotherapists in training; (3) the range of variables studied focuses on characteristics such as age, social class, or personality type, neglecting internal and personal characteristics; and (4) the majority of studies on the self of the therapist focus on a theoretical perspective to the detriment of transtheoretical research. This last limitation is further supported by research showing that the choice of theoretical orientation is in itself inherent to the person of the psychotherapist and thus inseparable from his or her personality, experiences, values, and personal philosophy (Norcross & Prochaska, 1983; Vasco, 1992). This finding had already been stated by Strupp (1978):

> The person of the therapist is far more important than his theoretical orientation . . . techniques are inert unless they form an integral part of the therapist as person. (p. 314)
>
> In the end, each therapist develops his or her own style and the "theoretical orientation" fades into the background. What remains salient is a unique personality combining artistry and skill. (p. 317)

Conscious of the neglected role of the psychotherapist in the research field (Garfield, 1997) and the unavoidable finding that some psychotherapists are simply better than others (Gelso & Hayes, 2007), two main lines of research have developed focusing on the study of the psychotherapist's development. The first concerns the international project organized by members of the Society for Psychotherapy Research (SPR Collaborative Research Network) that gathers research from almost 50 different countries (Rønnestad, Willutzki, & Tarragona, 2010). Using quantitative methodology, the study aims to examine the characteristics, practices, and experiences of psychotherapists from different countries and theoretical backgrounds. The second is based on qualitative methodology and has been developed by Skovholt and Rønnestad (1995), Jennings, Goh, Skovholt, Hanson, and Banerjee-Stevens (2003), and Sullivan, Skovholt, and Jennings (2005) in order to study representations of psychotherapists' development with different levels of experience, different theoretical orientations, and with an emphasis on psychotherapy expertise.

These studies do not assess psychotherapy results. Instead, they stress the importance of the person of the psychotherapist by challenging the psychotherapist's uniformity myth (Kiesler, 1966) underlying the continuities and discontinuities that occur in the professional development of psychotherapists. These studies do not intend to overlook the importance of other factors, such as the client's characteristics or the contributions of different theoretical orientations, but strive to promote a holistic understanding of the psychotherapist's effect on psychotherapy. In addition, the study of psychotherapists' representations of their professional development seems to be one of the privileged ways to access the wisdom that often remains locked in the psychotherapy offices. Gelso and Hayes (2007) state,

> Knowledge of how therapists' backgrounds, personalities, and experiences affect their work with patients has been based almost exclusively on therapists' personal reflections and anecdotes. Therapists often share their experiences and knowledge

> with trusted colleagues with whom they work closely, but much of this valuable clinical wisdom accrues, and atrophies, in the offices of individual therapists. It has been difficult to generate and retain a collective, cumulative wisdom about the person of the therapist because this information is transmitted so infrequently in public forums (e.g., symposia, workshops, and professional books and articles). (p. 113)

The study of the psychotherapist's development can be crucial in comprehending the complexities inherent in psychotherapy effectiveness because it provides an understanding of the relational dynamics that may interfere with the development of the psychotherapeutic process. On the other hand, in the genesis of these studies is a genuine interest in the accumulated psychotherapist archetypes, whether as a mechanism for the progressive differentiation of the elements embodied in the psychotherapeutic process or as an understanding of the preferred path to becoming fully human and competent therapists (Skovholt, Jennings, & Mullenbach, 2004). Rønnestad and Skovholt (2003) state, "If a more accurate and comprehensive conceptualization of therapist counselor development is attained, we can better arrest the negative avenues of professional development such as incompetence, impairment, burnout, and disillusionment" (p. 6).

The pertinence of the current study is also due to the fact that to date, there have been no published studies in Portugal concerning psychotherapists' representations of their own professional development. The results of the current study are discussed considering international psychotherapist development research.

The Current Study

The aim of this study was to analyze representations of psychotherapists from different theoretical and practical backgrounds who are recognized by their peers as experts and also to analyze the experiences perceived as being crucial to their professional development. Research suggests that experienced and recognized psychotherapists in different areas of mental health, the informant-rich cases, are an important source for identifying salient variables (Patton, 1990) that contribute to psychotherapeutic effectiveness (Jennings & Skovholt, 1999).

In the current study, we used qualitative methodology because it is considered a preferred method for exploratory phases of research and it allows in-depth study of complex phenomena such as the construction of meaning of the whole process that being and becoming a psychotherapist involves. The use of qualitative methods is especially relevant when we want to access the experiential world of individuals, through concepts, languages, and meanings, which are less likely to be captured by quantitative methodologies (Polkinghorne, 2005).

A phenomenological approach was also used because it privileged the procedural construction of meanings of the psychotherapist's development. In this analysis, we do not intend to draw a developmental trajectory of psychotherapists but, rather, to analyze the perceived contribution of therapeutic as well as extratherapeutic experiences on the psychotherapist's professional development.

Method

PARTICIPANTS

The sample selection strategy is considered purposeful. In order to identify information-rich cases (Patton, 1990), we used the peer-nomination technique, in which nine psychotherapists from different orientations identified colleagues who they considered good psychotherapists and who they would consult for personal psychotherapy. Twenty-three therapists gathered more consensus among their peers. Some of these therapists were also engaged in teaching and/or supervision activities as faculty and in psychotherapy associations or societies.

Participants were recruited through telephone contact and via e-mail. From a total of 23 contacted psychotherapists, 20 agreed to participate in the study. The ages ranged from 35 to 77 years (M = 50.35 years, SD = 9.95), and years of experience ranged between 10 and 44 years (M = 21.4 years, SD = 8.79). Eleven therapists were female, and 9 were male. With regard to professional background, 16 were psychologists, 3 were psychiatrists, and 1 was a general practitioner. Regarding theoretical orientations, 4 were identified predominantly with the cognitive–behavioral model (cb), 5 with the constructivist model (c), 3 with the humanist approach (h), 4 with the psychoanalytic approach (p), and 4 with the systemic approach (s).

INSTRUMENTS AND PROCEDURE

For the construction of the interview guide, we used a specific type of semistructured interview, conceptualized as expert interview (Flick, 1998). This type of interview restricts its focus to thematic analysis in which the individual is clearly recognized. The semistructured interview is a flexible and detailed data collection method (McLeod, 1995) that allows a deeper exploration of themes and to monitor the relevance of content. The interview developed is composed of 16 open-ended questions, grouped into the following eight main themes (Carvalho & Matos, 2006):

1. Motivations to choose psychology/psychiatry as a career
2. Motivations to become a psychotherapist
3. Development as a psychotherapist (major changes, change agents, personal style, and characteristics that remain stable)
4. Current conceptualization of the process of therapeutic change and the main characteristics of the psychotherapist that best contribute to the psychotherapeutic process and the promotion of change in psychotherapy

5. Impact of being a psychotherapist on private and relational life
6. Impact of personal and relational experiences on psychotherapeutic practice
7. Current difficulties in practice
8. Future aspirations as a psychotherapist

The interviews were conducted in psychotherapists' work contexts (except two interviews) and were on average 50 minutes in duration. At the beginning of the interview, the general purpose of the study was explained, participation was consented to, and consent for audio recording of the interview was requested. The interviews were then transcribed taking into account the discursive nature of the narratives.

DATA ANALYSIS

During data collection, interviews were successively transcribed and then pre-analyzed by both authors of the study. This procedure allowed a reflection of questions that could be included or reformulated so as to collect important data that spontaneously emerged in previous interviews. Data analysis was conducted using the grounded theory method (Glaser & Strauss, 1967; Strauss & Corbin, 1990). Grounded theory, as the name implies, is a method of qualitative analysis, which aims at the construction of theory based on data through the use of a set of systematic and inductive procedures (Strauss & Corbin, 1990). This procedure allowed, at first, to collect sections of text that expressed different meanings and stages of the psychotherapist's development because participants could explore the same theme in different questions. Then these sections were organized into descriptive categories and emerging themes. The categories were titled according to the description made by the participants in the study. This nomination process is referred to as the in vivo *coding* method (Glaser, 1978) and is encouraged to maintain proximity to the data. Throughout the process of analysis, higher ranking categories emerged according to their ability to group the concepts and categories previously defined. It is a method of increasing complexity and abstraction because the grounded theory comparative method (Glaser & Strauss, 1967; Strauss & Corbin, 1990) requires continuous reflection and reformulation of previously analyzed data. However, data analysis did not entail an inductive linear perspective from concrete to abstract but, rather, a cyclic perspective, which entails a return to the data until the construction of the participants' narrative essence, designated the *core story* (Charmaz, 2000; Strauss & Corbin, 1990). The adopted methodology was based on a constructivist perspective of grounded theory because the analytical process reflects the construction of meanings that therapists ascribe to their experiences, as opposed to a positivist perspective of discovering truth (Charmaz, 2000). This process is not free from the subjectivity of the investigator; therefore, strategies were adopted for conducting cross-validation analysis. The first strategy relates to the need to include a peer debriefer (Creswell, 2003), who reviews the entire analysis process, from the organization of the coding themes, categories, and subcategories to the interpretation and discussion of results. The entire process of encoding and data interpretation was carried out in partnership by the authors, with the supervisor of the study being assigned to the study as peer debriefer. The second strategy relates to actively seeking to maintain closeness to the data by in vivo coding, graphic representation of the results, or via the use of the psychotherapists' narratives in the presentation of results. The third strategy involves constant reflection and dialectical analysis of data through the use of the bracketing technique. These strategies are considered by different researchers and methodologists as important techniques to validate data in scientific qualitative research (Creswell, 2003; Fischer, 2009; Flick, 1998; Williams & Morrow, 2009).

Results

Two major themes emerged from the analysis: (1) relational experiences in psychotherapist development and (2) phases and changes of the psychotherapists' development. The first theme is organized into two subthemes, namely relational experiences in the *professional domain* and relational experiences in the *personal domain*, which contributed to the development of psychotherapists. The second theme is also divided into *professional domain* and *personal domain*. Finally, the core story (Charmaz, 2000; Strauss & Corbin, 1990) is identified because it is the element that emerges from the narratives as being more representative of how psychotherapists attributed meaning to their experiences and their developmental process. Furthermore, being transversal in the analysis, it represents a synthesis and integration of the two aforementioned themes of the development of the psychotherapist.

Given that the qualitative analysis does not end at the categorization and codification of the data but also extends to the writing process, we seek to present this co-constructed narrative of the experiences of psychotherapists.

To assist the reader in understanding the content analysis, a summary table of the subthemes, emerging categories, and subcategories is presented for each of the themes (see Figs. 4.1 and 4.2).

Theme 1: Relational Experiences of Psychotherapist Development

SUBTHEME 1: RELATIONAL EXPERIENCES IN THE PROFESSIONAL DOMAIN THAT CONTRIBUTED TO THE PSYCHOTHERAPIST'S DEVELOPMENT

In psychotherapeutic practice, experiences signifying as being the most striking ones arise in the context of interaction with clients. The relational nature of psychotherapy is understood by psychotherapists as educational and transformative in the sense that the shared experience of the psychotherapeutic situation is constituted as a privileged space for professional development. In this theme, three categories emerged: (1) experiences with positive impact on the psychotherapeutic practice; (2) experiences with negative impact on the psychotherapeutic practice; and (3) factors validated by the psychotherapeutic experience, considered crucial in the psychotherapeutic process.

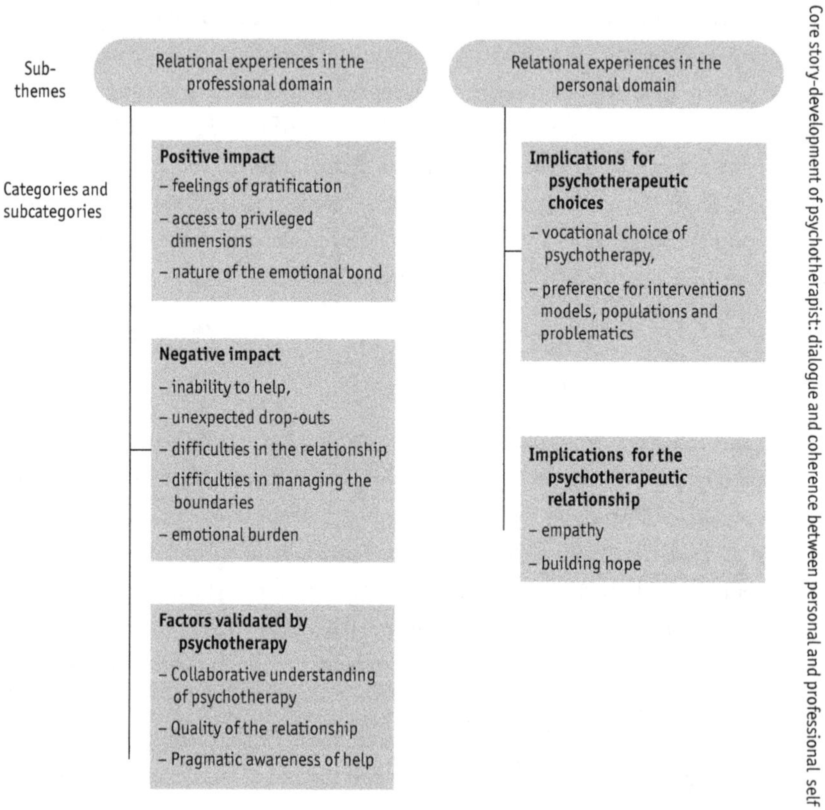

FIGURE 4.1 Relational experiences in the professional domain: subthemes, categories, and subcategories.

Experiences with Positive Impact on the Psychotherapeutic Practice

The following are understood as having a positive and reinforcing impact on the practice of psychotherapy: (1) experiences that promote a feeling of gratification for the help provided in situations of great suffering and in which the psychotherapist perceives a sense of usefulness, (2) experiences of access to privileged dimensions of human experience through the clients, and (3) the nature of the emotional bond.

The perception of success in following difficult cases that provoke high emotional activation in psychotherapists (among other processes, due to the vicarious experience of suffering) is felt as reinforcing psychological commitment to clinical practice, particularly in the early stages of psychotherapeutic practice. These experiences come to be so significant that they can determine the preference of the psychotherapist for certain clinical populations and even the decision of continuing as a psychotherapist. One interviewee referred to a difficult case as a central marker of the resolution of his distress. It was based on inappropriate expectations in his role as a psychotherapist and made him question whether he should continue his clinical practice (C1M)[3]. Some processes are represented as milestones in transitions of the developmental phase. Consider, for example, the case of a psychotherapist who has in her bag photographs from a client whose process represented a milestone in the therapist's ability to establish the psychotherapeutic relationship (s1f), or the case of another psychotherapist who keeps a drawing on his office wall concerning a difficult process of great emotional activation (c1m).

The access to privileged dimensions of human experience is also regarded by the participants as having a positive impact on psychotherapeutic practice, particularly witnessing the client's fighting capacity, as well as the interest aroused by the *idiosyncratic philosophizing* of the client (h1m):

> The more charming side of psychotherapy is that you have windows to the most interesting aspects of people—that is, the ability to face and fight against an extremely adverse situation. (c2m)

The nature of the emotional connection that psychotherapists establish with certain clients and access to significant material of the client's experience is also considered a turning point in their history as psychotherapists:

> The [most striking] moments are the ones of patients or people with deprivation histories or disorganized attachment to close figures that become emotionally activated, and attach to us in a very particular way while having great esteem toward us. These patients then allow themselves, the remembering and activation of certain memories, and we try to work with them through these life events. It is a privilege to have access to such stories. (cb2m)

Experiences with Negative Impact on the Psychotherapeutic Practice

On the other hand, other dimensions are regarded as having a negative impact on the psychotherapeutic practice and in the development of the psychotherapist, insofar as they may compromise the practice, namely the perception of inability to help, particularly when associated with high expectations of the power of the psychotherapist to provide help; dropouts from psychotherapy when they are unexpected and are represented as a threat to the ability of assessment of the psychotherapeutic progress; and difficulties in establishing the psychotherapeutic relationship with certain clients with certain problems (issues), described by a psychotherapist as a *terrible* event (cb1f) and expressed in the following statement:

> To feel that they [the clients] needed to be helped, but, on the other hand, to wish they did not return because it was too hard for me . . . some sessions are too painful from the human point of view, because we are not able to distance ourselves, we are always very attentive to any phrase or any words that we can say that can be interpreted in the wrong way and throw everything away [risk everything]. (s2f)

Other experiences believed by psychotherapists as having a negative impact on the psychotherapeutic practice and on the development of the psychotherapist are the difficulties in managing the limits (boundaries) of psychotherapy with clients, particularly in situations of harassment, stalking, or approach beyond the limits of psychotherapy and attempts at manipulating, especially in marital psychotherapy; and the emotional burden that the relational experience involving dramatic situations and the experiencing of human suffering at its limit may cause in the psychotherapist, which is reflected in the following narrative:

> We have to absorb a lot of negative emotionality, that passes through us. . . . We carry the voice of patients with us, emotions are with us and it takes hours to drain out of the body, hours. . . . We touch the absurdity of life, we are there with the absurd in our arms and, sometimes, it takes hours to free ourselves of this. (c2m)

These experiences are perceived as being negative due to the difficulty in managing emotions, particularly in the early stages of practice. Supervision and peer discussion are represented as being optimal moments because they offer the security and tranquility necessary for the exercise of clinical practice, particularly through the confrontation with new perspectives on intervention. Moreover, they help psychotherapists in the management of the emotional charge raised in confrontation with situations/limits of human suffering. These ideas are expressed in the following statement:

> That sharing is almost like a catharsis, ready ok, lets unload . . . we bring that emotional charge, so we have a colleague with whom we will unload and we'll talk about what we feel, what we think, and the doubts that we have. . . . This helps a lot, it seems that. . . .Phew, it took a weight off my back. (s2f)

Factors Validated by Psychotherapeutic Experience Considered Crucial in the Psychotherapeutic Process

Synthesis and integration of experiences arising from the psychotherapeutic practice contribute to the validation of the determinants of the psychotherapeutic change process. Some of them are already addressed in theoretical training, but they are reinforced by accumulated practice, particularly (1) the importance of clients' personal meaning (sense) of their problems, which brings us to a collaborative understanding of the psychotherapeutic process well expressed in the statement, "the good hypothesis is the useful hypothesis, not necessarily the true hypothesis!" (s3f); and (2) the importance of the quality of the psychotherapeutic relationship as a determining factor of the process.

Another factor that emerges from accumulated and reflexive practice is the pragmatic awareness of help—that is, the emerging knowledge from meeting multiple clients and their stories that are preserved in the memory of the psychotherapist, becoming important resources in conducting new processes:

> I've done very complicated crossings with other people, and so I've been the boatman to many people. And I can tell many stories that have a lot of clinical validity, which help a lot of people to realize their experiences and feel validated in their difficulties, so this is in fact an important added value and that doesn't come in the manuals, it is the learning of the pragmatics of clinical intervention. (c2m)

SUBTHEME 2: RELATIONAL EXPERIENCES IN THE PERSONAL DOMAIN THAT CONTRIBUTED TO THE DEVELOPMENT OF THE PSYCHOTHERAPIST

Regarding personal experiences of the psychotherapist, events underlying normative and non-normative transitions were signaled as formative in becoming and being a psychotherapist. In this subtheme, two categories emerged: implications for psychotherapeutic choices and implications for psychotherapeutic relationship.

As one participant told us, these are the "lights and shadows" of the personal trajectory (s4f) that are projected in the psychotherapeutic setting:

> The person matures, will pass important phases of the life cycle, in personal, marital, and family terms. Clearly, I think that is a very important factor in the maturation of a psychotherapist and the growth of a psychotherapist. (s4f)

Implications for Psychotherapeutic Choices

The permeability between personal and cultural life events and decisions in the professional sphere is represented in the vocational choice of psychotherapy and in the preference for certain intervention models and clinical populations.

Regarding the vocational decision for psychotherapy, experiences in the context of peers and family that promoted reflection and questioning as well as events that triggered personal crises (e.g., relational disruptions and losses) were cited as motivating the interest in and motivation for understanding human behavior:

> I had a period of personal crisis, I was very depressed, my relationship ended, anyway it was a pretty difficult phase for me, it was a period of questioning and, suddenly, I found that I became fascinated with how people function. (c1m)

In Portugal, the April Revolution in 1974 marked the overthrow of the dictatorial regime and the establishment of democracy. The revolution also signified a cultural and political shift that enhanced creative questions, debates, and concerns of social intervention and was represented by some psychotherapists as a context favorable to the emergence of interest in the social sciences and humanities.

Personal experiences had an impact on the preference for certain theoretical models, populations, and problems. A psychotherapist reported the impact of the birth of his daughter on his willingness to continue to assist children in a more analogical way (c1m). Another psychotherapist told us about the relationship between the death of his father and his interest in existential issues (cb3m).

Implications for the Psychotherapeutic Relationship

Interviewees also signaled the impact that certain life experiences had in the construction and meaning of the psychotherapeutic relationship, particularly with regard to empathy and building hope:

> With age and time, life brings us things that helps us to better understand the world of other people. (h3m)

> I went through various tragedies in life, maybe the fact that I have always managed to deal with things in a more constructive, positive way and with a smile, I think it helps when I watch others in their suffering. . . . My competencies, my strengths helped me to understand others, to support them to discover their own strengths and skills and, perhaps, to be more convincing in the transmission of these strengths and skills. (s1f)

Theme 2: Phases and Changes of the Psychotherapist's Development

SUBTHEME 1: PHASES AND CHANGES IN THE DEVELOPMENT OF THE PSYCHOTHERAPIST IN THE PROFESSIONAL DOMAIN

Psychotherapists said that in the course of their development, they built different representations about psychotherapy and their role as psychotherapists. These changes are perceived as being significant and in sharp contrast to previous representations. These changes are present in the expression mentioned by two of the respondents as night and day (p1m and cb2m). The representations of the main changes were organized into five categories.

Each category is defined by bipolar dimensions, which describe a movement of change underlying the development of the psychotherapists' representations. However, these dimensions do not imply a static and exclusive developmental state or phase but, rather, are represented by psychotherapists as developmental paths of an erratic and constant dialogue of personal and professional structures of the psychotherapist's self. Thus, they are dialectic categories looking for consistency between the challenges offered by the practice and the sense of identity of the psychotherapist. These domains are spontaneous references in the narrative of the participants when questioned about their changes as psychotherapists and about their views of psychotherapy. The following categories were identified:

1. Potentialities and limitations of psychotherapy and psychotherapists: *Super Psychotherapist versus Human Psychotherapist*
2. Attentional focus on the evaluation of the psychotherapist's performance: *Psychotherapist Auto versus Psychotherapist Inter*

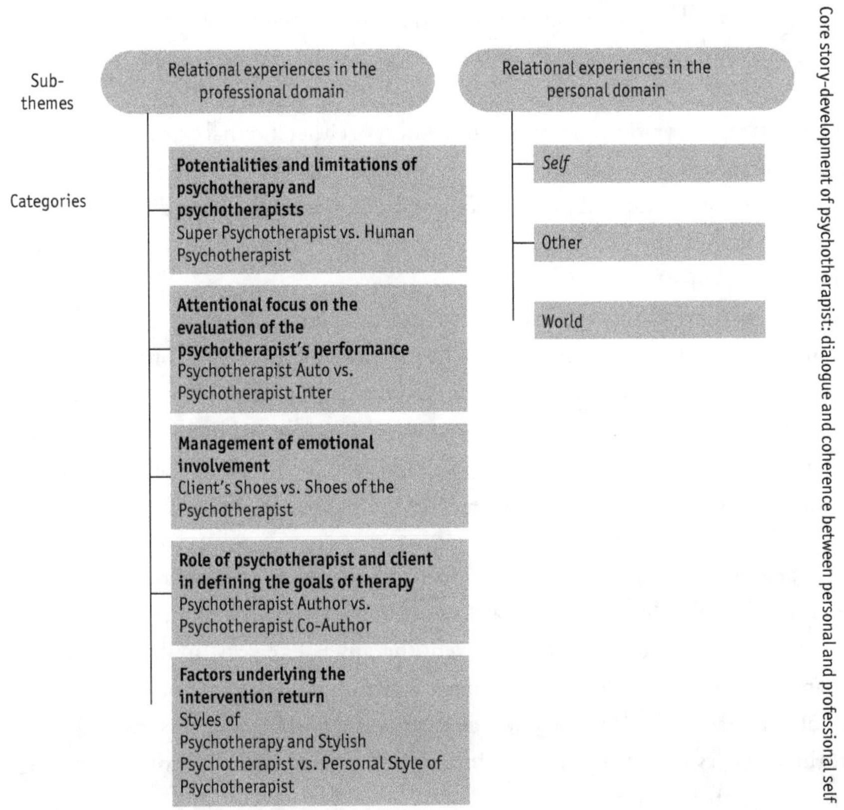

FIGURE 4.2 Phases and changes of the psychotherapist's development: subthemes, categories, and subcategories.

3. Management of emotional involvement: *Client's Shoes versus Shoes of the Psychotherapist*
4. Role of psychotherapist and client in defining the goals of therapy: *Psychotherapist Author versus Psychotherapist Coauthor*
5. Factors underlying the intervention (external and internal focus): *Styles of Psychotherapy and Stylish Psychotherapist versus Personal Style of Psychotherapist*

Potentialities and Limitations of Psychotherapy and Psychotherapists: Super Psychotherapist Versus Human Psychotherapist

The potentialities and limitations of psychotherapy and psychotherapists are, at the beginning of clinical practice, represented by an *idealized fantasy* (p1m) of *naive omnipotence* (c1m) and *salvation of the other* (c1m):

> It's like a very, very strong illusion that we are going to change the world, or that we change people, we have a fabulous arsenal, or we have fabulous nuclear weapons to change people. (c2m)

> There is very much the myth of psychotherapy, as if a person possesses magic, a bright crown around the head that distinguishes them from others! (c3f).

These initial representations emerge in the context of either internal expectations about the psychotherapeutic role or external and sociocultural expectations about psychotherapeutic practice. The psychotherapist incorporates what we call the *Super Psychotherapist*, and clinical practice is mythologized in terms of the ability to help and promote change in clients.

These expectations promote high anxiety and insecurity, especially in the face of non-immediate results socially imposed on the psychotherapist. In the course of clinical practice, the progressive realization of the limited nature of psychotherapeutic help, the construction of what we call the *Human Psychotherapist*, is seized by the growing complexity of the possibilities of psychotherapeutic space and the role of the psychotherapist in the process. Two of the interviewees refer to this change as follows:

> In the beginning I had a somewhat idealized vision, a little more omnipotent. . . . I thought that psychotherapy could solve all the ills of a person and, today, I don't think any of that. . . . Psychotherapy is like yeast in cakes, if the eggs are not there, if the flour is not there, if the ingredients are not there, you can put the yeast in and the cake will not be as it could be, and this limitation of reality, I guess I started to accept, integrate and know that the contribution I can give is limited. (p3f)

> Nowadays, I have a lot more security because I don't feel pressed to solve the world's problems, and I think that the problem of youth is that we think we can help people and that everything will be resolved. . . . Today I don't have this weight on my shoulders. (cb1f)

A magical definition of psychotherapy, the psychotherapist's superhuman power, and the underlying distress of the illusions of salvation are progressively replaced by the awareness of the possibilities and limitations of psychotherapy and the humanization of the psychotherapist as a provider of help. The understanding of the limits of psychotherapy results from (1) the acceptance that some problems fall outside of the psychological domain of intervention and that clients may benefit from a referral to other professionals or even to other psychotherapists, (2) the understanding of suffering as inevitable in life and human existence, and (3) the acceptance of uncertainty and ambiguity in the psychotherapeutic process. Understanding the limits is particularly expressed in the following statements by a psychotherapist:

> I better accept suffering in the lives of people and in my own life. Lives are suffered, there is no going back to it, we are not going to [take it away]. Suffering will continue to exist, whether there are psychotherapists or not. (c1m)

> I am less rushed than I was 10 years ago also . . . I think that I dealt less with the ambiguity; therapy involves us dealing with the ambiguity, not realizing what is ahead, unable to make sense of the case and to be able to deal with this ambiguity. (c1m)
>
> Fundamental characteristics of a psychotherapist? Humility regarding own knowledge and the ability to help the other to create change. (s3f)

Attentional Focus in the Assessment of the Psychotherapist's Performance: Psychotherapist Auto Versus Psychotherapist Inter

Continuing a perception of unlimited power in psychotherapeutic help in the beginning of practice, characterized by *Super Psychotherapist*, produces what we call the *Psychotherapist Auto*, self-centered on his or her abilities and competencies to promote help in psychotherapy. Gains and setbacks in the process are primarily attributed to the psychotherapist's own performance. This self-focus is felt as promoting high anxiety, distress, and fear of making mistakes that have iatrogenic implications. These emotional reactions inhibit a holistic and relational understanding of the psychotherapeutic process. The following statements exemplify this attentional focus:

> At the beginning, I was so scared and had so much fear of not being able to do things well, I was so worried about what I was saying, what I did, what I thought, what I felt, basically there was a giant eye on myself that did not let me be available to others. (p3f)
>
> I lived with an intense anxiety, that is, for me it was highly uncomfortable. . . . There was a time when I considered quitting, I suffered a lot from therapy. Imagine, the day before therapy I began to get tense. (c1m)

Progressively psychotherapeutic effectiveness is no longer understood as being exclusively dependent on the performance of the psychotherapist and on the theoretical models, and a relational understanding of psychotherapy emerges. The attentional focus of the psychotherapist turns to the dialogical interaction in psychotherapy. A movement to what we call the *Psychotherapist Inter* is in progress.

A sense of greater security and serenity in the management of errors and psychotherapeutic impasses is increasingly developed with experience and a continuous reflexive stance. Psychotherapists perceive self-efficacy particularly in challenging therapeutic processes. The progressive decentering of the Psychotherapist Auto toward the Psychotherapist Inter extends the psychotherapeutic space. Psychotherapy becomes more complex, and the psychotherapist *discovers* the client and his or her importance in the evolution of the process. Within a broader and relational conception of change, the Psychotherapist Inter has more room to allow him- or herself to improvise and to risk innovation/creativity. Clients become important agents of learning, and the psychotherapeutic relationship becomes an important indicator of psychotherapeutic progress. The Psychotherapist Inter is now more available to the other and to the complex sphere of psychotherapeutic relationships:

> I actually had a lot of fear of not being up to the situation, which ended by not being available for the relationship, I was more concerned with me than with the person and with the relationship, and I think that it passed, fortunately! . . . I think now I can take pleasure in the situation, which at the time I could not because of fear. (p3f)

Managing Emotional Involvement and Proximity: Client's Shoes Versus Shoes of Psychotherapist

One of the factors that psychotherapists consensually indicated as being more influential in psychotherapeutic success is empathy. As an essential quality of the psychotherapeutic relationship, empathy is characterized as a difficult and complex process, given the encounter between two epistemic realities, client and psychotherapist; the management of emotional charge potentiated by the vicarious experience of suffering; and the difficulty establishing a genuine relationship of unconditional support:

> Am I really able to understand this person? I think that is one of the hardest things to do . . . understanding, empathy. There aren't many encounters with others that are genuinely open, with a total availability to others, it happens few times . . . to be unconditionally on the side of people is not something so easy, we are accustomed to believe very conditionally. (cb3m)

The polarization of this category, *Client's Shoes versus Shoes of Psychotherapist*, emerges from the definition of empathy as a metaphor for the capacity of the psychotherapist to put him- or herself in the shoes of the client knowing that the shoes are not his or her own, meaning not to lose his or her own references (Rogers, 1975; Skovholt & Rønnestad, 1995). To wear the "shoes of the client" as an empathic exercise without the "as if" condition can lead to identification with the client and projection of own experiences. This is perceived as problematic, either because of the impact it can have on the quality of emotional support provided to clients or because of the effect on psychotherapists' personal lives.

"Absorbing negative emotionality" (c2m), the "weight of the stories" (c4f), and "sleeping with the cases" (c3f) are statements that point to the risk of overidentification—that is, to permanently wearing the client's shoes, which can contaminate other contexts of psychotherapists' personal experience.

The movement that allows the psychotherapist to understand the frame of reference of the client requires the learning of an optimal emotional distancing in the psychotherapeutic relationship. "Close the door, remove the client's shoes" protects the psychotherapist from emotional overinvolvement and appears to be an important achievement in obtaining security in the role of a psychotherapist, as expressed in the following statements:

> It seems that this is an achievement to not to be afflicted with, to not be anxious with the anxiety of our patients, not to get depressed with the depressions of the clients, but still stay attuned. . . . Empathize with the person, without letting us invade. (p2f)

> From an early age, I learned that I can't take things home, and this causes the person to have to set limits . . . and it is the only way that I have to continue to enthuse myself and be touched by the situations, but without getting depressed or carrying it for the rest of my life. . . . To continue to be there one hundred percent we have to protect ourselves somehow. (cb1f)

Role of the Psychotherapist and Client in Defining the Goals of Therapy: Psychotherapist Author Versus Psychotherapist Coauthor

At the beginning of practice, the definition of the aims of therapy tends to be paradoxically imposed by psychotherapists. We say "paradoxically" because it is precisely at the beginning of practice, with less experience, that psychotherapists need to lead therapy and to have certainty in the intervention and the results to be achieved. Although, as one of the participants mentioned, if dealing with fragile and misleading representations,

> When I entered the first session, I soon had all the responses. . . . I think that because of this felt omnipotence in the first session . . . . . ., "I know what I will do next time," but in fact do not know. (c1m)

Thus, the search for objectivity and safety of practice, validated by personal and cultural expectations of the unlimited power of the psychotherapist, underlies the emergence of what we call the *Psychotherapist Author.* The Psychotherapist Author is characterized by a unified definition of the aims of therapy, namely
(1) by a concern with diagnosis and rapid identification of the problem; (2) by the need to observe rapid changes and to "see things work" (cb2m); (3) by the directivity and imposition in conducting the psychotherapeutic process; and (4) by the structuring and programming of the practice, particularly by referencing textbook treatments and structured and planned interventions:

> In the beginning, it was a little more rigid, one thing you learn in a certain way, leads to the first interview, looking to follow those steps, the person is very attached to a script in the beginning, it is for the sake of safety and security. . . . Then the person

> forgets them, but integrates them in such a way that they seem to arise naturally, I can't think "Now I will use a paradoxical strategy!" (s4f)

> [In the beginning] maybe I was more involved in the desire to heal, inhibited less my desire to steer the situation a little, and I have learned to be more silent, more able to accept that one has to do more internal work, more slowly, and therefore greater tolerance. . . . The young often get anxious, because results fail, or strive so much that it seems that they want to be the authors of the improvement of the patients, who after all have to learn to manage their conflicts themselves, to understand what is happening with them. (p2f)

With the expansion of the role of the client, a collaborative and shared definition of psychotherapy comes about through what we call *Psychotherapist Coauthor*: This movement is characterized by the reinvention of variables such as timing and client's alternative contexts of change and by relinquishing the total and absolute control of the psychotherapeutic journey, considered erratic, undefined, and endowed with a dialogical complexity, evident in the following statement:

> We get out of that attitude in which we have the knowledge that the other person lacks. . . . We enter a more collaborative one, to know each other and help each other to achieve what you want, and not what I think he should reach, is a colossal shift. . . . It gives us a whole way of being with the person that is totally different and I think more rewarding for me in this case . . . to be open to each other, to the phenomenological experience that the other person brings. (cb1f)

The Psychotherapist Coauthor is also defined by epistemic opening and humility. Finally, the Psychotherapist Coauthor distributes the power in therapy and considers the client as an essential agent in the definition of psychotherapeutic success:

> There was another thing that came later; which was that I started to become aware of things that clients themselves taught me. . . . I think at the beginning I did not even let them teach me. (s3f)

Underlying Factors to the Psychotherapist's Intervention: Styles of Psychotherapy and Psychotherapists Stylish Versus Personal Style of Psychotherapist

Throughout their training, psychotherapists have access to ways of thinking about psychotherapy, either through theoretical models or through senior psychotherapists and trainers. This is represented by psychotherapists in the beginning of clinical practice as being of conceptual and theoretical clarity. They tend to become fascinated with the models that give a sense of apparent security in the face of the initial chaos fostered by the complexity of the psychotherapeutic intervention:

> Let's say that I believed in the model in a very naive way, for three, four years. It was nice, it gave me that fantasy, that innocent security of the early years, convinced that I could do anything, that I had solutions for everything, so it helped me in that sense, it gave me a certain determination in the intervention that helped. (c2m)

> I think there is a phase of a certain initial fascination with the model, with the theory, with the possibilities, seeing senior people speak to us of their work, after that there comes the awareness that this is not as easy as it seems. . . to be with a client is a difficult thing, which requires a lot of training, requires a personal reflection on how we are and how we behave, the felt difficulties . . . there is an awareness of a personal path that has to be completed [executed]. (h2m)

The guiding factors of intervention at the beginning of psychotherapeutic practice are initially inspired by the use of theoretical models and textbook practices due to the structure they provide (*Psychotherapy Styles*) and the simulation of senior psychotherapists and in questioning before difficulties or impasses (*Psychotherapists Stylish*).

Given the adoption of external references in the definition of authenticity, the practice is increasingly felt as stiff and uncomfortable, formatted, and with the feeling of "performing a role" (cb3m). The progressive awareness of (1) the nonlinear character of the psychotherapeutic process and (2) the diversification of theoretical models, in terms of trainers, models, and intervention strategies and techniques more in line with the psychotherapist's genuine self, allow a more spontaneous, flexible, and individualized therapy.

The Personal Style of the Psychotherapist appears to result, thus, from the synthesis and integration of theoretical influences and personal styles of the psychotherapists observed, as well as from the use of personal characteristics in practice, such as the use of humor, metaphors, and self-disclosure:

> I was indoctrinated with self-control and the absence of complete openness on the part of the psychotherapist, the total absence of transfer and countertransference and indoctrinated with the manual that is "you have to be the manual and not yourself." The big difference in principle from that time to now is that I'm much more at ease being myself and saying what I feel and what I think, as an important factor in the psychotherapeutic relationship and change, in favor of the patient, not for my well-being. (c2m)

The genuineness and authenticity arise as a corollary of integration and search for congruence between personal and professional experiences, and they inspire creativity and satisfaction with the challenge that the permanent attempt to understand the other demands. Consider the following descriptions:

> It's funny . . . I was remembering an expression that Figo [soccer player] has used, that maybe is similar to what I feel at this moment . . . [when he] was asked if

> he was going to play that game being angry or afraid he responded in a way that I think is very funny: "No I'll play as I always play the game, for enjoyment." . . . This is how I play, that's how I like to play and I'm going to play like that and that gives me pleasure, in fact, to do psychotherapy today! It is curious because it is a radical change from six or seven years ago, it gives me joy, sometimes I even forget myself! . . . I would like to be able to see me ten years ago, because . . . WOW! (c1m)
>
> On the other hand, when we want someone to find himself and pop out of the internal packages that limit, meaning that their identity comes to the surface, we also have to be ourselves, despite the technique. Pretense, hypocrisy, patting yourself on the back, do not fit in this relationship. (p4m)

Finally, the psychotherapist has space to reinvent him- or herself and to be there 100% (cb1f), being able to be with his or her client in a true way, "without masks, without being artificial and . . . without defenses, fears" (h2).

SUBTHEME 2: PHASES AND CHANGES OF THE PSYCHOTHERAPIST'S DEVELOPMENT IN THE PERSONAL DOMAIN

For psychotherapists, the nature of change does not take place only in the professional field but also in the personal domain. This subtheme is organized into three categories that represent precisely the implications that the practice takes on: representations of the self, representations of the other, and representations of the world.

Representations of the Self

The trips that the psychotherapy takes to the world of others, embodied in the process of empathy present during the psychotherapeutic encounter, seem to promote the development of a sense of tolerance, "a less superficial and deeper understanding" (h1m) of the human being, which is reflected in the self through self-knowledge and acceptance of the psychotherapist's personal characteristics. A psychotherapist describes the impact of being a psychotherapist on her personal life as follows:

> From the personal point of view, I feel that therapy [being a therapist] helped me to grow and live in a more peaceful, more serene, less troubled, less anxious way. Here's a question that I think is very important, to be aware of my own inner world, of my own fears, anguishes, concerns, not to escape it, to take it as mine. (h2m)

It is interesting to note that the understanding and acceptance of the therapist by the client constitutes one of the objectives to promote in psychotherapeutic help, and it seems to be a spontaneous result in the development of the psychotherapist. Despite the client's role being clearly differentiated from the role of the psychotherapist, the relational dialectic seems to constitute itself as an opportunity for a deep knowledge of self in relationship. As a psychotherapist told us, "We're doing a psychotherapeutic process with our clients and we are ourselves doing [receiving] psychotherapy" (s2f).

Vicarious experience of suffering and of human limits also has implications for the relativization of priorities and the devaluation of what some psychotherapists have defined as "trivial" problems (s2f and cb3m). Putting their own personal experience in contrast with the experiences of some clients triggers, somehow, a sense of privilege and of relief and an appreciation of significant relationships such as family and friends:

> To perceive that life story, that person's problems and to feel selfishly well about my family, with the story that I have. . . . Sometimes, I really don't recognize what I have around me, for example. If you want, the effect it can have is of valuing. (c4f)

Representations of Other

With regard to the representations of the other, the main changes mentioned by the psychotherapists are the deep respect and admiration for the idiosyncrasies of the human being, so well expressed in the following statement:

> We think, before studying these things a little bit, we know some determinants and we are able to predict the behavior of people, and in fact it is not so! . . . We are dealing with a person we see as unique and unrepeatable, there is no equal in the world, and this I think is a challenge, it's exciting. (s4f)

This admiration for the human being has at least three implications for the personal experience of the psychotherapist. The first refers to a less rigid, more open and complex stance when encountering behavior that is in dissonance with his or her personal experience:

> Therapy [being a psychotherapist] ultimately influences our way of being in life, our values, philosophies, even existential aspects, choices that are made, the profound respect for people, and even a more comprehensive approach to certain behavior, which could sometimes be seen as shocking, strange, bizarre. But we get to look at them in another way, have a certain tolerance and understanding, this might be the great influence of therapy. Accept the diversity of people and recognize that people have a right to make choices in their lives and this is something that concerns them, and that I don't have to have an influence, or even often, an opinion. (h2m)

The second implication deals with a constructive approach to people's capacities for resilience, emotional survival, and the process of making sense of disruptive experiences:

> I worked with victims of torture ... it has been a fantastic learning experience . . . because it showed me the extent of almost human limit, that is one

> thing that interests me, they amazed me! How do people who we imagine are totally destroyed by the most blatant and the most terrible things—and, in fact, the side of torture is one side of an unimaginable violence, and how people are able to survive this, and to restructure and to live well, is a remarkable thing. (cb3m)

The third implication concerns the sense of hope and tolerance vis-à-vis others believing in the resolution of the problems:

> I think the big change that was taking place in me, in my personal relationships, was in acceptance. . . . I'm a very tolerant person. . . . I think that tolerance, tolerance for others, appears as a corollary of this whole process, this slow therapeutic relations broth. (h1m)

However, this same complexity inherent to the understanding of the other, "this deeper evaluation of psychological things" (h1m), is likely to promote anxiety and uncertainty:

> I like to feel that the complexity with which we can see things—on the one hand sometimes we feel anguish, but on the other hand there is a feeling of fullness, that we do not give interpretations to the banal or everyday or superficial things, that we seek to understand the logic of things, how people function and its complexity, that sometimes is distressing because we are powerless to change a number of things, even of people who are by our side, but that, on the other hand, . . . gives the notion that we are seeing things in some depth. (cb2m)

Participants also mentioned professional learnings that were felt as positive experiences as psychotherapists in their relationships, namely in marriage, divorce, and remarriage and in parenting, because they contributed to a less dramatic and more creative experience of emotional challenges. Negative impacts on the emotional availability to others were also reported, notably the most close and significant ones, due to the implications of emotional wear of the psychotherapeutic relationship:

> I think that during my divorce process, I managed to avoid a number of mistakes, I am absolutely sure, because theoretically I knew a lot about divorce and I think I managed to do a good job there. In terms of remarriage, there are many issues that arise and are unavoidable, and because I know they are unavoidable, I don't dramatize, therefore, any other person who does not know that a particular conflict is inevitable, can dramatize. (s1f)

Representations of the World

To be a psychotherapist has implications in the form of shaping the world. The contact with a variety of worlds, arising from clinical practice, promotes a more flexible view and perspective on the world:

> This access to people's lives, that they allow naturally, is extremely beneficial ... gives me a variability over the world, gives me flexibility, because people sometimes are in the same place, they live with the same people all the time, are at the same age, they become boring and extremely cynical. I think this is the natural antidote, I mean I somehow know that the world is diverse and that's good, it's nice, it's interesting and I prepare myself for this world. (cb3m)

This diversity also appears to promote a sense of acceptance of the imperfect and absurd nature of human existence:

> And life also has very absurd things, very violent things, very terrible things that have no explanation in the sense that they happen, we have to prepare ourselves for these things ... life is not fair, there is nothing productive in many things. (cb3m)

The interviewees also referred to social concerns, expressed by the problems reported in psychotherapy and that seem to constitute important information about the state of the world for some psychotherapists:

> Maybe the biggest impact is to think of society in these recent years, I am thinking "In which society do I live, which brings these problems?" ... "Why is it that people are like that?" "What is it that brings this transformation?" "What are we making of ourselves, of society and of the world, in the small portion that I can contribute?" (cb1f)

For other psychotherapists, worldviews are inspired by their theoretical models, and this sense of understanding goes beyond the psychotherapeutic setting and is part of the more general domain of personal experience, as expressed in the following statement:

> Through psychoanalysis, I realized what civilization was in general and how badly we comply. I noticed also the wars in which we live and how we could improve our own groups. It gave me opportunities for observation and understanding that I find very good. (p4m)

Core Story—Development of Psychotherapist: Dialogue and Coherence Between Personal and Professional Self

The core story unfolding in the interviews is the development of the psychotherapist as a progressive process of searching for consistency and coherence between personal and professional experiences. The professional development of a psychotherapist is intimately related to his or her construction as a person. This seems to be the most explicit representation by psychotherapists interviewed about their professional development:

> I don't see psychotherapy as having, psychotherapy is being. It's a process of incorporation, we have to breathe this . . . because, it is also our own personal development. We also are very involved in the things that we have within ourselves, who we are, in the understanding of what we are, and in using that same understanding. (p1m)

The psychotherapist is a professional of the relationship and as one psychotherapist said, "It is a matter of fundamental research, knowing the [self of the] psychotherapist, because we are the main tool of our work" (cb1f). This tool (psychotherapist) is embedded within relational stories, memories, constructions of realities, meanings, and idiosyncrasies, which are inevitably a part of how psychotherapists practice psychotherapy.

The development of the psychotherapist does not apply exclusively to the professional domain of developing technical skills but also refers to the domain of self-knowledge and acceptance of personal characteristics as important resources for the development of a personalized practice of psychotherapy. Self-knowledge and self-acceptance are even considered as important resources in the acceptance and understanding of the other: "If the person is not capable of self-knowledge, he hardly gets to know the other, and if you can't see the other, you are hardly able to be empathic" (s1f). One of the psychotherapists also told us about self-awareness present in the ability to read emotional resonances of the client:

> I read better the discomfort in a relational mode, that is, when I feel uncomfortable, rather than thinking I'm inappropriate, I think "Why I'm feeling this, why is this person making me feel. . . .why is the relationship with this person making me feel uncomfortable, what is she trying to say to me?" (c1m)

The synthesis and integration of experiences from the personal and professional field, as well as the personal appropriation of the professional role, form part of the characteristics considered important in practice. The construction of a personal style of intervention and the legitimization of the person of the psychotherapist are viewed as central markers of the maturing and developmental process:

> I'm much more myself [me] than I was in the past . . . and therefore, my well-being was legitimized in the relationship. My personal experience has been legitimized; the person who I am has become legitimized. (c2m)

The developmental process is represented as a lifelong process and what is considered vital is the curiosity, the openness to the phenomenological experience of the other. The fascination behind the understanding of the complexity and uniqueness of human primordial serves as gear lubricant of the unfinished development dynamics of the psychotherapist, as reported by one interviewee:

> Psychotherapy is a phenomenon of humanity. . . . To be a psychotherapist is one path, and it is a path that never is, nor ever will be finished, it is a path to be carried on throughout experience, throughout life. (p1m)

Discussion

The aim of this study was to analyze the representations of psychotherapists considered experts about the experiences perceived as being crucial to their professional development. It was not intended to draw developmental pathways but, rather, to analyze the variety of experience and changes that occur in therapeutic and nontherapeutic settings that contribute to the construction of being a psychotherapist. Two major themes emerged from the analysis: (1) relational experiences of psychotherapist development and (2) phases and changes of psychotherapist development.

The experiences that psychotherapists described as being more likely to promote change arise in interpersonal contexts in therapeutic or in personal relationships. This data is consistent with the findings from studies by Skovholt and Rønnestad (Rønnestad & Skovholt, 2003; Skovholt & Rønnestad, 1995), which claim that interpersonal experiences appear to be more important than impersonal sources of information such as seminars, work, and theories. Also, in Rønnestad and Orlinsky's (2005) international study, clinical experience with clients is considered to be most crucial in psychotherapist development, followed by personal psychotherapy, supervision, courses and seminars, and experiences in the personal life of the psychotherapist. This finding does not mean, however, that compelling theoretical training and quality supervision are not important to psychotherapist development and to psychotherapy effectiveness.

In the first subtheme, relational experiences in the professional domain that contributed to psychotherapist development, we find that the experiences felt with a more intense emotional tone represent the most significant moments for psychotherapist development. On the one hand, we note that experiences represented as having a positive impact and that reinforce practice were the ones that return a sense of usefulness and effectiveness. These include experiences that restore a sense of gratification, experiences of access to privileged dimensions of clients' experience, and emerging experiences that focus on the nature of the emotional bond that the psychotherapist develops with some clients. On the other hand, the sense of inability to help, unexpected client dropouts, difficulties in establishing the psychotherapeutic relationship, managing the limits of psychotherapy, and emotional distress caused by the practice seem to form developmental challenges that could trigger early withdrawal from practice or even psychotherapist burnout, which is a common professional hazard (Abreu, Stoll, Ramos, Baumgardt, & Kristensen, 2002).

Reflective and accumulated practice also seems to be represented as an important device for the validation of the determining factors in the psychotherapeutic process. The collaborative comprehension of the psychotherapeutic process, the importance of relationship quality, and pragmatic help, which is called context-sensitive knowledge (Rønnestad & Skovholt, 2003), are three of the characteristics identified by expert psychotherapists in the studies of Sullivan et al. (2005) and Rønnestad and Skovholt (2003). Because psychotherapy is a dialogic encounter between the psychotherapist's and client's realities, it is not surprising that the client is a mirror that constitutes the greatest reflection for the psychotherapist's practice. It is precisely the understanding and integration of these dialogical moments that is the central catalyst of developing a sense of self and being in psychotherapy.

With regard to the second subtheme, relational experiences in the personal domain that contributed to psychotherapist development, we find that many of the choices made in the psychotherapists' career, namely therapeutic orientations, preferred intervention populations, and the construction and meaning of the psychotherapeutic relationship (particularly with regard to empathy), were influenced by experiences in the personal domain. Rønnestad and Skovholt (2003) found that experienced psychotherapists reported a greater impact of personal life experiences on practice (namely experiences with a strong emotional tone, such as including stories of abandonment and also rigid and demanding family contexts). Although in the current study psychotherapists did not explicitly articulate which life events (particularly negative experiences) had implications for their practice, psychotherapists described how experiences that generate higher emotional stress in their personal life enhanced their psychotherapeutic practice and felt like gains, especially in terms of empathy and support.

In Rogers' (1975) ironically titled article, "Empathic: An Unappreciated Way of Being," he says that "the better integrated the therapist is within himself, the higher the degree of empathy he exhibits" (with clients) (p. 4). Being and becoming a psychotherapist is a process that goes beyond the realm of the theoretical models, techniques, and conceptual reading of psychotherapy, usually privileged in comparative studies (Reupert, 2006), and is part of a more complex domain of increasing differentiation and personalization of psychotherapeutic practice. Thus, this process is represented as continuing and unfinished because it draws on the dialectic between therapeutic and nontherapeutic experiences, the definition of psychotherapy, therapeutic change, the helping relationship, and the psychotherapist's role being inherent to the psychotherapist's developmental history. It seems, therefore, that the continued pursuit of coherence between the relational challenges of psychotherapeutic practice and the psychotherapist's personal experience should be subjected to a deeper understanding, given its implications for clinical practice.

For the second theme, stages and changes in the development of psychotherapists, we present a figure that can help us analyze the categories along two main axes

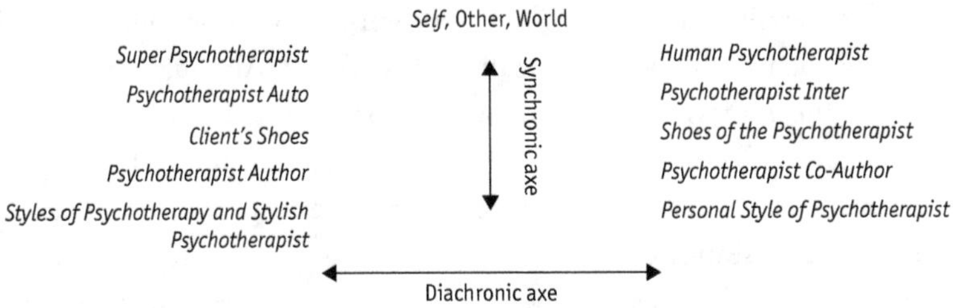

FIGURE 4.3 Synchronic and diachronic axes for organizing categories.

(Fig. 4.3), the diachronic and synchronic. The diachronic axis is implicit in the polarization of the categories and implies the temporality of change and the promoting factors. The synchronic axis emphasizes the importance of an integrated and inclusive understanding of the areas analyzed—for example, the categories constructed cannot be understood as developmental bumps but, rather, as salient representations of the development of the psychotherapist.

On the diachronic axis, a movement of progressive differentiation of the psychotherapists' representations about their role in the psychotherapeutic space and process can be inferred. The supportive role of the psychotherapist is initially amplified, and the definition of psychotherapy effectiveness relies on technical expertise. This focus on the psychotherapist's *power* goes through the hetero-imposition of therapy goals, means, and the processes underlying an idealized goal. The search for an objective and safe practice, validated by further personal and sociocultural expectations, underlies the emergence of Psychotherapist Author. Conflict between practice and the integration of experiences that challenge the initial definition of the psychotherapist role and of psychotherapy occurs with the progressive introduction of the client space and its contingencies in the process. This represents the core promoter of change in psychotherapy. The accumulated and reflected practice, and as was stated by one of the psychotherapists interviewed, "the broth of slow therapeutic relationships," emerges as a challenging context for increasing complexity in the definition of help. The relational experiences and the cognitive and emotional movement that understanding clients demand appear to be agents for the differentiation of categories from a temporal perspective. The experience in itself is not a differentiating factor of the psychotherapist's expertise. However, as mentioned by Goldberg (1992), experience is no guarantee of wisdom but constitutes itself as an excellent opportunity.

The conflict between psychotherapy and the psychotherapists' limitations inherent to the movement of building a Psychotherapist Human implies the acceptance of uncertainty and ambiguity as well as the acceptance that professional practice does not exclusively depend on the psychotherapists' technical and theoretical expertise (Matos, 2011). Rønnestad and Skovholt (1991, as cited in Skovholt, Hanson, Jennings, & Grier, 2004) reported that one of the mistakes of inexperienced psychotherapists is precisely premature closure—for example, when facing the ambiguity of psychotherapeutic practice, psychotherapists cling to simplistic solutions, theories, or frameworks in order to avoid feeling cognitively and emotionally overwhelmed. Although this strategy can inhibit anxiety and professional uncertainty, it appears that this same ambiguity and anxiety can induce reflection and opening. Neufeldt, Karno, and Nelson (1996) state that reflection is the enhancing of the conversion of experience into expertise.

Another important feature of psychotherapists in this study relates to the progressive learning of managing emotional involvement. These results are in line with the findings of Rønnestad and Skovholt (2003). The authors report that in the early stages of development, psychotherapists tend to overidentify themselves with clients, and this overinvolvement tends to block the construction of a helpful therapeutic relationship. Moreover, the authors report that learning how to manage emotional involvement is quite difficult but crucial in order to help psychotherapists deal with human suffering throughout their career. This developmental competence is called *boundaried generosity* (Skovholt et al., 2004).

As a corollary of learning obtained throughout training, mimicking the psychotherapist's masters fosters the gradual learning of a personal style of intervention. The self-knowledge promoted in a relational context allows psychotherapists to be more spontaneous, with personal characteristics appearing to be indicators of genuineness and transparency in the psychotherapeutic relationship. As mentioned previously, we are not stating that psychotherapists do not need to learn techniques and theoretical models. However, as noted by Skovholt et al. (2004), training in technical skills, although constituting an important part of becoming an expert psychotherapist, is not enough. Also, as noted by Orlinsky and Rønnestad (2005), the conflict between more than one therapy and psychotherapeutic practice modalities at the beginning of training seems to be followed by a theoretical opening associated with representations of greater developmental progress in psychotherapeutic practice. Thus, the movement inherent in the development of the person of the psychotherapist looks beyond the technical domain and engages in the logic of human and humanized development.

From the synchronic standpoint, the categories inherent to the Human Psychotherapist, Inter Psychotherapist, the Client's Shoes, the Psychotherapist Coauthor, and Psychotherapist's Personal Style reflect a more limited power of the psychotherapist but also a broader image of the psychotherapist's potentialities. The client shares this power. On the one hand, the relationship that the client establishes with the psychotherapist is an indicator of success. On the other hand, the relationship that the psychotherapist establishes with the client is a central promoter of development. It is also interesting to note that self-knowledge conveyed through psychotherapeutic practice, conflicts with uncertainty, openness to ambiguity, and the adoption of the other as internal reference expands to the psychotherapist's personal life. This second subtheme, phases and changes of the psychotherapist's development in the personal sphere, is an indicator of professional development as integral to the development of the psychotherapist as a person. The admiration of clients' fighting capacities and clients' resilience in the face of traumatic situations appears to enhance curiosity toward others and a sense of tolerance and genuine understanding. In the same sense, Rønnestad and Skovholt (2003) identified the extensive experience of suffering as a promoter of human variability recognition, acceptance, and appreciation. Throughout the analysis, from both a synchronic and a diachronic perspective, it can be seen that developmental experiences are more likely to happen on an inter- and intrapersonal logic, with the technical skills component being less emphasized.

Even in the psychotherapists' training, it seems that the most obvious implications of this study relate to the need to promote openness to uncertainty and ambiguity and a reflective attitude toward the difficulties and challenges of psychotherapeutic practice among novice psychotherapists. *Premature closure* may interfere with the psychotherapist's development, which, apart from losing the potential psychotherapeutic relationship, not only causes ineffective assistance but also causes iatrogenic consequences in the clients' lives. The psychotherapists' training should focus not only on the cognitive component but also on emotional and relational professional development because the relational component is the most determining factor of successful psychotherapy (Jennings & Skovholt, 1999). Given the challenging nature of psychotherapeutic experiences, practice can foster increasing levels of complexity during the integration of learning and, alternatively, may carry risks, given the vicarious experience of traumatic situations and the psychotherapist's own personal challenges. The incorporation of professional experiences promoting reflection on practice, self-knowledge, and the integration of personal experiences in the curriculum could help psychotherapists to manage psychotherapeutic emotional experiences because these constitute unique opportunities to humanize psychotherapist training (Matos, 2011). In 1910, Freud recognized that no psychoanalyst would go further than what is allowed by his or her complexes and internal resistances (p. 145). Psychotherapy will always be a meeting of two or more selves, the world and the other's; as Mahoney (1991) stated, our choices are neither random nor irrelevant, and we will be wise to examine the patterns and preferences of our own options. This implies the awareness, as much as possible, of the implications of the way psychotherapists give meaning to clients' lives and to the psychotherapeutic process.

A second implication stresses the importance of the humanization of psychotherapists in psychotherapy research, particularly concerning the need to deepen the comprehension of the impact of the personal and relational story on how psychotherapists personalize their practice and signify their role. The introduction of personal characteristics as important variables in being and becoming a psychotherapist can help in understanding the complex interactions that are established between clients and psychotherapists, whether in research processes or in results. How psychotherapists regulate their personal relationships and attachments, how they regulate their emotions, how they perceive and manage countertransference behaviors, how they perceive their relational skills, and the degree of satisfaction in their most significant relational contexts may be important topics for further investigation of the association between the quality of relational experiences and events in personal experience (Barreto & Matos, 2012; Carvalho & Matos, 2010, 2012; Matos, 2011). This study also emphasizes the fact that being and becoming a psychotherapist is a lifelong process; therefore, this requires the existence of training devices that include both theoretical and technical updates and both personal development and supervision, according to the logic of integral development.

The results of this study should be evaluated in light of several limitations. The first limitation is that given the qualitative nature of the exploratory study presented, the data cannot be generalized to other psychotherapists. A second limitation relates to the process of identification of the sample. With the peer-nomination technique, we sought to minimize the effect of psychotherapists' institutional knowledge by gathering consensus among nine key informants from different geographical points of the country; this is a not representative sample of psychotherapists recognized as experts in Portugal.

The delimitations of this study are associated with the qualitative methodology. We sought to adopt a critical, reflective hermeneutics and to reduce the subjective nature of the process involving the encoding and interpretation of data through the use of validation strategies. However, we are aware that the entire coding process could have undergone changes, and the emergence of new categories in another encoding process is likely. This is a limitation because the qualitative methodology is fundamentally interpretive (Creswell, 1998), which allows greater proximity and depth to more complex research topics but restricts and limits data replication.

To conclude, we stress the contribution of this study to highlight the synthesis of the personal and professional dimensions in understanding the complex task of being and becoming a psychotherapist; after all, as Skovholt et al. (2004) stated, "Expertise is not about narrow skill development. It is becoming, over a long time, fully human" (p. 140).

Acknowledgments

This research was partially supported by a PhD research grant of the first author (SFRH/BD/22333/2005), by a research project (PTDC/PSI/65416/2006), and by PEst-C/PSI/UI0050/2011 financed by the Portuguese Foundation for Science and Technology (FCT). This chapter was also supported by FEDER funds through the COMPETE program under the project FCOMP-01-0124-FEDER-022714.

Notes

1. This study was originally published in Portuguese in Carvalho and Matos (2011a, 2011b). The *Journal Psicologia: Ciência e Profissão* authorized the use of its contents in this chapter.

2. We highlight the central contribution of revisions to the main studies of the impact of characteristics of the psychotherapist in the results of different psychotherapies that have been published in the *Handbook of Psychotherapy and Behavior Change* during the past 30 years (Beutler, Crago, & Azrimendi, 1986; Beutler et al., 1994, 2004; Parloff, Waskow, & Wolf, 1978). However,

despite the concern, especially referred to in the last two issues (Beutler et al., 1994, 2004) to include extratherapeutic characteristics (traits) and specific features (states) in the review, the authors concluded that in the past 20 years there has been a declining emphasis on investigations of the characteristics of the psychotherapist that are not associated with specific effects of treatment.

3. Each transcribed narrative was assigned a code that contains three types of information. The first is on the theoretical orientation (cb, cognitive–behavioral; c, constructivist; h, humanism; p, psychoanalytic/dynamic; s, systemic). The second piece of information concerns the number of interviews conducted within the same model. The third piece of information corresponds to the sex of the respondent (m, male; f, female). For example, in "p1m," "p" corresponds to the psychoanalytic orientation, "1" to the number of the interview within the psychoanalytical model, and "m" to male.

References

Abreu, K. L., Stoll, I., Ramos, L. S., Baumgardt, R. A., & Kristensen, C. H. (2002). Estresse ocupacional e síndrome de burnout no exercício profissional da psicologia. *Psicologia: Ciência e Profissão, 22*, 22–29.

Ahn, H., & Wampold, B. E. (2001). Where oh where are the specific ingredients? A meta-analysis of component studies in counseling and psychotherapy. *Journal of Counseling Psychology, 48*(3), 251–257.

Barreto, J., & Matos, P. M. (2012). *Mentalizing countertransference: A contribution to further research on countertransference management*. Communication presented at the 3rd Joint Meeting of the European and the United Kingdom Chapters of the Society for Psychotherapy Research, Porto, Portugal.

Beutler, L. E., & Castonguay, L. G. (2006). The task force on empirically based principals of therapeutical change. In L. C. Castonguay & L. E. Beutler (Eds.), *Principles of therapeutical change that work* (pp. 3–12). New York, NY: Oxford University Press.

Beutler, L. E., Crago, M., & Azrimendi, T. G. (1986). Research on therapist variables in psychotherapy. In S. L. Garfield & A. E. Bergin (Eds.), *Handbook of psychotherapy and behavior change* (3rd ed., pp. 257–310). New York, NY: Wiley.

Beutler, L. E., Machado, P. P., & Neufeldt, S. A. (1994). Therapist variables. In A. Bergin & S. Garfield (Eds.), *Handbook of psychotherapy and behavior change* (pp. 229–269). New York, NY: Wiley.

Beutler, L. E., Malik, M., Alimohamed, S., Harwood, T. M., Talebi, H., Noble, S., & Wong, E. (2004). Therapist variables. In M. J. Lambert (Ed.), *Handbook of psychotherapy and behavior change* (5th ed., pp. 227–306). New York, NY: Wiley.

Carvalho, H. M., & Matos, P. M. (2006). *Entrevista sobre o psicoterapeuta: Manuscrito não publicado*. Faculdade de Psicologia e de Ciências da Educação da Universidade do Porto, Porto, Portugal.

Carvalho, H. M., & Matos, P. M. (2010). *Attachment and secure base representations in psychotherapists: The mediating role of emotion regulation*. Paper presented at the 41th annual meeting of the Society for Psychotherapy Research, Asilomar, CA.

Carvalho, H. M., & Matos, P. M. (2011a). Ser e Tornar-se Psicoterapeuta Parte I: Diálogo entre Experiências Pessoais e Profissionais [Being and becoming a psychotherapist Part I: Dialogue between personal and professional experiences]. *Psicologia: Ciência e Profissâo, 31*(1), 80–95.

Carvalho, H. M., & Matos, P. M. (2011b). Ser e tornar-se psicoterapeuta parte II: Diálogo entre mudanças pessoais e profissionais [Being and becoming a psychotherapist Part II: Dialogue between personal and professional changes]. *Psicologia: Ciência e Profissâo, 31*(4), 778–799.

Carvalho, H. M., & Matos, P. M. (2012). *A secure base: Implications of psychotherapist's attachment experiences*. Paper presented at the third joint meeting of the SPR European and UK chapters, Porto, Portugal.

Castonguay, L. G., Goldfried, M. R., Wiser, S., Raue, P. J., & Hayes, A. M. (1996). Predicting the effect of cognitive therapy for depression: A study of unique and common factors. *Journal of Consulting and Clinical Psychology, 64*(3), 497–504.

Charmaz, K. (2000). Grounded theory: Objectivist and constructivist methods. In N. D. Y. Lincoln (Ed.), *Handbook of qualitative research* (2nd ed., pp. 509–535). Thousand Oaks, CA: Sage.

Creswell, J. W. (1998). *Qualitative inquiry and research design: Choosing among five traditions*. Thousand Oaks, CA: Sage.

Creswell, J. W. (2003). *Research design: Qualitative, quantitative, and mixed methods approaches* (2nd ed.). Thousand Oaks, CA: Sage.

Del Re, A. C., Flückiger, C., Horvath, A. O., Symonds, D., & Wampold, B. E. (2012). Therapist effects in the therapeutic alliance–outcome relationship: A restricted-maximum likelihood meta-analysis. *Clinical Psychology Review, 32*(7), 642–649. doi:10.1016/j.cpr.2012.07.002

Fischer, C. T. (2009). Bracketing in qualitative research: Conceptual and practical matters. *Psychotherapy Research, 19*(4–5), 583–590.

Flick, U. (1998). *An introduction to qualitative research*. London, England: Sage.

Freud, S. (1910/1959). The future prospects of psycho-analytic therapy. In J. Strachey (Ed.), (1978) *The Standard Edition of the Complete Psychological Works of Sigmund Freud* (Vol. 11, pp. 87-172). London: Hogarth Press.

Garfield, S. L. (1997). The therapist as a neglected variable in psychotherapy research. *Clinical Psychology: Science and Practice, 4*(1), 40–43.

Gelso, C. J., & Hayes, J. A. (2002). The management of countertransference. In J. Norcross (Ed.), *Psychotherapy relationships that work* (pp. 267–284). New York, NY: Oxford University Press.

Gelso, C. J., & Hayes, J. A. (2007). *Countertransference and the therapist's inner experience: Perils and possibilities*. Mahwah, NJ: Erlbaum.

Glaser, B. G. (1978). *Theoretical sensitivity*. Mill Valley, CA: Sociology Press.

Glaser, B. G., & Strauss, A. L. (1967). *The discovery of grounded theory: Strategies for qualitative research*. New York, NY: Aldine.

Goldberg, C. (1992). *The seasoned psychotherapist: Triumph over adversity*. New York, NY: Norton.

Hayes, J., Riker, J., & Ingram, K. (1997). Countertransference behavior and management in brief counseling: A field study. *Psychotherapy Research, 7*(2), 145–153.

Hill, C. E., & Lambert, M. J. (2004). Methodological issues in studying psychotherapy processes and outcomes. In J. M. Lambert (Ed.), *Handbook of psychotherapy and behavior change* (5th ed., pp. 84–135). New York, NY: Wiley.

Jennings, L., Goh, M., Skovholt, T. M., Hanson, M., & Banerjee-Stevens, D. (2003). Multiple factors in the development of the expert counselor and therapist. *Journal of Career Development, 30*(1), 59–72.

Jennings, L., & Skovholt, T. M. (1999). The cognitive, emotional, and relational characteristics of master therapists. *Journal of Counseling Psychology, 46*(1), 3–11.

Kiesler, D. J. (1966). Some myths of psychotherapy research and the search for a paradigm. *Psychological Bulletin, 65*(2), 110–136.

Lambert, M. J. (1989). The individual therapist's contribution to psychotherapy process and outcome. *Clinical Psychology Review, 9*(4), 469–485.

Laska, K. M., Smith, T. L., Wislocki, A. P., Minami, T., & Wampold, B. E. (2013). Uniformity of evidence-based treatments in practice? Therapist effects in the delivery of cognitive processing therapy for PTSD. *Journal of Counseling Psychology, 60*(1), 31–41.

Luborsky, L., McLellan, A. T., Woody, G. E., Obrien, C. P., & Auerbach, A. (1985). Therapist success and its determinants. *Archives of General Psychiatry, 42*(6), 602–611.

Mahoney, M. J. (1991). *Human change processes: The scientific foundations of psychotherapy.* New York, NY: Basic Books.

Matos, P. M. (2011). Das famílias dos clientes às famílias dos psicoterapeutas: questões sobre o desenvolvimento dos psicoterapeutas. In P. M. Matos, C. Duarte, & M. E. Costa (Eds.), *Temas do desenvolvimento e de intervenção psicológica com famílias*. Porto, Portugal: LivPsic.

McLeod, J. (1995). *Doing counselling research.* London, England: Sage.

Mohr, D. C. (1995). Negative outcome in psychotherapy: A critical review. *Clinical Psychology: Science and Practice, 2*(1), 1–27.

Neufeldt, S. A., Karno, M. P., & Nelson, M. L. (1996). A qualitative study of experts' conceptualization of supervisee reflectivity. *Journal of Counseling Psychology, 43*(1), 3–9.

Norcross, J. C. (2002). Empirically supported therapy relationships. In J. C. Norcross (Ed.), *Psychotherapy relationships that work: Therapist contribution and responsiveness to patient needs* (pp. 3–16). New York, NY: Oxford University Press.

Norcross, J. C., & Prochaska, J. O. (1983). Clinicians theoretical orientations—Selection, utilization, and efficacy. *Professional Psychology: Research and Practice, 14*(2), 197–208.

Orlinsky, D. E. (1989). Researchers' images of psychotherapy: Their origins and influence on research. *Clinical Psychology Review, 9*(4), 413–441.

Orlinsky, D. E., & Howard, K. I. (1986). Process and outcome in psychotherapy. In S. L. Garfield & A. E. Bergin (Eds.), *Handbook of psychotherapy and behavior change* (4th ed., pp. 311–384). New York, NY: Wiley.

Orlinsky, D. E., & Rønnestad, M. H. (2005). *How psychotherapists develop: A study of therapeutic work and professional growth.* Washington, DC: American Psychological Association.

Parloff, M., Waskow, I., & Wolf, B. (1978). Research on therapist variables in relation to process and outcome. In S. L. Garfield & A. E. Bergin (Eds.), *Handbook of psychotherapy and behavior change: An empirical analysis* (2nd ed., pp. 233–282). New York, NY: Wiley.

Patton, M. Q. (1990). *Qualitative evaluation and research methods* (2nd ed.). Newbury Park, CA: Sage.

Polkinghorne, D. E. (2005). Language and meaning: Data collection in qualitative research. *Journal of Counseling Psychology, 52*(2), 137–145.

Radeke, J. T., & Mahoney, M. J. (2000). Comparing the personal lives of psychotherapists and research psychologists. *Professional Psychology: Research and Practice, 31*(1), 82–84.

Reupert, A. (2006). The counsellor's self in therapy: An inevitable presence. *International Journal for the Advancement of Counselling, 28*(1), 95–105.

Rogers, C. R. (1975). Empathic: An unappreciated way of being. *The Counseling Psychologist, 5*(2), 2–10. doi:10.1177/001100007500500202

Rønnestad, M. H., & Orlinsky, D. E. (2005). Clinical implications: Training, supervision and practice. In D. E. Orlinsky & M. H. Rønnestad (Eds.), *How psychotherapists develop: A study of therapeutic work and professional growth* (pp. 181–201). Washington, DC: American Psychological Association.

Rønnestad, M. H., & Skovholt, T. M. (2003). The journey of the counselor and therapist: Research findings and perspectives on professional development. *Journal of Career Development, 30*(1), 5–44.

Rønnestad, M. H., Willutzki, U., & Tarragona, M. (2010). David E. Orlinsky: Developing psychotherapy research, researching psychotherapist. In L. G. Castonguay, J. C. Muran, L. Angus, A. J. Hayes, N. Ladany, & T. Anderson (Eds.), *Bringing psychotherapy research to life: Understanding through the work of leading clinical researchers* (pp. 233–243). Washington, DC: American Psychological Association.

Skovholt, T. M., Hanson, M., Jennings, L., & Grier, T. L. (2004). Expertise in therapy and counseling. In T. M. Skovholt & L. Jennings (Eds.), *Master therapists: Exploring expertise in therapy and counseling* (pp. 17–30). Boston, MA: Allyn & Bacon.

Skovholt, T. M., Jennings, L., & Mullenbach, M. (2004). Portrait of the master therapist: Developmental model of the highly-functioning self. In T. M. Skovholt & L. Jennings (Eds.), *Master therapists: Exploring expertise in therapy and counseling* (pp. 125–146). New York, NY: Allyn & Bacon.

Skovholt, T. M., & Rønnestad, M. H. (1995). *The evolving professional self: Stages and themes in therapist and counselor development.* New York, NY: Wiley.

Strauss, A., & Corbin, J. (1990). *Basics of qualitative research: Grounded theory procedures and techniques.* Newbury Park, CA: Sage.

Strupp, H. (1978). The therapist's theoretical orientation: An overrated variable. *Psychotherapy: Theory, Research and Practice, 15*(4), 314–317.

Sullivan, M. F., Skovholt, T. M., & Jennings, L. (2005). Master therapists' construction of the therapy relationship. *Journal of Mental Health Counseling, 27*(1), 48–70.

Vasco, A. B. (1992). *Psicoterapeuta conhece-te a ti próprio: Características, crenças metateóricas, estilos terapêuticos e desenvolvimento epistemológico dos psicoterapeutas Portugueses.* Dissertação de doutoramento, Faculdade de Psicologia e de Ciências da Educação da Universidade de Lisboa, Lisboa, Portugal.

Wampold, B. E. (2001). *The great psychotherapy debate: Models, methods, and findings.* Mahwah, NJ: Erlbaum.

Wampold, B. E. (2006). The psychotherapist. In J. C. Norcross, R. Levant, & L. Beutler (Eds.), *Evidence-based practices in mental health* (pp. 200–208). Washington, DC: American Psychological Association.

Wampold, B. E., & Bolt, D. M. (2006): Therapist effects: Clever ways to make them (and everything else) disappear. *Psychotherapy Research, 16*(2), 184–187.

Williams, E. N., & Morrow, S. L. (2009). Achieving trustworthiness in qualitative research: A pan-paradigmatic perspective. *Psychotherapy Research, 19*(4–5), 576–582.

5 Psychotherapy Expertise in Singapore

A QUALITATIVE INVESTIGATION[1]

Len Jennings, Vilma D'Rozario, Michael Goh, Ashley Sovereign, Megan Brogger, and Thomas M. Skovholt

THERE IS A GREAT need for international discussion regarding the training of psychologists and psychotherapists as psychology moves towards globalization (Goh & A. Tan, 2002; Leung, 2003). Calls to internationalize psychology and psychotherapy (Leong & Ponterotto, 2003) and for psychology and psychotherapy to attain global relevance (Kogan, 2000; Marsella, 1998) have refreshed the discussion around global issues and applications of psychotherapy. Although there is some international research on therapist factors such as the worldwide survey of nearly 4000 therapists conducted by Orlinsky and Ronnestad (2005), international research on therapist expertise is lacking.

This study joins recent efforts to define psychotherapy practice in the Southeast Asian country of Singapore (A. Tan & Goh, 2002; E. Tan, 2004; Yeo, 2006). In the first book on the practice of psychology in Singapore, Goh and Tan (2002) forecasted future challenges that may confront psychological practice in Singapore given organizational and professional identity concerns, diversity of training programs and models, lack of clear competency benchmarks, and lack of local research. As well, E. Tan (2004) noted how Western theories and models have been adapted for use in counseling practice in Singapore and called for research at the local level.

In the current study, we explore characteristics of expert or master therapists in Singapore by employing similar methodology used in a study of master therapists in the United States (Jennings & Skovholt, 1999). In their qualitative study, Jennings and Skovholt found that master therapists had developed highly desirable characteristics across the cognitive, emotional, and relational domains. The researchers noted that, among other characteristics, master therapists were avid learners, emotionally mature, and had a keen sense of judgment pertaining to the timing and intensity of their interventions. A limitation of the Jennings and Skovholt study was a lack of diversity in the research sample and little emphasis on cultural competence. Goh (2005) and others (Coleman, 1998; Fuertes, Bartolomeo, & Nichols, 2001; S. Sue, 1998; D. W. Sue & D. Sue, 2008) have argued that the exploration of psychotherapy expertise must include the concept of multicultural competency.

But why should psychotherapists outside of Singapore care about psychotherapy in this island nation in Southeast Asia? Singapore is an independent island nation situated in Southeast Asia between Malaysia and Indonesia. A former British colony that gained independence in 1965, Singapore's free port trading status at the crossroads of East and West attracted settlers from China, India, and the Malay Peninsula. Her current population of 4.4 million residents comprise Chinese (77%), Malay (14%), Indian (8%), and others (1%; for example, Eurasians, Japanese, and Korean). Sternberg (2002) firmly believed that if any successful multicultural application of psychology were to be discovered, Singapore would be a likely source. Sternberg further noted that Singapore's small geographic size belies the huge influence the country has in the region and around the world on economic, sociopolitical, and educational issues.

We believe that much can be learned about the international practice of psychotherapy by studying the characteristics and therapy practice of expert therapists from different regions around the world. Expert therapists are exemplars and key informants about the practice of psychotherapy. Studying master therapists in the highly diverse setting of Singapore is an ideal place to begin building an understanding of psychotherapy expertise from both an international and multicultural perspective. As such, this study should yield valuable data that informs the practice of psychotherapy in a multicultural context. Moreover, qualitative methodology, with its emphasis on discovery and understanding, is a logical approach to explore the little known phenomenon of psychotherapy expertise in Singapore (Patton, 2002). To better understand psychotherapy expertise in Singapore, we pose the following research question: What are the personal characteristics and therapy practices of expert psychotherapists practicing in Singapore?

Method

PARTICIPANTS

The master therapists (5 men, 4 women) ranged in age from 40 to 59 years ($M = 50.56$ years, $SD = 6.19$). Their number of years practicing psychotherapy ranged from 10 to 34 years ($M = 18.44$ years, $SD = 7.06$). As for formal training, there were two Ph.D. clinical psychologists, one Ph.D. counseling psychologist, one MSW social worker, two M.A.-level therapists, two B.A.-level therapists, and one therapist with extensive applied training (e.g., extensive training with Jay Haley) and 34 years of experience, but holding no formal degree. The primary theoretical orientations identified by the master therapists were divided among family systems (n = 5), psychodynamic (n = 2), existential–humanistic (n = 2), with several therapists incorporating other approaches as well, such as cognitive–behavioral, solution-focused, and Jungian therapy. Regarding ethnicity, of the nine Singaporean participants, seven were of Chinese descent, one of Indonesian–Chinese decent, and one of East Indian descent. Regarding training, four of the nine obtained their training in the United States, one in the United States and New Zealand, one in the United States and the Philippines, one in Canada, one in England, and, finally, one obtained her doctoral training in Singapore.

RESEARCHERS

Of the three researchers involved in the consensual data analysis team, two doctoral-level psychologists had previous experience working together coding data through a consensual process. One of the psychologists taught graduate-level counseling psychology for approximately 2 years at a Singaporean university. The third data analyst was a doctoral student who had completed a doctoral qualitative research course. Before the study began, biases and concerns of the analysts were revealed in order to monitor them during the analysis process. For example, one analyst was concerned about the intrusion of themes found in an earlier study conducted on master therapists. The second analyst shared a concern that being from a Western country may influence her ability to understand the cultural nuances embedded in the participants' stories. The third analyst posed a potential concern about the inherent power differential due to her student status. Strategies for dealing with this power differential as well as researchers' biases and concerns were initially discussed and revisited during the course of the data analysis process. In addition, we employed a Singaporean auditor, currently teaching graduate-level counseling psychology for an American university, to monitor each stage of our analysis process. The auditor, a psychologist and academician, had previous experience with qualitative inquiry and had taught and practiced in both Singapore and the United States. We asked the auditor to pay particular attention to the accuracy of our cultural perceptions of the data.

INTERVIEW PROTOCOL

The participants were asked to respond to 18 open-ended questions (see the Appendix) designed to highlight the personal characteristics and therapy practices of Singaporean master therapists. The questions were virtually identical to those used in the Jennings and Skovholt (1999) study and were mostly derived from the literature on counselor effectiveness and expertise. The interviewing followed an interview guide format (Patton, 2002) in which all the questions were posed (not necessarily in order), followed by extemporaneous probes designed to elicit even greater detail on the topic at hand.

PROCEDURE

Recruitment

Borrowing the sampling methodology of the Jennings and Skovholt (1999) study, a combination of a peer nomination process and snowball sampling (Patton, 2002) strategy was used to identify Singaporean master therapists. To begin the nomination process, one of our researchers, a Singaporean psychologist teaching counseling psychology for a university in Singapore, electronically mailed her professional colleagues from a variety of sources including the Singapore Counseling Association, the Singapore Psychological Society, and a list of field supervisors affiliated with a M.A. counseling psychology program in Singapore. The use of many therapists to begin the nomination process is in contrast to the original study on master therapists (Jennings & Skovholt, 1999) in which three key informants began the snowball sampling process. Our goal was to initially "cast a wide net" by soliciting more therapists nominations at the beginning of the nomination process. We used this sampling strategy to decrease the possibility of only a small subset of deserving therapists being recognized by their peers. The e-mail letter invited counseling professionals to nominate three colleagues they believed were expert or master therapists or counselors.

It should be noted that in this study, we used the terms counselor and therapist interchangeably. We made this decision after reviewing the limited literature in Singapore on the terms that helping professionals use to describe themselves, and after consulting with psychotherapy practitioners and educators in Singapore. In an effort to use the appropriate terminology in our initial correspondence, sampling, and interviews, we learned that the term counselor was better understood, more widely used, and potentially most inclusive of exemplars for our study. However, in this article, readers will note the more frequent use of the term therapist, especially when referring to master or expert therapists, in order to be consistent with the literature on expertise in psychotherapy.

Nomination of master therapists was based on the following criteria: (a) This person is considered to be a "master counselor"; (b) This person is most frequently thought of when referring a close family member or a dear friend to a counselor because the person is considered to be the "best of the best"; and (c) One would have full confidence in seeing this counselor for one's own personal counseling. Those nominated as master therapists were then contacted via e-mail or telephone and asked to nominate three master therapists as well. As expected with the snowball sampling method, over the course of the sampling process, a number of key names were repeatedly mentioned and made up the core participant pool (Patton, 2002). A total of 127 nominations were cast by 45 therapists/key informants, which led to the identification of 47 master therapists.

From this process, therapists receiving three or more nominations yielded nine potential participants. This cutoff seemed optimal because the majority of nominees (81%) received one or two votes, whereas only a handful or so of the nominees (19%) received 3 or more nominations, creating a level of distinction within the group of 47 nominated therapists. In addition, interviewing nine participants provided the desired balance between depth of exploration and breadth of participant viewpoints. The nine therapists receiving the most nominations among the pool of 47 peer-nominated Singaporean master therapists were invited to participate in a 90-minute face-to-face interview. All nine therapists agreed to an interview conducted by the first author and his Singaporean colleague. The interviews were conducted in English, the official language of education and business in Singapore.

Data Analysis

Videotaped interviews were transcribed and characteristics in common among these master therapists were identified primarily through grounded theory procedures (Strauss & Corbin, 1998). We employed grounded theory as our overall framework because we preferred to begin at the "ground level," analyzing transcriptions line-by-line through open coding, and then moving from lower-level concepts toward higher-level theorizing through the development of themes and categories as recommended by Strauss and Corbin.

We also borrowed several analytic procedures found in consensual qualitative research (CQR) methodology—particularly decision-making by consensus (Hill et al., 2005; Hill, Thompson, & Williams, 1997). Working on one transcription at a time, each researcher individually coded the transcription at the concept level, which was often a phrase or two representing the most elemental unit of meaning that could be coded (Strauss & Corbin, 1998). Then the researchers met and worked toward consensus to determine the best concept for each quotation. Next, the research team organized the codes into themes for each master therapist, creating themes within each case. This data analytic process was repeated until all nine transcripts had been analyzed for themes within each case.

The researchers then conducted a cross-case analysis (Patton, 2002) by combining like themes among all nine interviews and tallied the number of quotations representing each theme as well as the number of therapists represented in that particular theme. Of the 45 preliminary themes, 8 were eliminated because they were associated with a low number of quotations (10 or less) by only a few therapists (3 or less) and/or because they could not be consolidated with another theme. At this point, some data were reassigned to a more appropriate theme by the research team. The 37 themes were further sorted and consolidated into 16 themes, increasing the robustness of the consolidated themes due to the increased number of participants and quotations represented in each consolidated theme. As a result, each theme was represented by at least four of the nine participants. Next, the researchers arranged the 16 themes into four categories. The auditor was then asked to examine the placement of the themes within categories. The auditor made several recommendations that improved the final organization of the thematic structure of the results. In Table 5.1, the 16 themes within four categories are highlighted and include the number of participants represented in each theme.

TABLE 5.1

Themes Grouped into Categories

Category and Theme	No. of Participants with Theme
Personal characteristics	
1. Empathic	6
2. Nonjudgmental	5
3. Respectful	6
Developmental influences	
4. Experience	8
5. Self-awareness	6
6. Humility	8
7. Self-doubt	4
Approach to practice	
8. Balance between support and challenge	4
9. Flexible therapeutic stance	8
10. Empowerment/strength-based approach	4
11. Primacy of the therapeutic alliance	8
12. Comfortable addressing spirituality	5
13. Embraces working within a multicultural context	5
On-going professional growth	
14. Professional development practices	9
15. Benefits of teaching/training others	6
16. Challenges to professional development in Singapore	5

Qualitative Meta-Analysis

In an effort to further the import of the current study's findings as they relate to cross-cultural psychotherapy, we conducted a qualitative meta-analysis (Timulak, 2007) to compare Jennings and Skovholt's (1999) Minnesota data with the current study. A qualitative meta-analysis is aimed at obtaining "a more comprehensive representation of investigated phenomenon," which "can be accomplished by treating the findings of primary qualitative studies, categories, abstracted descriptions, and vivid narrative paradigmatic examples as data for further analysis" (Timulak, 2007, pp. 305–306). In order to do this, domains, categories, and themes from the included studies are gathered and then grouped together based on their common meanings. These groupings are called meta-analytic categories, which are essentially meta-descriptions of the similar content between studies (Timulak, 2007).

For the qualitative meta-analysis, the same three researchers that made up the consensual data analysis team from the current study worked toward consensus to identify themes between the Minnesota and Singapore studies that were strongly related, moderately related, or divergent. In order to determine this, the researchers returned to the themes and/or quotes from each manuscript and compared content. Divergent themes were those remaining themes that had no overlap with the themes from the other study. As such, divergent themes were noted, but not given a meta-analytic category, as they were independent from those in either study. Once consensus was made on which themes' content hung together and the strength of their associations, the themes across studies for the strongly and moderately related categories were reviewed to suggest a label for the combined category. The meta-analytic categories provided a common description and summary for the themes from both studies. Themes were considered strongly related between studies if the content was nearly exact and moderately related between studies if the content was similar, but somewhat differentiated.

Results

The interview data indicated that Singaporean master therapists possess numerous characteristics in the following four categories: Personal Characteristics, Developmental Influences, Approach to Practice, and Ongoing Professional Growth. Presented below are one or two quotations that best represent each of the 16 themes. The reader should note that due to the self-report nature of the findings, the following descriptions reflect the master therapists' self-perceptions.

PERSONAL CHARACTERISTICS

The main thrust of this category highlights the Singaporean master therapists' characteristics that allow for building a safe, therapeutic encounter with clients. The three themes in this category are empathic, nonjudgmental, and respectful.

Empathic

Master therapists spoke of possessing a great empathy for their clients. As one master therapist explained, once the client felt genuinely understood and accepted in whatever circumstances, true change and healing began:

> A number of my clients came because they were quite confused about situations and they were also often self-blaming, they weren't doing things right . . . or they were partly messing themselves up. And in the course of listening to them and seeing their situation, [I] helped them be able to be more empathetic to themselves by communicating empathy to them. . . . So then they began to have this clearer sense

> of their own worth or their own abilities and resources. I realize that when I work with my clients, I do attempt to put myself into their situation . . . [and] help them to see what they are already doing to get in touch with what good changes they have already made.

Nonjudgmental

Another personal characteristic was the nonjudgmental attitude of the master therapists. This trait can produce a sense of safety for clients. For example, one master therapist described how clients could share their feelings free of judgment:

> I would say that they felt relieved after the first session because a lot of things that they said to people, even before they finish, they're slammed. But when they come here . . . they felt a sense that they could talk about their issues without being judged, without being evaluated as a person. So even if there is no solution, they are actually happy that they could come to a place and say all they want about their struggles and problems.

Respectful

The master therapists were mindful of their impact on clients and the importance of working with clients in a respectful manner. Respect for clients, whoever they are and whatever their issues may be, was a pervasive theme among these master therapists. For example, one therapist said:

> I mean I want to do justice to this person, because he comes to me not just because of any problem but a very personal problem, so I must take that person seriously. It's not like objects that you can play around with, they are human beings. Human beings with emotions that can react. I think we ought to treat [them] with a lot of respect.

DEVELOPMENTAL INFLUENCES

This category highlights the Singaporean master therapists' experiences and qualities that served as a catalyst in their development of expertise in psychotherapy. The four themes in this category are experience, self-awareness, humility, and self-doubt.

Experience

The interviewees described a journey, explaining the many elements that created and influenced their path to expertise. When exploring elements of expertise, experience was mentioned frequently as an important factor. One master therapist made the point that there were no quick developmental influences and no guarantee that experience alone leads to expertise:

> I think years of experience are important because it takes a long time to develop and store information to work from. It also takes an equally long time or perhaps even longer time to develop a store of experiences to respond from. So there is no short cut. I think we can fast track the development of counselors with very specific training, and in a concerted manner, a structured manner, but how do you make up for the experience? Beyond the experience, there is a certain maturity that is needed in one's life. And that interacts with one's role as a counselor or a therapist. I can't think of a way of making up for that. Having said that, the advance of years does not make one a wise person.

One master therapist captured the impact of learning from ordinary life experiences on his professional development:

> I constantly have an interest in growth and development . . . and I enjoy the process of learning. So I think this is what keeps me alive. Learning not just in terms of what is written from counseling, or literature, or psychology, but learning from life itself. I draw a lot of lessons from the radio, the BBC World Service, because it just opens up the world in a very concise manner. So I think that's important because therapy is about life and so if you can't relate to life and you can only relate to the psychology of life then I think you would have lost touch with the humanity that's involved.

Self-Awareness

Self-awareness seemed to serve many purposes in the development and maintenance of expertise such as recognizing one's limitations and areas of growth. Additionally, the master therapists spoke of how their self-awareness has served them well when conducting therapy. One master described it as recognizing your internal processes when working with clients—being able to be a participant/observer of interactions with clients:

> Whatever we are hearing from our clients impacts us as therapists and it triggers off our inner conversation. . . . How may I be reacting to that experience? And how would I listen to my inner conversation to utilize that and to respond to the client, because that helps me to connect, at some level, with the client's experience as well. . . . What if I am going to react adversely to the situation? Am I going to transfer that to my client? Or can I hold . . . and perhaps use that possible reaction to empathize with the client?

Humility

The master therapists recognized humility as another important component in the development of expertise. Recognizing one's limits may serve as a source of motivation and growth. One master therapist described the importance of the humbling process of recognizing and learning from one's mistakes:

> Nobody becomes an expert by first becoming an expert. I think therapists do not acknowledge the fact that they failed many times or they have made mistakes. It's hard to acknowledge that, but I think all of us failed, all of us learn from our mistakes. I think the earlier we acknowledge it the better it is for ourselves because it's from there that we learn how to do better.

Self-Doubt

Despite their experience and reputation, some of the master therapists spoke to another issue related to the development of expertise—periodic self-doubt and how this feeling motivated them to keep growing their clinical skills. One master therapist said:

> I feel like I'm always trying to catch up, that I should be able to do more than what I'm able to do now. But there's still so much out there . . . that I haven't grasped.

Despite having developed a high degree of competence, experiencing self-doubt still occurred:

> I guess maybe a bit more confident now than I was before when I first started. Although having said that, you are still thinking "What am I doing here?" There are days when it's just a bummer day. I was just thinking that I should stop doing this and open a pasta shop. Yeah and someone would say, "All your pasta would get stuck together so maybe you should stick to what you are doing!"

APPROACH TO PRACTICE

Although the master therapists were somewhat diverse in theoretical orientations and therapeutic styles, the following six themes were identified as important among the therapists in conducting therapy: balance between support and challenge, flexible therapeutic stance, empowerment/strength-based approach, primacy of the therapeutic alliance, comfortable addressing spirituality, and embraces working within a multicultural context.

Balance Between Support and Challenge

Many of the master therapists spoke of the importance of maintaining a balance between support and challenge when working with clients. One interesting way of conceptualizing this balancing act included the following dance metaphor:

> It's the ability to follow the client and to lead the client. And dance with the client. You cannot move too far ahead of clients, so the steps must be kind of in sync. Like I have a client who wanted to work on her issues but each time we come close to it she blocks and she goes off elsewhere. Now there are times when I pursue and then she blocks again. So after a bit I notice that I'm not getting anywhere. And I step back and let her lead and she might start reading her written notes because that was her way of coping with the intensity. So I would then just go along and pick up what she was saying that would help her experience herself positively. I let that tension go down a bit. And then I see if she's ready to engage in something more serious.

Flexible Therapeutic Stance

The master therapists described a flexible approach in their work with clients. If client variables required them to adapt their style, they did. For example, one master therapist described how one theory does not fit all:

> Because at one point you may be so bowled over by one theory and operate and think from there. But then over time you realize Hey! You know, some clients just don't go that way. . . . And then you learn something new and incorporate that.

Empowerment/Strength-Based Approach

A number of master therapists spoke about their clients' internal resources and how the therapist's task was to reinforce these strengths and bring them to bear in dealing with the problem at hand. One master therapist said:

> Look at where they are and the strengths they have. And it's good to make them know that they can do something, there is something in them. It's not like everything is down and in doubt. So they still have something working for them. How can they build on that and look at whatever they can do better in?

Primacy of the Therapeutic Alliance

Many of the master therapists acknowledged the importance of the therapeutic relationship. The impact of the relationship varied from a necessary condition in the therapeutic process to the relationship being the actual source of healing. For example, one therapist said:

> I think that [the relationship] is the start of the healing process. To have the sense that you are not alone, there is someone who cares, there is someone to help, there is someone whom you can relate with. . . . That breaking away from the isolation, connecting with someone and creating that meaning, that understanding of the situation for themselves. I think that starts the healing process.

Another therapist noted that although Singaporean therapists are exposed to many current training opportunities on psychotherapy technique, relationship skills are needed the most:

> We in Singapore, we are exposed to a lot of mainstream [psychotherapies], whatever is happening in town, people will go by the droves to learn. And it is good to learn this, but what they will experience is, by the third or fourth session, the toolbox is empty. You have used all the fancy questions and the nice techniques [but what about] the relationship? The relationship becomes much more important. It sustains the whole counseling process.

Comfortable Addressing Spirituality

Beyond observance of any particular religion, many master therapists spoke of a broad personal spiritual mindset, which primarily functioned as a backdrop when working with clients, but also included some therapists privately praying for clients. One described the impact of a spiritual identity on his therapeutic approach:

> I look at people and appreciate that we are essentially spiritual beings. . . . It's not hooked up with any particular religion. . . . I mean spirituality in a broader context. When I work with people I need to appreciate that we are not just here as physical beings. The material existence is only part of our being and there is a spiritual dimension in all of us that can be transcendent, that's connected to some other being somewhere, whatever you call it. Especially in our local context, there is a high percentage of people who are very religious. . . . We should get in touch with [clients' religious beliefs] and see how that affects the way they view their life, themselves, their problems and . . . how that might be a resource to empower them.

Embraces Working Within a Multicultural Context

A number of master therapists spoke of the importance of cultural awareness in their work and the challenges of adapting Western therapeutic approaches to Eastern values and systems. One therapist spoke about adapting his individualistic training to incorporate more systemic thinking:

> But somehow, being influenced by the earlier training in therapy, and being in a very intrapsychic, very individually focused or even reductionistic in orientation, is a bit unfortunate. And yet, when we think about people and their experience in culture, and about the Asian context, we cannot ignore context, we cannot ignore the fact that we are connected to other parts, you know, in our human experience. So even the "self" is not an individual self, it's the "self" in relation to. I need to take a multiple perspective orientation that there are multiple realities, multiple truths, multiple perspectives and that whatever I see, I need to see more than one.

One master therapist stressed the importance of not imposing Western values (e.g., autonomy, assertiveness) when working within a Singaporean context.

> Families have structure, hierarchy, and in the Asian context you are not about to ask a young fellow to speak his mind and let his father know exactly how he feels, without, in the first place, asking the father, "Is it ok for the son to say whatever he wants to say?" You have got to respect the hierarchy.

ONGOING PROFESSIONAL GROWTH

This category illustrates the importance of continuing education on retaining and growing one's expertise as well as enhancing self and others' development through teaching and training opportunities. In addition, significant challenges to professional development in Singapore are noted.

Professional Development Practices

Professional development, a key factor in developing and maintaining expertise, was not limited to conferences, literature, or textbooks. One master therapist believed that therapists should extend beyond their areas of practice to broaden development:

> Experienced counselors could just be happy with what they have, just stay at the same level, go for every course that does the same kind of training. Whereas I think really good counselors have a taste for different schools of thought, and integrate what they learned. So it's not a very stale kind of thing . . . you must be willing to go beyond what you are doing, to learn from others.

A senior-level master therapist spoke to the practice of extended breaks from work in order to dedicate time to training and professional development:

> I have incorporated within my own professional life periods when I would go away to different places for exposure. I take a sabbatical leave. I make that a part of my professional life cycle, [and] go away for some refreshment, have some time to think.

Benefits of Teaching/Training Others

Now highly regarded and seasoned, the master therapists have much to offer other therapists. Many of the master therapists viewed teaching and training as an opportunity to hone their own skills and to reflect upon their practice:

> When I do more training and teaching, my thoughts get challenged by the trainees. That has actually been a very helpful experience for me. When I do training I have to be responsible for what it is that I say. I need to know what I'm saying and why I'm saying it. Likewise, when I show my tapes during teaching, being able to say why I'm doing what I'm doing. I think just being able to articulate that has been helpful for me. It clears my mind.

Challenges to Professional Development in Singapore

During the interviews, master therapists identified several "professional growth edges" in the Singapore psychotherapy profession. For instance, a training need recognized by several therapists was that of basic counseling skills. One master therapist explained that basic counseling skills are not natural for many Singaporean trainees:

> The American and British [trainers] took basic skills for granted because that's their natural language and they are more adapted to it. I think basically they are more gentle and what's the word? More "tactful," whereas in our local context, you have to teach [Singaporean therapists] the basic skills. But they still go back to how they normally talk. It has to be a very vigorous way of training to get to a different modality of working.

There also appeared to be a lack of opportunity for therapy and supervision for psychotherapists in Singapore. Other barriers to growing one's clinical skills were related to workplace demands such as high standards for productivity while balancing clinical duties with increasing administrative responsibilities. Finally, one therapist suggested the need for agencies to provide opportunities for therapists to get feedback on their work and skills:

> What happened when they completed the training, they wanted to continue to hone their skills, but because when they went back to the agencies, the staffs were not able to "spar with them," or reinforce the learning, or help them to practice what they had learned. So there was no feedback.

QUALITATIVE META-ANALYSIS RESULTS

Findings from the qualitative meta-analysis between the current study and the Jennings and Skovholt (1999) study indicated a great deal of correspondence regarding the personal characteristics, developmental influences, and therapy practices of psychotherapy experts. As shown in Table 5.2, of the 25 themes between the two studies, themes numbered 1–12 were considered strongly related between studies and themes numbered 13–20 were moderately related between studies. The strongly and moderately related meta-analytic categories derived from the 20 overlapping themes were relationship, therapeutic alliance, experience, professional development, humility, and self-awareness. The 5 remaining themes, numbered 21–25, were not related between the studies and were called divergent themes (see Table 5.2).

Discussion

In our effort to more fully understand psychotherapy expertise in Singapore, we learned some of the nuances of psychotherapy practice in an Asian country, identified a number of characteristics of these highly regarded therapists, and were impressed by the multicultural milieu in which these master therapists work. We will now discuss the 16 themes in relationship to the literature and suggest implications of the findings on the research and practice of psychotherapy. In addition, we will briefly compare the current findings to those of the Minnesota study on master therapists (Jennings & Skovholt, 1999).

PERSONAL CHARACTERISTICS

When analyzing the data, we were struck by how little the Singaporean therapists spoke about their personal selves. Instead, these master therapists talked more about the process of doing therapy. Even when asked directly, "What is therapeutic about you?" some of them were hesitant to talk about themselves. In the section on Developmental Influences, we discuss possible cultural values (e.g., humility) in Singapore that may help account for this phenomenon.

The first three themes (empathic, nonjudgmental, and respectful) identified for master therapists in Singapore are strikingly similar to Carl Rogers' (1961) original core conditions of unconditional positive regard, being nonjudgmental, and empathy. Ironically, several master therapists suggested that many Singaporean therapists struggle with basic

TABLE 5.2

Qualitative Meta-Analytic Categories of Expert Characteristics and Themes from Minnesota and Singapore[a]

Degree of Relationship	Meta-Analytic Category	Themes from Minnesota Study (Jennings & Skovholt, 1999)	Themes from Singapore Study (Jennings et al., 2008)
Strongly related between studies	Relationship: Experts engage with their clients in an empathic and nonjudgmental way and use relational skills to guide their sense of timing, pacing, and dosage of interventions. This ultimately serves to create a safe and secure therapeutic atmosphere.	(1) Master therapists possess strong relational skills (2) Experts at using exceptional relational skills	(3) Empathic (4) Nonjudgmental (5) Respectful (6) Balance between support and challenge (7) Flexible therapeutic stance
Strongly related between studies	Therapeutic alliance: Ranging from a necessary condition to the intervention itself, experts support their client's strength and growth through the therapeutic alliance.	(8) Believes in the therapeutic alliance	(9) Primacy of therapeutic alliance (10) Empowerment/strength-based approach
Strongly related between studies	Experience: Experts draw on life and work experiences to inform and advance their skills.	(11) Accumulated experience is a major resource	(12) Experience
Moderately related between studies	Professional development: Experts value ongoing learning both within and outside their area of practice and benefit from articulating their work when teaching students.	(13) Voracious learners	(14) Benefits of teaching and training others (15) Professional development practices

Moderately related between studies	Humility: Experts have a healthy perspective on their sense of importance and recognize their limits of competence.	(16) Mentally healthy and mature	(17) Humility
Moderately related between studies	Self-awareness: Experts are open to reflection and feedback from many sources to help them recognize their limitations and areas of growth.	(18) Emotionally receptive (19) Aware of how their emotional health impacts the quality of work	(20) Self-awareness
Not related between studies (divergent)	—	(21) Values cognitive complexity and ambiguity of the human condition	(22) Challenges to professional development (23) Embraces working within a multicultural context (24) Comfortable addressing spirituality (25) Self-doubt

[a]All themes from each study are included:

- Strongly related (themes 1–12): Content between studies was nearly exact.
- Moderately related (themes 13–20): Content between studies was similar but somewhat differentiated.
- Not related (themes 21–25): Themes that had no overlap with the themes from the other study.

counseling skills. It was suggested that a surge in interest by Singaporeans to become psychotherapists has not necessarily been met with a concomitant rise in standards or requirements for practice. Master therapists suggested greater attention to foundational training (e.g., Rogers) versus the more coveted specialized training du jour.

DEVELOPMENTAL INFLUENCES

For many of these Singaporean expert therapists, life appeared to serve as a laboratory for growth and development. Some seemed intensively tied into learning from living. This meant seeking out experiences that stretched them and opened up new worlds. With the richness of experience there was, an always present, self-awareness. Here the expert appeared to be using the self like a musical instrument, always tuning the self and hearing how experience influences one's capacity to better understand life and experience deep compassion.

As indicated in the qualitative meta-analysis, experience and self-awareness were themes found in the Minnesota study as well. In addition, the focus the Singaporean therapists placed on experience and self-awareness is supported by the literature that addresses cross-cultural effectiveness. This literature suggests that individuals who are effective with diverse populations are highly self-aware (Sue & Torino, 2005), intentionally seek out culturally diverse experiences (Hammer, Bennett, & Wiseman, 2003), and constantly process these interactions and encounters (Earley & Ang, 2003).

In regard to humility and self-doubt, Singaporean master therapists appeared to take this type of self-critique to an elevated level, in a generalized Asian manner that accentuates modesty, humility, collective versus individual pride, and avoidance of self-praise and self-promotion (Wang, Brislin, Wang, Williams, & Chao, 2000). In particular, there seemed to be a philosophy operating for some that one needs to remember his or her shortcomings, in order to keep motivated, and so as to progressively advance one's skills. Anecdotally, it is interesting to note that we encountered some resistance to the peer nomination process for this study in Singapore. Several therapists alluded to a dilemma; to accept nomination as a master therapist suggests immodesty and, therefore, disqualifies one from being a master therapist. Humility was a characteristic of the Minnesotan master therapists as well.

APPROACH TO PRACTICE

In this category, the first two themes of balance between support and challenge and flexible therapy stance reflected a sophisticated practitioner who was not afraid to practice in new and even seemingly paradoxical ways and one who had a keen openness to different therapeutic stances. These themes support Norcross's (2002) concept of relationship stances in which he suggests that choice of relationship stance depends on a multitude of factors, including the client's readiness for change, preferences, reactivity level, and motivational level. Therefore, therapists would do well to be flexible in their approach, and alter their relationship stances (e.g., more supportive or challenging stance) according to what will be the most therapeutic for their clients. Similarly, Singaporean master therapists articulated a comfort in shifting their therapy stance and sought a balance between supporting and challenging clients. Relating therapist flexibility to multicultural practice, S. Sue (1998) used a computer science term called "dynamic sizing" to describe how therapists need to be flexible in adjusting their knowledge about people, cultures, and psychopathology in order to know when a generalization is appropriate and when therapists need to pay attention to individual differences. Indeed, Draguns (2002) reminds us that psychotherapy often occurs at the junction where both therapist and client present universal, group-specific, as well as unique characteristics—sometimes all at once. Singaporean master therapists appeared to have the flexibility and multicultural awareness to thrive in this nexus.

Singaporean master therapists' focus on empowerment and a strength-based approach also aligns with the current emphasis on positive psychology as an appropriate framework for working with diverse populations (Constantine & Sue, 2006; Gerstein, 2006). Gable and Haidt (2005) defined positive psychology as "the study of conditions and processes that contribute to the flourishing or optimal functioning of people" (p. 104). In practice, positive psychology supports the amplification of strengths rather than the repairing of weaknesses by focusing on such subjective experiences as well-being, contentment, skill, perseverance, mindfulness, and wisdom (Seligman & Csikszentmihalyi, 2000). Similarly, a number of master therapists reported facilitating client empowerment by helping them identify, expand, and utilize their internal resources and personal strengths.

In regard to the primacy of the therapeutic alliance, the current findings seem to support the work by Wampold (2001), who emphasized common factors such as establishment of rapport, warmth, and a therapeutic relationship as being more critical for psychotherapy success than any particular theoretical orientation. Missing in the literature is a description of the methods expert therapists use to navigate the challenges of building a therapeutic alliance with culturally diverse clients. For example, conventional psychotherapy cultural rules suggest that therapeutic boundaries preclude accepting gifts from clients. Yet, in some communities of color or ethnicity, gift giving and gift receiving is an indication of cultural competence (Schank & Skovholt, 2006). Similarly, some cultural factors such as power imbalance and inherent mistrust make establishing working alliances difficult (Lo & Fung, 2003). Cardemil and Battle (2003) suggested that discussing racial and ethnic differences with clients can enhance the therapeutic alliance. Similar to the Minnesotan master therapists, we learned how important the therapeutic alliance was to the Singaporean master therapists. Further research is needed to discover the specific ways the Singaporean experts negotiate cross-cultural challenges in order to build and maintain the therapeutic alliance.

The centrality of spirituality in the master therapists' lives, as well as in their therapy sessions, was clearly evident. This may not come as a surprise given Singapore's multi-religious population where every major religious holiday, whether of majority or minority groups, is observed. Many of the master therapists shared that they were very comfortable addressing spirituality and religion in their own lives, in their clients' lives, and in the therapy session. Singapore master therapists expressed one of the key themes in the role of diversity in psychotherapy as outlined by D. W. Sue, Bingham, Porché-Burke, and Vasquez (1999). D. W. Sue and associates noted how psychotherapists in the United States have tended to overlook the role of spirituality and religion in clients' lives either due to ignorance or fear of offending. We are encouraged by the master therapists' willingness to address spirituality in their psychotherapy practice.

Likewise, Singaporean master therapists' embracement of their work within a multicultural framework is commendable. Singaporean master therapists appeared to be respectful of social and cultural norms that influence the clients and the contexts in which they practice. Hermans and Kempen (1998) aptly compare trying to do research in this globalizing context with trying to study "moving cultures" (p. 1111). This is particularly true for Singapore, where many therapists are trained within Western traditions, in Western countries (particularly the United States, United Kingdom, and Australia), and immersed in Western psychotherapy textbooks and literature abroad and at home. These therapists appeared to be very knowledgeable about helping others within an integration of Western and Asian customs, traditions, and cultural taboos. We could summarize this by saying these master therapists seemed to be psychotherapy innovators, navigating emic (culture-specific) and etic (culture-general) dimensions in their clients as well as integrating East–West philosophies in helping and healing.

ONGOING PROFESSIONAL GROWTH

Singaporean master therapists shared a passion for continuing education in their field. This passion is similar to how the Minnesotan master therapists were described as voracious learners. The Singaporean master therapists spoke of the benefits of teaching others for their own professional development. Their willingness to assume this responsibility is similar to the role of "professional elder" that Skovholt and Ronnestad (1995, p. 66) described in their in-depth study on therapist development. These authors suggested that teaching is "as impactful as being the recipient of wisdom from other wise elders" (p. 66). The role of teacher and "professional elder" takes on an even greater saliency in a small country like Singapore, with fewer human resources available.

The three challenges to professional development in Singapore—lack of basic counseling skills, limited supervision and therapy for therapists, and workplace barriers to professional growth—are indicative of the growing pains of a profession within a society that is rapidly developing. In the brief 40-year history of this small island nation, growing from a fishing village to one of the most vibrant economies in the world, it may be argued that Singapore emphasized business, technology, industrial, and productivity—skills that enhanced the economy rather than the social or interpersonal skills of its citizens

(Green & Sakamoto, 2001). In such a "high-tech" society, the gains made by psychotherapy professionals in Singapore, especially the master therapists nominated in this study, are, therefore, quite remarkable.

In their examination of psychology in Singapore, Goh and A. Tan (2002) forecasted many of the professional identity issues, training and credentialing concerns, and growing pains that emerged in this study. It is noteworthy that in a sample of Singaporean master therapists that included psychologists, family therapists, mental health practitioners, and a social worker, there was strong agreement regarding training needs and professional development concerns—particularly around the importance of clinical supervision, self-care and burnout prevention, the need for psychotherapy opportunities for therapists, and continuing education. In a country like Singapore with limited human resources, nurturing resilient and healthy psychotherapists is critical.

QUALITATIVE META-ANALYSIS COMPARISONS

As mentioned previously, of the 25 themes between the two studies, 12 were considered strongly related and 8 moderately related, leaving 5 themes that were not related between the studies. As such, there appears to be greater similarity between the Minnesotan and Singaporean experts than differences. These findings suggest that there may be underlying universal characteristics of expert psychotherapists, regardless of cultural or nationality differences. However, more research studying psychotherapy experts from various cultures is needed to determine whether this explanation has merit. In addition, it is unclear how much the Western training of the Singaporean master therapists confounds these overlapping themes. Nonetheless, the convergence of themes in the areas of relationship, therapeutic alliance, experience, professional development, humility, and self-awareness bolsters the importance of these six areas in the professional lives of expert psychotherapists.

To highlight cross-cultural findings, the five divergent themes noted in the qualitative meta-analysis will be discussed. Four of the five divergent themes were found in the Singapore study, but not in the Minnesota sample. These four divergent themes were challenges to professional development, embraces working within a multicultural context, comfortable addressing spirituality, and self-doubt. The fifth divergent theme, valuing the cognitive complexity and ambiguity of the human condition, was present in the Minnesota sample, but not in the Singapore sample.

Challenges to professional development, the first divergent theme, included concerns about workplace barriers to professional growth such as balancing clinical demands with administrative responsibilities. It is hypothesized that this divergence may be due to a difference related to practice settings given that most of the Singaporean master therapists were employed in community mental health settings, whereas the Minnesotan participants were engaged in private practice. Another possible explanation as to why these master therapists emphasized professional challenges may be due to the participants' willingness to educate a perceived foreigner about the context of psychotherapy practices in Singapore. Related to their comfort working within a multicultural context, these master therapists may have served as "cultural brokers" intending to help the American researcher understand the cultural nuances of the Singaporean workplace.

The second divergent theme was that Singaporean therapists embraced working within a multicultural context more often than did Minnesotan therapists. Despite recent emphasis on training and competency in the area of multicultural psychotherapy practice, Minnesotan master therapists (all from the dominant, Euro-American culture) did not specifically speak to this issue. One explanation for this difference could be that Singapore's population is more ethnically and racially diverse. At the time of the data collection for the Minnesota study (1996), the state population was over 90% Caucasian. Less experience with diverse clients as compared to the Singaporean therapists may have contributed to the absence of this topic among the Minnesotan participants.

Comfort addressing the topic of spirituality with clients was the third divergent theme found in the Singapore study. As mentioned earlier, Sue et al. (1999) suggested that psychotherapists in the United States often overlook the role of spirituality and religion in clients' lives due to ignorance or fear of offending. Furthermore, empirical research in this area highlights a widening gap between American clients' spirituality and psychologists' ability to discuss, incorporate, and treat these issues (Delaney, Miller, & Bisonó, 2007). Delaney et al. claimed this widening gap underlines "the need to emphasize religious issues in the cultural competency training of psychologists" (p. 543). The researchers further asserted, "religion is a defining aspect of the diversity that psychologists will encounter in practice and one that is particularly central in understanding and treating many ethnic groups" (p. 544). Singapore is a country in which religious practices (particularly Animism, Buddhism, Hinduism, and Islam) and their places of worship occupy many street corners in this small island nation. Therefore, it may not be surprising that Singaporean master therapists described being comfortable addressing spirituality with clients.

Self-doubt was the final divergent theme found in the Singapore study. This theme is not necessarily a negative representation of these master therapists. Indeed, this theme seemed to capture their ability to candidly reflect upon their professional development. One possible explanation for this finding is that the two samples of therapists were at slightly different stages in their professional development. The average number of years of practice for the Singaporean experts was 18.4 compared to 29.5 for the Minnesotan experts. It is possible that such a gap in experience may account for therapists who still, on occasion, question their competence versus more seasoned therapists who have been able to let go of self-doubt. In a study identifying therapists' developmental experiences throughout their profession, Skovholt and Ronnestad (1995) found that therapists with 25–35 years of experience have developed a profound sense of competence in the role of therapist. Skovholt and Ronnestad describe the "integrity" stage this way:

> The enormous effort that went into building oneself professionally and the many lessons from successful and unsuccessful experience, over thousands of hours of work, have produced an intense acceptance of oneself as a competent professional in this field. . . . Twenty-five years later, acceptance has replaced pervasive anxiety. Only now does the individual fully understand the numerous ways anxiety, expressed earlier, is now absent. (p. 88)

The divergent theme from the Minnesota study, valuing the cognitive complexity and the ambiguity of the human condition, did not lend itself to immediate, cogent explanations. Because hypotheses offered here would be purely speculative, further research is needed to explore the meaning and significance of this difference.

LIMITATIONS

The use of only one criterion for defining mastery is a limitation of the current study. Although the use of multiple methods for measuring expertise is preferable and would increase validity of the construct, we believe this study contributes to the literature because it is a beginning step in the exploration of psychotherapy expertise in Singapore. It is our hope that future research will take the broad findings that we offer here and begin to refine our understanding of Singaporean therapy expertise, as well as explore the criteria for expertise in an increasingly complex manner. For example, the use of client input in the selection of experts, although difficult to obtain, would provide another extremely important perspective on the concept of psychotherapy expertise. Another limitation was the risk of potential bias due to two of the current authors' involvement in a previous study on master therapists. To help control for this bias, an auditor was employed, biases were bracketed at the beginning of the study, and research team members were vigilant in their focus on minimizing the intrusion of prior master therapist findings. A final limitation was the use of a virtually identical interview protocol drawn from the original study on master therapists. Greater flexibility with the interview questions may have allowed us to explore new avenues, especially related to culture.

IMPLICATIONS FOR PRACTICE

Psychotherapists can learn much from Singaporean master therapists who practice in an extremely diverse country. One lesson is the importance of continually keeping the client's cultural context in mind. The deep respect Singaporean master therapists have for their clients is another characteristic that will serve practitioners working with a diverse clientele. Another implication for practice pertains to the openness Singaporean master therapists appear to have when exploring their clients' spirituality issues. Practitioners who have previously avoided the topic of spirituality may want to consider the benefits of working with clients' spiritual concerns. The final implication relates to the sheer determination Singaporean master therapists demonstrated when seeking professional growth opportunities in a country with limited opportunities. Their desire to build an expertise base in psychotherapy, despite serious challenges, is inspiring and suggests that striving for expertise takes a great deal of passion and determination.

IMPLICATIONS FOR FUTURE RESEARCH

The present study adds another portrait of expertise to existing qualitative research on therapist development and mastery (Jennings & Skovholt, 1999; Orlinsky & Ronnestad, 2005; Ronnestad & Skovholt, 2003; Skovholt & Jennings, 2004, Skovholt & Ronnestad, 1995). In particular, the themes of self-doubt, spirituality, and embraces working within a multicultural context are new contributions to the therapist expertise literature and warrant further investigation. When additional qualitative studies on expert therapists become available, qualitative meta-analysis methodology (Timulak, 2007) holds much promise as a tool to help consolidate our understanding of psychotherapy expertise.

Future researchers can explore in greater detail the multicultural practices of these Singaporean exemplars. For example, how do Singaporean master therapists manage the challenging task of building and maintaining therapeutic alliances with clients who are culturally different from the therapists? Likewise, greater emphasis needs to be placed on obtaining culturally diverse and culturally competent participants for future studies on expert therapists in the United States. Finally, international studies are encouraged so that we can continue to deepen our understanding of psychotherapy practice and expertise from a wide variety of cultures. With international databases, we may obtain a better understanding of the universal characteristics of expertise as well as the culturally specific applications of psychotherapy.

Note

1. This chapter is reproduced with permission by the journal *Psychotherapy Research* and Taylor & Francis (http://www.tandfonline) from Jennings, L., D'Rozario, V., Goh, M., Sovereign, A., Brogger, M., & Skovholt, T. (2008). Psychotherapy expertise in Singapore: A qualitative investigation. *Psychotherapy Research, 18*(5), 508–522.

References

Cardemil, E. V., & Battle, C. L. (2003). Guess who's coming to therapy? Getting comfortable with conversations about race and ethnicity in psychotherapy. *Professional Psychology: Research and Practice, 34*(3), 278–286.

Coleman, H. L. K. (1998). General and multicultural counseling: Apples and oranges? *Journal of Multicultural Counseling and Development, 26*, 147–156.

Constantine, M. G., & Sue, D. W. (2006). Factors contributing to optimal human functioning in people of color in the United States. *The Counseling Psychologist, 34*, 228–244.

Delaney, H. D., Miller, R. M., & Bisonó, A. M. (2007). Religiosity and spirituality among psychologists: A survey of clinician members of the American Psychological Association. *Professional Psychology: Research and Practice, 38*(5), 538–546.

Draguns, J. G. (2002). Universal and cultural aspects of counseling and psychotherapy. In P. Pedersen, J. G. Draguns, W. J. Lonner, & J. E. Trimble (Eds.), *Counseling across cultures* (5th ed.). Thousand Oaks, CA: Sage.

Earley, P. C., & Ang, S. (2003). *Cultural intelligence: Individual interactions across cultures*. Palo Alto, CA: Stanford University Press.

Fuertes, J. N., Bartolomeo, M., & Nichols, C. M. (2001). Future research directions in the study of counselor multicultural competency. *Journal of Multicultural Counseling and Development, 29*, 3–12.

Gable, S. L., & Haidt, J. (2005). What (and why) is positive psychology? *Review of General Psychology, 9*(2), 103–110.

Gerstein, L. H. (2006). Counseling psychology's commitment to strengths: Rhetoric or reality? *The Counseling Psychologist, 34*, 276–292.

Goh, M. (2005). Cultural competence and master therapists: An inextricable relationship. *Journal of Mental Health Counseling, 27*, 71–81.

Goh, M., & Tan, A. G. (2002). Envisioning the future of psychology in Singapore. In A. G. Tan & M. Goh (Eds.), *Psychology in Singapore: Issues of an emerging discipline* (pp. 60–82). Singapore: McGraw-Hill.

Green, A., & Sakamoto, A. (2001). Models of high skills in national competition strategies. In P. Brown, A. Green, & H. Lauder (Eds.), *High skills: Globalization competitiveness, and skill formation*. London, England: Oxford University Press.

Hammer, M. R., Bennett, M. J., & Wiseman, R. (2003). Measuring intercultural sensitivity: The Intercultural Development Inventory. *International Journal of Intercultural Relations, 27*, 421–443.

Hermans, H. J. M., & Kempen, H. J. G. (1998). Moving cultures: The perilous problems of cultural dichotomies in a globalizing society. *American Psychologist, 53*, 1111–1120.

Hill, C. E., Knox, S., Thompson, B. J., Williams, E. N., Hess, S. A., & Ladany, N. (2005). Consensual qualitative research: An update. *Journal of Counseling Psychology, 52*, 196–205.

Hill, C. E., Thompson, B., & Williams, E. N. (1997). A guide to conducting consensual qualitative research. *The Counseling Psychologist, 25*(4), 517–572.

Jennings, L., & Skovholt, T. M. (1999). The cognitive, emotional, and relational characteristics of master therapists. *Journal of Counseling Psychology, 46*, 3–11.

Jennings, L., D'Rozario, V., Goh, M., Sovereign, A., Brogger, M., & Skovholt, T. (2008). Psychotherapy expertise in Singapore: A qualitative investigation. *Psychotherapy Research, 18*(5), 508–522.

Kogan, M. J. (2000). Internationalizing psychology's curriculum. *Monitor on Psychology, 31*(9), 53.

Leong, F. T. L., & Ponterotto, J. G. (2003). A proposal for internationalizing counseling psychology in the United States: Rationales, recommendations, and challenges. *The Counseling Psychologist, 31*, 381–395.

Leung, S. A. (2003). A journey worth traveling: Globalization of counseling psychology. *The Counseling Psychologist, 31*(4), 412–419.

Lo, H. T., & Fung, K. P. (2003). Culturally competent psychotherapy. *Canadian Journal of Psychiatry, 48*(3), 161–170.

Marsella, A. (1998). Toward a "global-community psychology": Meeting the needs of a changing world. *American Psychologist, 53*(12), 1282–1291.

Norcross, J. C. (2002). *Psychotherapy relationships that work: Therapist contributions and responsiveness to patients*. New York, NY: Oxford University Press.

Orlinsky, D. E., & Ronnestad, M. H. (2005). *How psychotherapists develop: A study of therapeutic work and professional growth*. Washington, DC: American Psychological Association.

Patton, M. Q. (2002). *Qualitative research and evaluation methods* (3rd ed.). Newbury Park, CA: Sage.

Rogers, C. (1961). *On becoming a person: A therapist's view of psychotherapy*. London, England: Constable.

Ronnestad, M. H., & Skovholt, T. M. (2003). The journey of the counselor and therapist: Research findings and perspectives on development. *Journal of Career Development, 30*(1), 5–44.

Schank, J., & Skovholt, T. M. (2006). *Ethics in small communities: Challenges and rewards for psychologists*. Washington, DC: American Psychological Association.

Seligman, M. E. P., & Csikszentmihalyi, M. (2000). Positive psychology: An introduction. *American Psychologist, 55*(1), 5–14.

Skovholt, T. M., & Jennings, L. (2004). *Master therapists: Exploring expertise in therapy and counseling*. Boston, MA: Allyn & Bacon.

Skovholt, T. M., & Ronnestad, M. H. (1995). *The evolving professional self*. Chichester, England: Wiley.

Sternberg, R. J. (2002). Preface. In A. G. Tan & M. Goh (Eds.), *Psychology in Singapore: Issues of an emerging discipline* (pp. xi–xiii). Singapore: McGraw-Hill.

Strauss, A., & Corbin, J. (1998). *Basics of qualitative research: Techniques and procedures for developing grounded theory* (2nd ed.). Thousand Oaks, CA: Sage.

Sue, D. W., Bingham, R. P., Porché-Burke, L., & Vasquez, M. (1999). The diversification of psychology: A multinational revolution. *American Psychologist, 54*, 1061–1069.

Sue, D. W., & Sue, D. (2008). *Counseling the culturally diverse: Theory and practice* (5th ed.). New York, NY: Wiley.

Sue, D. W., & Torino, G. C. (2005). Racial–cultural competence: Awareness, knowledge, and skills. In R. T. Carter (Ed.), *Racial–cultural psychology and counseling: Training and practice, Volume 2*. Hoboken, NJ: Wiley.

Sue, S. (1998). In search of cultural competence in psychotherapy and counseling. *American Psychologist, 53*, 440–448.

Tan, A. G., & Goh, M. (Eds.). (2002). *Psychology in Singapore: Issues of an emerging discipline* (pp. 60–82). Singapore: McGraw-Hill.

Tan, E. (2004). *Counseling in schools: Theories, processes, and techniques*. Singapore: McGraw-Hill.

Timulak, L. (2007). Identifying core categories of client-identified impact of helpful events in psychotherapy: A qualitative meta-analysis. *Psychotherapy Research 17*(3), 305–314.

Wampold, B. E. (2001). *The great psychotherapy debate: Model, methods, and findings*. Mahwah, NJ: Erlbaum.

Wang, M. M., Brislin, R. W., Wang, W., Williams, D., & Chao, J. H. (2000). *Turning bricks into jade: Critical incidents for mutual understanding among Chinese and Americans*. Yarmouth, ME: Intercultural Press.

Yeo, A. (2006). *Labyrinth of therapeutic encounters: Collected essays on counselling and psychotherapy*. Singapore: Counselling and Care Centre.

6 Personal and Professional Characteristics of Japanese Master Therapists

A QUALITATIVE INVESTIGATION ON EXPERTISE IN PSYCHOTHERAPY AND COUNSELING IN JAPAN

Tatsuya Hirai and Michael Goh

Introduction

In this chapter, we present a study that qualitatively explored the characteristics of Japanese master therapists, extracted particular experiences conducive to optimal therapist development, and examined similarities and differences between Japanese and American master therapists.

In the past 20 years, a considerable number of research studies have been conducted to examine characteristics and behaviors of exceptionally competent psychotherapists, or "master therapists." Major topics regarding master therapist research are as follows: general characteristics (Blatt, Sanislow, Zuroff, & Pilkonis, 1996; Jennings, Goh, Skovholt, & Banerjee-Stevens, 2003; Jennings & Skovholt, 1999; Skovholt, Rønnestad, & Jennings, 1997), ethical values (Jennings, Sovereign, Bottorff, Mussell, & Vye, 2005), working alliance (Raue, Castonguay, & Goldfried, 1993; Sullivan, Skovholt, & Jennings, 2005), group therapy (Kivlighan & Quigley, 1991), power issues (Murphy, Cheng, & Werner-Wilson, 2006), and cultural competence (Goh, 2005).

IMPORTANCE OF MASTER THERAPIST STUDY

Why are master therapist research studies important? First, by examining characteristics and behaviors of master therapists, we can clarify important factors conducive to highly effective therapy. Second, by investigating expertise of various master therapists, we can distinguish both universal and idiosyncratic components of expertise in counseling and therapy. Third, through examining the development process of master therapists, it becomes clearer what kinds of life events and professional experiences positively or negatively impact optimal therapist development. Accordingly, we can design effective educational curriculum for counselor education. Fourth, we can illustrate the power of psychotherapy in its most optimal state.

WHY STUDY MASTER THERAPISTS IN JAPAN?

The body of master therapist research began with an original lack of diversity, as Jennings and Skovholt (1999) noted when the first studies emerged. Given the expanding practice of psychotherapy throughout the world and yet the potential problems in transnational applications (Watters, 2010), it is increasingly important to understand how culture animates the therapeutic process. The chapters in this book reflect how the field is adding cultural nuance to our understanding of optimal therapeutic relationships. In this regard, Japan makes for a fascinating study. Regarded as one of the most unique and homogenous places in the world by geography, history, and tradition, Japan is at once aggressively modern and fiercely traditional. Japan reflects a hybridization of multiple cultures. Although the influence of the Western psychological practices is clearly present, there is also evidence of intentional Japanese cultural modeling that emerges. Discovering how some of the best therapists in Japan do their work is both to add to the internationalization of master therapist research and to uncover how culture is put to work in their therapeutic work.

We proceed now to explore the characteristics of master therapists in Japan. Specifically, personal and professional characteristics of 10 Japanese master therapists were investigated through in-depth interviews. In addition, influential experiences of master therapists that contributed to their therapist development were explored. Third, cross-cultural similarities and differences between Japanese and American master therapists are illustrated. Thus, main research questions in this study are as follows:

1. What are the personal and professional characteristics of Japanese master therapists?
2. What kind of experiences and learning have contributed to the development of Japanese master therapists?
3. What are some cross-cultural similarities and differences between Japanese and American master therapists?

Literature Review

BRIEF HISTORY OF COUNSELING AND PSYCHOTHERAPY IN JAPAN

Before Western forms of counseling and psychotherapy were introduced to Japan, Japan already had indigenous forms of therapy, called Naikan therapy and Morita therapy. Morita therapy was established by Shoma Morita, a Japanese psychiatrist, in the early 1920s (Kondo, 1976). According to Kitanishi (2005), Morita therapy assumes that the problem exacerbates when the client pays too much attention to the problem. Therefore, Morita therapy encourages the client to alleviate attention from his or her problem and accept things as they are, including his or her suffering and problems. Morita therapy treatment is usually offered in a residential setting, in which the client is first introduced to absolute bed rest and isolation for 1 week. Then, the client is guided through gradual restoration, engagement in physical work activities, and experience of normal daily life. Through this process, the client is instructed to write a diary for self-awareness and supervision from the therapist. The target clients for Morita therapy are those with anxiety disorder, social phobia, and obsessive–compulsive disorder.

In 1941, Ishin Yoshimoto, who was a civilian and a monk, invented Naikan therapy mainly based on Buddhist philosophies (Kawahara, 2005). Naikan can be translated to "introspection" or "self-examination" in English, and in this therapy, the client is expected to go through intensive introspection about his or her whole life, beginning from early stages of development. During the introspection, the client is instructed to examine how he or she has been cared for by parents and other people in life, what he or she has done for them in return, and what kind of troubles and worries he or she has caused them. Because the main purpose of Naikan therapy is introspection, instruction and supervision from the therapist are purposefully minimal. According to Tseng, Chang, and Nishizono (2005), Naikan therapy aims to help the client grow psychologically from narcissistic to more empathic to and appreciative of others.

The first form of psychotherapy introduced to Japan was psychoanalysis, which was introduced by Heisaku Kosawa, who studied psychoanalysis in Vienna and became the first psychoanalyst in Japan in 1934 (Japan Psychoanalytical Association, 2008). Kosawa advanced the field of psychotherapy in Japan and educated a number of psychiatrists who later had a major impact on the development of psychotherapy. At the same time, however, psychoanalysis was confined primarily to studies and practiced exclusively among doctors and not among other helping professionals.

After World War II, an educational mission was sent to Japan from the United States to promote liberal education and to reform school curriculum accordingly in the late 1940s (Hayashi, Kuno, Osawa, Shimizu, & Suetake, 1992). At that time, the concepts of counseling and guidance services were first introduced to Japan. In 1951 and 1952, American psychologists held 3-month-long student personnel services (SPS) workshops in three major universities in Japan. These intensive SPS workshops established the foundation of counseling services in Japan, and Japanese workshop participants later founded student counseling centers at a number of Japanese colleges and universities (Hayashi et al., 1992).

In 1961, Carl Rogers visited Japan and offered a number of workshops throughout the country during his 6-week visit. This visit had a major impact on the development of counseling in Japan because client-centered therapy brought by Rogers appealed not only to counselors and psychologists but also to a variety of helping professionals in business, governmental, educational, and other clinical settings (Hayashi et al., 1992). Client-centered therapy had one of the most influential roles in the development of counseling in Japan in that it opened counseling to helping professionals in various fields as well as to the general public.

After client-centered therapy was introduced, other psychotherapy/counseling approaches were introduced to Japan. The introduction of additional approaches is illustrated in the following chronology of the introduction of various organizations related to psychotherapy and counseling:

- Japan Psychoanalytical Association (1955)
- Japanese Association of Behavioral Therapy (1974)
- Japanese Association of Humanistic Psychology (1982)
- Association of Japanese Clinical Psychology (1982)
- Japan Association of Group Psychotherapy (1983)
- Japanese Association for Family Therapy (1984)
- Japanese Association of Brief Psychotherapy (1995)
- Japanese Association for Cognitive Therapy (2001)

Among these associations, the Association of Japanese Clinical Psychology (AJCP) is the largest and most influential in Japan, with 12,033 full members and 5537 associate members (Association of Japanese Clinical Psychology, 2007). In fact, the AJCP is the largest organization among all psychological associations in Japan.

Regarding licensure as a psychotherapist/counselor, there is no national licensing system in Japan as yet. In 1998, however, the Japanese Certification Board for Clinical Psychologists (JCBCP) was founded by leading clinical psychologists and academicians, and it started to certify clinical psychologists based on its certification system. In order to be certified as a clinical psychologist, it is required to complete 2 years of a master's program in clinical psychology accredited by JCBCP and to accumulate a prescribed number of clinical hours during and/or after the graduate program. In 1990, the Ministry of Education acknowledged JCBCP as an official foundation. As of 2007, there were 15,097 certified clinical psychologists in Japan (Japanese Certification Board for Clinical Psychologist, 2007).

In approximately the past 10 years, counseling services have become much more accepted and well known to the Japanese public. This is partly because the Ministry of Education, Culture, Sports, Science, and Technology started to provide a significant budget for the assignment of school counselors to every public junior and senior high school in Japan in 1995 (Ministry of Education, Culture, Sports, Science, and Technology,

2007). This was because the Ministry of Education, Culture, Sports, Science, and Technology perceived an urgency to solve increasingly serious problems in schools, such as school phobia, bullying, and deterioration of class management.

Along with the development of counseling services in Japan, a few other changes had taken place. First, the word "counseling" started to appear more often in the media, such as newspapers, magazines, and books. The word "counselor" was even used for non-psychologists, such as cosmetologists and financial planners. The image of counselor started to be portrayed in TV dramas, novels, and comic books. As a result of these changes, counseling services have become more familiar to the general public.

In Japan, certain stigma for counseling services still exists. Especially within the older generation, there is a negative image of counseling in which only people with severe mental health problems seek the services of a counselor. Increasingly more Japanese people are using counseling services, but many of them are not accustomed to the idea of paying money for psychological services. Therefore, many Japanese people use free counseling services that are embedded in their own organizations, such as schools, universities, and companies, rather than private counseling services. Except for psychotherapy and clinical assessment in psychiatry, psychological services are not covered by medical insurance. That is why it is still difficult for psychologists to make a living as private practitioners, except in Tokyo. Despite these limitations, it is expected that the use of counseling services will continue to grow in the field of education, career, medicine, and community services.

JAPANESE STUDIES RELATED TO MASTER THERAPIST RESEARCH

The number of research studies related to master therapists is quite limited in Japan. In fact, there are currently only three published research articles on this topic (Shinpo, 1998, 1999; Takeshima, Sugiwaka, Nishimura, Yamamoto, & Agari,1993). In this section, we critically review these research studies and clarify methodological concerns.

Takeshima et al. (1993) conducted a survey study of the manner in which years of clinical experience demonstrated an impact on the contents and skills of psychotherapy. A survey questionnaire was created based on several different questionnaires, such as the Therapist Orientation Questionnaire (Sundland & Baker, 1962), Fey's Questionnaire (Fey, 1958), and the Usual Therapeutic Practice Scale (Wallach & Strupp, 1964). This survey questionnaire consisted of 65 questions, including questions related to clinical experience, average number of therapy sessions in a week, problems and issues of patients, therapeutic orientations, and therapeutic attitudes and behaviors.

The questionnaire was sent to 500 psychotherapists or psychiatrists who belonged to the three largest professional psychotherapy/psychiatry associations in Japan. Response rate was 44.5%, and the researchers decided to use responses from 212 subjects, after excluding five insufficient responses. Subjects were then divided into four groups, depending on the years of clinical experience (clinical experience <4 years, 5–10 years, 11–15 years, and >16 years).

A chi-square analysis (the number of therapeutic skills used in therapy × years of experience) revealed that the therapists with more experience used a greater variety of therapeutic skills. In addition, a factor analysis regarding therapeutic attitudes and behaviors revealed four major factors: psychodynamic framework of understanding clients, active treatment planning, therapist's directiveness, and flexibility in therapeutic relationship.

Results from a 4 × 4 analysis of variance showed that regardless of therapeutic orientations, (1) therapists with more clinical experience depend less on the psychodynamic framework; (2) therapists with more experience are more active in treatment planning; (3) therapists with less experience tend to be more directive, whereas those with more experience tend to be less directive and more accepting; and (4) therapists with more than 11 years of experience have much fewer differences in therapeutic skills compared with therapists with less experience.

This study was important in that the researchers gained information regarding therapeutic practice from a considerably large number of psychotherapists and psychiatrists. It was also notable that they compared the differences of therapeutic attitudes and behaviors based on length of clinical experience, which helps us understand the unique characteristics of expert therapists more clearly.

The study had several weaknesses. First, no data were reported regarding reliability and validity of the questionnaire in the study. Because the researchers created an original questionnaire based on several different questionnaires, checks for reliability and validity are essential. Second, it was regrettable that more than half of the subjects were psychiatrists ($n = 128$), and the number of psychotherapists was smaller ($n = 85$). Because the nature of work between psychiatrists and psychotherapists is considerably different, the results of the study could also have been quite different if only psychotherapists as subjects were selected. In other words, generalizability of the study to psychotherapists is limited. Third, as Rønnestad and Skovholt (2003) noted, therapists with more years of experience are not necessarily more competent. Therefore, characteristics of therapists with more experience may or may not be characteristics of master therapists in general.

In another study, Shinpo (1998) qualitatively analyzed the therapeutic process of a Japanese master therapist by reviewing videotaped consecutive therapy sessions from two different clients. The master therapist in this study was a Japanese clinical psychologist in her 40s with more than 15 years of clinical experience. In addition to videotaping the session, the researcher interviewed the master therapist regarding her treatment planning, decision-making process, philosophy of her therapy, and therapeutic orientations. The researcher created four frames of reference for qualitative analysis: getting clues, setting working hypotheses, making decisions, and performing interventions. Protocol analyses were conducted by using videotaped therapy sessions and audiotaped interviews. Qualitative analysis identified five characteristics of this master therapist: (1) existence of long-term and stable treatment planning, (2) use of multiple levels of information in selecting specific skills and interventions, (3) keen observation, (4) flexible adaptation to situational change, and (5) high level of sensibility to client's feelings and interpersonal patterns.

Although the study by Shinpo (1998) is one of only a few research studies on this topic in Japan, it has some serious weaknesses. First, the definition of master therapist is not sufficient. In the article, the author defined master therapist as a therapist with more than 10 years of clinical experience. However, years of experience does not necessarily correspond to expertise in therapy (Rønnestad & Skovholt, 2003). Therefore, master therapist should be defined in a way that is closely related to expertise. Second, the selection process of the master therapist is unclear. The manner in which this therapist was selected was not described in the article, nor were the standards of selection indicated. Although some information regarding this therapist, such as clinical work history, current work, educational and training experiences in therapy, and therapeutic orientation, was provided, justification for selecting this particular therapist as a master therapist was weak. Third, because only one therapist was analyzed in this research, results need to be considered tentative at best. Fourth, the author did not specify what kind of qualitative analysis method was used but merely mentioned that protocol analysis was done and categories and themes were extracted. Thus, information regarding the analysis method was insufficient. In addition, the author stated that the analysis was conducted mostly by himself, which introduces threats to validity of the analysis and categorization.

Shinpo (1999) conducted a similar research study the following year. In this study, Shinpo interviewed two counselors with intermediate experience (clinical experience between 7 and 10 years). First, actual therapy sessions of these therapists were videotaped. Second, the researcher interviewed them while reviewing the recorded session together and asked the therapists how they paid attention to important clues in the session, how they generated working hypotheses, and how they selected specific interventions and carried them out. These interviews were all tape-recorded. Third, interview contents were qualitatively analyzed until categories and themes emerged. Then, the results were compared to those of Shinpo's previous study of master therapists (Shinpo, 1998) to clarify similarities and differences between intermediate therapists and master therapists.

According to Shinpo (1999), similarities between intermediate and master therapists are (1) a high level of coordination among short-, middle-, and long-term treatment planning and (2) well-integrated use of different therapeutic skills. In terms of differences, master therapists had (1) a higher level of sensitivity and meta-cognition, (2) a larger number of channels for receiving information and a smoother decision-making process, (3) a higher ability to vividly recall and describe therapy sessions, and (4) a higher ability to create and execute extemporaneous and creative interventions.

Shinpo's (1999) study possesses several weaknesses. First, qualitative analysis was conducted mostly by one researcher, which weakens the validity of analysis. Second, selection criteria of two intermediate therapists were not explained in the study. If two therapists were selected merely by a convenience sampling or connections with the researcher, this research may have serious selection bias. Third, results are severely limited because this research had only two subjects. Fourth, the age range of four clients in this study was limited to 22–28 years, which further limits generalizability of the results. Fifth, the qualitative analysis method was not clearly defined. It appears that the researcher created an analysis method of his own, and there was no reference to well-established standard qualitative methods such as the grounded theory approach (Strauss & Corbin, 1990) or consensual qualitative research method (Hill, Thompson, & Williams, 1997). Thus, we call into question the validity of Shinpo's analysis method.

SUMMARY

The purpose of this section was to critically examine past research studies regarding characteristics and behaviors of Japanese master therapists. Critical review of Japanese qualitative research revealed that the amount of research done in Japan is quite limited. Methodologically, qualitative studies done in Japan interviewed only a few therapists, which greatly limits the transferability of the studies. It is desirable to interview as many therapists as US master therapists studies to increase transferability and trustworthiness of the Japanese studies. Third, the Japanese studies focused on only therapists' behavioral and cognitive functioning, failing to examine more internal personal characteristics.

Overall, we believe that conducting both qualitative and quantitative master therapist studies internationally is necessary to further develop this research field. International comparison studies can offer insight into how theories and practices may be similar and different from culture to culture, and they facilitate the development of optimal therapy practice for each culture while identifying universally effective aspects of therapy and counseling.

Methods

DATA COLLECTION

In this study, 11 Japanese master therapists were selected from throughout Japan. The selection process for Japanese master therapists utilized a peer-nomination procedure similar to the sampling methodology in the Jennings and Skovholt (1999) study but expanded the nomination to a national level. To begin the nomination procedure, board members of the three largest Japanese professional associations relating to clinical psychology were approached by invitation letters. One of these associations was the Association of Japanese Clinical Psychology with more than 19,000 members. Most of the members are professional clinical psychologists, university faculty members, or graduate students in clinical/counseling psychology programs. The second association was the Japanese Society of Certified Clinical Psychologists, which has approximately 20,000 members. This is a professional association that consists of certified Japanese clinical psychologists. The third association was the Foundation of the Japanese Certification Board for Clinical Psychologists. This association was founded in 1988 as a credentialing body whose task was to certify Japanese clinical psychologists. Its board members are mainly university professors in the field of clinical/counseling psychology. These three associations were selected as sources for nominees due to their size, their broad range of influence, and because they are most representative of the professionals engaged in clinical psychology and psychotherapy in Japan. In addition, it was believed that the board members of these associations would have knowledge of Japanese psychotherapists in breadth and depth. Because the board members are actively involved with various activities, such as organizing professional conferences at which a number of therapists present actual therapy cases, providing supervision for a number of psychotherapists, and setting important guidelines and curriculum for therapy training, they are a logical source of contacts and referrals. Moreover, a majority of these board members are pioneers in the field of clinical psychology in Japan, and they have developed the practice, research, and training of psychotherapy as a team for half a century.

The number of board members for these three associations was 25, 23, and 28, respectively. A total of 76 board members were contacted via postal invitation letters. In the invitation letters, the purpose, method, and procedure of this research project were delineated, and respondents were asked to nominate three master therapists. Borrowing from the Jennings and Skovholt (1999) study, each respondent was asked to nominate three master therapists based on the following criteria: (1) This person is considered to be a "master therapist," (2) this person is most frequently thought of when referring a close family member or a dear friend to a therapist because the person is considered to be the "best of the best," and (3) one would have full confidence in seeing this therapist for one's own personal therapy. It was particularly emphasized that the names and other identifiable information of nominated therapists were to be kept strictly anonymous. Postal letter, rather than e-mail letter, was selected because sending an e-mail message to someone who is not an acquaintance could be regarded as impolite in Japanese culture. As a method to contact someone for the first time, postal letter is a more polite and preferred way in Japan. Approximately 3 weeks after the first invitation letter was mailed, the researcher mailed the second letter as a reminder for those who had not yet responded to the request. Consequently, 52 of 77 board members responded to the invitation letters, and the response rate was 68.4%. The total number of master therapists nominated through this process was 70. Of 70 different therapists, 51 therapists received one nomination, five therapists received two nominations, three therapists received three nominations, three therapists received four nominations, three therapists received five nominations, three therapists received six nominations, and the remaining two therapists received seven and nine nominations, respectively.

A minimum of four nominations was chosen as the cutoff point for the master therapist interview group. A total of 11 therapists received four or more nominations; this number of therapists was considered as optimal when balancing the breadth of various therapists and depth of each interview. The percentage of therapists who received four or more nominations yielded 16% of all the therapists nominated and accounted for 47% of the total number of nominations (61 of 131). The mean number of nominations for the 11 selected master therapists was 5.5, within the range of nominations between four and nine.

TABLE 6.1

Number of Nominations Received by Japanese Nominees

No. of Nominations	1	2	3	4	5	6	7	8	9
No. of Nominees	51	5	3	3	3	3	1	0	1

RESPONDENTS

Subsequently, these 11 therapists, having received four or more nominations, were contacted via postal invitation letters to participate in a 90-minute, in-depth interview. All but 1 therapist agreed to participate. Of the 10 master therapists who were interviewed, 2 were female and 8 were male. With regard to their educational level, 7 were Ph.D. clinical psychologists, 1 was an M.A. clinical psychologist, and 4 were psychiatrists (2 of them were both psychiatrists and clinical psychologists). Eight of 10 master therapists held licensure as Japanese clinical psychologists. Their ages ranged from 58 to 85 years (M = 72.2 years, SD = 7.66 years), and their years of experience ranged from 34 to 60 years (M = 46.1 years, SD = 6.90 years). In terms of the theoretical orientation, 3 identified themselves as psychoanalysts, 6 as integrationists, and 1 created his own therapeutic approach integrating the body and the mind. Six therapists were university professors teaching clinical psychology to graduate students while also practicing psychotherapy on a regular basis. Four were practicing clinical psychologists/psychiatrists working for a hospital or a private clinic (Tables 6.1–6.3).

The primary interview method used for this research was a semistructured interview questionnaire with 17 open-ended questions. This questionnaire was used as an interview guide, which gave a certain level of structure to efficiently capture the essence of the research questions while leaving room to be flexible and conversational according to the nature of the individual interview and the master therapist. Thus, although the interview followed the interview guide questionnaire in general, the order and the wordings of these questions were modified for each master therapist.

The interview guide questionnaire was created as follows. First, the authors prepared 20 interview questions based on past research and discussion with two other Japanese clinical psychologists. Sixteen questions were translated from the Jennings and Skovholt (1999) study, and 4 questions were added to clarify the factors that facilitated the development of master therapists and ways to incorporate those factors into the therapist

TABLE 6.2

Age Range of Japanese Master Therapists

Age range (years)	51–60	61–70	71–80	81–90
No. of master therapists	1	2	5	2

TABLE 6.3

Demographic Information of Japanese Master Therapists

Therapist No.	Years of Experience	Education	License(s)	Orientation
1	60	Ph.D.	CP	Integrative
2	40	Ph.D.	CP	Integrative
3	45	Ph.D.	CP	Integrative
4	43	M.D.	CP, MD	Integrative
5	34	M.D.	CP, MD	Psychoanalytic
6	50	Ph.D.	CP	Psychodynamic
7	49	M.D., Ph.D.	MD	Integrative
8	45	M.A.	CP	Integrative
9	50	Ph.D.	CP	Integrative
10	45	M.D.	MD	Psychoanalytic

CP, clinical psychologist; MD, medical doctor (psychiatrist).

training. Subsequently, we asked two experienced senior psychotherapists to participate in a pilot interview, using these guiding questions to determine whether the wording and the content of the interview questions were sound and appropriate for Japanese master therapists. After the pilot interviews, the authors inquired about the appropriateness of the interview questions, and based on the feedback, the authors revised the questionnaire.

INTERVIEW PROTOCOL

Interviews were conducted in Japanese at the respondent's clinic or laboratory, and all interviews were audiotaped. The duration of the interview was approximately 110 minutes on average and conducted in Japanese.

DATA ANALYSIS

After all the interviews were conducted, the digitally recorded interview data were transcribed in Japanese. Based on the transcription, common characteristics of Japanese master therapists were extracted mainly through the grounded theory approach (Strauss & Corbin, 1990). This approach was employed because we preferred to start the analysis from the direct experiences of master therapists rather than imposing prior assumptions and hypotheses. Thus, the data analysis in this research proceeded from identifying the smallest unit of data, called concepts, to synthesizing into broader themes, categories, and domains, the largest unit in the analysis. We also employed core procedures of consensual qualitative research methodology (Hill et al., 1997, 2005). Instead of one researcher conducting all the analysis, we had a team of four clinical psychologists who collaboratively analyzed the data. We had two male researchers (one of whom was the author) and one female researcher, as well as one male auditor who was a senior psychologist. All researchers are professional clinical psychologists and university faculty members, and they have extensive experience in qualitative analysis. As recommended by Hill et al. (1997, 2005), the auditor observed the entire analysis process and provided feedback and comments at various stages of the analysis.

To begin the analysis, each of the three researchers individually read the transcription line by line and wrote a few words that best represented the core meaning of the smallest unit of data, which was usually one to several lines. After each researcher completed this coding process, the three researchers came together and discussed whether a concise concept was chosen for an appropriate quotation. A concept was employed only when consensus was achieved among the three researchers. Each concept and the corresponding quotation were recorded to a computer by using a qualitative analysis computer software called MAXqda. After the concepts were extracted by this process for all 10 transcriptions, each concept and the corresponding quotation were printed out on the same card. At this point, a total of 825 concepts were identified.

Next, the researchers proceeded to perform a cross-case analysis (Patton, 2002), in which the researchers carefully read all the concepts and these were sorted into various different groupings based on the content similarities of concepts until appropriate groupings emerged. These groupings were organized from smaller to larger units, such as themes, categories, and domains. This process was again conducted using a team effort with three researchers and one auditor. Different groupings and naming were discussed until all the researchers reached a consensus. From this process, 79 preliminary themes and 18 preliminary categories were identified.

After 1 week of engaging in this process, researchers held another research meeting and re-examined the data for more concise and robust groupings. Themes that had a small number of quotations (≤5) and a small number of therapists endorsing them (≤3) were eliminated. In addition, based on the feedback from the auditor and further discussion among the researchers, some units of data cards were reassigned to a different group and/or more appropriate descriptors were employed for themes and categories. As a result, 18 themes and five categories were determined through a process of consensus.

Results

From the qualitative analysis of the interview data, five categories emerged: (1) cultivating abundant learning, (2) perceptive understanding of self and others, (3) effective intervention, (4) relationship-building with the client, and (5) therapist's humanity. In this section, each category and its subordinating themes are explained, and representative quotes from the interviews are provided (Table 6.4).

TABLE 6.4

Categories and Themes of Japanese Master Therapists

Category A: Cultivating Abundant Learning
1. Proactive learning style
2. Abound in ingenuity
3. Diligently manage massive learning
4. Learning from great mentors
5. Existence of supportive environment

Category B: Perceptive Understanding of Self and Others
6. In-depth self-reflection
7. Finely tuned understanding of the client
8. Being able to take a comprehensive view of the client
9. Capacity to embrace antinomy

Category C: Effective Intervention
10. Perform at a high level of therapeutic effectiveness
11. Multidimensional therapeutic approach
12. Precise yet flexible intervention

Category D: Relationship-Building with the Client
13. Deep respect for the client
14. Being open toward the client
15. Active engagement in the mutually therapeutic relationship

Category E: Therapist's Humanity
16. Therapist's personality
17. High level of resilience
18. Respect for the profundity of human beings

CATEGORY A: CULTIVATING ABUNDANT LEARNING

This category indicates that Japanese master therapists possess proactive and creative learning styles, which enable them to process massive amounts of information and stay open to new learning opportunities.

Theme 1: Proactive Learning Style

Japanese master therapists maintain high levels of curiosity and professionalism that motivate them toward proactive learning. Rather than remaining passive and waiting for someone to teach them, they creatively seize every opportunity to learn about human minds. One therapist explained his passionate efforts to learn a wide range of therapeutic approaches in order to be as helpful as possible for his different clients:

> There is no absolute recipe regarding what to do to facilitate people change. So, when I heard that psychoanalysis was quite effective, I tried it, and I learned that it is effective for some people but not at all for others. Then, I sought out another effective approach, and I had practiced behavioral approach for a while, which was indeed effective. However, I found out that certain clients could not benefit from this approach, so I made a lot of efforts to learn another approach: image therapy.

Theme 2: Abound in Ingenuity

Japanese master therapists seem to be interested in learning something new and in creating a new body of knowledge and practice based on that new learning. One of the therapists described the renewal process of his therapy style in which he discarded his previous style and started over again in order to refresh himself and become more flexible:

> It may be necessary to get hooked on a particular therapeutic style first, in order to be free from its limitations eventually. Learning a certain style is an entrance, but there is a different exit. . . . First, people may cling to a certain style to create a form. The older the therapist becomes, however, the harder it becomes to break the form. When you break the form you created, you have to start over again from the beginning, which is true self with only flesh and blood, nothing else. Therefore, this renewal process may require certain level of ego strength . . . capacity to break and start over.

During the therapy process as well, master therapists seek for something new. One of the master therapists described how carefully he pays attention to both new materials and changes in the client:

> One of the indications when therapy is going well is that you can find new materials in the therapy session. Something new is always happening during the session, such as you hearing something you have not heard before, or the client talking about the same episode from a different point of view. That is when I feel that the therapy is going well, and I feel a sense of satisfaction somewhere in my mind, such as "Oh, this is interesting!" or "Good, something new is emerging here." In that sense, conducting a therapy is about discovering something new.

As described previously, Japanese master therapists continue to seek something new in the client and the therapy process, as well as engage themselves in the process of renewing therapeutic style and the therapist him- or herself.

Theme 3: Diligently Manage Massive Learning

The master therapists interviewed emphasized that there is no shortcut to becoming a competent therapist, but that it is important to maintain quiet dedication to massive and lifelong learning. A group of therapists mentioned that there is no end goal in learning. One therapist explained it as follows:

> When I compare my present self with myself 20 years ago, I think I can see things today that I did not see then. However, I am more aware of the fact that there are so many things that I don't know or I don't see, which makes me realize more clearly how ignorant I am.

On the same theme, another therapist put it this way:

> Strictly speaking, there is no place where you can say, "I have been there, I have done that"' or "I have achieved this much." It is just that I am here today tentatively on this ever-lasting continuum of learning. Once you become narcissistic, you just slip down from this process. It takes so much effort to stay on this learning continuum, but it takes only a second to fall down from it . . . and this is a challenge for us on this path [as a psychotherapist].

Theme 4: Learning from Great Mentors

Most of the master therapists mentioned the importance of learning from their great mentors. One master therapist explained the importance of great mentors as follows:

> The most important and influential experiences were encounters with a great mentor. It was not necessarily establishing a formal relationship as a great mentor and an apprentice, but meeting someone you respect as a great mentor. This process of devoting myself to the great mentor, and then departing from him/her was important to me.

Regarding therapist development, one master therapist stated the following:

> Someone I see as growing well as a therapist has some kind of life master. It does not have to be a supervisor but someone you can look up to or someone you hold admiration for. I have this impression that a therapist who has this kind of great mentor is becoming a competent therapist.

Theme 5: Existence of Supportive Environment

Although Japanese master therapists emphasized the importance of self-discipline and personal efforts, they were also cognizant of there being a supportive environment, which facilitates one's development. This supportive environment includes supervisors, significant others such as parents, and happenstance that led them to a particular direction, in addition to the great mentors noted in the previous theme. A master therapist mentioned the impact of loving parents:

> When I think of a master therapist, I can see that his/her parents must have truly loved this person and raised him/her preciously and warmly. Because of that upbringing, a master therapist has a capacity to trust others. Regardless of the situation, he/she can fundamentally trust people . . . and I think this [trust in people] plays an important role in therapy, because psychotherapy is based on encountering with someone, and making use of one's personality. So, in that situation, one's most fundamental essence shows itself, I think.

CATEGORY B: PERCEPTIVE UNDERSTANDING OF SELF AND OTHERS

This category illustrates the importance of in-depth self-reflection, understanding the client with both depth and breadth, and the capacity to hold seemingly contradicting aspects and synthesize them into a deeper knowing or understanding.

Theme 6: In-depth Self-Reflection

Japanese master therapists repeatedly stressed the importance of self-reflection in order to examine one's motivation to become a therapist, as well as embrace parts of oneself that are difficult to accept. One master therapist explained as follows:

> One can only understand another depending on how deeply one is willing to dig one's well, called mind. In other words, the therapist can enter the depth of the client's mind in proportion to the depth of mind the therapist was able to explore. Thus, unless you are in touch with your own pain and darkness, you cannot truly touch the client's depth of mind, even if you may be able to find them from a far.

Another therapist mentioned the importance of examining one's own motivation to become a therapist:

> In order to become a good therapist, I think the most important thing is to confront the "self." In particular, examining your own motivation is important, such as why you want to do psychotherapy, or why you are interested in this work. . . . If you could confront your own blind spots through supervision or personal counseling, then you may be able to make some change, and then, you may be able to become a therapist who can truly be of service to others.

Theme 7: Finely Tuned Understanding of the Client

This theme indicates precise understanding of the client through empathy, awareness of the client's subtle signs and details, careful understanding of the client based on facts, and accurate and rapid processing of a rich variety of information. One therapist described precise empathy as an important characteristic of master therapists as follows:

> What is important is how closely you can empathize with the client. . . . Even when you are saying something very appropriate or giving good advice, if you don't understand the client's feelings, then the expression of your remark becomes harsh, and the client won't receive your remark. If the client has feelings of envy or hatred, then the more you say something appropriate, the more the client wants to deny what you say. Thus, it is extremely important to express your ideas while you take the client's current feelings into consideration.

Another therapist described how he pays attention to subtle and detailed information of the client as follows:

> For example, let's say I posed a question to the client. The vibration of the sound travels through the space between the therapist and the client, enters the drum membrane of the client's ear, is processed in his/her brain, and the client responds. If you pay careful attention to the time between the question and the response, you can sense whether a certain thought process is intervened, such as different kind of thoughts are suppressed or denied, by the subtle time gap. If this gap is always happening, then the brain must be fatigued, and there is a possibility of clinical depression, even if the client is smiling on the surface. But if the client has been talking and only a part of the conversation has a subtle gap, then it means that certain thoughts are omitted. I think it is important to pay attention to such a subtle detail . . . "God exists in subtlety" so to speak. Important things exist in a corner. What you can see on the surface is like a table of contents.

Theme 8: Being Able to Take a Comprehensive View of the Client

This theme indicates the therapist's ability to look at the client and the therapy process in a broader perspective. More concretely, this theme includes elements such as a high competency in case formulation, objective monitoring of the therapy process, and an ability to grasp client change over time. The following therapist described how she monitors the therapy process:

> It is important to always have a relative viewpoint [in therapy]. It is no doubt that creating a working alliance, as well as getting in touch with the client's deep inner

> world is important. However, some therapists pay too much attention to these aspects. I think it is important to ponder what the current therapy session might mean for the client, in relation to the client's continuum of past, present, and future. Further, it would help maintain this balance if the therapist could monitor the therapy process from a relative perspective.

Theme 9: Capacity to Embrace Antinomy

This theme means the capacity to embrace different aspects that seem contradictory to each other and find a balance between them. Examples of this balance include a balance between acceptance and challenge, the therapist's professional self and personal self, expertise and ordinariness, theory and practice, and effectiveness and side effects. One therapist described the balance between acceptance and challenge in the following way:

> If you continue doing play therapy, it will surely happen that the clients demand to play more after the session time is over. It is challenge for the therapist, then, to decline the request with a sense of acceptance. Acceptive decline . . . you have to be able to live this paradox. Of course, just saying it is not enough. You need to experience the paradox, and live through it.

Another therapist summarized the importance of this theme as follows:

> There is a metaphor which says, warm heart and cool head. I think that the gist of psychotherapy is how we live through various paradoxes, such as intellect and sensibility, or focus and wholeness, with a moment-to-moment assessment as well as a good sense of balance.

CATEGORY C: EFFECTIVE INTERVENTION

This category illustrates how master therapists provide effective interventions for the client. Master therapists perform at a high level of therapeutic effectiveness, while working on multidimensional aspects of the client simultaneously, and offer precise and flexible interventions to maximize the benefits for the client.

Theme 10: Perform at a High Level of Therapeutic Effectiveness

Master therapists described the ability to produce therapeutic effectiveness as one of the characteristics of master therapists. Not only do they provide highly effective therapy but also they are interested in pursuing efficient therapy, which means producing high effectiveness while moderating time and keeping the load for the client at a minimum. One therapist described this therapeutic efficacy as follows:

> I think that the clients who come to counseling often have a vicious circle in his/her cognitive, behavioral, and/or interpersonal realm. Therefore, if one part changes, then other parts could cyclically change. When the client is relatively well functioning, cognitive shift could invite more personal change, or just a little bit of behavioral change could change the client and his/her interpersonal patterns. . . . So, I think it is most important that the therapist could be a catalyst for this kind of positive cyclical change.

Theme 11: Multidimensional Therapeutic Approach

Master therapists reported that they attempt to simultaneously work on different aspects of the client, such as parts and the whole, or body and mind. One of the master therapists described his approach as follows:

> I have come to use language that transcends body and mind. In other words, I tend to use words that impinge on both body and mind, such as joyful or relaxing. When we use a wordy language, it is too intellectual and does not reach to the body. I pay attention to the use of these words, because I am trying to relate to the being before body and mind is differentiated.

Theme 12: Precise Yet Flexible Intervention

This theme indicates the therapist's precise intervention, such as exceptional verbal ability, using questions and clarification to facilitate the client's change and natural inner healing power and delicate yet flexible intervention to respect the client's pace. One of the master therapists described his efforts to provide effective questions and clarification for optimal client's change as follows:

> Particularly in the intake interview, some therapists ask questions based on the therapist's theoretical background or associations, but this kind of question would not be considered as appropriate and competent. Appropriate questions start from what the client talked about, and the ones that the client feels natural to be asked in that context, although the client has not asked those questions by themselves. And while answering these questions, the client is gradually encouraged to get in touch with the psychological area where she/he has not been clearly aware of . . . it is also important that the interaction between the two should be somewhat asymmetrical. Rather than responding to the client on the same level, the therapist should post questions from a bit different level, so that the client feels it is natural to answer that question, but it also requires the client to reflect on him-/herself a bit deeper. Once, one of my clients told me as follows: "You listen to my story well, then bring the itchy part that is unreachable for me to light, and describe that part using my words." When the session is going well, maybe I am able to interact this way.

CATEGORY D: RELATIONSHIP-BUILDING WITH THE CLIENT

This category describes how master therapists viewed relationship-building, trust, and respect to be essential and central to the therapeutic relationship.

Theme 13: Deep Respect for the Client

This theme illustrates therapist's respectful attitude toward the client, including the master therapist's trust in the client's inner power to change, a belief that the main character in therapy is the client, a willingness to stretch for the client's welfare, and respect for human diversity. One therapist described how he views his client as a potentially independent and capable person, and believes in the client's inner capacity, as follows:

> What I am consciously valuing is that I try to constantly see the client as a self-reliant person who can count on himself/herself, become aware of his/her own needs and feelings, and take care of them. Of course, asking for help as necessary is included as a characteristic of a self-reliant person. Even if the client may not be able to behave this way at present, I still see the client holding capacity to be a self-reliant person in the future. . . . And I think it is also important whether we can consistently sustain the belief in the client's capacity for self-reliance, even when the client's pathology is quite severe.

Theme 14: Being Open Toward the Client

In order to build a trustful relationship with the client, Japanese master therapists asserted that it is important for the therapist to be authentic and to describe the therapist's thoughts and feelings in a genuine way without hurting the client. One of the master therapists mentioned that he tries to be as open as possible with the client so that trust develops between the two:

> I try to be as honest and candid as possible in front of the client, although there is a fine line between this and consequently hurting the client, and we should be careful about this. One of the clients whom I have been been seeing for a long period of time, and who is a female therapist with a borderline personality disorder, got better through therapy, and when the termination of the therapy was approaching, she said that she was thankful to me because her condition is much better, but there was one word that she wanted to leave to me. She told me, "The mouth is the gate of evil." I think she was implying that my candid communication sometimes hurt the client. But when the therapy process is going well, communication between the two gradually becomes candid as in this example. If the process hadn't been going well, then the client would get angry and leave the therapy. . . . When the therapy is going well, the feeling that it is OK to communicate straightforwardly occurs in each other's heart.

Theme 15: Active Engagement in the Mutually Therapeutic Relationship

This theme describes the characteristics of master therapists' construction of trustful relationships with clients. More concretely, this theme illustrates the master therapist's capacity to build relational connection with the client at an early stage of therapy, the therapist's deep connection with the client, and emphasis on mutual dynamic process in the therapeutic relationship. One of the master therapists asserted the ability to form a positive relationship at an early stage as one of the important characteristics of master therapists:

> When a master therapist meets someone, she/he can connect with the person at a fundamental level in a relatively short period of time. The client can feel safe or trustful when she/he goes to that therapist.

In relation to mutual dynamic process in the therapeutic relationship, another therapist described his experience of intersubjectivity between the client and the therapist and asserted that accurate and deep empathy is possible when optimal mutual interaction is happening between the two:

> When the client and the therapist are in the therapy session, and the therapist is wondering what to say, I imagined someone called "Mr. Atmosphere-in-the-Space of the Therapy Session" [which is a figurative metaphor of intersubjectivity, or co-created space between the therapist and the client]. And when this "Mr. Atmosphere-in-the-Space" gradually came down to the bottom of his heart, and reached a certain feeling, then I verbalized that feeling. . . . Let's say a client is very angry and saying something extrapunitive. The therapist is fed up with listening to the client's story. This is rather a superficial communication. However, when we go down the shared field between the two, we gradually become aware of the possibility that the client is feeling very lonely because whatever he says is not accepted by the society. . . . And it is relatively easy to do this because Japanese is not a subject-prominent language, so we could describe certain feelings and softly share them between the two by not using the subject, such as "lonely, isn't it?"

CATEGORY E: THERAPIST'S HUMANITY

This category describes personal characteristics of Japanese master therapists. It includes Japanese master therapists' personalities, their high level of resilience, and their respect for the profundity of the human being.

Theme 16: Therapist's Personality

Japanese master therapists described various personality characteristics as important components of master therapists. Those personality characteristics are grouped into modesty, absence of self-centeredness and dominance, sincerity, and stability. Particularly, modesty and paucity of self-centeredness were most frequently mentioned by Japanese master therapists. Using a figure from Buddhism, one of the master therapists described the image of master therapist as follows:

> It is difficult to describe a perfect image of a master therapist, but for me, the image of "Myoko-nin" [a term used in Buddhism, which connotes a pious Buddhist who is modest, honest, and idyllic] is closest to the image of an ideal master therapist. "Myoko-nin" is someone with whom you can feel comfortable, warm, and at home when you go to see that person. At the same time, "Myoko-nin" remains inconspicuous, and he does not speak until he is asked to do so. But if someone asks something to him, he listens well and interacts with that person with sincerity. There is a paucity of self-centeredness and dominance for this kind person. Without self-centeredness and dominance, people can become more well-rounded in their personality.

Theme 17: High Level of Resilience

Another important theme of master therapists' humanity is their high degree of resilience. Japanese master therapists seem to have experienced some kind of difficulties in their childhood and/or adolescence, but they have learned important lessons from those difficult experiences and have been enriched by them in some way. It appears that Japanese master therapists place importance on facing the difficulty and sustaining themselves in a difficult situation. Regarding difficult experiences in youth, one therapist briefly described his sense of alienation as follows: "From my childhood, I had sensed that I was alienated from other people." Another therapist mentioned the importance of facing one's own neurotic part and making use of it, as an example of deepening oneself through difficult process:

> Being sophisticated [as a therapist] means to make good use of your own neurotic part. The neurotic part is your sensitive part, and people make that part insensitive when it is painful to face. If you desensitize to it, though, your sensitivity wouldn't develop. Thus, what is important is how we can be able to utilize that sensitive part in a positive way. In the long run, people have suppressed various parts of their lives, and you need to release, or come to terms with those parts if you want to use them for other people. The process of releasing the sensitive parts could be scary, and those who are afraid of this process continue to suppress those parts, which desensitize their various senses, and the interactions with the client remain somewhat ineffective.

Theme 18: Respect for the Profundity of Human Beings

This theme describes the master therapists' deep respect and sense of awe with regard to the profundity of human beings and their minds. A number of master therapists warned against the therapists' possible arrogance that they can completely understand the human mind with psychological explanations alone. One therapist asserted that the human mind is not completely graspable:

> Eastern people assume that mind is beyond our comprehension. . . . You know "Yui-shiki" ["Consciousness-Only"] in Buddhism? That concept asserts that what we can recognize is just a tiny part of the whole truth.

Discussion

In this section, results of this study are summarized and discussed in relation to the three main research questions, and they are compared with results of existing literature on master therapist research.

CATEGORY A: CULTIVATING ABUNDANT LEARNING

Japanese master therapists appear to spontaneously cultivate new learning opportunities, such as learning various different therapeutic approaches, actively learning from supervision and case conferences, and studying abroad. They are motivated by their strong curiosity and will to become exceptionally competent therapists. In addition, they seem to be always looking for something new in their learning experiences as well as in the therapy process, and they are fascinated with creatively inventing new therapeutic approaches. It is assumed that their strong curiosity for new learning has led many of the Japanese master therapists to study abroad and to introduce new knowledge and skills to the community of Japanese clinical psychology.

These themes coincide with the master therapists' characteristic as "voracious learners" in the Jennings and Skovholt's study (1999), which described master therapists' love for learning, voracious appetite for knowledge, and eagerness for new experiences. In addition, as Mullenbach and Skovholt (2004) noted, master therapists' love of learning and curiosity for new experiences is a powerful source of energy and renewal for their continuous professional development. Another source of Japanese master therapists' proactive learning style is their strong aspirations and will to become exceptionally competent therapists. This tendency is discussed in Skovholt, Jennings, and Mullenbach's (2004) study, which suggested that master therapists possess an intense will to grow and to live professionally competent lives.

CATEGORY B: PERCEPTIVE UNDERSTANDING OF SELF AND OTHERS

Japanese master therapists appear to possess outstanding cognitive abilities to understand themselves and others. Regarding self-understanding, Japanese master therapists recognize the importance of self-reflection, including having courage to process one's own pain, suffering, and other negative feelings and aspects inside. They also emphasized that this process is important to examine the therapists' possible self-centered motivations to help others and overcome those motivations to be genuinely altruistic. Moreover, Japanese master therapists utilize self-reflection during the therapy process, in which they monitor their own moment-to-moment feelings and sensations as an important source of information, and use the information in the therapy process.

This emphasis on self-reflection was illustrated in Jennings and Skovholt's (1999) study, in which they reported self-awareness and reflectivity as characteristics of master therapists. Similarly, Sullivan et al. (2005) described the "use of self" in the therapy relationship. In their study, it was reported that master therapists are aware of their own power in the relationship, accept their emotions, and use themselves as a whole as agents for change.

The emphasis on self-reflection also coincides with Naikan therapy, which is a traditional Japanese therapy based on Buddhist philosophies (Kawahara, 2005). Naikan literally means "introspection" or "self-examination" in English. Naikan therapy expects the client to thoroughly examine his or her whole life, beginning from early childhood, in relation to the connection with important people in his or her life. In addition, Naikan therapy is done mostly by the client alone, and the therapist occasionally meets with the client to listen to his or her self-examination. From the procedure of this traditional Japanese therapy, it can be seen that the solitary self-examination as well as the awareness of connection with others have been valued in Japanese society.

Many Japanese master therapists reiterated the importance of possessing a capacity to embrace antinomy, including the ability to find an optimal balance between acceptance and challenge, personal self and professional self, theory and practice, positive effects and side effects of psychotherapy, and expertise and ordinariness. They emphasize the importance of moving flexibly without being caught in one direction, and they warn against our temptations to prematurely reach clear-cut answers by employing dualism. This characteristic is indeed mentioned in several master therapist research studies. Jennings and Skovholt (1999) reported that master therapists value complexity and the ambiguity of the human condition, and Skovholt et al. (2004) similarly mentioned master therapists' embrace of complex ambiguity. In terms of the therapeutic relationship, Sullivan et al. (2005) described a balance between a safe and a challenging relationship. Skovholt et al. aptly used the term "paradox characteristics" to describe the previously mentioned characteristics.

CATEGORY C: EFFECTIVE INTERVENTION

As one of the most important characteristics of master therapists, Japanese respondents reported that master therapists are able to perform at a high level of therapeutic effectiveness while using multidimensional and flexible therapeutic interventions. Japanese master therapists are aware of time and cost-effectiveness, and they have become increasingly innovative, which allows them to perform at maximum effectiveness with a minimum load for the client. Japanese master therapists also simultaneously pay attention to different levels of client information, such as body and mind, detailed parts and comprehensive whole, as well as cognition and emotions. In addition, according to the client's functioning, needs, and pace, Japanese master therapists flexibly choose the most appropriate interventions for the client.

Regarding the multidimensional and flexible therapeutic interventions, similar results are reported in other master therapist studies. Based on the qualitative analysis of Japanese master therapists, Shinpo (1998) reported that Japanese master therapists utilize multiple levels of information in selecting specific skills and interventions, and they can flexibly adapt to a situational change in therapy. In a similar study in which Japanese master therapists and intermediate therapists were contrasted, Shinpo (1999) illustrated that master therapists possess a larger number of channels for receiving information and smoother decision-making process and also a higher ability to create and execute extemporaneous and creative interventions. In addition, Takeshima et al. (1993) reported that therapists with greater experience use a wider variety of therapeutic skills.

As one of the Japanese master therapists asserted in this study, it appears that the differences between therapeutic orientations and therapist interventions become less distinct. This may mean that therapists become free from specific theories, skills, and orientations as they develop and gain more flexibility and creativity in their therapeutic styles. This tendency is supported by other master therapist studies. For instance, Eells, Lombart, Kendjelic, Turner, and Lucas (2005) analyzed case formulations of expert therapists and discovered that expert therapists showed fewer differences based on therapeutic orientations compared to novice and experienced therapists.

In terms of placing a value on a high level of effectiveness as master therapists, it parallels with value on competence in the study by Jennings et al. (2005). They reported that American master therapists value being competent as well as maintaining competency as a therapist, which lead them to a lifelong learning process of psychotherapy and the human mind. Similarly, Takeshima et al. (1993) reported that therapists with more than 11 years of experience had far fewer differences in the use of therapeutic skills compared to therapists with less experience.

CATEGORY D: RELATIONSHIP-BUILDING WITH THE CLIENT

Japanese master therapists repeatedly expressed their deep respect for the client. In summary, they believe in and actively seek out the client's strengths, inner resources, and power to change. Based on this belief, they see that the main character in the therapy is the client, and the therapist's role is to serve the client from the sidelines so that the client can spontaneously tell his or her stories and realize his or her inner potential. In addition, Japanese master therapists appear to respect the client's diverse values, lifestyles, and symptoms.

These beliefs and attitudes of Japanese master therapists coincide with the master therapists' characteristics described by Jennings and Skovholt (1999). They described a number of the master therapists' beliefs about human nature, such as their firm belief in the client's competence and ability to change, and respect for the client's right to self-determination. Jennings et al. (2005) described the master therapist's respect for the client's autonomy in their research on the master therapist's ethical values as follows:

> Master therapists appear to greatly respect the phenomenological worldviews of their clients and hold the belief that for change to occur, clients, for the most part, need to be allowed to determine the direction of the therapeutic process.

Based on the belief that the main character in the therapeutic endeavor is the client, Japanese master therapists emphasize the therapist's role to assist the client from the sideline. This result has similarity with results from other master therapist studies. For example, in their investigation of the client's emotional experiencing and the master therapist's therapeutic intervention, Wiser and Goldfried (1993) reported that affiliative, noncontrolling interpersonal stances, reflections, and acknowledgments, and also highlighting minimal, nonspecific contents, contributed to the client's maintaining high emotional experiencing. This means that the therapist's supportive and nondominant interventions were effective in maintaining the client's emotional experiencing. Japanese research regarding therapist development also showed a similar result (Takeshima et al., 1999). Takeshima et al.'s survey of 212 Japanese psychotherapists revealed that therapists with less experience tended to be more directive, whereas therapists with more experience were less directive and more accepting in therapy.

CATEGORY E: THERAPIST'S HUMANITY

This category described the master therapists' personal characteristics, including their personality, resilience, and respect for the profundity of the human being. Regarding the Japanese master therapists' personality characteristics, the most frequently reported ones were modesty, sincerity, and lack of self-centeredness and a sense of dominance. Japanese master therapists contend that the more we learn, the more we become aware of our ignorance and the profundity of human beings, which naturally keeps us modest. They also emphasized the importance of overcoming one's self-centeredness and dominance because they are aware that a considerable number of Japanese therapists are unconsciously operating under the influence of self-centeredness and dominance and that it is challenging to accept and overcome them. Japanese master therapists consider lack of self-centeredness and dominance as one of the important characteristics of master therapists because it is difficult to reach this stage.

Regarding this characteristic, Jennings et al. (2005) reported "nonmaleficence" as an important ethical value of master therapists. They warned against therapists who unconsciously use the client for their own emotional needs, and they asserted that humility counterbalances the potential for arrogance and grandiosity. Similarly, Skovholt et al. (2004) cited "genuine humbleness" as one of the emotional central characteristics of master therapists; they wrote, "Arrogance and its first cousin, self-centeredness, are seen as dangerous stance for the therapist and are, therefore, actively resisted" (p. 136). Although lack of self-centeredness appears to be more important to Japanese master therapists and is more frequently cited by them, it is also an important factor for American master therapists.

One potentially effective method to overcome self-centeredness is Naikan therapy, a traditional Japanese therapy based in Buddhism (Kawahara, 2005). In summary, this process helps the client to realize how his or her life is interconnected with other people's kindness and care and that it is not possible to live alone. Thus, Naikan therapy could be an effective way for the therapist to resolve his or her self-centeredness; Tseng et al. (2005) asserted that Naikan therapy helps the individual to grow psychologically from being self-centered to empathic and appreciative of others.

CROSS-CULTURAL COMPARISON OF JAPANESE AND AMERICAN MASTER THERAPISTS

In this section, cross-cultural similarities and differences between Japanese and American master therapists are discussed, and salient characteristics of Japanese master therapists are examined.

Common Characteristics Between Japanese and American Master Therapists

Overall, it appears that the characteristics of Japanese master therapist have many commonalities with those of the American master therapists included in the Skovholt et al. study (2004). Similar themes are strong interests in new learning, importance of self-awareness and reflection, acceptance of ambiguity, and exceptional ability to form trustful relationships. It is instructive to clarify that master therapists may hold similar important characteristics beyond cultural differences. At the same time, however, similar themes may have different emphasis and importance depending on the culture. For example, judging from the number of quotes and their magnitude, it appears that the existence of great mentors has much stronger influence on Japanese master therapists than on American master therapists. This may be due to the fact that Japanese society has a more hierarchical societal structure and/or values strong bonds between great mentors and apprentice, described as "Amae" relationship by Doi (1971). Similarly, modesty plays a much stronger role for Japanese master therapists, although humility was mentioned in American master therapist research (Skovholt et al., 2004). Thus, future master therapist research would benefit from cross-cultural comparison of international master therapist research studies to deepen the understanding of master therapists. It is important to not only clarify similarities and differences of master therapists in different nations but also examine the differences of priority and magnitude of similar themes. By doing so, we can understand subtle differences and universal qualities of master therapists between cultures.

Culturally Different Characteristics of Japanese and American Master Therapists

Although there are many similarities between Japanese and American master therapists, it also appears that some characteristics are unique to Japanese master therapists, or the degree of emphasis on certain characteristics is different between two cultures.

First, Japanese master therapists seem to place more value on understanding the client without depending on the verbal interaction between the client and the therapist. For example, as cited in the Results section, one of the Japanese master therapists expressed his efforts to empathize with the client while keeping the verbal exchange to a minimum. He even said, "It is my belief that listening to the detailed content is not necessarily imperative for therapy." Another therapist described how he tries to understand the client's condition from subtle nonverbal cues during the conversation by saying, "If you pay careful attention to the time between the question and the response, you can sense whether a certain thought process is involved, such as different kinds of thoughts are suppressed or denied, by the subtle time gap." A different therapist also valued the minimalist approach as follows:

> To me, the ideal is that the client's load is kept at a minimum. Thus, it is not desirable to continue seeing the client more than necessary, or having the client share what is confidential and what the client does not usually disclose.

What is clear from the previous examples is that Japanese master therapists appear to consider it ideal to understand the client while keeping verbal exchange at a minimum. This tendency may be explained from high-context/low-context communication style proposed by Hall (1976). According to Hall, a high-context (HC) communication or message is one that is anchored in the physical context (situation) or internalized in the person, and less reliance is placed on the explicit code or message content. Instead, an HC communication relies heavily on nonverbal messages and the group identification/understanding shared by those communicating. Subtlety is a highly prized art in HC cultures, including Japanese culture. Therefore, it is possible that the Japanese client would feel more understood if the therapist could empathize with the client without too much verbal interaction. Likewise, it is possible that Japanese master therapists try to understand the client's feelings as accurately as possible through nonverbal information while keeping the verbal exchange to a minimum so that the therapist can build a working alliance more quickly with the client. Of course, American master therapists also collect information from nonverbal cues and use the information for understanding the client. However, it appears that Japanese master therapists place more value on this matter than do American master therapists.

Second, Japanese master therapists seem to value intersubjectivity or mutual process between the therapist and the client. In addition, the boundary between the Japanese therapist and the Japanese client seems to be thinner. For example, when asked about his successful therapy session, a Japanese master therapist described the session as follows: "[When the therapy is going well] I feel that the therapeutic process gets deeper, and I have this sense that the 'self' and 'other' are merged into one." Another Japanese master therapist described the important psychological space between the therapist and the client as follows:

> What I value most is this space between us, the space we share, and we breathe the space together. This space can be described as a psychological space between us, and it is created through mingling each other's inner psychological space.

From these examples, it appears that Japanese master therapists' boundaries are more porous that those of American master therapists, and empathy and understanding seem to occur in the space between the therapist and the client rather than in the therapist's mind. This difference can be explained by individual/group orientations. Pedersen (2000) noted that US culture and society are based on the concept of individualism and that the uniqueness of each individual is valued, and individual identities are considered rather solid and separate from each other. On the other hand, in many non-Western cultures, identity is not seen apart from the group orientation. In those cultures, the psychosocial unit of operation tends to be the family, group, or collective society (Sue & Sue, 2007). Similarly, it seems that the psychological unit during the therapy is not necessarily the separate client and therapist but, rather, a shared psychological space or "merged being" for Japanese master therapists.

Third, Japanese master therapists respect the profundity of the human mind and assert that what we can perceive is just a small part of an immense human inner world. In addition, it appears that Japanese master therapists respect the unconsciousness or unknown parts of the human mind and feel comfortable leaving it as it is. One of the master therapists described this point as follows: "Eastern people assume that mind is beyond our comprehension. . . . You know 'Yui-shiki' in Buddhism? That concept asserts that what we can recognize is just a tiny part of the whole truth." Another therapist mentioned the same theme as follows:

> [The human mind is] something like an unfathomable, boundless, and uncertain space. Regarding this human mind, we tend to assume that it is mostly explainable by psychological theories. However, that is simply our assumption, and the reality could be quite different when we think about it with calm and objective mind. Thus, the more I have gained experience, the more I have come to be awed by life itself, rather than feeling like I have come to understand life much more clearly.

Whereas Western psychology has attempted to bring light to the unconscious, clarify its mechanism, and verbalize it, Eastern cultures, including the Japanese culture, respect the unknown and consider it to be even arrogant that the human mind or life is explainable. This difference can be explained by using the model proposed by Kluckhohn and Strodtback (1961). They stated that people make assumptions about how they relate to nature. Traditional Western thinking believes in mastery and control over nature. In Asian cultures, however, people view the relationship with nature as harmonious. In these cultures, then, people tend to accommodate and/or avoid direct confrontation with nature because they need to achieve balance and harmony with the environment. If we apply this model to the human mind, nature can be described as an unknown part of the human mind. In the counseling process, Western therapists and clients may tend to believe that any unknown parts should be brought up to a level of consciousness, and both parties in the process must take an active part in solving problems via agency and self-control. Japanese therapists, on the other hand, may tend to respect the mystery of the human mind. One of the Japanese master therapists contrasted this difference as follows:

> For Western people, it may be that there is a thick wall between unconsciousness and consciousness. Thus, they try to pull down this wall, and try to achieve self-actualization by enlarging the world of consciousness. On the other hand, Eastern people do not have to enlarge the conscious world. It is fine if the wall between the conscious and the unconscious is thin. Unless the interaction between the two is smooth through symbolization or festivals in the community, it does not matter whether unconscious is brought into consciousness or not.

Fourth, Japanese master therapists reported their great mentors as one of the most influential learning opportunities, and it appears that this learning is not limited to cognitive and/or technical learning but also includes relational learning with emotional attachment. In this sense, the impact from their great mentors was not limited to learning about therapy but also included a more holistic human encounter. It was also stated by several master therapists that there exists a learning process from their great mentors in which they first had a strong attachment to their great mentors and fully learned from them, followed by the "graduation" from them and acquiring of new great mentors and creating one's own method. This learning process is quite similar to the Japanese traditional learning process called *Shu-ha-ri* (守破離), taught in Kendo (Japanese art of fencing). Shu-ha-ri describes a three-step process of mastering certain traditional Japanese art, such as Kendo, flower arrangement, and Kabuki. The first step is called *Shu* (protect), in which the apprentice first closely learns from his or her great mentor and masters his or her skills and attitudes. The second step is called *Ha* (break), which means leaving the great mentor, freeing him- or herself to other great mentors and learning opportunities. The final step is called *Ri* (Away), which means to create his or her own style, independent from the great mentor. It would be instructive to examine the learning process in different traditional Japanese arts and how we can apply these methods to therapist training to ensure a culturally appropriate training model.

LIMITATIONS OF THE STUDY

One possible limitation is that the study employed a one-shot sampling method, instead of the snowball sampling method, due to the concern that the snowball sampling method might increase the risk of Japanese therapists selecting certain therapists based on moral indebtedness rather than on more objective standards because Japanese society is considered to be more hierarchical than American society. Because of this difference in the nomination procedure, our findings may or may not be comparable to those of other master therapist studies that employed a snowball sampling nomination method.

Another limitation is the possible generation gap between the master therapists in this study and younger, but competent, therapists and also the degree of generalizability of this research to therapist development in a younger generation. Most master therapists in this study were from the first generation of psychotherapists who studied psychotherapy abroad and brought both knowledge and techniques to Japan and constructed basic structures, such as academic associations and professional credentials, for the development of psychotherapy in Japan. On the other hand, entry- and middle-level Japanese therapists received their education at a time when training opportunities were already relatively well-established and various therapeutic approaches were available to learn. Therefore, the developmental processes for current master therapists and prospective master therapists in younger generations could be different. Considering the fact that the average age of master therapists in this study was relative high ($M = 72.2$ years, $SD = 7.66$ years), it may be interesting to examine the characteristics and developmental process of young, but competent, Japanese therapists.

Another limitation is the fact that the master therapists in this study were selected through the single selection method of peer nomination. Although it would be more complex and time-consuming, the representativeness and validity of master therapists would be more robust if we could employ multiple selection methods, such as nominations by clients, assessment of actual case descriptions and formulations, and/or assessment of actual video-recorded therapy sessions.

Note that the results of this study may not transfer beyond the context of this sample group. This is because the study employed an information-rich qualitative study method instead of a representative sampling method used in quantitative studies (Patton, 2002).

IMPLICATIONS AND RECOMMENDATIONS

In this section, four recommendations for future master therapist research and four recommendations for therapist training are offered.

Research Recommendation 1: Future research could benefit from further examination of the impact of one's great mentors for the development of psychotherapists.

It was quite striking that most of the Japanese master therapists mentioned their great mentor as one of the most influential aspects in their professional and personal development. It is also noteworthy that master therapists gave greater emphasis to the personal or relational impact they had from their great mentor, such as values, attitude, emotional support, and philosophy of life, rather than cognitive or technical learning. In this sense, future master therapist researchers may want to closely examine the learning process from great mentors, as well as the specific lessons learned from the great mentors.

> *Research Recommendation 2*: Future research should possibly examine the process of being aware of one's self-centered motivation and setting oneself free from it.

Japanese master therapists are keenly aware of the risk of self-centered motivation behind their helping behaviors and also the difficulty of being aware of and remaining free from that motivation. As a means to be aware of their own self-centeredness, master therapists suggested in-depth self-reflection through individual self-introspection, clinical supervision, and/or personal therapy. However, it appears that there are various ways to be aware of one's self-centeredness as well as a gradual process of becoming free from it. More in-depth study is necessary to examine the change process from self-centeredness to genuine caring and also to clarify different methods to facilitate this change. This future research is particularly important because Japanese master therapists emphasized the difficulty of the process while pointing out the possible large number of therapists who may be operating from the self-centered motivation.

> *Research Recommendation 3*: Future research could further examine the important role of the "study-abroad" experiences of Japanese master therapists.

It is notable that more than half of Japanese master therapists had some experience studying abroad, and many of them reported that this experience had a critical influence on their professional development and career. Thus, it would be beneficial to further examine how and what master therapists learned from their study-abroad experiences, how they overcame difficulties in a different culture, how they dealt with re-entry culture shock in their home country, and how they integrated clinical and cultural experiences in both Japan and overseas and subsequently synthesized their study-abroad experiences to positive learning opportunities.

> *Research Recommendation 4*: Future research could clarify universal aspects of expertise between master therapists and other experts, as well as differentiate characteristics between master therapists and experienced therapists, while distinguishing unique characteristics of master therapists.

As one of the Japanese master therapists noted, one of the characteristics of master therapists is to find both connection and commonalities with experts in other fields. Chi, Glaser, and Farr (1988) outlined seven characteristics of expert performers, and it appears that some of these characteristics may have commonalities with Japanese master therapist characteristics described in this study, such as perceiving large meaningful patterns, seeing a problem at a deeper level, and having strong self-monitoring skills. Thus, it appears to be important to clarify common characteristics between experts in different professions while distinguishing unique characteristics of master therapists. In addition, it is also important to distinguish different characteristics between master therapists and experienced therapists. It is conceivable that some of the characteristics of master therapists are common to experienced therapists, other characteristics are the same in qualities but different in their degree, and some characteristics are qualitatively unique to master therapists. In order to achieve this, comparative study between Japanese master therapists and experienced therapists would be necessary.

> *Training Recommendation 1*: Training programs can equally emphasize the importance of assessing both psychopathology and strengths of the client.

More than half of the Japanese master therapists mentioned the importance of capitalizing on the client's strengths and spontaneous healing power. However, in the current therapist training in Japanese graduate schools, understanding of the client is heavily skewed to the assessment of client weaknesses and psychopathology, and there is much less opportunity to learn how to assess and utilize the client's positive qualities. In this sense, Japanese therapist training could benefit from incorporating the positive psychology movement (Seligman, 1998) and positive psychological interventions (Magyar-Moe, 2009) so that novice therapists could develop a more balanced view of clients and learn how to capitalize on the clients' strengths and resources.

> *Training Recommendation 2*: Training programs can offer more opportunities for novice therapists to learn from mentors and masters in a holistic way.

As the supervision system has improved in Japanese therapist training systems, novice therapists have had greater opportunity to receive formal and systematic supervision from more experienced therapists. This means that the purpose, duration, and boundary of supervision have become clearer. It is also important to note that supervision is currently more limited to technical or conceptual teaching and discussion of cases. Considering the results arising from the fact that master therapists learned significantly from their great mentors personally and holistically, this "formalization" of a supervision system may not be so beneficial for trainees. It may prove to be of greater benefit to prepare opportunities for novice therapists to find their favorite great mentors, allowing them to spend significant time with their great mentors so that trainees can learn from their great mentors in a more personal and holistic manner.

> *Training Recommendation 3*: Training programs can introduce a progressive therapist development model in which novice therapists first have opportunities to choose therapeutic approaches that fit their interests and values and then become independent from them and create their own approach.

Several Japanese master therapists emphasized that it is important to first be immersed in a particular approach, become independent from it, and then create one's own therapeutic style. This means that optimal learning is different for therapists depending on their development phases. Thus, a sample of an ideal training curriculum could be that novice therapists first have opportunities to familiarize themselves with various therapeutic approaches through both theoretical and experiential studies. Second, based on their interests and values, they choose a particular approach to master. As they accumulate experiences and develop as a therapist, they can gradually become independent from the approach and create their own styles with more creativity and flexibility. Especially for relatively experienced therapists, it appears that opportunities for renewal are important in order to keep their motivation fresh and continue spontaneous learning. Therefore, it is recommended that training programs introduce this kind of progressive therapist development model and offer various ongoing professional development opportunities so that experienced therapists can stay creative and novel in their therapeutic styles.

> *Training Recommendation 4*: Training programs can explore the positive use of study-abroad programs for therapist development.

More than half of Japanese master therapists experienced study abroad, and many of them reported it as being one of the most influential experiences in their development. From the interviews, it appears that studying abroad has a number of advantages for a therapist-in-training and contributes to the develop of important characteristics identified by master therapists, such as spontaneous and creative learning opportunities, finding one's great mentors, opportunities for deep self-introspection, developing one's tolerance and acceptance of ambiguity, gaining comprehensive and multiple perspectives on understanding people, and developing a high level of resilience. Despite this excellent opportunity for therapist development, the current number of Japanese graduate students or novice therapists who are willing to study abroad is relatively small. Thus, it is recommended that Japanese therapist training programs highlight the advantages of studying abroad and provide more opportunities of this nature for young therapists, thus leading to optimal therapist development.

Conclusion

MAIN CHARACTERISTICS OF JAPANESE MASTER THERAPISTS

Based on the findings of this study, important characteristics of Japanese master therapists were clarified. First, as a foundation, they possess positive personality traits, such as modesty, warmth, sincerity, absence of self-centeredness, and resilience. Based on these characteristics, they are able to build trustful relationships with their clients, both at an early stage and throughout the therapy process. Second, they possess exceptional ability to perceive and process various cognitive (i.e., case formulation, objective monitoring of the therapy process, and keen observation of the client's verbal and nonverbal cues) and emotional (i.e., accurate empathy and use of the therapist's feelings during the session) information from the client, the therapist him- or herself, and the therapy process. This perceptive capacity to understand appears to make it possible to perform at a high level of therapeutic effectiveness, maintaining a flexible therapeutic stance depending on the client. Third, master therapists are able to continuously learn from their experiences, stimulated by their curiosity and creativity as well as their sense of responsibility and discipline as professionals.

THREE IMPORTANT DOMAINS FOR JAPANESE MASTER THERAPIST DEVELOPMENT

Close examination of interviews with Japanese master therapists reveals three domains that are crucial for optimal professional development: self, others, and human nature. First, the "self" domain refers to characteristics related to the individual therapist, such as personality, values, and will. Specifically, it appears that personal characteristics such as curiosity, creativity, modesty, warmth, sincerity, and resilience, as well as a high degree of professionalism and will to become an expert therapist, are important ingredients related to the self domain. Second, the "others" domain pertains to important and influential people around the therapist who contribute to an optimal learning process, such as great mentors, clients, and colleagues. It is apparent from the results that one of the greatest influences on Japanese master therapist development is the existence of great mentors. Other Japanese master therapists reported that they have learned much from their clients and the mutual process between the client and the therapist. Other master therapists also mentioned their colleagues and how much they have learned from case conferences and informal conversations with colleagues. The third domain is "human nature," which connotes a sense of awe to something greater than self or others, such as profundity of the human mind, including the unconscious, as well as complexity of life. A number of Japanese master therapists repeatedly mentioned the complex, profound, and immense nature of human beings and their minds, and the importance of getting in contact with

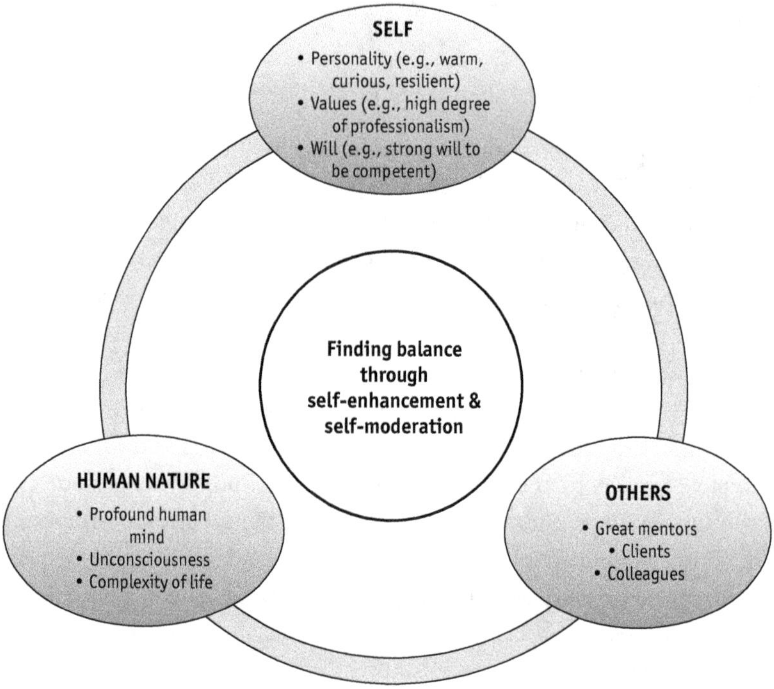

FIGURE 6.1 Three important domains for optimal development of Japanese master therapists.

the profundity of human nature so that we can stay modest without being arrogant about what we know and what we do as psychotherapists.

Japanese master therapists emphasized the importance of these three domains; in addition, they placed a high importance on finding a balance among these three domains through self-enhancement and self-moderation. Self-enhancement means to gain more knowledge and skills and also gain confidence and expertise as a psychotherapist. Self-moderation, on the other hand, means to realize what one knows is just a part of the whole truth, and the existence of oneself is trivial in relation to the immensity and profundity of human beings. In this sense, self-enhancement helps us to feel confident and competent, while self-moderation keeps us from being arrogant and self-centered. Thus, the combination of these seemingly contradicting concepts is important. In short, according to Japanese master therapists, optimal development occurs when the therapist makes best use of the three important domains—self, others, and human nature—while finding a balance between these domains through self-enhancement and self-moderation (Fig. 6.1).

SPIRAL MODEL OF JAPANESE MASTER THERAPIST DEVELOPMENT

From this study, it appears that the developmental process of Japanese master therapists may not be linear or stepwise but, rather, spiral. For example, a number of master

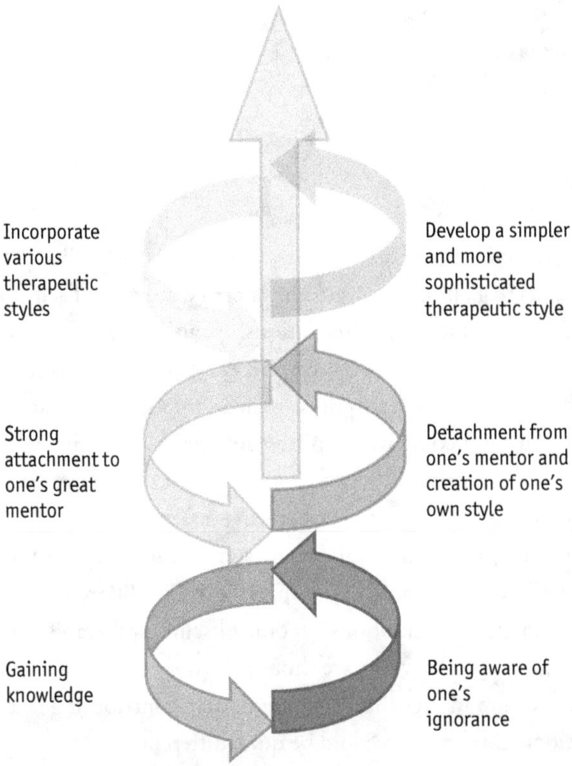

FIGURE 6.2 Spiral developmental model of Japanese master therapists.

therapists described their changes in therapeutic style as starting from a lay helper, gaining expertise as professionals, and returning to a seemingly ordinary therapy style. Other therapists illustrated their learning process from great mentors as a process of strong attachment, subsequent detachment from great mentors, followed by creation of their own styles and, later, encounters with new great mentors. Another therapist described his changing awareness about this knowledge as starting from ignorance, gaining knowledge, being deeply aware of one's ignorance, and staying modest and motivated to learn more. These changing processes may appear to be a return to the starting point, if we see the process from a two-dimensional viewpoint, but we can be aware that they are in fact coming back to a similar but higher point, if we see the process from a three-dimensional viewpoint. In addition, it appears that a self-reflection process including the utilization of clinical supervision, self-introspection, and personal therapy would help the therapist to see his or her developmental process from a three-dimensional viewpoint (Fig. 6.2):

Develop a simpler and more sophisticated therapeutic style
Incorporate various therapeutic styles
Detachment from one's mentor and creation of one's own style

Being aware of one's ignorance
Strong attachment to one's great mentor
Gaining knowledge

Summary and Final Remarks

Regarding the characteristics of Japanese master therapists, it has been clarified that certain personality traits (e.g., modesty, warmth, sincerity, absence of self-centeredness, and resilience), the ability to build a trustful relationship with the client, the exceptional ability to perceive and process various cognitive and emotional information during therapy, and a high level of therapeutic effectiveness are main important characteristics.

Regarding cross-cultural comparison, both similarities and differences were found in master therapist characteristics. It is noteworthy that many characteristics of Japanese master therapists are similar to those of American master therapists. This may mean that at the later stage of therapist development, master therapists could possibly transcend cultural differences and share more similarities, just like differences in actual therapy among different theoretical orientations become obscure as therapists become more experienced. At the same time, however, we should be aware that even when characteristics of Japanese and American master therapists are similar, contributing factors/experiences as well as its developmental process could be quite different.

It was our intention to contribute to the internationalization of master therapist research. This study showed complex and intriguing characteristics of Japanese master therapists while clarifying both similarities and differences of master therapists in two cultures. It is our hope that further international master therapist studies will be conducted, both in depth and breadth, inviting participation of more master therapists from different cultures. This would surely contribute to a deeper understanding of people in different cultures, which is one of the most important missions of psychology today.

References

Association of Japanese Clinical Psychology (2007, December 10). *History*. Retrieved from http://www.ajcp.info/en/history.htm

Blatt, S. J., Sanislow, C. A., Zuroff, D. C., & Pilkonis, P. A. (1996). Characteristics of effective therapists: Further analysis of data from the National Institute of Mental Health Treatment of Depression Collaborative Research Program. *Journal of Consulting and Clinical Psychology, 64*, 1276–1284.

Chi, M. T., Glaser, R., & Farr, M. J. (Eds.). (1988). *The nature of expertise*. Hillsdale, NJ: Erlbaum.

Doi, T. (1971). Amae no kouzou [The structure of dependence]. Tokyo: Kobundo.

Eells, T. D., Lombart, K. G., Kendjelic, E. M., Turner, L. C., & Lucas, C. P. (2005). The quality of psychotherapy case formulations: A comparison of expert, experienced, and novice cognitive–behavioral and psychodynamic therapists. *Journal of Consulting and Clinical Psychology, 73*(4), 579.

Fey, W. F. (1958). Doctrine and experience: Their influence upon the psychotherapist. *Journal of Consulting Psychology, 22*(6), 403–406.

Goh, M. (2005). Cultural competence and master therapists: An inextricable relationship. *Journal of Mental Health Counseling, 27*(1), 71–81.

Hall, E. T. (1976). *Beyond culture*. New York, NY: Anchor Press.

Hayashi, S., Kuno, T., Osawa, M., Shimizu, M., & Suetake, Y. (1992). The client-centered therapy and person-centered approach in Japan: Historical development, current status, and perspectives. *Journal of Humanistic Psychology, 32*(2), 115–136.

Hill, C. E., Knox, S., Thompson, B. J., Williams, E. N., Hess, S. A., & Ladany, N. (2005). Consensual qualitative research: An update. *Journal of Counseling Psychology, 52*(2), 196.

Hill, C. E., Thompson, B. J., & Williams, E. N. (1997). A guide to conducting consensual qualitative research. *The Counseling Psychologist, 25*(4), 517–572.

Japan Psychoanalytical Association. (2008, January 7). *Kaicho Aisatsu* [Remarks from the president of the association]. Retrieved from http://www.seishinbunseki.jp/society/greeting.html

Japanese Certification Board for Clinical Psychologists. (2007, December 10). *Rinsyo Shinrishi towa* [Characteristics of clinical psychologists]. Retrieved from http://fjcbcp.or.jp/rinshou/about-2

Jennings, L., Goh, M., Skovholt, T. M., & Banerjee-Stevens, D. (2003). Multiple factors in the development of expert counselors and therapists. *Journal of Career Development, 30*, 59–72.

Jennings, L., & Skovholt, T. M. (1999). The cognitive, emotional, and relational characteristics of master therapists. *Journal of Counseling Psychology, 46*(1), 3–11.

Jennings, L., Sovereign, A., Bottorff, N., Mussell, M. P., & Vye, C. (2005). Nine ethical values of master therapists. *Journal of Mental Health Counseling, 27*(1), 32–47.

Kawahara, R. (2005). Japanese Buddhist thought and Naikan therapy. In W. S. Tseng, S. C. Chang, & M. Nishizono (Eds.), *Asian culture and psychotherapy: Implications for East and West* (pp. 186–198). Honolulu, HI: University of Hawaii Press.

Kitanishi, K. (2005). The philosophical background of Morita therapy: Its application to therapy. In W. S. Tseng, S. C. Chang, & M. Nishizono (Eds.), *Asian culture and psychotherapy: Implications for East and West* (pp. 169–185). Honolulu, HI: University of Hawaii Press.

Kivlighan, D. M., & Quigley, S. T. (1991). Dimensions used by experienced and novice group therapists to conceptualizing group process. *Journal of Counseling Psychologist, 38*, 414–423.

Kluckhohn, F. R., & Strodtbeck, F. L. (1961). *Variations in value orientations*. Oxford, England: Row, Peterson.

Kondo, K. (1976). The origin of Morita therapy. In P. William (Ed.), *Culture-bound syndromes, ethnopsychiatry, and alternate therapies* (pp. 250–258). Honolulu, HI: University Press of Hawaii.

Magyar-Moe, J. L. (2009). *Therapist's guide to positive psychological interventions*. Burlington, MA: Academic Press.

Ministry of Education, Culture, Sports, Science, and Technology. (2007, December 10). *School counselor nit tsuite* [Regarding school counselors]. Retrieved from http://www.mext.go.jp/a_menu/shotou/seitoshidou/kyouiku/houkoku/07082308/002.htm

Mullenbach, M., & Skovholt, T. M. (2004). Emotional wellness and professional resiliency of master therapists. In T. M. Skovholt & L. Jennings (Eds.), *Master therapists: Exploring expertise in therapy and counseling* (pp. 77–106). Boston, MA: Allyn & Bacon.

Murphy, M. J., Cheng, W., & Werner-Wilson, R. J. (2006). Exploring master therapists' use of power in conversation. *Contemporary Family Therapy, 28*(4), 475–484.

Patton, M. Q. (2002). *Qualitative evaluation and research methods* (3rd ed.). Thousand Oaks, CA: Sage.

Pedersen, P. (2000). *A handbook of developing multicultural awareness* (3rd ed.). Alexandria, VA: American Counseling Association.

Raue, P. J., Castonguay, L. G., & Goldfried, M. R. (1993). The working alliance: A comparison of two therapists. *Psychotherapy Research, 3*(3), 197–207.

Rønnestad, M. H., & Skovholt, T. M. (2003). The journey of the counselor and therapist: Research findings and perspectives on professional development. *Journal of Career Development, 30*(1), 5–44.

Seligman, M. (1998). What is the good life. *APA Monitor, 29*(10), 2.

Shinpo, Y. (1998). Sinrimenstsubamen ni okeru kaunsera no ishiketteikatei ni kansuru kenkyu (1: Jyukurensya no mensetsubamen no bunseki wo toshite [Counselors' decision making process in therapy session (1): Session analysis of expert therapists]. *Taisho University Journal of Clinical Psychology, 1*, 35–54.

Shinpo, Y. (1999). Counselors' decision making process in therapy session: Comparison between intermediate and expert counselors. *Taisho University Journal of Clinical Psychology, 2*, 56–75.

Skovholt, T. M., Jennings, L., & Mullenbach, M. (2004). Portrait of the master therapist: Developmental model of the highly functioning self. In T. M. Skovholt & L. Jennings (Eds.), *Master therapists: Exploring expertise in therapy and counseling* (pp. 125–146). Boston, MA: Allyn & Bacon.

Skovholt, T. M., Rønnestad, M. H., & Jennings, L. (1997). Searching for expertise in counseling, psychotherapy, and professional psychology. *Educational Psychology Review, 9*(4), 361–369.

Strauss, A., & Corbin, J. M. (1990). *Basics of qualitative research: Grounded theory procedures and techniques*. Thousand Oaks, CA: Sage.

Sue, D. W., & Sue, D. (2007). *Counseling the culturally diverse* (5th ed.). Hoboken, NJ: Wiley.

Sullivan, M. F., Skovholt, T. M., & Jennings, L. (2005). Master therapists' construction of the therapy relationship. *Journal of Mental Health Counseling, 27*(1), 48–70.

Sundland, D. M. & Barker, E. N. (1962). The orientation of psychotherapists. *Journal of Consulting Psychology, 26*(3), 201-212.

Takeshima, A., Sugiwaka, H., Nishiura, R., Yamamoto, A., & Agari, I. (1993). Seishin ryoho ni okeru rinsyokeiken nensu to chiryosya no koudou to taido [Relationships between the years of clinical experience and the behaviors and attitudes of therapists in psychotherapy]. *Japanese Journal of Counseling Science*, 26(2), 97–106.

Tseng, W. S., Chang, S. C, & Nishizono, M. (2005). *Asian culture and psychotherapy*. Honolulu, HI: University of Hawaii Press.

Wallach, M. S., & Strupp, H. H. (1964). Dimensions of psychotherapists' activity. *Journal of Consulting Psychology, 28*(2), 120.

Watters, E. (2010). *Crazy like us: The globalization of the American psyche*. New York, NY: Free Press.

Wiser, S., & Goldfried, M. R. (1993). A comparative study of emotional experiencing in psychodynamic–interpersonal and cognitive–behavioral therapies. *Journal of Consulting and Clinical Psychology, 61*, 892–895.

7 Characteristics of Korean Master Group Counselors[1]

Kyoung-In Kwon and Chang-Dai Kim

IN THE PAST FEW DECADES, many researchers have been interested in factors that contribute to effective counseling (Miller, 1993). Among them, counselor variables have been discussed as a main factor that affects counseling process and outcome (Berry & Sipps, 1991; Beulter, Machado, & Neufeldt, 1994; Cantor, 1991; Hill & O'Grady, 1985; Holloway & Wampold, 1986; Horvath & Greenberg, 1989; Kim, 2000; Propst, 1980). There is increasing empirical evidence supporting the effects of counselor variables on outcome (Kim, Wampold, & Bolt, 2006; Wampold & Brown, 2006). Wampold (2007) emphasized the importance of research on counselor variables, showing that the counselor rather than the type of treatment is what makes differences in counseling outcomes. He asserted that knowledge of characteristics of exemplary counselors is a prerequisite for research on the effects of counselor factors.

Counselor variables have been examined mainly in the areas of counselor training and supervision by utilizing developmental stage models. These developmental stage models are premised on the view that the level of counselor expertise advances through processes similar to the human psychological development (Skovholt & Rønnestad, 1995). Many different models on counselor development exist (Blocher, 1993; Fleming, 1953; Hess, 1987; Hill, Charles, & Reed, 1981; Hogan, 1964; Loganbill, Hardy, & Delworth, 1982; Stoltenberg & Delworth, 1987; Skovholt & Rønnestad, 1995; Worthington, 1984; Yogev, 1982). These models have great value in that they provide useful information about unique characteristics of counselors in different developmental stages. However, there are some limitations as well.

Previous research on counselor development has been conducted mostly within individual counseling and supervision (Hogan, 1964; Stoltenberg & Delworth, 1987; Worthington, 1984), reflecting the reality in practice that supervision is usually provided for individual counseling. There is little research on counselor development in other counseling modalities or settings such as group counseling. Group counseling is an effective counseling modality that has different characteristics from individual counseling (Corey & Corey, 2000; Lee & Kim, 1998; Lee, Kim, Seol, Kim, & Kim, 2002). Although the history of group counseling in Korea is relatively short compared to that of individual counseling, group counseling has grown rapidly and appears to continue to grow in popularity (Lee et al., 2002). Kim (2000) mentioned that group counseling would be widely used in Korea due to the Korean culture that values "we" and others' perspectives, along with its unique therapeutic benefits. Kim also asserted that group counseling is an area in which Korean counseling makes an international contribution, given that group counseling is considered a secondary treatment modality in comparison to individual counseling in the United States and Europe. In Korea, there is a high demand for group counseling in various settings. Group counseling is also considered a core component of counseling training programs.

Most of the past research on counselor development focused on the discrete characteristics of each stage, and there was less research focus on expertise development processes or the transition from one stage to the next. Contributing situations, facilitating factors, or specific strategies in the development of counselor expertise have not been examined. One reason that previous research on counselor development only focused on distinctive characteristics of each stage, particularly the novice stage, seems to be that the primary goal of such research was to improve supervision. In other words, examining the characteristics of counselor development itself was not the focus in most of the previous research. Thus, empirical research on counselors' development itself is needed.

A considerable amount of empirical studies have been conducted in regard to counselors' cognitive characteristics. Since the late 1980s, many studies have been conducted in this line of research. One of the topics in this area of research is the effect of counselor experience on the level of competence in case conceptualization (Chi, Glaser, & Farr, 1988; Cummings, Hallberg, Martin, Slemon, & Hiebert, 1990; Martin, Slemon, Hiebett, Hallberg, & Cummings, 1989). However, these studies explain counselor development only for the cognitive aspect. Skovholt and Rønnestad (1992) asserted that counselor competence should be viewed from an integrated perspective as competence develops through a combination of clinical experience, relational and emotional characteristics of the counselor, as well as the integration of their own inner experiences. An integrative developmental model appears to fit best in investigating the components of counselor competence.

Recent research endeavors on counselor development have started to look at highly skilled counselors or experts. An exemplary study is by Jennings and Skovholt (1999);

these authors investigated the developmental characteristics of master counselors or senior counselors who have been designated as "the expert among experts" by other counselors. Exploring the expertise of those counselors who have reached the final stage of counselor development is valuable, providing useful information for counselor training and education. For instance, the findings on the master counselors' characteristics can be used as objectives in counselor training programs or as evaluation criteria for counselor competency. Skovholt and Jennings (2004) found that while there are commonalities shared by experts in different professional fields, some characteristics are unique to each field. Group counseling experts may also possess unique characteristics that are distinctive from those of individual counseling experts. The goal of the current study is to identify the characteristics of master group counselors in Korea who have reached the final stage of counselor development.

The present study attempted to address the limitations of previous studies as follows. First, this study examined the characteristics of group counselors, while most of the previous studies on counselor development and supervision were conducted within individual counseling and supervision. Second, instead of focusing only on the discrete characteristics of each counselor's developmental stage, this study investigated the developmental process of group counselors. Specifically, this study examined group counselors' strategies, challenges, coping methods, and facilitative and hindering factors for growth in the process of their development. Third, this study takes an integrated stance in investigating counselor characteristics by giving attention to emotional, relational, and intrapersonal as well as cognitive characteristics. Fourth, this study examined group counselors in the final stage of counselor development, which will provide information on concrete learning goals and core components of counselor training.

The current research used a sample of master group counselors. The master group counselor is defined as someone who has reached the final stage of group expertise development. The dictionary definition of "master" (大家) is "a person who has profound knowledge in one's professional domain." Despite the lack of conceptual clarity, the term "master" is frequently used by mental health professionals, referring to counselors who are "the best of the best" among fellow practitioners (Jennings & Skovholt, 1999). In search for an adequate term to describe group counselors with extraordinary skills and qualities, the term "master" was selected in this study (Goldberg, 1992; Jennings & Skovholt, 1999). Considering the short history of group counseling in Korea, the number of experts in this field is small and the use of the term "master" may be controversial. However, if we were to consider 1970 as the year that group counseling was first introduced in Korea (Lee et al., 2002), over 40 years have passed. It is more than enough time for a novice group counselor to develop into a high-level expert counselor, allowing for the exploration of life span development of group counselors. Guided by previous research on master counselors (Jennings & Skovholt, 1999), counseling experience, experience as a group counselor, and acknowledgment from fellow experts were used as a selection criteria. The research questions of this study are as follows. First, what are the personal and professional characteristics of master group counselors in Korea? Second, what are the facilitating factors, hindering factors, and strategies used for the development of group counseling expertise?

Methods

PARTICIPANTS

Key Informants

The peer nomination method through snowball sampling was used to select master group counselors. The selection criteria for key informants were (1) active involvement in counselor training, (2) consistent involvement in Korean counseling associations, and (3) reputation as a well-known counselor. Representativeness in geographical location, educational background, and gender were considered in determining key informants. Four Ph.D. holders in counseling psychology (two men, two women) were selected as the key informants of this study. The key informants had an average of 24 years ($SD = 2.8$) of clinical experience. They were actively involved in professional associations in Korea such as Group Counseling Association, Korean Counseling Psychological Association, and Korean Counseling Association. The key informants have written books and conducted research on group counseling. They also have experience as group counselors. In terms of work settings, one worked as a professor, two private practitioners, and one was both an academic and a practitioner.

Master Group Counselors

Five group counselors (four men, one woman) were selected as master group counselors for this study. Three held Ph.D.'s in counseling psychology or counselor education, and two held M.A. degrees in psychology. All held professional licenses from the Korean Counseling Psychological Association and the Korean Counseling Association. Ages ranged from 46 to 63 years ($M = 52.6$, $SD = 6.5$). The average counseling experience was 26.2 years ($SD = 5.4$). Experience as a group counselor ranged between 12 and 35 years ($M = 21.6$, $SD = 9.0$). One worked as a university professor and four as private practitioners. In regard to theoretical orientation, the participants reportedly use humanistic approaches with an integration of other theories such as cognitive–behavioral theory and object relations theory.

PROCEDURE

Recruitment

This study used peer nomination and a snowball sampling method to select master group counselors (Jennings & Skovholt, 1999; Patton, 1990). The final five participants were determined from an initial sample of individuals who were nominated more than once.

Peer nomination is an effective and widely used method to identify exemplary personal and interpersonal characteristics of counselors (Anastasi & Urbina, 1997; Cole & White, 1993; Hillerbrand & Claiborn, 1990; Luborsky, McLellan, Woody, O'Brien, & Auerbach, 1985; Serbin, Lyons, Marchessault, Schartzman, & Ledingham, 1987). Luborsky et al. (1985) addressed the utility of this method for counseling research, stating that counselors are able to identify potentially competent counselors and discern who are more or less competent. The participant selection process is illustrated in Table 7.1.

The nomination process continued until no new names emerged (Patton, 1990). As a result, 27 counselors were nominated. Among them, one counselor received 11 nominations, one received six nominations, one received five nominations, one received four nominations, four received three nominations, seven received two nominations, and 12 received one nomination. Five counselors with the most nominations were selected for

TABLE 7.1

Selection Process of Master Group Counselors

Process	Content
Selection of key informants	Two men, two women Involvement in counselor training Participation in counseling associations in Korea Reputation as a well-known counselor
Nomination of master group counselors by key informants	Each key informant nominated three master group counselors among Korean group counselors by using the following nomination criteria: The person is thought to be the best group counselor. The person is frequently considered to be an expert counselor when referring a close relative or friend to group counseling. The person whose group the nominator would think of participating.
Nominations by the nominated	The nominated master group counselor nominates three master counselors, excluding oneself (repeat this process).
End of nominations: The core subject pool formed.	The nomination process continues until certain individuals are repeatedly nominated and new names rarely emerge.
Finalization of master group counselors (cutoff decision)	The number of participants is determined.

the final participants. Specifically, along with those with 11, six, five, and four nominations, one of those with three nominations was included. Among those who received three nominations, a professional identity as a group counselor was less prominent. They reported that they were more actively involved in other areas than group counseling, such as individual counseling, research, and teaching. In order to identify group-counseling experts among the four, the nomination order was converted into scores and the one with the highest score was chosen.

Development of an Interview Schedule

An interview schedule was created to maintain consistency among the interviews with the five master group counselors. The interview questions were developed based on the research questions and a literature review. Literature on counselor effectiveness, counselor characteristics, developmental stages of counselors, and group counseling was reviewed (Goldberg, 1992; Harrington, 1988; Jackson & Thompson, 1971; Luborsky et al., 1985; Miller, 1993; Schwebel & Coster, 1998; Skovholt & Jennings, 2004; Wicas & Mahan, 1966). In particular, three articles informed the development of interview questions: (1) an article regarding life-span theory on events that influence counselor development (Baltes, Reese, & Lipsitt, 1980); (2) a study on critical incidents that facilitated the developmental process of counselors (Skovholt & McCarthy, 1998); and (3) a study on the characteristics of master therapists (Jennings & Skovholt, 1999).

Initial interview questions were developed by two experienced group counselors based on a literature review. These questions were reviewed by two other group counselors and then revised based on their feedback. This revised version of the interview questions was reviewed again by two doctoral-level qualitative researchers experienced in grounded theory research. At the same time, 12 master's and doctorate-level counselors who had professional interest in group counseling were asked what questions they would like to ask a master group counselor. Forty-five questions were collected through this process and were categorized into similar topics.

After combining the feedback from the two qualitative researchers and responses from the 12 master's and doctorate-level counselors, a second version of the interview schedule was developed. This second version of the interview schedule consisted of 20 questions. The interview questions were piloted with one of the group counselors who had received three nominations during the sampling process. The 3-hour pilot interview was audiotaped and transcribed. The transcribed data were then analyzed by using the grounded theory method. Based on the results of the pilot study, the third version of the interview schedule was created. Another pilot interview was conducted with an experienced group counselor who had more than 15 years of group counseling experience. Based on the results of the second pilot study and feedback from two professors in counseling, the final version of the interview schedule was created, as shown in Table 7.2.

TABLE 7.2

Interview Schedule

Main Questions	Subquestions
What are characteristics of master group counselors?	• In your opinion, what is the biggest difference between master group counselors and master counselors providing individual counseling? • Let us say two group counselors receive similar training. Why does one become a master group counselor while the other one becomes an ordinary group counselor? • As a group counselor, what makes you therapeutic? • What made you choose group counseling? • What does group counseling mean to you?
What developmental process does a counselor go through to become a master group counselor?	• How are you different from the time you first began group counseling? • We would like to understand your developmental process of becoming an exceptional group counselor. What developmental stages did you go through? • If you were to write an autobiography as a group counselor, what are the major events (or people) you must include in the book?
What are some unique characteristics of the process of becoming a master group counselor?	• If there was anything unique about your learning experience as a group counselor, what was it? • What were the frustrations you had experienced as a group counselor and how did you overcome them? • What is the most difficult client like? Is there a special strategy you use to deal with such difficult clients whom others may not deal with effectively? • What was the critical experience that brought about a great spike in your growth as a group counselor? • Do you have any special way to maintain and advance your expertise?
Questions regarding the decisions of future group counselors	• If your child (or a significant person in your life) tells you that he/she wants to become a group counselor, how would you react? If he/she is firm in his/her decision, what would you suggest specifically? • What are the qualities of a person you believe should rather not become a group counselor? • How important is "experience" in developing an exceptional expertise? What are some other important factors other than experience?

Interview

Guba and Lincoln (1981) asserted that participants themselves are the best evaluators to determine whether the categories created by researchers adequately reflect the participants' experiences. Thus, the use of a follow-up interview increases the validity of the results of the qualitative analysis. The present study added an additional follow-up interview to the interview follow-up design (Jennings & Skovholt, 1999) in order to increase validity through dialogue. Consequently, three interviews were conducted with each participant.

The interviews occurred from September 2006 to December 2006. The number of the interview sessions with each participant varied from three to five. The total duration of the interviews per person ranged from 6 to 10 hours. Additional communication through e-mail and phone occurred as needed. Procedures of the interviews are described in Table 7.3.

TABLE 7.3

Interview Procedures

Interview Type	Procedures	Duration
First interview	• The interviewer met with each of the five participants. • The interviewer conducted interviews by using the interview schedule. • For some, the first interview was conducted over two sessions.	2½–4 hours
Second interview	• Had the first follow-up interviews. • Showed the participants the paradigm model and the table of concepts, subcategories, and categories that emerged through open coding and axial coding of grounded theory prior to the interviews.	30 minutes to 2 hours
Third interview	• Had the second follow-up interviews. • Research findings were sent to the participants via e-mail for review prior to the interviews. Participants reviewed the direct quotations from their previous interviews that were cited in each concept to determine if they were appropriately applied. Participants also reviewed the results to determine if there was anything to add or remove. • Participants were asked if they have anything to share additionally. • Participants were asked to share their thoughts on the findings of the current study. • This interview occurred in one or two sessions.	2–4 hours

Data Analysis

The data were analyzed by using grounded theory. Grounded theory is useful when the concepts to explain a certain phenomenon have not been identified, when little is known about relations among concepts, when relevant and irrelevant variables for a certain phenomenon have not been specified, when theories for a certain phenomenon do not exist, or when existing theories need to be modified or clarified (Strauss & Corbin, 1998). The grounded theory approach appeared to be appropriate for this study as there is little research on Korean group counselors' developmental process. Grounded theory seemed to be useful in identifying new concepts to explain master group counselors' in Korea developmental process and finding relations among the concepts.

A content analysis was conducted by using the coding procedures suggested by Strauss and Corbin (1998). The data were analyzed in the order of open coding, axial coding, and selective coding. Open coding refers to the process of identifying and naming concepts through reading the raw data and categorizing related events, objects, and interactions together (Strauss & Corbin, 1998). This coding process occurred through continuous questioning and comparison. The properties and dimensions of categories were continuously refined through line-by-line coding. When a meaningful or interesting statement came up, it was given a concept label. Original words used by the participants were maintained when possible. The researcher interpreted the meaning of participants' statements and labeled concepts. An example of a concept label is shown below:

> That I experienced group counseling for the first time . . . and that I had found there what I had struggled to find for approximately 10 years of my youth . . . that is unforgettable. (Case 1)—Code: Intense First Group Counseling Experience

Axial coding systematically links the concepts that emerge from open coding and develops well-defined and dense categories. Axial coding reveals relationships among categories. The researchers conducted category analysis and developed a paradigm model that explains relationships among categories. Through the paradigm model, the researchers refined the categories to be more dense and found similarities and differences among the categories. Ideas or new discoveries during this process were recorded in memos or diagrams. Relationships among categories were checked repeatedly throughout continuous revisions. Using the coding paradigm described by Strauss and Corbin (1998), data were analyzed into conditions, context, action/interactional strategies and consequences. Main themes related to the characteristics of master group counselors were presented in the paradigm analysis.

In the initial labeling stage, the principal investigator and an experienced doctoral-level counselor, knowledgeable in grounded theory, coded the data independently. The researchers compared their coding results and developed the final concepts and categories collaboratively. Additionally, the results of the axial coding resulted in the development of a paradigm model that was then reviewed by an experienced qualitative researcher.

Such a review process took place repeatedly. To check whether the findings accurately reflected the participants' responses, the second and third follow-up interviews were conducted. Finally, the applicability of the results was assessed by two licensed group counselors.

Results

The open coding procedure produced a total of 65 concepts, 28 subcategories, and 13 categories that emerged from the data. Axial coding was performed by using a coding paradigm proposed by Strauss and Corbin (1998), which consists of conditions, context, action/interactional strategies, and consequences. As a result, a paradigm model was constructed as illustrated in Fig. 7.1. Through this paradigm model, this study investigated master group counselors' reasons for choosing group counseling as their clinical expertise, their experience of being immersed in the process of group counseling, situations that contributed to their expertise development, factors that influenced strategies for acquiring expertise, interactive strategies for growth, and exceptional expertise as the consequence.

MAIN THEMES OF THE CHARACTERISTICS OF THE MASTER GROUP COUNSELOR DEVELOPMENT

Based on the proposed paradigm model above, nine themes emerged as follows: (1) reasons for choosing group counseling, (2) phenomenon of being immersed in group counseling, (3) mentors, (4) frustrations and coping, (5) contributions of pain, (6) deficiency and anxiety, (7) strategies for growth, (8) personal characteristics, and (9) professional characteristics (Box 7.1).

Reasons for Choosing Group Counseling

One of the reasons the master group counselors chose group counseling as their area of specialty was their *intense first group counseling experience*. When the first experience with group counseling was either very enjoyable or shocking, the impact of such an experience appears to have a continuing effect on their development. In addition, master group counselors had *personal transformative experience through group counseling* and that such a transformative experience led to conviction and trust in the process of group counseling. Some participants chose group counseling as they experienced unique therapeutic effects of group counseling. As for *unique therapeutic factors of group counseling*, the participants mentioned universality, sense of belonging, the power of feedback and confrontations provided by the group leader and group members, experience of collaborating with others to help someone, and the ability of the group to bring dramatic changes in

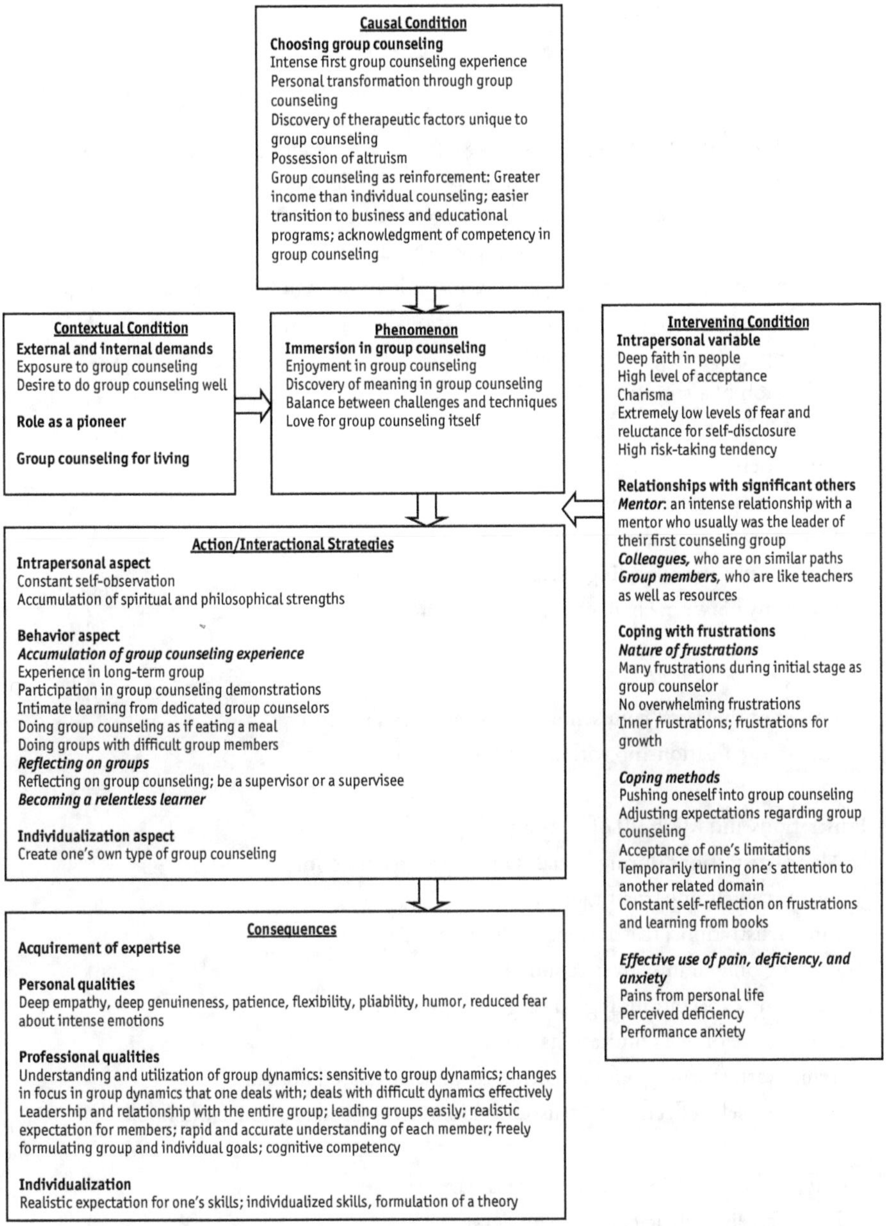

FIGURE 7.1 Paradigm model on the characteristics of master group counselors.

group members. Other incentives also affected their decision to choose group counseling as their professional specialty. Participants stated that *group counseling is more lucrative than individual counseling, group counseling can easily turn into educational or other programs,* and *the presence of reinforcements such as positive feedback about their competence as a group counselor* were important reasons for choosing group counseling. Altruistic

BOX 7.1

MAIN THEMES IN THE DEVELOPMENT OF MASTER GROUP COUNSELORS

Reasons for Choosing Group Counseling
- Intense first group counseling experience
- Personal transformation through group counseling
- Discovery of therapeutic factors unique to group counseling
- Group counseling as reinforcement: Greater income than individual counseling; easier transition to business and educational programs; acknowledgment of competency in group counseling
- Possession of altruism

Being Immersed in Group Counseling
- Enjoyment in group counseling
- Discovery of meaning in group counseling
- Love for group counseling itself
- Harmony between challenges and techniques

Mentors
- Leader of their first counseling group becomes a mentor
- An intense relationship with a mentor

Frustrations and Methods of Coping
- Many frustrations during initial stage as group counselor
- No overwhelming frustrations
- Inner frustrations; frustrations for growth
- Pushing oneself into group counseling
- Adjusting expectations regarding group counseling
- Acceptance of one's limitations
- Temporarily turning one's attention to another related domain
- Constant self-reflection on frustrations and continued learning from books

Positive Effects of Pain, Deficiency, and Anxiety
- Pain, perceived deficiency, and anxiety

Situations That Contributed to the Acquirement of Exceptional Expertise
- External and internal demands
- Role as a pioneer
- Group counseling for living

Strategies for Growth

- Participation in long-term group
- Participation in group counseling demonstrations
- Close learning from dedicated group counselors
- Doing group counseling consistently and frequently as if eating a meal
- Doing groups with difficult group members
- Constant self-observation
- Accumulation of spiritual and philosophical strengths
- Accumulation of group counseling experience
- Reflecting on group counseling; being a supervisor and a supervisee
- Becoming an endless lifelong learner
- Creating one's own style of group counseling

Personal Characteristics

- Very little fear and reluctance for self-disclosure
- Preference and striving for new and diverse experience
- High risk-taking tendency
- Having patience and not hurrying
- Deep faith in people
- High level of acceptance
- Deep empathy, deep genuineness, flexibility and pliability, sense of humor that processes burdens and pains of life productively, ability to reduce fear about intense emotions

Professional Characteristics

- Acquired sensitivity to see group dynamics
- Changes in their view on what are important group dynamics
- Deals with difficult dynamics effectively
- Has leadership and relationships with the entire group
- Easily and comfortably leads groups
- Freely formulates group and individual goals
- Extends group counseling as the solution for organizational, societal, and national issues
- Respects resistance
- Rapidly and accurately understands each member
- Cognitive competence: Great amount of information, integration of information, discerned application, great memory
- Has realistic expectation for one's skills
- Possesses individualized skills
- Formulates one's own counseling theory

motivation of wanting to share with others the positive experience they had with group counseling also played an important role in their inclination toward group counseling:

> It was more than just good. I was saved. My case was a bit extreme. In short, I spent away my younger days trying to find the meaning of life but couldn't find it. Then in my first group counseling—when I was 32 years old, I found it. The very thing I could not find in philosophy books or my studies was revealed to me through my experience in group counseling.
>
> Group helps me see myself and make changes better. Compared to individual counseling, group counseling does more to show who I am and help me realize ways to change myself little by little. It shows me ways to change how I am in more concrete ways than any religion or philosophy that I took interest, throughout my life.
>
> The greatest therapeutic factor of group counseling is feedback from the group. Compared to individual counseling, it gives extremely powerful feedback. In addition, in individual counseling, counselors deal with what the clients tell them. There, clients can have a defensive stance and hide themselves to a certain degree. But in group counseling, that doesn't work. You somehow end up revealing yourself.
>
> It's great that I get paid about 20–30% more when I do group counseling than other programs. That's a big incentive.

Being Immersed in Group Counseling

Master group counselors shared the experience of *being immersed in group counseling*. Four characteristics were observed under this theme. First, master group counselors enjoy group counseling. Second, they attribute special meanings to group counseling, which varies from group as an efficient method to a professional area worthwhile to make a whole commitment of their life. Third, they find meaning and satisfaction from group counseling. Fourth, they feel group counseling has challenges, but they are manageable and controllable.

> Group counseling was my life. I spent the golden days of my life doing group counseling. Most of my life's time . . . I don't mind spending the rest of my life for group counseling. That's the only thing I know how to do, and that's my only hobby. I can give everything up but that, I cannot.
>
> As I get older, group counseling is becoming more than rewarding. Group counseling is fun. There's nothing more fun than this.
>
> More than the outcome, the fact that I get to do such a meaningful work is simply a blessing in itself. The fact that I am at such a place . . . I'm the most alive there.
>
> It was an extremely difficult task for me. Expansion—that can be done through reading more books. But doing group counseling was a bit hard for me. But when

> I actually did it, and when it goes well at times, I felt good thinking to myself, "Hey, I'm able to do even this kind of stuff!"

Mentors

Master group counselors' mentors were often "leaders of groups they participated in during the earlier stages" of their counselor development. Their relationship continued on to become a lasting relationship and played as an important role model for life and group leadership. Master group counselors described their mentors as a parent, teacher, provider of emotional support, and an influential person in life's decisions. It was evident that master group counselors had "intense relationship experiences" with their mentors.

> My first group counseling was with Teacher ooo . . . . It lasted for two days, one night at ooo thermal spring resort. I think of him the most often. Whenever I do individual or group counseling, he gave me support, saying I did well. Sometimes we drink soju [Korean whiskey] together. Well, he doesn't drink that much now because of his diabetes. So recently, we just drink a glass or two. When I talk about counseling, he provides great support. I'm the most indebted to him in my journey of becoming a counselor. He always showed me trust and faith. I think whom you meet at your first group counseling is important.
>
> Meeting Teacher ooo, faith in Christianity, and counseling . . . these three things are like the Holy Trinity to me.

Frustrations and Coping Methods

In answering the question of whether master group counselors also experienced frustrations during their development, they reported that they had many frustrations when they were a novice group counselor. They underwent hardships due to their lack of counseling techniques, excessive expectations for group counseling or the group members, theories and techniques that were not yet internalized, and involuntary group members. At times, these hardships were too overwhelming that they would cry alone and ask themselves why they were doing group counseling. However, they *endured the process without getting too overwhelmed even though the frustrations were intense*. Gradually, the nature of their frustrations changed from external problems such as evaluation and difficult group members to internal ones such as questioning whether they are effectively managing their role as a group counselor.

> When I first began group counseling, these people were not motivated and unwilling to talk. They didn't open up, express their feelings, or give feedback to others. Running group with those kinds of people was so hard. I would go into my room and cry because it was so difficult at first.

> It's not that I didn't have any overwhelming problems. They were really about to overwhelm me, but I just could not let myself get overwhelmed.
>
> Personally, I didn't have that many frustrations coming from the outside. My biggest frustration was internal, whether I am mature enough to be a group counselor. That question made me feel endless frustration.

Master group counselors actively dealt with challenges by *pushing themselves even more deeply into group counseling*. For instance, one participant stated that he participated in long-term group counseling when he felt burdened by group counseling. Participants reported that many of their frustrations stem from excessive or inadequate expectations for group or group members. Gradually, master group counselors adjusted their level of expectations. In addition, they overcame challenges by "confronting and accepting their limitations." Some master group counselors reported that the *experience of turning attention to other counseling domains temporarily* gave greater depth and strength to their life as a group counselor. Master group counselors also indicated that they have *continually reflected on their frustrations, and used professional books to overcome difficulties.*

> I pushed myself even harder into the position that I had to do group counseling. I intentionally pushed myself to do the two and a half years of group counseling. It was like, let's try until it works out.
>
> I had this idea of how group should be, and I tried really hard to make that happen. So when that did not happen, I was dissatisfied—much more frequently than now. But not anymore! There are definitely more active groups as well as those that aren't so active. Now I would just openly acknowledge the situation and try to help each other find meaning behind such situations. That's how I do it now.
>
> I have limitations. I can make mistakes and do wrong, so there can be group members that might get disappointed at me. Basically, I don't have the illusion that I must be perfect as a leader. Just because some members are disappointed at me or that they are not fully healed does not mean that I am totally incompetent. I may be somewhat incompetent, and lack in some ways, but counselors should accept themselves as they are.
>
> I would just turn my eyes to other things. Like, science. My heart goes out to science. When I think too much about people, I get tired. It's hard. When I tell people that I relieve my stress through science, they laugh. But it really gives me rest. People are too complex. (Is science simple?) Oh, of course it's complex. But when I do science, I don't have to think about people. So it helps me to rest.

Positive Effects of Pain, Deficiency, and Anxiety from Personal Life

It was found that *pain, deficiency, and anxiety in their personal life* facilitated master group counselors' professional development and growth. In addition to the numerous trainings, clinical experience, and encounters with great mentors, these counselors also experienced various hardships of life, such as family conflicts, frustrations in family dynamics, and painful losses. Master group counselors reported that although they had wanted to avoid those hardships, these experiences actually had motivated them to become more deeply immersed within group counseling and helped them to understand their group members better. Participants stated that conflicts or difficulties with their family helped them discover some important aspects of themselves and formulate their own theories of group counseling. In addition, some participants stated that their continuous effort to integrate theory and practice and continued pursuit of training regarding group-counseling techniques was their way of coping with their deficiency or anxiety, rather than a conscious strategy to become a master counselor or to acquire expertise.

> I got married and for the first three years of my marriage, I lived that kind of life. I didn't go to work. So I thought about just going off to a rural area and live quietly without a child. My wife agreed at first, but then after a while she said she didn't want to go to a rural place. And then whenever my relatives gathered for national holidays, she would get upset that we didn't have children. My younger sibling had two kids. I'm the first son of eight children. She would get so mad at me and start a fight. [Laugh] I would fight back, of course. Before I got married, I thought I was so nice and gentle. But I realized that I am easily angered as well, and that I am pretty demanding toward my wife. I realized many of my limitations through marriage. Anyway, the fact that I saw my limits was a huge event for me as a group counselor. [Researchers' note: Overcoming coerciveness is considered very important in the individualized group counseling theory.]
>
> My family was strict and conservative. My mom in particular was very strict in educating her children since she had gone through Japanese-style education. In addition to the Confucian Korean culture, my mom's razor-sharp Japanese style had us grow up in a very stiff atmosphere. I didn't get much emotional support. My parents had big love for us, but that love did not get warmly expressed to us. Things had to be this and that way. I grew up with many do's and don'ts. . . . In Teacher OOO's group, I finally realized the value of my being after all those years of hearing things like "you can't do that." That's how I started counseling.
>
> Why do I try so hard to integrate theory and practice? Why do I struggle to explain? I must have something I am trying to control. You see, when I explain in words, I gain control. I probably have anxiety. I should just live the way my body wants to for once.
>
> I think to myself that when I meet someone who is in extreme pain, I can console that person only to the degree of pain I have experienced. In that sense, I think how I digest all the life's tasks—whether I wanted it or not—and pain is extremely critical.

Situations That Contributed to the Acquisition of Expertise

Both internal and external demands contributed to the master group counselors' expertise development. Master counselors entered group counseling with positive expectations that group counseling would be a good place for self-exploration and self-growth. However, external demands also played a role in developing expertise with group counseling. For instance, one participant reported a situation in which he had no choice other than leading a group. Interestingly, these external demands seemed to turn into internal desire at a certain point. In other words, even though these counselors may have started group counseling due to external factors, at some point they made an internal decision to consider group counseling as their specialty. For some, group counseling became a way to make a living, which contributed to their commitment to group counseling. Finally, their role as a pioneer in Korean group counseling seemed to have facilitated their expertise in the field.

> My eyes opened up a bit more to group counseling. That's when I came to this field and got stuck here. In my case, situations worked out well and the timing was good. It was almost like you just end up doing group no matter what. Well, once I was in, I wanted to do well. External demands don't remain forever. At some point, it turns into strong internal needs, and that's how I can go on.
>
> If you fail one group counseling session, your money's gone. People stop coming to you. It's always a life and death matter. If I don't solve problems that come up during a group counseling session with concrete skills, it's hard for me to make a living.
>
> When I was going around company trainings to give lectures, OOO asked me to run a sensitivity training. But back then, no one in Korea knew how to do it. Then I came across Dr. OOO, who had experienced group counseling in the United States. So I went to him and asked if he could help facilitate the group. He wanted to participate as a member instead. He said he didn't get trained to be a facilitator so he wouldn't do it. I said, "But you are the only one in Korea who has done it. What can we do?" He finally said he would do it if I came in as a helper since he doesn't know anything about the company. So, on the condition that I let him in the company training, I went in as a helper when I knew nothing about what it meant to be a group facilitator. I had never done group counseling before.

Strategies for Growth

Master group counselors employed various strategies to acquire expertise. Among them, accumulating group-counseling experience was the most time- and energy-consuming strategy. All five participants had participated in a long-term counseling group that lasted more than two years as either a group leader or group member. Another noteworthy strategy was *participation in group counseling demonstrations as a group leader and groups that are open to public for observation as a group member*, through which they were able to affirm their counselor identity and grow further as a group counselor. They also had an *intense learning experience with another group counselor who had devoted their entire life to group counseling*. One participant stated that he "did group counseling as often as eating a meal" and had "copious experience with involuntary group members."

> For two years and a half, group counseling proved to be a positive asset and I really liked my group members then. They were really motivated. Of course, there were several who weren't. You know, people tend to have their own fantasies about such a group, and they sometimes enjoy it. But all in all, the process wasn't easy at all. You would need that kind of process in order to become an expert. It will take an experience of being totally immersed for a certain duration of time.
>
> They did demonstrations at OOO University three times. When I participated in all three, everyone who is considered good at group counseling in Korea demonstrated their group counseling three times in public. When I saw them demonstrate, I realized that there weren't huge difference between those people and me. Sometimes, I felt that I would be much sharper than them. Seeing that, I realized that I don't really have to be so low in confidence. That really gave me strength.
>
> When I think about my relationship with my advisor, it was something like an apprenticeship. Back then, he didn't have that many students under him. So he took me everywhere he went and made me participate. And at some point, he let me even lead his group. So I saw group counseling run since I was really young.
>
> It has been almost six years since I have been just doing only group counseling. Ever since 1972, I spent about three to four months a year in a group. If I were to count everyone who I have worked together in a three-nights-four-days group, it will probably reach about 15,000. The time I spent in group counseling is longer than the time I spent with my wife after getting married.
>
> In my group, there were difficult people who didn't want to be in a group. They were there because they had to. They were upset at just being there. Not because there was something wrong with the group, but because they were told that they had problems that needed to get fixed. . . . I did group counseling with all different kinds of people.

Participants identified *continuous self-observation* and *accumulation of spiritual and philosophical strength* as fundamental to acquiring their expertise. They valued self-reflection and reflection on their group work. It appeared that the master group counselors used an immediate *reflection-in-action* method to continuously reflect on themselves as well as their interventions for group work. As for their limitations, master group counselors addressed their *lack of systematic supervision experience*, stating that they got involved with group counseling when it was first introduced in Korea.

Nonetheless, these master group counselors appeared to be *relentless learners* who continuously engaged in learning and *strived to create their own group counseling style.*

> An important thing is counselor's self-exploration. You can only see in others as much as you see in yourself. When you run group counseling, you need to observe more people than individual counseling, so it's actually quite harder and busier. So if you are not sensitive enough . . . you need to look at many people, not just one member. So you need to divide your energy. You need to focus here, but also need to read other people's reactions. I had to utilize all those different skill sets—isn't that self-exploration?
>
> I feel like I didn't study that hard when I studied counseling. After quitting OOO University, I studied Buddhism. For three years, I just had my psychology book open and moved around elsewhere. And Teacher OOO told me that if you don't get to study abroad after two trials, then at least come to OOO. I thought if I go abroad, my Buddhist mindset will become stagnant again. And I thought about spending several years just reading books. I thought, "Do I really need to endure those years and study counseling?" Those were my concerns. . . . I thought a lot about the fact that I am a person before I am a counselor. Actually, I did not really live up to my expectation. So it's really embarrassing to talk about these things.
>
> There is a fixed evaluations sheet kind of thing. So even though I don't get formal evaluations group-wise, I always look back at the sheet. I evaluate myself all the time. For example, I check to see if I skipped working with the group member because I was concerned about potential resistance.
>
> I actually think my big weakness is that I wasn't really supervised systematically. Back then, we didn't really have experts who could actually supervise. Group counselors were even rarer at my school or counseling center.
>
> It was just really fun to find out more efficient ways for solving life's problems. It may sound obvious, but a good learner would not hold on to the old ways when there is a more efficient way. That is not how a conscientious counselor should be. Another thing is that I have greed for new stuff. As OOO said, I am still anxious to learn.
>
> I constantly want to create my own thoughts these days. I want to find my own stuff—that way, "self" can be created. It's boring to constantly talk about someone else's story. I guess I want to do things through my own voice. But it's sad that it becomes a fiction on one hand. When I talk about the Circle (an integrative model of counseling), I want to verify each part of the model—what is it exactly? What are the experiences that provide such things? If I offer A, does B really happen? Now that there is a model, I want to see it unfold in reality.

Personal Characteristics

Master group counselors had *very little fear and reluctance toward self-disclosure.* This seems to be the case because group counseling is conducted in the presence of many people, and the group counselor frequently needs to use himself as a tool to run the group. They expressed their *liking for new and diverse experience* or at least they tried to pursue such experiences. They also appeared to have high risk-taking tendency and were *an expert at waiting* patiently.

> I am free and honest. I am honest because I am free. Because of that, group members participate being more honest as well. As much I feel comfortable and honest in my group, the group atmosphere, too, becomes that way and members open up comfortably. So that probably works as a therapeutic factor. I personally consider that part of me as a strength as a counselor—as a group counselor. Sometimes I think to myself perhaps I am too honest.
>
> It is easier to choose clients when doing individual counseling. Nonetheless, we can still choose members for group counseling as well. We usually go through a screening process. Nevertheless, there are many times when we cannot do screening. For instance, an entire group may be referred, and this actually happens quite often. Therefore, group leaders should be able to deal with all kinds of personalities, pathologies, and disabilities. Relatively speaking, group counselors need to have greater ability to take in more variety.
>
> I keep throwing myself into difficult situations. I tell myself, "This is a good thing!" And keep throwing myself into these situations even when I get scared at times. I also feel ambivalent about doing demonstrations. It's a more intense situation than just teaching. I want to keep throwing myself into challenging situations so I can continue to grow. Get yelled at for things I did wrong or messed up. It's more like "Let's see how I deal with difficult situations" than "Let's see how well I do."
>
> Do group counselors really wait? I don't think so. It's more like watching for the right moment, and that's not right. Watching for the right moment is not waiting. Giving more time alone does not mean waiting. It's really being with that person. *That* is waiting.

All of the participants possessed *deep faith in people, high level of acceptance, empathy, sincerity*, and *flexibility with time and counseling approaches*. Many of them did not think they were a humorous person but that they actually had the *wit to productively process the pains and burdens of group counseling*. They also showed *relatively low fear for varied intense emotions.*

> In the beginning, when I was in my early thirties and participated in group counseling as a member, I would look at the faces of other members and think to myself, "How can I spend three nights and four days with those kinds of people?" I considered them insignificant. But then as the group counseling continued, I came to realize that one human being is just amazing, so precious, and functioning well in his

own way. Also, in group counseling, you become more popular the more you talk bad about yourself. Hearing other people's problems made me value them more, because these people are trying to accept their problems and live well. Then you realize how precious the grass and trees in the field are. . . . You feel grateful that you exist in this universe. You realize you exist because they exist. You can be less lonely because they exist. You start expressing gratitude to others.

Someone told me that I am very accepting. I guess that's a compliment. Helping clients accept themselves 120%. But it's not enough just to make them accept themselves well. You need to help clients to affirm who they are as a person.

Genuinely deep empathy means accepting the person as a whole while listening to him talk. Once the ability to take in [another's] life is obtained, everything grows, you can truly empathize. It's not just taking in feelings.

I don't try to be funny intentionally. When people are so fixed on one thought, I just look at that from a whole new perspective. When people laugh at my "humor," they are not just laughing because my humor was funny. It's sort of like a laugh of enlightenment. . . . And when the whole group is tensed up, I don't try to break the tension by being funny. I just give my honest feedback, and it appears to be humorous.

I experienced such diverse groups with so many people that when someone expresses some emotion or problem, it's familiar to me and I can easily understand from their situation.

Professional Characteristics

The most remarkable professional characteristic of master group counselors was their *ability to deeply understand and effectively use the group dynamics*. As their expertise matured, their *eyes became more sensitive toward group dynamics*, and *group dynamics that they focus on have changed*. In addition, they *became more adept at dealing with difficult group dynamics*. Effective individual counselors also have the skills to form strong relationships with clients, but master group counselors appeared to have developed an additional *ability to build relationships with the group as a whole and to facilitate relationships among group members*. Master group counselors reported that they were anxious about group counseling as a novice group counselor, but as time passed, they were able to gain a *comfortable and light attitude toward leading groups*. In addition, they now *freely formulate individual and group goals*. They even *extended group counseling as a solution to organizational, societal, and national issues*.

I can see the dynamics of the group—I can see very detailed, very minute flows or processes within the group. I guess that's the best part—that I can see such things now. I can pick out themes that can be dealt meaningfully within the group more than I did before. I become more accepting and more sensitive, as if my eyes have become a microscope.

In individual counseling, the role of an empathizer or acceptor is very important. In group counseling, you also need to play the role of a mediator, participant, or confronter. In other words, you need counseling skills and coaching skills, as well as leadership skills. The counselor needs to be extremely experienced, because with group counseling, you never know who will be talking about what a minute later. If there are 15 participants, one facilitator must be able to feel the feelings that 15 participants are feeling, and then be able to keep his composure on top of that.

It was hard when trusting relationships were not formed. But now I don't make a big deal out of that. Now I say, "It's natural that we don't feel close. It's natural that we can't trust each other. It's natural that you are fearful now. That is all natural. Let's say we are afraid when we are. Let's say 'I'm still awkward.' " I wasn't like this before. Back then, I wanted people to open up quickly and that's why it was hard for me.

I think I can set goals more quickly now. I believe this is very important. I form the shape and size of goals that can actually be achieved, considering the person's context and life. That is so important. A novice counselor who becomes an expert counselor? I think that's possible when I see myself now.

Although our nation is divided into north and south, it will become unified one day. I don't think there is any better way to recover our nation's cultural homogeneity than group counseling.

These master group counselors respected resistance and considered it as an important element for group work. They emphasized that *quick and accurate understanding of each individual* is needed for effective group leadership. Master group counselors also showed cognitive competency. They seemed to have the ability to *process great amounts of information*, to integrate various kinds of information, and to use the information differentially, as well as possess a *terrific memory*. Ultimately, master group counselors seem to have developed toward individuation, which is characterized by their *realistic expectations about one's abilities, individualized and specialized skills*, and *formulation of one's own counseling theory*.

Respecting resistance is important, but resistance is definitely "data." How we like another person shows the nature of the interpersonal relationship. At the same time, resistance is also a very illuminating evidence of what the relationship is like. Respect? Sure. But it's more like data. It's more than just "an important tool." Without it, what do we work with?

I believe understanding one individual as opposed to understanding group dynamics is very different. Oh, you need to first figure out what the dynamics are like—or what is really going on in the group process. And to do so, you need to be able to understand each individual first.

In the old days, I would come home after doing group counseling all day and lie down in my bed at night and recover everything that had happened in the group that day. I had gone through image training, so I would just replay my group as if I were watching a movie. I think, back then, I was able to recover every word exchanged within the group. Through that, I would be able to figure out the characteristics of my group members. That is not just good memory—that requires great concentration.

Time to time, when you seem to have come across an unsolvable problem, it is good to have few of your own "secret methods" that frequently work well for you. For me it's di-identification method, body-focused methods, and experiential methods.

Discussion

The current study investigated personal and professional characteristics of master group counselors in Korea, identified facilitating and impeding factors, and major strategies in the process of expertise development. The findings on master group counselors are compared with the results from existing studies on counselor characteristics. In addition, several recommendations are offered for training and research in the Korean group counseling context.

Most of research on counselor characteristics and counselor development has focused on individual counseling. Thus, our findings on master group counselors were compared with individual counselors' development and characteristics. Finding a precise dividing line between the characteristics of group counselors and those of individual counselors is not possible because they both are grounded in the common identity of a counselor. However, certain characteristics seem to be more emphasized for group counselors. For the comparison, three studies that examined the characteristics of individual counselors in the later developmental stages were used. The comparison studies are Jennings and Skovholt's (1999) study on master counselors, Goldberg's (1992) study on seasoned psychotherapists, and Albert's (1997) study on professional counselors.

Master counselors in both areas show flexibility and sensitivity. They also have similar cognitive and relational characteristics. Regarding cognitive attributes, both individual and group counseling experts were relentless learners with accumulated experiences in counseling. Master group counselors in the current study showed high cognitive abilities. Similar to master counselors in individual counseling and their cognitive complexity, master group counselors showed abilities to process enormous amounts of information, integrate different pieces of information, pull out relevant information, utilize the information differentially, and possessed a good memory. Considering emotional characteristics, master counselors in both individual and group counseling had high emotional receptivity. In regard to relational characteristics, both individual and group master counselors have strong relationship skills and use these skills to build a therapeutic working alliance. They are able to empathize with others deeply and do not fear intense emotions.

Some characteristics were unique to master group counselors. Little fear and resistance were critical characteristics of the master group counselors. Although this is true for individual counseling experts, the comfort of self-disclosure seems to be more emphasized in master group counselors. This may be related to the open and revealing nature of group counseling, where counseling is conducted in the presence of multiple group members. Master group counselors in this study utilized themselves as an important instrument within the group and were open about their mistakes or weaknesses. Such attitude appears to influence the atmosphere of their group. The master group counselors' openness and comfort for self-disclosure is also shown in their willingness to demonstrate their group work in front of others for training purposes.

Master group counselors showed eagerness for new learning and experiences. This seems to be similar to master individual counselors' appreciation for the ambiguity of the human condition (Jennings & Skovholt, 1999). Because group counselors work with group members with a variety of characteristics, this reinforces the master group counselors' interest in and pursuit of new learning and experiences.

Compared to master counselors in individual counseling, a high risk-taking tendency was emphasized in master group counselors. This may be related to the therapeutic characteristic of a group format where trying new behaviors is encouraged. Group counselors often employ experiments as a vital intervention technique. Often times, group counselors need to take a risk when dealing with unpredictable and daring processes.

There are some unique skills required for group counselors. For instance, group counselors should be able to understand the entire group beyond individual clients, as well as recognize and utilize group dynamics. Such tasks are challenging even for master group counselors and can only be achieved through countless clinical experiences and learning. With increased experience, group counselors appear to build a more delicate sense for group dynamics and learn to effectively deal with difficult dynamics. The ability to see and deal with group dynamics was emphasized by master group counselors. Understandably, this focus on group dynamics differentiates group counseling from individual counseling expertise.

Both group and individual counseling experts show excellent skills in building relationships and utilizing them therapeutically. However, group counselors are expected to have more complex relationship skills, such as skills in facilitating interactions among group members and building a. . .group-as-a-whole relationship. This is often called effective leadership or charisma—the relational competence that can positively affect the entire group.

Several factors appeared to facilitate the expertise development of master group counselors: *mentors; intense first group counseling experience; personal transformation through group counseling; discovery of therapeutic factors of group counseling; altruism; group counseling as reinforcement; frustrations of group counseling and methods for coping; effective use of pain, deficiencies, and anxiety from personal life; external and internal demands; role as a pioneer*; and *group counseling for living.*

Hindrances in the expertise development of Korean master group counselors were the lack of systematic supervision and that early frustrations as group counselors were quite intense. The lack of supervision was an inevitable limitation faced by the first or second generation of group counselors in Korea. Due to the lack of systematic group counseling training programs that would prepare novice group counselors for developmental challenges, the Korean group counselors may have experienced their early frustrations more intensely.

Main strategies for growth chosen by Korean master group counselors were *participating in long-term group counseling of more than two years, participating in group counseling demonstrations and groups that are open to public for observation, engage in an intense learning experience with another group counselor who has given their entire life up for group counseling, did group counseling as often as eating a meal, lead numerous group counseling with difficult group members, engage in constant self-exploration, accumulate religious and philosophical strengths, reflect on group, become a voracious learner*, and *create my kind of group counseling*. These numerous strategies do not appear to be intentional efforts but seem to have occurred naturally during their immersion within group counseling. Such strategies are consistent with the strategies for professional development proposed by many group counseling experts from outside of Korea (Corey & Corey, 2000; Yalom, 1995).

The fact that all five participants had experienced long-term groups that lasted more than two years is remarkable. Through this experience, the master group counselors were able to witness the continuous process of group development and actual changes in group members, and develop a deeper understanding of the group. In addition, their participation in group counseling demonstrations and groups that are open to public for observation are unique to Korea. The master group counselors indicated that involvement in such groups was helpful as they received concrete feedback regarding their expertise and gained confidence as group counseling experts.

The *immersion in group counseling* phenomenon is the core phenomenon in the paradigm model of this study (Strauss & Corbin, 1998) and considered as the basis for many characteristics of master group counselors. Several points can be discussed regarding this phenomenon. Some of the reasons why the master group counselors became immersed in group counseling are consistent with the core components of counselor training, which includes experience of increased self-understanding and change, observation and modeling of an exceptional counselor's practice, and supervision that provides feedback on one's counseling style. It is notable that group counseling is an effective method that provides all these experiences at once. Another probable reason for their commitment to group counseling may be that they had a critical experience in group counseling. In particular, intense group counseling experiences as a group member during their beginning stage of development offered them an opportunity to witness how group counseling can change people including themselves. Such experiences appeared to have served to formulate goals for their own groups and given them the strength to persevere even in the face of frustrations and failures.

The master group counselors' immersion experience in group counseling appears to be similar to the state of "flow" (Csikszentmihalyi, 1990). Csikszentmihalyi's flow consists of nine elements: a balance between challenges and skills, clear goals, immediate feedback, focused concentration on the task, a sense of control, merge between action and awareness, loss of self-consciousness, an altered perception of time, and "auto telic" experience. According to Csikszentmihalyi, flow is defined as the optimal experiences that can occur when one focuses on a certain activity and the individual experiences feelings of enjoyment and self-fulfillment in the process. In fact, the master group counselors appeared to experience joy and self-fulfillment through group counseling. In addition to the four subcategories within the immersion experience of master group counselors (*enjoyment in group counseling, discovery of meaning in group counseling, harmony between challenges and techniques*, and *love for group counseling itself*), five elements of flow are also shown in the master group counselors.

First, in regard to immediate feedback, master group counselors seemed to receive immediate and concrete feedback regarding their work from their group members or organizations/corporations that had referred the group to the counselor. Such feedback served as reinforcement that had them continue group counseling. Second, these master group counselors showed a high level of concentration in group. While in group, the focus of their concentration appears to be limited to group counseling, and any unrelated thoughts, worries, or concerns are blocked from their awareness. Third, having a sense of control and confidence when faced with difficult situations seemed to be critical for counselors in bringing out positive counseling outcomes. Fourth, as one participant stated, the process of overcoming self-consciousness is a critical part of developing expertise. In the state of flow where people function at their optimal level, they invest all of their attention to the activity being performed, but do not pay attention to themselves. Fifth, master group counselors seemed to consider group counseling as an "auto telic" experience; group counseling became an activity that is as intrinsically rewarding, especially as they reached the latter stages of expertise development.

Csikszentmihalyi, Rathunde, and Whaleden (1993) assert that flow is not only related to individuals' current interest but also serves as a source of new goals. Thus, the master group counselors' skills and interests are prerequisites for experiencing flow in group and the flow in turn creates more conviction and affection for group counseling. In addition, the flow experience with group facilitates group counselors to seek goals that are more challenging and to experience enjoyment by achieving those goals. In that sense, the flow or an immersion experience in group counseling can be considered a core phenomenon, the prerequisite for expertise development, and a developmental strategy that generates higher goals.

IMPLICATIONS FOR TRAINING

Several practical suggestions can be made for training and supervision. First, training programs should provide information on the importance of early group counseling experiences and help them to gain positive experiences. Novice group counselors should be cautious when joining their first group counseling, and training programs should find experienced group counselors for leading training groups given the importance of early group experience. Second, participation in long-term group counseling is encouraged for future group counselors. Experiencing long-term group counseling as either a group leader or a member was identified as an effective way to facilitate master group counselors' growth as a group counselor. Third, mentorship or apprenticeship with an experienced group counselor is recommended. The master group counselors in this study advised novice counselors to find a group counselor who fits well with them and learn closely from the person for a few years after they obtained a basic understanding of what group counseling is. Fourth, graduate and internship programs should identify common challenges that novice group counselors experience and provide systematic supervision and support. Fifth, the value of spiritual and philosophical reflection should be emphasized to a greater degree in counseling training. Spiritual and philosophical reflection is often dismissed due to the difficulty in measuring the outcome. Yet, master group counselors' qualities such as deep trust in human beings, high acceptance, and empathy seemed to largely stem from their spiritual and philosophical contemplation. Sixth, the ability to adequately adjust expectations for group counseling and group members was an important characteristic of master group counselors. Thus, along with the efforts to add and build more skills and knowledge, group counselors should also learn how excessive expectations could interfere with effective group leadership. Seventh, group counseling training should teach different types of group dynamics as well as skills to deal with important group dynamics. Group counselors are distinct from individual counselors in many ways, but the most definite difference is that group counselors should, of course, understand and utilize group dynamics. Eighth, there should be a focus on both further development and accessibility in regard to supervision and practice opportunities for group counselors. Compared to supervision for individual counseling, supervision for group counseling is less developed. Research on supervisees' needs and the effective formats within group counseling is needed. Furthermore, training groups for experienced group counselors would be useful. Through training groups, group counselors can continue to grow as a group counselor and maintain their competency.

LIMITATIONS AND FUTURE RESEARCH

This study also has some limitations. First, the current study utilized retrospective data. Retrospective data have an advantage of illuminating more meaningful past experiences. However, some information may have been forgotten or distorted due to the passage of time. Future research should use different types or sources of data, such as observations and group members' report. Second, the current study focused on master group counselors who have already acquired expertise. Further study on the developmental processes of group counselors by using a longitudinal study design is recommended. Third, this study was conducted with five group counselors who were nominated as the best of the best by fellow counselors regardless of their theoretical orientation, clinical settings, and clientele. Future research is recommended to explore master group counselors' attributes by theoretical orientation, clinical settings, and different client populations.

Note

1. This chapter is a revised version of Kwon, K., & Kim, C. (2007). The analysis on the characteristics of Korean master group counselor. *Korean Journal of Counseling, 8*, 979–1010. Adapted with permission from the Korean Counseling Association.

References

Albert, G. (1997). What are the characteristics of effective psychotherapist? The experts speak. *Journal of Practical Psychology and Behavioral Health, 3*, 36–44.

Anastasi, A., & Urbina, S. (1997). *Psychological testing* (7th ed.). Englewood Cliffs, NJ: Prentice-Hall.

Baltes, P. B., Reese, H. W., & Lippsitt, L. P. (1980). Life-span developmental psychology. *Annual Review of Psychology, 31*, 65–110.

Berry, G. W., & Sipps, G. J. (1991). Interactive effects of counselor–client similarity and client self-esteem on termination type and number of sessions. *Journal of Counseling Psychology, 38*, 120–125.

Beulter, L. E., Machado, P. P., & Neufeldt, S. A. (1994). Therapist variables. In S. L. Garfied & A. E. Bergin (Eds.), *Handbook of psychotherapy and behavior change* (4th ed., pp. 229–268). New York, NY: Wiley.

Blocher, D. H. (1993). Toward a cognitive developmental approach to counseling supervision. *The Counseling Psychologist, 11*(1), 27–34.

Cantor, D. W. (1991). Women as therapists: What we already know. In D. W. Cantor (Ed.), *Women as therapists: A multitheoretical casebook* (pp. 3–19). New York, NY: Springer.

Chi, M. T. H., Glaser, R., & Farr, M. J. (1988). *The nature of expertise*. Hillsdale, NJ: Erlbaum.

Cole, D. A., & White, K. (1993). Structure of peer impression of children's competencies: Validation of the peer nomination of multiple competencies. *Psychological Assessment, 5*, 449–456.

Corey, M. S., & Corey, G. (2000). *Group: Process and practice* (5th ed.; M. K. Kim, C. D. Kim, A. S. Park, J. G. Jeon, & S. M. Chun, Trans.). Seoul, South Korea: Sigma Press.

Csikszentmihalyi, M. (1990). *Flow: The psychology of optimal experience*. New York, NY: Harper & Row.

Csikszentmihalyi, M., Rathunde, K., & Whaleden, S. (1993). *Talented teenagers: The roots of success and failure*. New York, NY: Cambridge University Press.

Cummings, A. L., Hallberg, E. T., Martin, J., Slemon, A., & Hiebert, B. (1990). Implications of counselor conceptualizations for counselor education. *Counselor Education and Supervision, 30*, 120–134.

Fleming, J. (1953). The role of supervision in psychiatric training. *Bulletin of the Menninger Clinic, 17*, 157–159.

Goldberg, C. (1992). *The seasoned psychotherapist*. New York, NY: Norton.

Guba, E. G., & Lincoln, Y. S. (1981). *Effective evaluation*. San Francisco, CA: Jossey-Bass.

Harrington, K. M. (1988). *Personal characteristics of diplomates defined as master therapist*. Unpublished doctoral dissertation, University of Minnesota, Minneapolis, MN.

Hess, A. K. (1987). Psychotherapy supervision: Stages, Buber and theory of relationship. *Professional Psychology: Theory, Research, and Practice, 18*, 251–259.

Hill, C. E., Charles, D., & Reed, K. G. (1981). A longitudinal analysis of counseling skills during doctoral training in counseling psychology. *Journal of Counseling Psychology, 28*, 428–436.

Hill, C. E., & O' Grady, K. E. (1985). List of therapist intentions illustrated in a case study and with therapists of varying theoretical orientations. *Journal of Counseling Psychology, 32*, 3–22.

Hillerbrand, E. T., & Claiborn, C. D. (1990). Examining reasoning skill differences between expert and novice counselors. *Journal of Counseling and Development, 68*, 684–691.

Hogan, R. A. (1964). Issues and approaches in supervision. *Psychotherapy: Theory, Research and Practice, 1*, 139–141.

Holloway, E. L., & Wampold, B. E. (1986). Relation between conceptual level and counseling-related tasks: A meta-analysis. *Journal of Counseling Psychology, 33*, 310–319.

Horvath, A. O., & Greenberg, L. S. (1989). Development and validation of the Working Alliance Inventory. *Journal of Counseling Psychology, 56*, 885–892.

Jackson, M., & Thompson, C. L. (1971). Effective counselor: Characteristics and attitudes. *Journal of Counseling Psychology, 18*, 249–254.

Jennings, L., & Skovholt, T. M. (1999). Cognitive, emotional, and relational characteristics of master therapists. *Journal of Counseling Psychology, 46*, 3–11.

Kim, D. M., Wampold, B. E., & Bolt, D. M. (2006). Therapist effects in psychotherapy: A random effects modeling of NIMH TDCRP data. *Psychotherapy Research, 16*(2), 161–172.

Kim, K. H. (2000). *Research in counseling psychology*. Seoul, South Korea: Hakjisa.

Lee, H. D., Kim, S. H., Seol, K. M., Kim, C. D., & Kim, J. H. (2002). *Group counseling*. Seoul, South Korea: Jungang Aptitude Press.

Lee, J. H., & Kim, J. H. (1998). *Foundations of group counseling*. Seoul, South Korea: Bopmunsa.

Loganbill, C., Hardy, E., & Delworth, U. (1982). Supervision: A conceptual model. *The Counseling Psychologist, 10*(1), 3–42.

Luborsky, L., McLellan, T. A., Woody, G. E., O'Brien, C. P., & Auerbach, A. (1985). Therapist success and its determinants. *Archive of General Psychiatry, 42*, 602–611.

Martin, J., Selmon, A. G., Hiebert, B., Hallberg, E. T., & Cummings A. L. (1989). Conceptualization of novice and experienced counselors. *Journal of Counseling Psychology, 36*, 395–400.

Miller, A. (1993). Who are the best psychotherapist? *Psychotherapy in Private Practice, 12*, 1–18.

Patton, M. Q. (1990). *Qualitative evaluation and research methods* (2nd ed.). Newbury Park, CA: Sage.

Propst, L. R. (1980). The comparative efficacy of religious and nonreligious imagery for the treatment of mild depression in religious individuals. *Cognitive Therapy and Research, 4*, 167–178.

Schwebel, M., & Coster, J. (1998). Well-functioning in professional psychologists: As program heads see it. *Professional Psychology: Research and Practice, 29*(3), 284–292.

Serbin, L. A., Lyons, J. A., Marchessault, K., Schartzman, A. E., & Ledingham, J. E. (1987). Observational validation of a peer nomination technique for identifying aggressive, withdrawn, and aggressive/withdrawn children. *Journal of Counseling and Clinical Psychology, 55*, 109–110.

Skovholt, T. M., & Jennings, L. (2004). *Master therapists: Exploring expertise in therapy and counseling*. New York, NY: Pearson.

Skovholt, T. M., & McCarthy, P. R. (1998). Critical incidents: Catalysts for counselor development. *Journal of Counseling and Development, 67*(2), 69–72.

Skovholt, T. M., & Rønnestad, M. H. (1992). Themes in therapist and counselor development. *Journal of Counseling and Development, 70*, 505–515.

Skovholt, T. M., & Rønnestad, M. H. (1995). *The evolving professional self: Stages and themes in therapist and counselor development*. New York, NY: Wiley.

Stoltenberg, C. D., & Delworth, U. (1987). *Supervising counselors and therapists: A developmental approach*. San Francisco, CA: Jossey-Bass.

Strauss, A., & Corbin, J. (1998). *Basics of qualitative research: Grounded theory procedures and techniques* (2nd ed.). Thousand Oaks, CA: Sage.

Wampold, B. E. (2007). *Evidence based practice. Invitational workshop presentation*. Seoul–Gyeonggi–Incheon Counseling Association.

Wampold. B. E., & Brown, G. S. (2006). Estimating variability in outcomes attributable to therapists: A naturalistic study of outcomes in managed care. *Journal of Consulting and Clinical Psychology, 73*(5), 914–923.

Wicas, E. A., & Mahan, T. W. (1966). Characteristics of counselors rated effective by supervisors and peers. *Counselor Education and Supervision, 6*, 50–56.

Worthington, E. L., Jr. (1984). An empirical investigation of supervision of counselors as they gain experience. *Journal of Counseling Psychology, 31*, 63–75.

Yalom, I. D. (1995). *The theory and practice of group psychotherapy* (4th ed.). New York, NY: Basic Books.

Yogev, S. (1982). An eclectic model of supervision: A developmental sequence for beginning psychotherapy students. *Professional Psychology, 13*, 236–243.

8 Bringing It All Together

A QUALITATIVE META-ANALYSIS OF SEVEN MASTER THERAPISTS STUDIES FROM AROUND THE WORLD

Len Jennings, Ashley Sovereign, Salina Renninger, Michael Goh, Thomas M. Skovholt, Sharada Lakhan, and Heather Hessel

MUCH OF THE research exploring therapist factors and psychotherapy expertise reviewed in Chapter 1 has been restricted to a few countries, most frequently the United States. However, within the past decade, some quantitative studies, such as Orlinsky and Rønnestad's (2005) study of nearly 4000 therapists worldwide, are adding to our knowledge of therapist factors from an international perspective. With this ongoing study, current data collection is at 12,000 participants (M. H. Rønnestad, personal communication, May 30, 2015). Another large study is the N = 100 qualitative study of counselor/therapist development (Rønnestad & Skovholt, 2013; Skovholt & Rønnestad, 1992). A major limitation of both of these studies is the focus on normative professional development. Here, in Chapters 2–7 in this book, a crop of qualitative studies have followed the general format and methodology of the Jennings and Skovholt (1999) study to learn about master therapists in countries other than the United States.

In this concluding chapter, we share the results of a qualitative meta-analysis (QMA) on the seven studies that were presented in the previous six chapters and one in the Appendix. As a synopsis, we briefly highlight each of the original studies here. Jennings and Skovholt (1999) interviewed 10 peer-nominated master therapists and developed the cognitive, emotional, and relational (CER) model of master therapists. In 2007, Kwon and Kim interviewed a set of peer-nominated counselors in Korea who specialized in group counseling, and they created a model of group counselor development as well as described many efficacious personal and professional characteristics of these master group counselors. Smith (2008) explored the general characteristics of peer-nominated master couple therapists in Canada. Smith's research identified three themes for this population: personal development and self, professional development, and relationships. In 2010, Hirai focused on understanding the characteristics and attitudes toward professional influences of master therapists in Japan. Hirai organized the results into 18 themes within five categories: cultivating abundant learning opportunities, perceptive understanding of self and clients, effective intervention, relationship-building with clients, and therapist's humility. In Portugal, Carvalho and Matos (2011a, 2011b) used semistructured interviews to collect data from peer-nominated master therapists on a variety of themes, including professional development, professional motivation, attitudes on therapeutic change, and the intersection of the personal and professional life. Carvalho and Matos' "core story" described the development of a therapist "as a progressive process of searching for consistency and coherence between personal and professional experiences" (p. 29). Řiháček, Kahancová, Jennings, Roubal, and Vybíral (2015) studied nine Czech master therapists using the same methodology and interview questions as those used in the study by Jennings and Skovholt (1999). The authors organized 16 themes within six categories: humble attitude toward mastery, clients, and colleagues; relationship; awareness of one's needs, limits, and resources; continuous development; engagement; and awareness of the complexity of psychotherapeutic work. For a detailed summary of each study, see Table 8.1.

Significance

In addition to the studies just mentioned, Jennings and colleagues (2008) explored the personal characteristics of Singapore master therapists and conducted one of the first QMAs in counseling psychology, comparing Singaporean and US master therapists (see Chapter 5). Jennings et al.'s QMA revealed a significant overlap between the US and Singaporean characteristics of peer-nominated master therapists, suggesting a rich area for further exploration of common-core characteristics. The current study extends this line of research by using qualitative methods to create a QMA including research from Jennings and Skovholt (1999), Kwon and Kim (2007), Jennings et al. (2008), Smith (2008), Hirai (2010), Carvalho and Matos (2011a, 2011b), and Řiháček et al. (2015). In doing so, the current research answers multiple calls to internationalize psychology and psychotherapy (Gerstein, Heppner, Ægisdóttir, Leung, & Norsworthy, 2009; Kogan, 2000; Leong & Ponterotto, 2003; Marsella, 1998). Studying master therapists from various regions of the world begins to build our understanding of psychotherapy expertise from an international perspective. As noted in Chapter 1, psychological practitioners from the United States and around the world frequently traverse the globe whether for international education and exchange, for cross-national consultations and collaborations, or in response to natural

TABLE 8.1

Summary of Studies Included in Qualitative Meta-Analysis

Study Author(s)	Jennings and Skovholt (1999)	Kwon and Kim (2007)	Jennings et al. (2008)	Smith (2008)	Hirai (2010)	Carvalho and Matos (2011a, 2011b)	Řiháček et al. (2015)
Research Question(s)	What are the personal characteristics of master therapists? What are the characteristics of therapists considered outstanding by their professional colleagues?	What are the personal and professional characteristics of master group counselors? What are the facilitating and limiting factors as well as strategies of these master group counselors in their process of acquiring expertise?	What are the personal characteristics and therapy practices of expert therapists practicing in Singapore?	What personal characteristics, ideas, or experiences make a person a "master" at working therapeutically with couples?	What are the personal and professional characteristics of Japanese master therapists? What kind of experiences and learning have contributed to the development of Japanese master therapists? What are cross-cultural similarities and differences between Japanese and American master therapists?	What are the therapeutic and extratherapeutic experiences that contribute to a psychotherapist's professional development?	Does the Czech cultural context contribute a unique perspective on what it means to be a master therapist?
Country Represented	Population: Psychotherapists in a major Midwestern metropolitan area, USA	Population: Group counselors in Korea	Population: Psychotherapists practicing in Singapore	Population: Couple therapists in a major metropolitan area in the province of Ontario, Canada	Population: Japanese psychotherapists	Population: Psychotherapists practicing in Portugal	Population: Therapists practicing in the Czech Republic

(*continued*)

TABLE 8.1 (Continued)

Study Author(s)	Jennings and Skovholt (1999)	Kwon and Kim (2007)	Jennings et al. (2008)	Smith (2008)	Hirai (2010)	Carvalho and Matos (2011a, 2011b)	Řiháček et al. (2015)
Sample Selection	Participants: Snowball sampling/peer nomination First-round nominators: 3 well-regarded practitioners involved with training and with "long-standing involvement in the mental community"	Participants: Snowball sampling/peer nomination Key informants: 4	Participants: Snowball sampling/peer nomination First-round nominators: 47 therapists responded to a widespread, open call to submit nominations	Participants: Snowball sampling/peer nomination First-round nominators: 10 randomly selected from two professional registries + 3 practitioners with medical training	Participants: Peer nomination Nominators: 52 of 77 board members of three Japanese professional associations related to clinical psychology agreed to participate	Participants: Peer nomination First-round nominators: 9 therapists from different orientations	Participants: Peer nomination/ snowball sampling First-round nominators: 49 representatives from approved training programs in the Czech Republic
	Criteria: Considered a "master therapist" Considered to be the "best of the best" Would be confident to refer family and close friends and to work with this person in personal therapy	Criteria: Involvement in counselor training Participation in a counseling association in Korea Reputation as a well-known counselor	Criteria: See Jennings and Skovholt (1999)	Criteria: See Jennings and Skovholt (1999) and Sullivan et al. (2002) Nominator must be personally knowledgeable about the therapist's work	Criteria: See Jennings and Skovholt (1999)	Criteria: Asked to identify those they considered good psychotherapists and those whom they would consult for personal psychotherapy	Criteria: See Jennings and Skovholt (1999)

	Cutoff: Minimum of 4 nominations Result: 10 of 10 therapists agreed to participate (7 women, 3 men)	Cutoff: Minimum of 3 nominations Result: 5 identified (1 woman, 4 men)	Cutoff: Minimum of 3 nominations Result: 9 of 9 therapists agreed to participate (4 women, 5 men)	Cutoff: Minimum of 5 nominations Result: 9 of 11 therapists agreed to participate (6 women, 3 men)	Cutoff: Minimum of 4 nominations Result: 10 of 11 therapists agreed to participate (2 women, 8 men)	Cutoff: Does not specify Result: 20 of 23 agreed to participate (11 women, 9 men)	Cutoff: Minimum of 4 Result: 9 of 16 agreed to participate (2 women, 7 men)
Data Collection	Semistructured interviews • 16 open-ended interview questions • Instrument revised after pilot interview • Audiotaped interviews were transcribed verbatim • Follow-up comments on transcript of interview • Follow-up interview after 2 months to validate findings and provide feedback	Semistructured interviews • 4 main questions with 16 subquestions • Interview questions developed through a literature review and soliciting questions from doctorate-level counselors • Questions reorganized into 20 items • Two pilot studies conducted to refine the interview schedule	Semistructured interviews • 18 interview questions largely derived from Jennings and Skovholt (1999)	Semistructured interviews and written narrative • Participants asked to write a narrative about their experience and what it means to be a master couples' therapist • 14 open-ended interview questions moderately derived from Jennings and Skovholt (1999) but focused on couple therapists • Review of interview transcript • 15-minute interviews of randomly selected nominators for each master therapist	Semistructured interviews • Translated and used the interview questions from Jennings and Skovholt (1999) • Added 4 original questions about developmental influences and training • Instrument was revised after pilot interview	Semistructured interviews • 16 open-ended questions grouped into eight main themes • Interviews were audiotaped and transcribed	Semistructured interviews • Interviews followed the outline in the Jennings and Skovholt (1999) study, with the addition of a question mapping the meanings of the term "mastery" • Interviews lasted 45–120 minutes • Audiotaped interviews were transcribed and translated into English

(*continued*)

TABLE 8.1 (Continued)

Study Author(s)	Jennings and Skovholt (1999)	Kwon and Kim (2007)	Jennings et al. (2008)	Smith (2008)	Hirai (2010)	Carvalho and Matos (2011a, 2011b)	Řiháček et al. (2015)
Data Analysis	Grounded theory	Grounded theory	Grounded theory, elements of CQR	Grounded theory	Grounded theory, elements of CQR	Grounded theory	Thematic analysis, elements of CQR
High-Level Findings	Developed from 1043 concepts, conceptualized into 27 themes within 9 categories	9 main themes	16 themes organized into 4 categories	Data emerged into 3 themes	825 concepts, organized into 18 themes, and arranged into 5 categories	A core story along with 2 major themes emerged, each organized into two smaller domains	Initial codes organized into 40 working themes, which then were reduced to 16 themes organized into six domains
	• Voracious learners • Draw upon accumulated experiences • Value cognitive complexity and ambiguity • Emotionally receptive	• Reasons for choosing group counseling • Being immersed in group counseling • Mentors • Frustrations and methods of coping	• Personal characteristics • Developmental influences • Approach to practice • Ongoing professional growth	• Personal development and self • Professional development • Relationships	• Cultivating abundant learning opportunities • Perceptive understanding of self and clients • Effective intervention • Relationship-building with clients • Therapist's humility	• Relational experiences in psychotherapist development: Professional domain and personal domain • Phases and changes of the psychotherapist's development: Professional domain and personal domain	• Humble attitude toward mastery, clients, and colleagues • Relationship • Awareness of one's needs, limits, and resources

<table>
<tr>
<td>• Mentally healthy, mature, and attend to their emotional well-being
• Aware of how their emotional health impacts their work
• Possess strong relationship skills
• Believe in the working alliance
• Experts at utilizing their exceptional relational skills in therapy</td>
<td>• Contributions of pain, deficiency, and anxiety
• Situations that contributed to the acquirement of additional expertise
• Strategies for growth
• Personal characteristics
• Professional characteristics</td>
<td>• Core story: Development of the psychotherapist—dialogue and coherence between personal and professional self</td>
<td>• Continuous development
• Engagement
• Awareness of the complexity of psychotherapeutic work</td>
</tr>
</table>

and human-made disasters and crises. From a practical and ethical standpoint, it is culturally unsophisticated at best and hegemonic at worse to imagine that a US-centric view of psychotherapy is the best or only means to healing. We therefore seek to understand how the best of the best practitioners from various countries do their work. Through the analysis of these studies from seven different countries (United States, Canada, Czech Republic, Portugal, Singapore, Japan, and Korea), a global understanding of master therapists begins to take form.

Meta-analysis provides an important tool for taking stock of where a line of inquiry has arrived and where future inquiry is needed. As such, meta-analysis of qualitative data has gained momentum recently and offers an excellent way to examine the studies completed to date. As mentioned in Chapter 1, there is increased focus on the role of the therapist as a contributor to outcome in psychotherapy, and understanding the characteristics and traits of master therapists can lead to valuable insights at the expert end of the therapist development continuum. By gaining insights into master therapist characteristics on a global level, we hope to consolidate the available knowledge on the characteristics of master therapists and contribute to the internationalization of counseling and psychotherapy.

Methods

RESEARCHERS

All three researchers (the first three authors of this chapter) involved in the consensual data analysis team had prior experience coding data through a consensual process. Two had prior experience working together conducting a QMA. Before beginning to evaluate the data, the researchers discussed potential biases and concerns so that these could be monitored throughout the evaluation process. Timulak (2009) suggests that QMA requires a good deal of attention to bracketing because the nature of a QMA is to build on preexisting findings and theory. As such, researchers must endeavor to remain open to discovery despite the potential pull toward preexisting conceptions of the findings. Therefore, before we began our formal analysis, we each "bracketed" our possible preexisting bias or expectations regarding this research topic. One area of bias related to the fact that two of the researchers had prior experience working together on a QMA project that included two studies also included in this project. In addition, there was concern about whether three Western-born researchers from the United States could capture the cultural nuances that were embedded in the studies included in this current QMA and also whether manuscripts translated to English could capture those nuances. Other strategies to address these concerns were employed. Throughout the analysis process, we encouraged each other to take on the "devil's advocate" role and check whether or not we were gravitating toward familiar concepts, actually exploring new perspectives, or possibility viewing data from an ethnocentric perspective. These frequent check-ins aided in maintaining a fresh perspective on the data. Another issue related to working with translated materials. To ensure accuracy, two of the studies (Korea and Portugal) that required translation to English were carefully reviewed by another native speaker after the initial translation by the original authors. Recommendations from these reviews were shared with the original authors for consideration in the translated manuscript. Last, we employed an external Singaporean auditor, currently teaching at a university in the United States and familiar with this body of research, to help identify culturally nuanced-based information that we may have missed as well as to audit our work at critical junctures in the research process. This auditor has also engaged in research in Singapore, Korea, and Japan, in addition to the United States.

POSITIONALITY

One particular issue raised during the audit was the question of how to make meaning of this rich data set while bracketing for country and cultural contexts. We acknowledge that one of the tensions in cross-national research is having to at once account for what is culture-general and what is culture-specific. We decided against presenting any kind of matrix delineating country characteristics a priori to avoid simplifying and essentializing what are in fact complex cultural systems that each country represents. Hermans and Kempen (1998) described our globalizing world as one in which "East" and "West" are false dichotomies because trade, tourism, and technology have maximized contact and engagement in ways that hybridize cultures. They say it is difficult to conclude that any particular country characteristic is unique only to that country and further runs the risk of stereotyping countries and cultures in overly simplistic ways. Instead, we allowed each study to reveal the myriad cultural complexities and nuances as they were presented in therapeutic situations by the master therapists.

In a landmark international handbook on cross-cultural counseling (Gerstein et al., 2009), the counseling history and practices of 29 different countries are portrayed. Relative to the current QMA, Korea, Japan, Singapore, and Canada are represented in the handbook. Even though each country's case study was written by an author(s) within each country with firsthand knowledge and experience of mental health practices in those countries, these stories are often influenced by masters and doctoral students returning from overseas study, mostly from the United States. Although attention is given throughout the handbook to country characteristics such as ethnicity and religion and sociopolitical climate in each chapter, the dominant approach to psychotherapy in these 29 cases is still mostly understood via country-specific author or authors' lenses. With no disregard for the valuable insights offered by respected authors from multiple countries, in the current study, we did not want to be constrained by artificial country delimits but, rather, allowed for the individual and collective voices of master therapists from various countries to organically and inductively paint these country portraits for us in the way themes emerged in our QMA.

RESEARCH QUESTION

For the study presented in this chapter, researchers utilized a QMA to examine qualitative studies from seven countries to identify the personal and professional characteristics common to master therapists from around the world. The goal of the QMA was to synthesize findings from multiple international studies, thus strengthening the literature on universal qualities associated with master therapists.

PROCEDURE

One advantage of choosing QMA is the triangulation of results that occurs when comparing multiple studies. In addition, QMA is meant to expand the body of knowledge, providing interpretative, rather than aggregative, explanation of results. QMA is thought to go beyond a study in isolation to allow for incremental accumulation of knowledge (Schreiber, Crooks, & Noerager Stern, 1997). Although this approach can be viewed as reductive, it is not. Rather, differences between findings are retained, and the complexity of the results is heightened. Opportunity to observe common findings and unique cultural findings remains when engaged in QMA. In addition, when categories are examined across multiple studies, definitions are deepened and categories are better articulated and understood (Finfgeld, 2003).

Although we considered various QMA approaches, Timulak's (2009) method was chosen because his approach allowed for the findings of identified studies to be utilized as the unit of data. Initially, a wide net was cast to identify all possible studies that could be included in the QMA. This included studies that had been published in peer-reviewed journals and unpublished studies that the researchers became aware of due to their personal network of professionals familiar with the literature on therapist expertise and master therapists. We identified 14 qualitative research studies that explored some aspect of master therapists. In addition to the seven studies presented in this book and included in the QMA, there were another five studies that went into detail on some specific aspect of mastery (i.e., therapeutic alliance (Sullivan, Skovholt, & Jennings, 2005), self-care practices (Mullenbach & Skovholt, 2004), ethical values (Jennings, Sovereign, Bottorff, Mussell, & Vye, 2005), use of computer-based test interpretations (Shy, 2008), and spiritual development (Menigat, 2007)) and two other studies that asked specific questions regarding multicultural practices of expert therapists (Goh, Starkey, Skovholt, & Jennings, 2007; Jennings et al., 2012). Due to our interest in learning more about the general characteristics of master therapists, we eliminated these seven studies from our QMA because only one aspect of mastery was examined in each of the studies. The seven selected for inclusion in the QMA utilized a grounded theory approach to data analysis, and all asked a similar research question that focused on general characteristics of master therapists. In addition, all seven studies included in the QMA used some form of peer-nomination sampling process to identify master therapists. Note that the Korean study

(Kwon & Kim, 2007) included an extensive model of developmental factors of group master therapists. Instead of analyzing developmental factors, we analyzed the portions of their research that specifically addressed personal and professional characteristics of master therapists.

Once the studies were identified, the unit of analysis needed to be determined. The researchers first debated the relative merits and difficulties of attempting to evaluate the "raw" data (i.e., quoted excerpts from transcripts) from the studies. The researchers decided that it was important to honor the original authors' contextualization of their data because their interpretation likely included nuanced findings not readily visible to those conducting a secondary analysis. In addition, because the researchers did not have full access to all the raw data, any effort to reanalyze quotations from the initial publications would be incomplete. Thus, it was determined that the results (themes) from each study would be the unit of analysis. This allowed for a "level playing field" in that a common metric was used across the studies. However, we decided that quotations from themes that comprise a meta-category would be used to further formulate, refine, and illuminate the meta-categories.

DATA ANALYSIS

In the current study, we employed a combination of grounded theory (Corbin & Strauss, 2008) and consensual qualitative research (CQR) methods (Hill, 2012). Several procedures from grounded theory included open coding, constant comparative method, and the creation of theoretical models based on the data. Elements of CQR included consensual decision-making, importance of attending to group dynamics during the analysis, representativeness of the sample, and the use of an external auditor.

Two studies (Jennings & Skovholt, 1999; Jennings et al., 2008) included in the current QMA were reported on previously in an initial QMA comparison (Jennings et al., 2008). Thus, it was determined that the review of these two studies would be the place to begin our analysis. After becoming familiar with these two studies and the initial qualitative meta-analytic findings, the researchers analyzed the remaining five studies and sorted the themes of the new studies into the preexisting meta-analytic categories developed in the Jennings et al. (2008) QMA. Themes that did not fit in the original meta-analysis categories were labeled divergent. A team of three researchers (L.J., A.S., and S.R.) worked together until consensual agreement was achieved regarding the placement of themes into meta-categories. A table was constructed to represent the initial findings and then set aside for later review. Next, we decided to reanalyze the data from scratch by conducting a cross-case analysis, in which all 111 of the studies' themes were reconsidered and reorganized to help minimize "groupthink" and bias toward the initial categories. Researchers together grouped the themes into fresh meta-categories by placing like themes together to see what patterns emerged. This new grouping of themes was compared to the initial grouping of themes, and then the researchers worked to create synthesis across the two sets of findings. Discussion continued until consensus was achieved regarding final meta-categories (Table 8.2). Through this iterative, constant comparative analysis process, two new meta-categories were created (Distinctive Clinical Abilities and Cognitive Complexity and Intricate Conceptualization), and the original six meta-categories from the Jennings et al. (2008) QMA were significantly enhanced (for comparison, see Chapter 5, Table 5.2). Finally, the research team worked together to create a synthesis model of the eight meta-categories that is presented in the Discussion section. This process involved higher level theorizing about the relationship among the meta-categories. To account for apparent overlap among some of the meta-categories, we began the modeling process using Venn diagrams. We approximated the size of each circle representing a meta-category based on the number of themes each meta-category contained. Note that due to the qualitative nature of our work, the scale of the model was not intended to be precise and is for illustrative purposes only. From this higher level analysis, many models were configured and considered until we finally agreed on the Synthesis Model of Master Therapists from Around the World (see Fig. 8.1).

Results

This section highlights the following eight meta-categories: (1) Distinctive Clinical Abilities, (2) Professional Development, (3) Relational Orientation, (4) Cognitive Complexity and Intricate Conceptualization, (5) Pursuit of Deep Self Knowledge and Growth, (6) Therapeutic Alliance, (7) Humility, and (8) Experience. When selecting quotations, we chose quotations that best illustrated each meta-category and provided a balanced representation among the seven countries.

DISTINCTIVE CLINICAL ABILITIES META-CATEGORY (18 THEMES)

This category represents a variety of themes that illustrated these therapists' signature abilities. For example, it appears that master therapists use their relational skills to guide the timing, pacing, and dosage of interventions. Here, a Singaporean master therapist describes trying to be "in sync" with her client:

> It's the ability to follow the client and to lead the client. And dance with the client. You cannot move too far ahead of clients, so the steps must be kind of in sync. I have a client who wanted to work on her issues but each time we come close to it she blocks and she goes off elsewhere. Now there are times when I pursue and then she blocks again. So after a bit I notice that I'm not getting anywhere. And I step back and let her lead and she might start reading her written notes because that was her way of coping with the intensity. So I would then just go along and pick up what she was saying that would help her experience herself positively. I let that tension go down a bit. And then I see if she's ready to engage in something more serious.

TABLE 8.2

QMA Results

Meta-Analytic Category	Themes from US Study (Jennings & Skovholt, 1999)	Themes from Korea Study (Kwon & Kim, 2007)	Themes from Singapore Study (Jennings et al., 2008)	Themes from Canada Study (Smith, 2008)	Themes from Japan Study (Hirai, 2010)	Themes from Portugal Study (Carvalho, & Matos, 2011a, 2011b)	Themes from Czech Study (Řiháček et al., 2015)
Distinctive Clinical Abilities (18 themes): Experts use relational skills with clients to guide their sense of timing, pacing, and dosage of interventions. This ultimately serves to create a safe yet challenging therapeutic atmosphere. Experts have a capacity to hold and release intense client emotion.	• Expert at using exceptional relational skills in therapy	• Respects resistance • Rapidly and accurately understands each member • Having patience and not hurrying • Very little fear and reluctance for self-disclosure	• Flexible therapeutic stance • Balance between support and challenge	• Maintains connection in the face of conflict • Developing a strong ability to conceptualize • Developing a (customized) approach to couple psychotherapy	• Finely tuned understanding of client • Precise yet flexible intervention • Able to take a comprehensive view of client • Perform a high level of therapeutic effectiveness (emphasis on efficient)	• Managing emotional involvement: Shoes of the psychotherapist (not absorbing negative emotionality)	• Secure relationship • Providing an encouraging perspective • Judicious use of self-disclosure

(continued)

TABLE 8.2 (Continued)

Meta-Analytic Category	Themes from US Study (Jennings & Skovholt, 1999)	Themes from Korea Study (Kwon & Kim, 2007)	Themes from Singapore Study (Jennings et al., 2008)	Themes from Canada Study (Smith, 2008)	Themes from Japan Study (Hirai, 2010)	Themes from Portugal Study (Carvalho, & Matos, 2011a, 2011b)	Themes from Czech Study (Řiháček et al., 2015)
Professional Development (15 themes): Experts value ongoing learning both within and outside their area of practice and grow through the process of teaching others.	• Voracious learners	• High risk-taking tendency • Preference and striving for new and diverse experience	• Benefits of teaching and training others • Professional development practices • Challenges to professional development	• Teaching enhances understanding • The curious student: Commitment to ongoing learning • Importance of peer relationships (to learning or to professional development)	• Abound in ingenuity (emphasis on learning something new professionally) • Proactive learning style • Learning from great mentors • Diligently manage massive learning • Existence of supportive environment (emphasis on therapist getting support)	• Positive relational experiences in professional domain: Feelings of gratification	
Relational Orientation (15 themes): Experts engage with individuals (personally and professionally) in an empathic, .	• Master therapists possess strong relational skills (not just in therapy)	• Deep empathy, deep genuineness, flexibility and pliability, sense of humor that processes burdens and pains of life productively, ability	• Empathic • Nonjudgmental • Respectful	• Personal qualities that facilitate strong relationships	• Deep respect for client • Being open toward the client	• Positive relational experiences in professional domain: Access to privileged dimensions; nature of emotional bond • Negative relational experiences in	• Humility and humanity • Therapists' care and curiosity

respectful, and nonjudgmental way		to reduce fear about intense emotions • Has leadership and relationships with the entire group • Deep faith in people				professional domain: Difficulties in managing boundaries; emotional burden • Attentional focus: Psychotherapist interpersonal (as mastery develops, relational understanding of psychotherapy emerges)	
Cognitive Complexity and Intricate Conceptu-alization (15 themes): Experts have both a keen ability and interest in working with complex, contextual, and ambiguous phenomena. They embrace and work within multiple worldviews.	• Values cognitive complexity and ambiguity of the human condition	• COGNITIVE COMPETENCE: GREAT AMOUNT OF INFORMATION, INTEGRATION OF INFORMATION, DISCERNED APPLICATION, GREAT MEMORY • Changes in their view on what are important group dynamics • Acquired sensitivity to see group dynamics • Deals with difficult dynamics effectively • Formulates one's own counseling theory	• Comfortable addressing spirituality • Embraces working within a multicultural context		• Respect for the profundity of human beings • Capacity to embrace antinomy (embraces contradictions) • Multidimensional therapeutic approach	• Relational experiences in personal domain: Representation of the world • Relational experiences in personal domain: Representation of others	• Complex thinking about therapeutic change • Creative work with information

(*continued*)

TABLE 8.2 (Continued)

Meta-Analytic Category	Themes from US Study (Jennings & Skovholt, 1999)	Themes from Korea Study (Kwon & Kim, 2007)	Themes from Singapore Study (Jennings et al., 2008)	Themes from Canada Study (Smith, 2008)	Themes from Japan Study (Hirai, 2010)	Themes from Portugal Study (Carvalho, & Matos, 2011a, 2011b)	Themes from Czech Study (Řiháček et al., 2015)
Pursues Deep Self Knowledge and Growth (15 themes): Experts actively reflect and pursue feedback from many sources to grow personally and professionally.	• Emotionally receptive • Aware of how their emotional health impacts quality of work • Mentally healthy and mature: Congruent and self-aware		• Self-awareness	• Embracing personal growth and self-awareness • Striving to maintain emotional health • A natural fit evokes passion in their work	• In-depth self-reflection	• Relational experiences in personal domain: Representation of self • Relational experiences in personal domain that impact implications for psychotherapeutic choices: Vocational choice of psychotherapy; preference for intervention models, populations and therapeutic issues • Relational experiences in personal domain that impact implications for the psychotherapeutic relationship: Empathy; building hope	• Self-nurturing • Keeping a boundary between one's personal and professional lives • Awareness of one's weaknesses and limits • Personal therapy, education, and supervision

Therapeutic Alliance: (12 themes): Ranging from a necessary condition to the intervention itself, experts support their client's strength and growth through active and ongoing attention to the therapeutic alliance.	• Believes in the therapeutic alliance	• High level of acceptance (emphasis on helping clients accept self)	• Primacy of therapeutic alliance • Empowerment/ strength-based approach	• Belief in the importance of a strong therapeutic relationship • The alliance in couple therapy • Trusting the client and following the client's lead	• Active engagement in the mutually therapeutic relationship	• Relational experiences in professional domain validated by psychotherapy: Collaborative understanding of psychotherapy; quality of the relationship • Role in defining therapy goals: Psychotherapist coauth or (less need for control, more collaborative) • Negative relational experiences in professional domain: Inability to help; unexpected dropouts; difficulty in the relationship	• Relationship is healing
Humility (8 themes): Experts have a healthy perspective on their sense of importance and recognize their limits of competence.	• Mentally healthy and mature: Humility	• Has realistic expectation for one's skills	• Humility	• Confident, yet modest	• Therapist's personality	• Relational experience in the professional domain: Potentialities and limitations; human psychotherapist (humble)	• Striving for "good enough" • Humility and humanity

(*continued*)

TABLE 8.2 (Continued)

Meta-Analytic Category	Themes from US Study (Jennings & Skovholt, 1999)	Themes from Korea Study (Kwon & Kim, 2007)	Themes from Singapore Study (Jennings et al., 2008)	Themes from Canada Study (Smith, 2008)	Themes from Japan Study (Hirai, 2010)	Themes from Portugal Study (Carvalho, & Matos, 2011a, 2011b)	Themes from Czech Study (Řiháček et al., 2015)
Experience (7 themes): Experts draw on life and work experiences to inform and advance their skills.	• Accumulated experience is major resource		• Experience		• High level of resilience (learned from personal hardships/ experiences)	• Relational experiences in professional domain validated by psychotherapy: Pragmatic awareness of help • Underlying factors to the psychotherapists invention: Style of the psychotherapist	• Years of practice • Appreciation of diversity of life experiences
		Divergent • Easily and comfortably leads groups • Freely formulates group and individual goals • Extends group counseling as the solution for organizational, societal, and national issues • Possesses individualized skills	*Divergent* • Self-doubt				*Divergent* • Mastery is in-between the therapist and the client

Similarly, one US master therapist illustrated her striving for attunement with her client:

> You trust that you won't overrespond or underrespond. You see, if she [a client] had gotten mad at me, then I would have pulled back and done something else. Part of it is a gestalt concept of dosage. That you have to put out the right level of experiment. Because if it isn't enough, it is not going to get the adrenaline going and if it is too much, they get overwhelmed.

Another strength was the master therapist's ability to maintain focused attention when working with a client. This attention may contribute to the creation of a safe and secure therapeutic atmosphere necessary for change. Demonstrating a keen ability to focus, one Japanese master therapist stated,

> Let's say I posed a question to the client. The vibration of the sound travels through the space between the therapist and the client, enters the drum membrane of the client's ear, is processed in his/her brain, and the client responds. If you pay careful attention to the time between the question and the response, you can sense whether a certain thought process has intervened, such as different kind of thoughts are suppressed or denied, by the subtle time gap. If this gap is always happening, then the brain must be fatigued, and there is a possibility of clinical depression, even if the client is smiling on the surface. But if the client has been talking and only a part of the conversation has a subtle gap, then it means that certain thoughts are omitted. I think it is important to pay attention to such a subtle detail. . . . "God exists in subtlety," so to speak. Important things exist in a corner. What you can see on the surface is like a table of contents. Real contents belong to somewhere more clandestine.

Master therapists also seem to have a well-developed capacity to hold and also reduce the level of intense client emotion. A Canadian master therapist noted the importance of working effectively with clients' intense expression of feelings:

> I think I've got courage to do this work. Strong affect doesn't worry me. I love it. I really feel it's alive when [couples do the] emotional work. . . . So that may be a piece of it. . . . I think people are often afraid of intense emotion and conflict. And you really get people screaming at each other. And you have to do something about it . . . and a lot of people [therapists] just don't want to go there.

PROFESSIONAL DEVELOPMENT META-CATEGORY (15 THEMES)

Professional development is another robust meta-category. It is clear that experts value ongoing learning both within and outside their area of practice and that they perceive a substantial benefit from articulating their work when teaching students and other professionals. One Korean master therapist outlined a professional development strategy that required courage and an attitude of openness to growth:

> I keep throwing myself into difficult situations. I tell myself, "This is a good thing" and keep throwing myself into these situations even when I get scared at times. I also feel ambivalent about doing demonstrations. It's a more intense situation than just teaching. I want to keep throwing myself into challenging situations so I can continue to grow. Get yelled at for things I did wrong or messed up. It's more like "Let's see how I deal with difficult situations" than "Let's see how well I do."

A Canadian master therapist also shared the strategy of teaching a topic in order to deeply internalize related knowledge:

> If I can teach it, then I know it. And so, I kind of put myself into positions where I'm teaching things that I'm curious about learning better because it makes sure that I can articulate it. Then I know that I know it well. And I know it in such a deep way that it's just going to be second nature when I use it.

A Japanese master therapist articulated the way her adherence to theory and style evolved throughout her development as a therapist:

> It may be necessary to get hooked on a particular therapeutic style first, in order to be free from its limitations eventually. Learning a certain style is an entrance, but there is a different exit. . . . First, people may cling to a certain style to create a form. The older the therapist becomes, however, the harder it becomes to break the form. When you break the form you created, you have to start over again from the beginning, which is true self with only flesh and blood, nothing else. Therefore, this renewal process may require certain level of ego strength . . . capacity to break and start over.

RELATIONAL ORIENTATION META-CATEGORY (15 THEMES)

Participants seem to have highly developed relational attributes that enable them to connect well with others. In addition, some of the participants identified that their own emotional wounds seemed to increase their sensitivity and compassion for others, factors that play into the ability to develop strong relationships. One US master therapist shared a personal account of suffering and how this experience increased her sensitivity to others, and therefore her therapeutic effectiveness:

> I have been through a hard five years; during which time I sold my house, moved into another place, had my last surviving sibling die of a brain tumor and my mother and an aunt die. So I was picking myself up and was kind of holding on to myself for a while. And the interesting thing is, when I was in the most pain, I was a very good therapist. And it was like the bank robbers who sandpaper their skin so that they can really be sensitive to the movements of the machine they are trying to break open. . . . I think I was more sensitive to what my clients were doing.

Master therapists maintain an ongoing awareness of both the privilege and the responsibilities of their unique relationships with clients. They approach clients with a deep respect for their vulnerability and the experiences they have had prior to presenting for therapy. The participants presented themselves as consistently attending to the therapeutic relationship, in part as a strategy for helping to heal. A Portuguese master therapist said,

> The [most striking] moments are the ones of emotional activation of patients or when there are people with deprivation histories or disorganized attachment to close figures, and then they attach to us in a very particular way, and have great esteem toward us, and then they allow themselves the remembering and activation of certain memories, and we try to work with them through these life events. It is a privilege to have access to such stories.

Another master therapist from Portugal shared the emotional burden that is often a part of doing psychotherapy:

> We have to absorb a lot of negative emotionality that passes through us. . . . We carry the voice of patients with us, emotions are with us and it takes hours to drain out of the body, hours. . . . We touch the absurdity of life, we are there with the absurd in our arms and sometimes, it takes hours to free ourselves of this.

COGNITIVE COMPLEXITY AND INTRICATE CONCEPTUALIZATION META-CATEGORY (15 THEMES)

Another of the stronger meta-categories described master therapists' keen ability and interest in working with complex, contextual, and ambiguous phenomena. The master therapists were capable of understanding the multifaceted individual differences among clients, recognizing the influence of diverse environments and situations, and holding an awareness of the intricacies of clients' lives. A Portuguese master therapist spoke eloquently about the challenges that accompany this complex work:

> I like to feel that the complexity with which we can see things—on the one hand sometimes we feel anguish, but on the other hand there is a feeling of fullness, that we do not give interpretations to the banal or everyday or superficial things, that we seek to understand the logic of things, how people function . . . that sometimes is distressing because we are powerless to change a number of things . . . on the other hand, it gives the notion that we are seeing things in some depth.

One US master therapist spoke to the risks of cognitive complacency, highlighting the need to keep in mind the ever-changing landscape of therapeutic practice:

> None of us ever "arrive" when we're in this business of working with people. . . . There's always an AIDS, the thing around the corner. There's always that level of complexity. . . . And the minute you start thinking things are simple, you better quit [psychotherapy]. That [reminds me of] my favorite quote, by the way: "If the brain was simple enough for us to understand it, we'd be too simple to understand it."

A Korean master therapist described how he developed acute attunement to the subtleties involved in group therapy:

> I can see the dynamics of the group—I can see very detailed, very minute flows or processes within the group. I guess that's the best part—that I can see such things now. I can pick out themes that can be dealt meaningfully within the group more than I did before. I become more accepting and more sensitive, as if my eyes have become a microscope.

A Singaporean master therapist demonstrated cultural competency when addressing the complexities and challenges of adapting Western therapeutic approaches to Eastern values and systems:

> But somehow, being influenced by the earlier training in therapy, and being in a very intrapsychic, very individually focused or even reductionistic orientation, is a bit unfortunate. And yet, when we think about people and their experience in culture, and about the Asian context, we cannot ignore context, we cannot ignore the fact that we are connected to other parts in our human experience. So even the "self" is not an individual self, it's the "self" in relation to. I need to take a multiple perspective orientation that there are multiple realities, multiple truths, multiple perspectives and that whatever I see, I need to see more than one.

A Czech master therapist addressed the intricate interplay of art and science in psychotherapy:

> At first, [psychotherapy] has to become a science, and only after that it can be an art. I must learn something in a scientific way, I need a hypothesis, a paradigm to be grounded in. Then I can step out of this paradigm and look at it from a bird eye's view. And that's art, in my opinion. An art can connect the inconnectable. . . . And in my opinion, an artist is everyone who thinks in his own way and isn't afraid to break the structure.

PURSUIT OF DEEP SELF KNOWLEDGE AND GROWTH META-CATEGORY (15 THEMES)

This strong meta-analytic category captured the ways in which experts actively reflect and pursue feedback from many sources to grow personally and professionally. The masters described honing the instrument of psychotherapy (the self of the therapist) in order to best serve their clients, using information from as many sources as possible to do so. The participants verbalized the ways in which it is important to grow personally, not just professionally, as the therapist's authenticity plays a major role in the client's development and growth. For example, one US master therapist said,

> [I need to be] fully aware of myself and my own motivational system, what's moving me inside. . . . So I get a chance to look at myself on the outside over and over and over again, through personal therapy, through lots of supervision, through ongoing consultation. That helps incredibly.

A Portuguese master therapist noted,

> From the personal point of view, I feel that [being a therapist] helped me to grow and live in a more peaceful, more serene, less troubled, less anxious way. Here's [something] that I think is very important, to be aware of my own inner world, of my own fears, anguishes, concerns, not to escape it, to take it as mine.

One Czech master therapist demonstrated self-knowledge of a particular personal strength that positively impacts therapy:

> I think the greatest thing I was gifted with is that I am an optimist, that I believe in happy endings, that it all ends well with people. And this is reflected in my therapies, where I can bear the burden with [my clients]. I know that it is difficult now, but when they find new life opportunities and find their freedom, they will be good. And I think this is [my] strongest point.

THERAPEUTIC ALLIANCE META-CATEGORY (12 THEMES)

Although the meta-categories of Therapeutic Alliance and Relational Orientation are somewhat related, the QMA provided data that supported a distinction between these concepts. The therapeutic alliance, in this context, is conceptualized as a specific area of focus for the therapist, a strategic intervention beyond a general sense of the relationship with the client. Participants discussed the use of the therapeutic alliance in such a way that it ranged from a necessary condition to being the intervention itself. A Singaporean master therapist articulated a strong belief about the primacy of the alliance over theory or technique in facilitating client change:

> We in Singapore are exposed to a lot of mainstream [psychotherapies], whatever is happening in town, people will go by the droves to learn. And it is good to learn this, but what they will experience is that, by the third or fourth session, the toolbox is empty. You have used all the fancy questions and the nice techniques [but what about] the relationship? The relationship becomes much more important. It sustains the whole counseling process.

A Japanese master therapist used psychodynamic terms to describe the therapeutic function of the working alliance:

> [When the therapy is going well], the therapist can walk along with the client's inner story and be with that which the client brings to the therapy process. That is when the therapist is living the story and being with the client. This is what is called transference in psychoanalysis, and the therapeutic process is proceeding when the therapist is living the client's transference together.

HUMILITY META-CATEGORY (NINE THEMES)

Rather than having "expert" status inflate their self-image, the master therapists shared a healthy perspective on their sense of importance and recognized their limits of competence. A Canadian master therapist described discomfort with the idea of being designated an expert in the first place:

> The word "master" is I think a bit pretentious . . . I would say that I'm good at what I do, that's how I'd put it . . . I'm a good psychotherapist, I'm a good couple therapist. I know I'm good at it. There are a few things in life that I know I can do and I know I can do this.

A Singaporean master therapist referred to the essential role that failure plays in the development of professional expertise:

> Nobody becomes an expert by first becoming an expert. I think therapists do not acknowledge the fact that they failed many times or they have made mistakes. It's hard to acknowledge that, but I think all of us failed, all of us learn from our mistakes. I think the earlier we acknowledge it the better it is for ourselves because it's from there that we learn how to do better.

A Portuguese master therapist noted,

> In the beginning I had a somewhat idealized vision, a little more omnipotent . . . I thought that psychotherapy could solve all the ills of a person and, today, I don't think any of that . . . psychotherapy is like yeast in cakes, if the eggs are not there, if the flour is not there, if the ingredients are not there, you can put the yeast in and the cake will not be as it could be. And this limitation of reality, I guess I started to accept, integrate and know that the contribution I can give is limited.

Finally, a Czech master therapist said,

> Therapists' need to relate to people competes with their need for confirmation that they are excellent. So a therapist who aspires for being an excellent therapist [hasn't] resolved enough his or her narcissistic balance. . . . Well I think that if a therapist has a need to show off and become a famous expert, there is something wrong with it.

EXPERIENCE META-CATEGORY (SEVEN THEMES)

Although it is not surprising that the data revealed experts benefit from experience, the master therapists discussed the value of widely different types of experience beyond working with clients. The master therapists were able to integrate personal and professional lessons into their approach with clients, drawing on life and work experiences to inform and advance their skills. One US master therapist explained the importance of continually learning from experience:

> I don't think years of experience by itself does it . . . I might have the same year of experience 20 times. So [one] needs to put that together with good consultation and a good collegial system so that you actually are learning from what you're doing, [learning] more about yourself and about how you are impacting people.

A Japanese master therapist described how he or she seeks out and benefits from challenging but intimidating experiences:

> I can gain freshest and most state-of-the-art experience when I am standing on the edge or border, rather than keeping myself at the center. I can learn most when I am

there at the edge. Of course, I can say this retrospectively. Standing at the edge is quite challenging and unstable. Being at the center provides much more stability. So, standing at the edge means I always carry this sense of uncertainty, but it also provides something new.

Discussion

Compared to the first qualitative study of master therapists (Jennings & Skovholt, 1999) with 10 participants and 25 hours of interviews, this QMA represents studies from seven countries, 72 peer-nominated master therapists, hundreds of interview hours, and thousands of total research hours. We now have a more thorough and global understanding of the characteristics of master therapists. The current QMA significantly deepened and expanded the earlier meta-analytic categories developed in the Jennings et al. (2008) comparisons between US and Singapore master therapists as well as revealed two new meta-categories. In addition, the current findings support the earlier CER model of master therapists (Jennings & Skovholt, 1999), the more elaborate 2004 Portrait of Master Therapists (Skovholt, Jennings, & Mullenbach, 2004), and the 2013 Updated Portrait of Master Therapists (Jennings, Skovholt, Goh, & Lian, 2013). In this discussion, we explore the salience of these eight meta-categories, examine how these categories relate to the expertise and therapist factors literature, and present the Synthesis Model of Master Therapists from Around the World. Finally, recommendations for research and training are offered.

DISTINCTIVE CLINICAL ABILITIES

Early in the analysis, a number of themes in the Distinctive Clinical Abilities meta-category were housed in the Relational Orientation meta-category. In time, we were able to see that many of the themes within the Relational Orientation meta-category, although relational in nature, were actually appropriately described as interventions and skills employed by master therapists. What remained in the Relational Orientation meta-category were themes that represented general characteristics versus specific skills. Thus, in the final analysis, we added the meta-category of Distinctive Clinical Abilities to reflect the active, skillful application of various interventions, resulting in the study's strongest and most applied meta-category.

It is enlightening to learn what master therapists consider their most prized abilities. What we found impressive was not so much the specific techniques but, rather, the master therapists' ability to remain relationally attuned while introducing and facilitating needed change processes. From the Japanese study, for example, the exquisite attunement the master therapist displayed when listening for subtle gaps in the client's speech pattern was remarkable. This attunement helped this master therapist to tentatively conceptualize the client's struggle as depression. Findings from many studies on experts suggest they are able to engage in very specific and nuanced attention to their craft and have the capacity for intense concentration when practicing. In fact, this is one ability that separates experts from novices (Ericcson, 2006).

Many themes within this meta-category reflect this interaction of skills and relational characteristics. Another example of this is represented in the Korean "respects resistance" theme. It identifies the attitudinal characteristic of being respectful to nurture safety in the relationship, seemingly allowing the therapist to skillfully work with the client's resistance. Overall, this meta-category, with impressive themes such as "maintaining connection in the face of conflict," represents many sophisticated abilities of master therapists that may ultimately serve to create a safe and challenging atmosphere in which they can maximize their therapeutic strategies when working with clients.

PROFESSIONAL DEVELOPMENT

The strong meta-category of Professional Development emphasizes continuous learning. These master therapists eagerly take on learning opportunities and achieve professional growth from both work and leisure pursuits. We found it inspiring that these seasoned practitioners are still eager to grow and expand. Many of their stories revealed their intense pleasure in experiencing novel situations, and many shared their delight, not discomfort, in being a beginner. Themes such as "voracious learners" and "the curious student: Commitment to ongoing learning" stress the importance of keeping active in one's lifelong education. It is reassuring to know that, in part, the attainment of mastery is built on diligent, ongoing, and sustained effort. As Colvin (2010) notes, "Certain people put themselves through years or decades of punishing, intensive daily work that eventually makes them world-class great" (p. 204). It may be that these master therapists view their work as a calling. Duffy and Dik (2013) report that those who report that their chosen profession is a form of calling exhibit greater career commitment, work meaning, and career maturity.

Neimeyer, Taylor, and Cox (2012) note that the challenge of maintaining professional competence grows over time as new knowledge is created and existing knowledge becomes outdated. In addition, it has been found that psychologists who engage in regular professional development activities report positively on their experience, noting that they not only learn a great deal but also are able to apply new knowledge to their clinical practice. Master therapists' proactive pursuit of lifelong learning and their enjoyment of learning may contribute to their status as "masters" because they are likely to remain current in their knowledge base and this, in turn, may enhance their clinical capability.

COGNITIVE COMPLEXITY AND INTRICATE CONCEPTUALIZATION

First classified as a "divergent" theme in the Jennings et al. (2008) QMA, with the addition of five more studies to the analysis, this new meta-category became one of the strongest of the final eight meta-categories. Based on the current QMA, it is clear that dealing with complexity was a major strength of master therapists. These master therapists have the capacity to handle disparate data, convolutedness, paradoxes, and puzzles without needing to distill the complexity down to a simple answer. In fact, Paradoxical Characteristics were a central finding as part of the Portrait of the Master Therapist (Skovholt et al., 2004). In short, they are comfortable with ambiguity and appreciate the complexity of the human condition. This appreciation of complexity is evidenced by these master therapists, who have created their own personal counseling theories and methods that are consistent and internalized. An analogy is with the great artist who studied standard methods in school and then expanded to a personally distinct style. A biography of Georgia O'Keefe explores such an unfolding professional style (Lisle, 1987). These master therapists also expressed their comfort with complexity through working with spirituality and enjoying the richness and challenge of working across cultures. Our findings support the expertise literature which indicates that experts in general (Chi, Glaser, & Farr, 1988; Ericcson, Charness, Feltovich, & Hoffman, 2006), and in psychotherapy (Owen & Lindley, 2010), excel in the cognitive domain. With regard to intercultural competence, these findings also reflect the characteristics of multicultural master therapists in three US studies that portrayed multicultural master therapists as avid cultural learners, perpetually curious, cultural detectives and strategists, and often awed rather than intimated by cultural complexities (Goh, Skovholt, Yang, & Starkey, 2012). In addition, research on differences between expert and novice therapists suggest that experienced counselors have more complex schemata and tend to notice more subtle features of problems than novice counselors (Martin, Slemon, Hiebert, Hallberg, & Cummings, 1989).

Expert therapists' ability to operate in a more complex manner than novices and their appreciation and tolerance for complexity may be, in part, a result of possessing excellent self-regulatory processes. Research on development of expertise suggests that experts are able to maintain strategic awareness of the task in which they are engaged, self-monitor accurately, and adjust as necessary. They attend not only to outcome of performance but also to learning processes necessary to develop skill. As such, they engage in a feedback loop that enhances learning and involves a forethought phase (goal-setting and motivation), performance phase, and self-reflection phase. This engagement in a learning process, paired with knowledge, already attained skills, and personal motivation, serves to continually deepen and further their abilities (Zimmerman, 2006).

RELATIONAL ORIENTATION

This meta-category captures more of the general relational characteristics that the master therapists possess, such as warmth, empathy, and compassion, and an ongoing focus on the quality of relationships. Some of the participants appear to have further developed these qualities as a result of coping with personal difficulties, identifying how painful experiences enhanced their sensitivity to other people. The importance of high-quality, well-connected relationships was pervasive throughout the master therapist data. In fact, relational characteristics were embedded in other meta-categories, most notably in the Distinctive Clinical Abilities and Therapeutic Alliance meta-categories. We found that, beyond their work with clients, these master therapists strive to interact in a consistent, caring manner across all of their relationships. Whereas some of the master therapists described their role in their family of origin as a major influence on their relational nature, others described not being so relationally oriented when younger and needing to work at it. No matter how they developed these characteristics, the master therapists' relational strengths are now a major resource in their personal and professional lives. This finding supports previous research identifying the significant contribution that therapist's individual characteristics make to the quality of the therapeutic relationship and client outcomes (Ackerman & Hilsenroth, 2003; Del Re, Flückiger, Horvath, Symonds, & Wampold, 2012; Lambert & Barley, 2001; Norcross, 2010).

THERAPEUTIC ALLIANCE

The current findings support the work by Norcross (2011) and Wampold and Imel (2015), who emphasized common factors such as establishment of warmth, rapport, and a therapeutic relationship as being more critical for psychotherapy success than any particular theoretical orientation. The findings also support the work of Horvath and Greenberg (1994) on the importance of the therapeutic alliance. Research consistently demonstrates that the therapeutic alliance is a robust predictor of therapeutic outcome (Horvath & Symonds, 1991; Orlinsky, Rønnestad, & Willutzi, 2004). Employing meta-analytical methodology, Horvath, Del Re, Flückiger, and Symonds (2011) found a moderate relation (r = .27) between therapeutic alliance and outcome from data sources representing more than 14,000 clients. Recently, after an extensive review of the therapeutic alliance, Crits-Christoph, Connolly Gibbons, and Mukherjee (2013) concluded that "studies have generally found evidence that a variety of aspects of the therapeutic relationship (e.g., personal role investment, interactive coordination, expressive attunement, affective attitude) measured in treatment sessions correlate positively with therapy outcomes" (p. 308).

Master therapists in this study emphasized the importance of the therapeutic alliance as well, and their characteristics dovetail with many essential elements (e.g., empathy, personal investment, attunement with the client, and sensitivity-related "timing and dosage" of their interventions) of the therapeutic alliance. We particularly see correspondence with Sullivan et al.'s (2005) qualitative study in which the researchers explored the question of alliance-building of master therapists, resulting in the development of a model containing six categories within two domains: Responding, Collaborating, and Joining (Safe Relationship Domain); and Using Self, Engaging, and Objectivity (Challenging Relationship Domain).

PURSUIT OF DEEP SELF KNOWLEDGE AND GROWTH

Although there is some overlap between Professional Development and this meta-category, there is an important difference. Whereas the Professional Development meta-category emphasized growth in the clinical and professional domains, this meta-category is geared toward rich and profound personal, individual growth and a high level of self-awareness. That is, the Pursuit of Deep Self Knowledge and Growth meta-category emphasizes the importance of intensive reflection in order to learn and grow from experience. This meta-category began as "self-awareness" and was modified and refined as more information was integrated. As more studies were reviewed, what became apparent was that "self-awareness" did not capture the vigor and intense curiosity with which the master therapists pursued discovering more about themselves. What we found was that self-discovery was a means to improve both personally and professionally. It appears that the effort toward personal growth is not a chore but, rather, pleasurable, and the participants used a variety of creative strategies to accomplish this goal. Also, it appears that the master therapists were aware of how personal growth positively impacted their clinical work. For the master therapists, it seems that who they are and the work they do are inextricably linked, and they attend to developing their *person* of the therapist alongside developing their therapeutic abilities. Again, because therapist variables can have such a significant impact on therapeutic outcomes, it makes sense for therapists to seek diverse strategies for personal growth (Daw & Joseph, 2007) and for training programs to consider how to best assist therapists in developing all aspects of the self (Aponte et al., 2009). A qualitative study of 10 highly resilient therapists (Hou & Skovholt, 2016) may give clues regarding strategies for therapist personal growth. The major theme in this study was "a strong web of vibrant connectedness." These therapists are connected to others, self, and areas for their own development.

HUMILITY

For some, the term "master therapist" may conjure descriptions such as arrogant, conceited, and pompous. Contrary to these pejoratives, the master therapists in this QMA were described as down to earth, unassuming individuals who have a healthy perspective on the limits of their importance. Roffman (2013) describes humility as an active response to the client that is not focused on the therapist but, rather, on the client and the relationship. He suggests that a stance of humility allows for increased receptivity by the therapist and a curiosity about what is happening relationally that is part of deep engagement with a client. This concept of humility is reflected in "Theme 10: For the Practitioner There Is a Realignment from Self as Hero to Client as Hero" in the Minnesota N = 100 Qualitative Study of Counselor/Therapist Development (Rønnestad & Skovholt, 2013, p. 159). Humility seems to most often occur with time and is linked to the "series of humiliations" that all practitioners experience over time when even their intense efforts sometimes do not bear fruit. In an exhaustive outcome research study of the work of 70 psychotherapists, Nissen-Lie et al. (2015) found that professional self-doubt was a key variable in more positive client outcomes. For us, the humility and professional self-doubt seem to tap similar therapist qualities.

Although there is limited research on the topic of therapist humility, the relatively new concept of cultural humility is germane to this category. Therapists who exhibit high levels of cultural humility are typically other oriented rather than self-oriented. They are thought to demonstrate a high degree of respect and low levels of superiority about a client's culture and background (Hook, Davis, Owen, Worthington, & Utsey, 2013). Hook et al. developed the Cultural Humility Scale to measure this construct. Through a series of studies, they found that higher degrees of cultural humility positively related to a high-quality therapeutic alliance. In addition, they found that positive gains toward therapy goals were explained by the mediating effect of cultural humility through the working alliance.

The literature on expertise development may also shed light on the important role humility plays in therapist development. Zimmerman (2006) identified a self-regulatory process of expertise development. In this model, self-reflection plays a key role in the motivation to further develop one's abilities. For master therapists, humility may be an important trait that is an impetus for self-reflection, thus feeding motivation for further growth. In addition, Zimmerman identifies failure as inevitable during this process. Experts have a tendency to tolerate failures, making small corrections and adjustments as they learn from their missteps. Again, humility may be an important factor in tolerating failure and using it for further development. Later, when we present our Synthesis Model of Master Therapists from Around the World, we describe how therapist humility may act as a catalyst for personal and professional growth.

EXPERIENCE

The final meta-category supports Wampold and Brown's (2005) research that suggests experience alone as well therapist age, gender, and professional degree account for little of the variance in psychotherapy outcome factors. Our moderate findings on the importance of therapist experience support the extant literature on the impact of experience. That is, it appears that experience is a necessary but not a sufficient ingredient in the formulation of expertise. As Goldberg (1992) states, "Although being an experienced psychotherapist doesn't guarantee us wisdom, it does give us an excellent opportunity for it" (p. 147).

This meta-category supports the work of Ericcson (2006), who suggests that at least 10,000 hours of cultivating one's craft is needed to achieve expertise. Although there are some variations in this length of time, depending on one's area of expertise, 10 years or more is considered necessary for the development of expertise. In addition, it is not the mere passage of time that allows for expertise to develop. Rather, it is effort to engage in deliberate practice over several years that is key to expertise development. Once expertise is attained, it is essential to continue to deliberately practice to maintain expertise and to develop further as an expert. Experts tend to demonstrate high motivation for practice and for deep concentration while engaged in development. This is different than going through the motions of any task-specific behavior and involves continual efforts to identify optimal training activities that support growth in one's abilities. For master therapists, this may mean that each session is treated as an opportunity for deliberate practice, and with each session, development of expertise is building.

CULTURALLY DISTINCT FINDINGS

Many of the previous chapters contained rich, contextual descriptions of each country's cultural and counseling scene. In this section, we comment on some of the more culturally related findings based on our immersion in the transcriptions while analyzing the data. The authors of this chapter include one individual from a non-US background and others who have traveled and interacted with psychologists from various regions of the world. We also humbly claim to be multicultural counseling educators and allies. However, we are cautious, given our US-centric training, that our observations may still be colored by a predominant Western lens in our training and experience and, as such, should be read with this limitation in mind. Some of the examples presented here relate to the divergent themes such as self-doubt listed in Table 8.2, and some are concepts such as humility that are found in the list of meta-categories but appear to have a culturally unique expression and meaning.

It is interesting to note that in Singapore, there was an accentuation on the role of humility to keep the therapists' skills sharp. In addition to the common meaning of humility noted in the meta-category, master therapists in Singapore worried about getting complacent and full of oneself. In fact, there was a self-doubt theme found in the data from the Singapore participants that echoed these fears and seemed to contribute to their drive for excellence. Scholars have long argued about how Singaporean meritocracy has the potential to breed elitism, but the humility demonstrated by these Singapore master therapists reflects Confucian-style humility (Wong, 2013).

We believe the master therapists in the Czech Republic study also demonstrated humility when defining the concept of mastery as a shared effort between the therapist and the client rather than existing primarily in the skills or characteristics of the therapist. In another form of humility, the Czech master therapists emphasized "not standing out" among their colleagues. In fact, when exploring the very idea of research on the topic of master therapists, one of the Czech researchers half-jokingly said "master therapist is an American thing," meaning that such accolades that might set oneself apart from others are frowned upon in the Czech culture. This anecdotal example seems supported by a British psychotherapist who offered a review of Sperry and Carlson's (2014) book on master therapists (Boileau, 2014):

> How *Master Therapists Work* assumes that there is such a thing as a master therapist, backing up its claims in each chapter with extensively referenced global quantitative and qualitative research. Written with an American audience in mind, the authors may be unaware that this in itself presents an interesting challenge to British therapists. Can we be seen in public reading a manual which explains how to achieve mastery when training courses this side of the Atlantic seem to promote the client as expert and the counsellor as, at best, good enough? (p. 326)

Another interesting hypothesis for the reluctance to "stand out" in the Czech Republic is that it may be a remnant of the communist occupation of former Czechoslovakia. One of the researchers explained that the communist occupation was so demoralizing that a "culture of mediocrity" was developed in which demonstrating excellence in one's work could have negative consequences for the individual.

Whereas several studies highlighted the necessity of personal and professional development, participants in the Czech study more commonly referenced the importance of personal therapy. This may be a result of the prevalence of psychodynamic therapy approaches within the country. In addition, Czech master therapists were more measured in their use of self-disclosure. This may be a reflection of the humility described by Czech master therapists, as well as a component of the psychodynamic approach utilized by many of the Czech master therapists.

Another fascinating finding was that in the study performed in Japan, there was a striking emphasis placed on the nonverbal conveyance of therapist messages such as empathy and even an avoidance of too much verbal interaction. As one of the Japanese masters said, "God exists in subtlety." The Japanese master therapists also stated a comfort with leaving the unconscious as unconscious, whereas a therapist from a Western country (e.g., Canada, the United States, Portugal, and the Czech Republic) often strives to bring unconscious material to the client's awareness. Instead, the Japanese master therapists appeared very comfortable with the idea that not all of the unknown can be known. In addition, in Japan, it appears that the idea of paying for psychotherapy is not a popular notion, so Japanese master therapists expressed some pressure to be time-/cost-effective. These therapists were very aware of the expense of therapy and tried to do as much as possible in as short of time as possible—thus, there appeared to be less need to focus on client content and more emphasis on the therapy process.

The Korean master therapist study emphasized the finding that the master therapists in this study had little fear as therapists and enjoyed a high risk-taking tendency. In addition, it was noted that self-disclosure was more common among the Korean master therapists, who were more comfortable with it. It is not clear whether this may be because group therapists were the focus of study or whether there is something unique to Korean culture that might explain these findings, which diverged from those of other master therapist studies. The authors also noted that the therapists in their study frequently received immediate feedback from their group interventions and utilized high levels of concentration. Again, this may be a result of the type of skill necessary of an excellent group therapist.

The Korean study (Kwon & Kim, 2007) was conducted with a population of group therapists, and it is likely that sampling choice had a significant impact on the resulting themes compared to studies with therapists who engaged in more individual work. However, it is also possible that there is something about the particular sociocultural setting that facilitates greater acceptance of group interventions. Perhaps the unique divergent themes that arose from this study reflected a larger culture of belief in collective process over individual decision-making.

Other culturally unique findings include Singapore's embrace of spirituality and diversity. These master therapists were quite comfortable inviting the topic of spirituality into the therapy session. This is not surprising because Singapore prides itself in almost all tourism promotion material as a multireligious country. In fact, one of the pioneer counseling agencies in Singapore started in 1966 was a partnership of two churches in Singapore (Churches Counselling Centre, which is now named Counselling and Care Center) and, today, many providers of psychological services have religious affiliations even though their clientele do not have to necessarily associate with those religions. Japanese master therapists also made references to spiritual concepts and frequently mentioned principles from Buddhism when describing their work. Interestingly, there was little mention of spirituality in the transcriptions of master therapists from Portugal, Canada, the United States, and the Czech Republic. Only as recently as 2007 did the American Psychological Association pass a resolution on religion and religion-based and/or religion-derived discrimination (American Psychological Association, 2007). This reflects years of complicated and uncomfortable juxtapositions where religion has at times been the rationale and justification for prejudice and also the target and victim of prejudice (Donahue & Nielsen, 2005; Hill & Pargament, 2003).

Regarding cultural competency, none of the other countries' master therapists were as vocal as Singapore master therapists regarding the importance of working across cultures and valuing diversity. Singapore master therapists also shared challenges in continuing their professional development due to the low numbers of supervisors available. Moreover, Singapore's small size as a country made it challenging for these therapists to pursue their own therapy due to the belief that "everyone knows everyone" in the field and the potential loss of privacy. Finally, we also noticed that master therapists in Japan and Korea emphasized the importance of having a great mentor. We considered that this may relate to a hierarchical societal structure that prizes the role of elders and thus may make strong mentoring relationships more likely, valuable, or sustainable. The notion of *Senpai* (mentor) and *kohai* (protégé) is a relationship many Japanese grow accustomed to beginning in the schooling years (Davies & Ikeno, 2002). Similarly, respect for the elderly is known to be a virtue in Korean society even as it is fast eroding (Han, 1996).

SYNTHESIS MODEL OF MASTER THERAPISTS FROM AROUND THE WORLD

Throughout the analysis process, we were able to continually refine the meta-categories, striving to make more fine-grained distinctions between categories. The use of the constant comparative method helped to produce these types of distinctions. However, we found that it was impossible to reach a point at which we had completely non-overlapping meta-categories. This could be seen as an indication that our analysis was incomplete, as a limitation of qualitative research methods to produce fine-grained distinctions, or, we posit, as an indication of the interrelationship and inherent complexity of some of these meta-categories. In this section, we first introduce the Synthesis Model of Master Therapists from Around the World (Fig. 8.1). Next, we describe the overlap found among several of the meta-categories during our analysis and offer hypotheses regarding possible connections among the eight meta-categories. Finally, we elaborate on the Synthesis Model of Master Therapists from Around the World that was developed in our advanced/final stage of analysis of the eight meta-categories.

When viewing the Synthesis Model of Master Therapists from Around the World, there are three ways to understand the model. First, each circle in Fig. 8.1 represents one of the eight meta-categories. Second, there are two major clusters of meta-categories, some with observed overlap. The cluster of three meta-categories on the left represent the learning domain—that is, learning processes and opportunities that helped the therapist grow personally and professionally and likely influence (see arrow) the meta-categories clustered to the right. The cluster of four meta-categories on the right represent the therapy domain—that is, therapists' approaches to practice and personal attributes (i.e., Cognitive Complexity and Relational Orientation) that enhance their interventions. Third, the meta-category of Humility is influenced most directly by the Cognitive Complexity and Intricate Conceptualization meta-category and secondarily from other therapy domain meta-categories as well. To complete the loop, the Humility meta-category influences

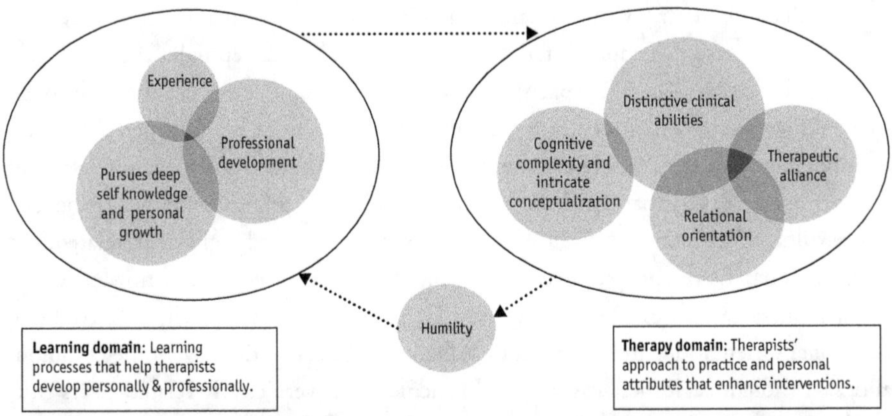

FIGURE 8.1 Synthesis Model of Master Therapists from Around the World and the complexity → humility → development growth loop.

the learning domain meta-categories on the left. We propose that with master therapists, this loop represents a never-ending growth process. Next, we address the overlap found in several of the meta-categories, and later we explain the "growth loop" inherent in our Synthesis Model of Master Therapists from Around the World.

EXPLANATION OF OVERLAP AMONG META-CATEGORIES

As mentioned previously, prior to creating the Distinctive Clinical Abilities meta-category, many of these themes resided in the Relationship Orientation meta-category. Even when the new meta-category was created, many of the Distinctive Clinical Abilities themes still had elements of Relational Orientation and Therapeutic Alliance characteristics. We use the following quote by a Singapore master therapist to illustrate what we view as inextricable overlap:

> It's the ability to follow the client and to lead the client. And dance with the client. You cannot move too far ahead of clients, so the steps must be kind of in sync. I have a client who wanted to work on her issues but each time we come close to it she blocks and she goes off elsewhere. Now there are times when I pursue and then she blocks again. So after a bit I notice that I'm not getting anywhere. And I step back and let her lead and she might start reading her written notes because that was her way of coping with the intensity. So I would then just go along and pick up what she was saying that would help her experience herself positively. I let that tension go down a bit. And then I see if she's ready to engage in something more serious.

In this quote, we see the *clinical abilities* of timing, pacing, and dosage. Moreover, we perceive the *relational orientation* characteristics of respect and patience serving to maintain and enhance the *therapeutic alliance.*

We also found that Distinctive Clinical Abilities had some overlap with the Cognitive Complexity and Intricate Conceptualization meta-category. The main overlap here is related to these master therapists' stated importance of case conceptualization skills and the need for strong cognitive capacities to understand clients' complex issues. Although we could have simply included case conceptualization skills in the Distinctive Clinical Abilities meta-category, we believe the emphasis master therapists placed on these skills set them apart in a way that should be highlighted. Also, the cognitive complexity needed to be skillful at case conceptualization at the expert level seemed highly interrelated.

Professional Development, Experience, and Pursuit of Deep Self Knowledge and Growth meta-categories also overlap, similar to how Distinctive Clinical Abilities, Relational Orientation, and Therapeutic Alliance meta-categories have some commonalities. Although each meta-category held themes that were clearly related to its title, we found that there were some situations in which it was difficult to determine if the reported experience was impactful on a personal level, professional level, or both. It also made sense to us that it is often artificial and simplistic to make distinctions as to the impact of many of life's most formative events (i.e., these formative events can have a pervasive and inextricable impact on both personal and professional selves). In summary, we believe that recognizing the apparent overlap offers a more accurate view of the inherent complexity and interrelatedness of these themes.

COMPLEXITY → HUMILITY → DEVELOPMENT GROWTH LOOP INHERENT IN THE SYNTHESIS MODEL OF MASTER THERAPISTS FROM AROUND THE WORLD

Now we propose a process that illustrates how some of these meta-categories influence each other in ways that advance professional growth. In this process model, the most pivotal meta-category is Humility. The Humility meta-category seems to have connections with several meta-categories, with the strongest related to the Cognitive Complexity and Intricate Conceptualization meta-category. It seems that those who are on the "cutting edge" of knowledge realize just how much they still do not know about their field. We hypothesize that because these master therapists "know that they don't know," their appreciation of the complexity inherent in the human condition serves to keep them humble. In addition, dealing with the elusive and complex nature of human problems puts the master therapists face to face with their limits and increases humility as well. These therapists, we posit, are acutely aware of their limitations and the complexity they are up against, and they realize that they need to continue placing themselves in new learning situations in order to continue to develop professionally and stay sharp in their field. In addition, their motivation to improve is likely related to caring and compassion for their clients and wanting to better help them (Relational Orientation).

Humility may also serve as a major avenue for professional growth because it can keep the person open to feedback instead of having a position that "my truth is the truth." There is no need for feedback if one's method is simply how it is done. Professional struggles can be very positive for long-term development. As part of an earlier N = 100 qualitative study, Skovholt and Rønnestad (1995) noted that

> a prerequisite for achieving professional identity is having experienced uncertainty and anxiety, and having experienced the discomfort of not feeling competent. We found in the narratives of all our senior informants . . . the themes of struggle, uncertainty and hardship. (p. 136)

Hence, these master therapists do not view mastery as an end point but, rather, a never-ending process. In short, we believe that the master therapists' healthy sense of humility promotes continued self-reflection, self-assessment, and personal and professional development. A description of the potential mechanism for this cycle of development is provided by Zimmerman (2006), who highlights the importance of covert cognitive and affective processes embedded in self-reflective-based development cycles.

The final area of influence noted in the synthesis model is the impact of Professional Development on Distinctive Clinical Abilities. We believe that the many ways these master therapists develop professionally (e.g., continuing education units, teaching, supervision, peer consultation, and personal therapy) lead to specific clinical abilities. Once engaged in providing therapy with clients, master therapists try new interventions and strategies acquired through professional development. Here is where additional feedback on the impact and effectiveness of one's work can be gathered. Miller, Hubble, and Duncan (2007) focused on the findings from the expertise literature on the importance of constantly attending to feedback regarding one's performance, regardless of experience and level of competence, arguing that practitioners may feel less compelled to request this feedback after they have reached a certain level of competency. In contrast, expert clinicians show intentional effort toward uncovering problems in the therapeutic relationship earlier rather than later (Miller et al., 2007). Similarly, in our theorized growth loop, master therapists realize some interventions could have gone more smoothly or produced better outcomes, and they genuinely strive to recognize their weaknesses and limitations. We believe this honest appraisal is facilitated by their humility and then leads to continued movement around the "growth loop."

Inspired by Hirai and Goh's spiral developmental model of Japanese master therapists presented in Chapter 6, we also use a spiral to represent therapist growth. The major difference between the spiral models is that Hirai and Goh emphasize the influence of mentors in the expert therapist's development whereas we hypothesize that the complexity—humility interaction is a major catalyst in expert therapist development. We put forth that striving for psychotherapy mastery is a never-ending, intensely stimulating, yet humbling process and, from a three-dimensional perspective, may be conceptualized as an upward developmental spiral (Fig. 8.2). The spiral model helps to illustrate

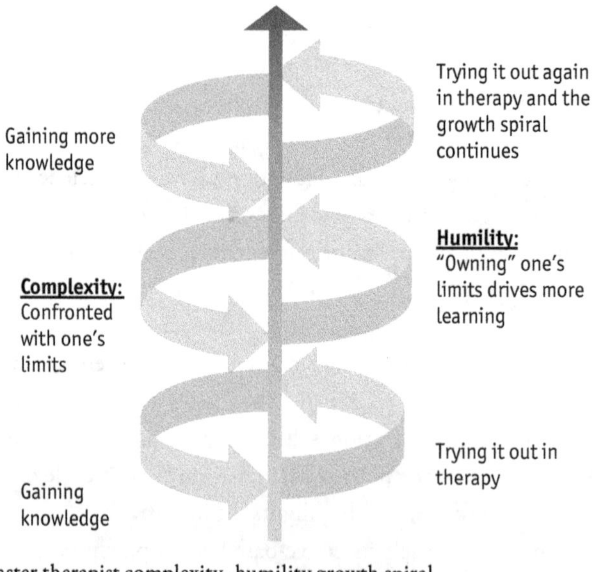

FIGURE 8.2 Master therapist complexity–humility growth spiral.

the increasing expertise that is the result of the complexity → humility → development growth loop.

IMPLICATIONS FOR TRAINING

The current QMA provides some suggestions for how counseling and therapy professions can train therapists to reach the heights of their abilities and strive for mastery in order to best serve their clients. First, it is important to acknowledge that therapist training programs cannot turn out "master therapists" upon graduation. Experience, deep self-knowledge over time, and failure are all necessary components of mastery and may be beyond the scope of what can be accomplished in a few years. Graduate programs are tasked with a focus on content learning, basic competencies, tracking measurable progress, and gatekeeping. Therefore, any training endeavor undertaken in graduate programs is more about planting seeds for future self-development. Not all therapists-in-training will become masters, but effective graduate programs and clinical supervisors may assist students in identifying and nurturing the necessary characteristics to develop expertise.

One way training programs may consider using the current findings related to those considered to be on the expertise end of the professional development continuum is to do what Covey (2003) calls "begin with the end in mind" (p. 40). That is, training programs may want to start by identifying salient values and characteristics of seasoned expert therapists. With that perspective in mind, we might ask what are the values and characteristics related to professional growth that these master therapists embrace, and how might we cultivate these in trainees? First and foremost, master therapists are voracious learners. Programs may benefit from exploring the ways in which we as trainers can enhance, rather than impede, students' natural desire for learning. Second, these master therapists have an appreciation for ambiguity and complexity in life. How do we encourage this, especially in a field that often emphasizes manualized approaches, evidenced-based treatments, and environments (graduate training programs) that demand quantitative, measurable evaluations of student competency? It is important to note that we are not suggesting de-emphasizing the importance of accountability or recommending to do away with assessment of skills and knowledge of trainees. However, we are encouraging training programs to find ways to help develop other, broader therapist characteristics that we believe are vital to optimal performance as a therapist (e.g., the ability to self-reflect, openness, caring, self-care, compassion, tolerance for ambiguity, appreciation for complexity, and humility).

In seeking to admit students who will become quality therapists, training programs face an absence of empirical evidence to guide admission decisions (Hill & Knox, 2014). Therefore, quantitative exam cutoff scores, years of experience in the field, or other measures may be used to begin initial screening of applicants. In the experience of the authors, however, as the selection process unfolds, personal characteristics demonstrated by an applicant (either in interviews or in a personal statement) gain more weight in consideration. The provision of psychotherapy is incredibly complex work with ill-defined problems, in the context of unique individual and contextual variables, and it is well understood that tolerating ambiguity is a valuable characteristic for a psychotherapist (Trull & Prinstein, 2012). Given the QMA findings with regard to characteristics such as humility and capacity for cognitive complexity, admission committees may want to increase wariness of applicants who present as overly confident in their current knowledge and abilities. Although there are certainly multiple, nuanced, and cultural impacts on how applicants present themselves to programs for consideration, the international nature of the meta-categories may speak to the ways in which certain personal characteristics transcend culturally bound expectations for training applicants. Given the conceptual link between characteristics such as tolerance for ambiguity and openness to learning, some have argued for a more formal, focused assessment of tolerance for ambiguity to be a part of medical school admissions (Geller, 2013). A similar screening for specific personal characteristics that may influence a student's openness to psychological training, and therefore professional development, may be warranted.

Beyond acquiring the knowledge, skills, and attitudes that reflect the scientific foundations of the profession and a solid grounding in evidence-based practices, students may benefit from training programs that address the process of learning in addition to necessary content. Courses that provide opportunities to experience and reflect upon deeper self-knowledge and that can demonstrate the impact of the self of the therapist on the therapeutic process may help students understand the clinical value of therapist insight and self-development (Skovholt & Starkey, 2010). Strategies that help trainees to recognize, cope with, and embrace ambiguous and complex phenomena, as well as to facilitate professional development and lifelong learning (Elman, Illfelder-Kaye, & Robiner, 2005), may have a greater impact on future learning than factual data that frequently become obsolete (Hall, 2015). The QMA suggests that students would benefit from a safe and challenging learning environment that emphasizes risk-taking, trying new things, and learning from failure. Faculty members and supervisors who model personal and professional advancement by seeking out ongoing challenges in their areas of expertise may help provide a supportive culture designed for optimum risk-taking and growth (Rønnestad & Orlinsky, 2005). Last, we encourage faculty to begin a conversation regarding how to better incorporate training related to these meta-categories.

FUTURE RESEARCH

Although peer nomination has demonstrated good psychometric support (Anastasi & Urbina, 1997) for identifying experts in the seven exploratory studies included in the current QMA, we believe the next stage of expertise research will entail the use of outcome-related measures and multiple criteria to strengthen the selection of master therapists. Hill, Spiegel, Hoffman, Kivlighan, and Gelso (2015) suggest several criteria that can be used to assess expertise: "performance as assessed by relationship expertise and interventions expertise, cognitive processing, client outcomes, experience, reputation, and the person of the therapist" (p. 2). In concert with quantitative studies such as that by Wampold and Brown (2005), it would be powerful to conduct a study in which peer-nominated therapists who consistently produce outstanding results using therapy outcome data are identified and then qualitatively interviewed. The next stage of therapist expertise research, although challenging, will be to employ multiple indices to identify master therapists. We believe that our proposed model of psychotherapy expertise, based on peer nominations, has helped to set the stage for more comprehensive research in this area.

Considering other ways to study psychotherapy expertise, it may be helpful to also identify a group of average therapists—those who perform adequately but are less consistent in obtaining superior results. Then, interview each set of therapists to identify differences in perspective. In addition, it may be useful to engage in case analysis. Research that asks experts to record their thought processes as they make decisions about behaviors while practicing has been useful in identifying how expertise is developed (Zimmerman, 2006). A similar process might be utilized with varied levels of therapists to examine their thought and decision-making processes as they engage in therapeutic endeavors. Also, because much of the expert's actions rely on tacit knowledge, efforts to overcome this limit in future studies are warranted.

LIMITATIONS

One limitation of the qualitative meta-analysis was that our findings emphasized more common (potentially universal) characteristics than cultural characteristics among these international master therapists. This may be due partly to the CQR data analysis team of Western researchers who may have unwittingly perceived more universal versus cultural variables in the data. In addition, we did not specifically group and then compare characteristics between Eastern (Japan, Singapore, and Korea) and Western (United States, Canada, Czech Republic, and Portugal) master therapists. Future research is needed to explore these important comparisons.

A second limitation is that in some instances, peer-nomination processes have been shown to be less effective in identifying experts than other strategies that directly assess abilities prior to determining expertise status (Ericsson, 2006). although there are findings suggesting that peer nomination can also be successful (Anastasi & Urbina, 1997), this remains a limitation of the sampling methods used in all the studies.

Conclusion

When comparing the current findings to those of previous master therapist research, our findings support earlier conceptualizations of mastery, such as the CER model of master

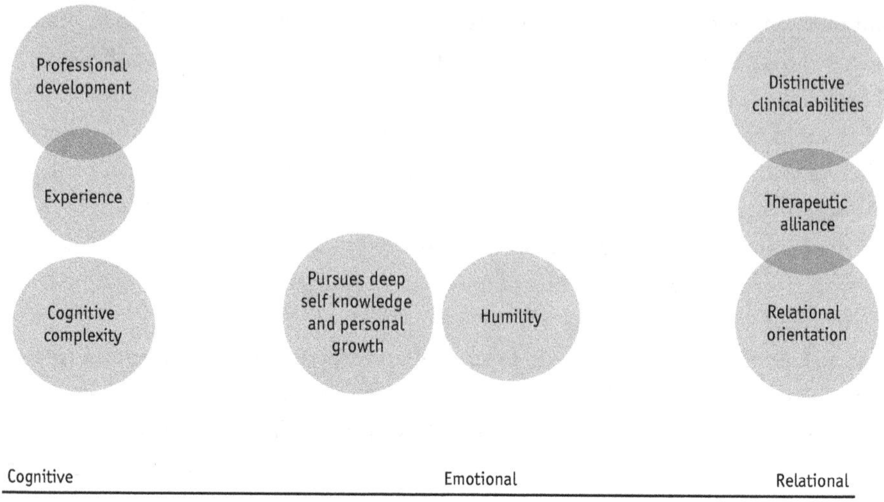

FIGURE 8.3 Comparison of eight meta-categories with the cognitive, emotional, and relational (CER) model of master therapists.

therapists (Jennings & Skovholt, 1999; Jennings et al., 2013; Skovholt et al., 2004). A comparison provided by Fig. 8.3 shows that each of the eight meta-categories aligns well with one of the three domains, supporting the ongoing utility and relevance of the CER model of master therapists.

Our findings also support the psychotherapy research literature in regard to the importance of the therapeutic alliance (Horvath & Greenberg, 1994), cognitive complexity (Owen & Lindley, 2010), professional development (Neimeyer, Taylor, & Philip, 2010), and the person of the therapist (i.e., therapist effect (Baldwin & Imel, 2013)) as major factors for optimal functioning as a psychotherapist. In addition, our findings support the existing literature that indicates that experience is necessary, but not sufficient, for the development of psychotherapy expertise (Wampold & Brown, 2005). An important contribution of our study is an in-depth, global understanding of the personal and professional characteristics of master therapists. A major contribution is the development of the Synthesis Model of Master Therapists from Around the World that emphasizes the importance of the complexity → humility → development growth loop. Finally, the rich narratives that qualitative research provides bring to life the many subtle yet sublime teachings of these master therapists. We hope that you can find some inspiration, affirmation, and benefit from their teachings as well.

REFERENCES

Ackerman, S. J., & Hilsenroth, M. J. (2003). A review of therapist characteristics and techniques positively impacting the therapeutic alliance. *Clinical Psychology Review, 23*(1), 1–33.

American Psychological Association Council of Representatives. (2007, August). *Resolution on religious, religion-based and/or religion-derived prejudice*. Washington, DC: Author.

Anastasi, A., & Urbina, S. (1997). *Psychological testing* (7th ed.). Englewood Cliffs, NJ: Prentice-Hall.

Aponte, H. J., Powell, F. D., Brooks, S., Watson, M. F., Litzke, C., Lawless, J., & Johnson, E. (2009). Training the person of the therapist in an academic setting. *Journal of Marital and Family Therapy, 35*(4), 381–394.

Baldwin, S. A., & Imel, Z. (2013). Therapist effects. In M. J. Lambert (Ed.), *Bergin and Garfield's handbook of psychotherapy and behavioral change* (6th ed., pp. 258–297). New York, NY: Wiley.

Boileau, G. (2014). Book review: How master therapists work: Effecting change from the first through the last session and beyond. *Counselling and Psychotherapy Research, 14*, 326–327. doi:10.1080/14733145.2014.917534 326-327

Carvalho, H. M., & Matos, P. M. (2011a). Ser e tornar-se psicoterapeuta parte I: Diálogo entre experiências pessoais e profissionais [Being and becoming a psychotherapist Part I: Dialogue between personal and professional experiences]. *Psicologia: Ciência e Profissâo, 31*(1), 80–95.

Carvalho, H. M., & Matos, P. M. (2011b). Ser e tornar-se psicoterapeuta parte II: Diálogo entre mudanças pessoais e profissionais [Being and becoming a psychotherapist Part II: Dialogue between personal and professional changes]. *Psicologia: Ciência e Profissâo, 31*(4), 778–799.

Chi, M., Glaser, R., & Farr, M. (Eds.). (1988). *The nature of expertise*. Hillsdale, NJ: Erlbaum.

Colvin, G. (2010). *Talent is overrated*. New York, NY: Portfolio Penguin Group.

Corbin, J., & Strauss, A. (2008). *Basics of qualitative research* (3rd ed.). Thousand Oaks, CA: Sage.

Covey, S. (2003). *The seven habits of highly effective people: Personal workbook*. New York, NY: Fireside.

Crits-Christoph, P., Connolly Gibbons, M. B., & Mukherjee, D. (2013). Psychotherapy process–outcome research. In M. J. Lambert (Ed.), *Bergin and Garfield's handbook of psychotherapy and behavior change* (6th ed., pp. 298–340). Hoboken, NJ: Wiley.

Davies, R. J., & Ikeno, O. (2002). *The Japanese mind: Understanding contemporary Japanese culture*. Boston, MA: Tuttle.

Daw, B., & Joseph, S. (2007). Qualified therapists' experience of personal therapy. *Counselling and Psychotherapy Research, 7*(4), 227–232.

Del Re, A. C., Flückiger, C., Horvath, A. O., Symonds, D., & Wampold, B. E. (2012). Therapist effects in the therapeutic alliance–outcome relationship: A restricted-maximum likelihood meta-analysis. *Clinical Psychology Review, 32*(7), 642–649.

Donahue, M. J., & Nielsen, M. E. (2005). Religion, attitudes, and social behavior. In R. F. Paloutizian & C. L. Park (Eds.), *Handbook of the psychology of religion and spirituality* (pp. 274–291). New York: Guilford.

Duffy, R. D., & Dik, B. J. (2013). Research on calling: What have we learned and where are we going? *Journal of Vocational Behavior, 83*, 428–436.

Elman, N. S., Illfelder-Kaye, J., & Robiner, W. N. (2005). Professional development: Training for professionalism as a foundation for competent practice in psychology. *Professional Psychology: Research and Practice, 36*(4), 367–375.

Ericcson, K. A. (2006). The influence of experience and deliberate practice on the development of superior expert performance. In K. A. Ericsson, N. Charness, P. J. Feltovich, & R. R. Hoffman (Eds.), *The Cambridge handbook of expertise and expert performance* (pp. 683–703). New York, NY: Cambridge University Press.

Ericsson, K. A., Charness, N., Feltovich, P., & Hoffman, R. (Eds.). (2006). *The Cambridge handbook of expertise and expert performance*. New York, NY: Cambridge University Press.

Finfgeld, D. (2003). Metasynthesis: The state of the art—So far. *Qualitative Health Research, 13*(7), 893–904.

Geller, G. (2013). Tolerance for ambiguity: An ethics-based criterion for medical student selection. *Academic Medicine, 88*(5), 581–584.

Gerstein, L. H., Heppner, P. P., Ægisdóttir, S., Leung, S. A., & Norsworthy, K. L. (2009). *International handbook of cross-cultural counseling: Cultural assumptions and practices worldwide*. Thousand Oaks, CA: Sage.

Goh, M., Skovholt, T. M., Yang, A., & Starkey, M. (2012). Developing habits of culturally competent practice. In T. M. Skovholt (Ed.), *Becoming a therapist: On the path to mastery* (pp. 79–100). Hoboken, NJ: Wiley.

Goh, M., Starkey, M. T., Skovholt, T. M., & Jennings, L. (2007). *In search of cultural competence in mental health: A study of expert multicultural counselors and therapists*. Unpublished manuscript, University of Minnesota, Minneapolis, MN.

Goldberg, C. (1992). *The seasoned psychotherapist: Triumph over adversity*. New York, NY: Norton.

Hall, J. E. (2015). Licensure and certification. In R. L. Cautin & S. O. Lilienfeld (Eds.), *The encyclopedia of clinical psychology* (pp. 1675–1683). Hoboken, NJ: Wiley Blackwell.

Han, G. (1996). Tradition and modernity in the culture of aging in Korea. *Korea Journal of Population and Aging, 25*(1), 41–57.

Hermans, H. J. M., & Kempen, H. J. G. (1998). Moving cultures: The perilous problems of cultural dichotomies in a globalizing society. *American Psychologist, 53*, 1111–1120.

Hill, C. (Ed.). (2012). *Consensual qualitative research: A practical resource for investigating social science phenomena*. Washington, DC: American Psychological Association.

Hill, C. E., & Knox, S. (2014). Training and supervision in psychotherapy. In M. Lambert (Ed.), *Bergin and Garfield's handbook of psychotherapy and behavior change* (pp. 775–812). Hoboken, NJ: Wiley.

Hill, C. E., Spiegel, S. B., Hoffman, M. A., Kivlighan, D., & Gelso, C. J. (2015, June). *Expertise in psychotherapy revisited*. Paper presented at the 46th International Annual Meeting of Society for Psychotherapy Research, Philadelphia, PA.

Hill, P. C., & Pargament, K. I. (2003). Advances in the conceptualization and measurement of religion and spirituality: Implications for physical and mental health research. *American Psychologist, 58*, 64–74.

Hirai, T. (2010). *Personal and professional characteristics of Japanese master therapists: A qualitative investigation on expertise in psychotherapy and counseling in Japan*. Unpublished doctoral dissertation, University of Minnesota, Minneapolis, MN.

Hook, J. N., Davis, D. E., Owen, J., Worthington, E. L., Jr., & Utsey, S. O. (2013). Cultural humility: Measuring openness to culturally diverse clients. *Journal of Counseling Psychology, 60*(3), 353–366. doi:10.1037/a0032595

Horvath, A., & Greenberg, L. (1994). *The working alliance: Theory, research, and practice* (Wiley Series on Personality Processes). Oxford, England: Wiley.

Horvath, A., & Symonds, B. (1991). Relationship between working alliance and outcome in psychotherapy: A meta-analysis. *Journal of Counseling Psychology, 38*, 139–149.

Horvath, A. O., Del Re, A. C., Flückiger, C., & Symonds, D. (2011). Alliance in individual psychotherapy. *Psychotherapy, 48*(1), 9–16.

Hou, J., & Skovholt, T. M. (2016). *Characteristics of highly resilient therapists*. Manuscript submitted for publication.

Jennings, L., D'Rozario, V., Goh, M., Sovereign, A., Brogger, M., & Skovholt, T. (2008). Psychotherapy expertise in Singapore: A qualitative investigation. *Psychotherapy Research, 18*(5), 508–522.

Jennings, L., Gulden, A., Oien, M., D'Rozario, V., Goh, M., & Skovholt, T. M. (2012). Multicultural knowledge and skills of Singaporean master therapists. *Journal of Asia Pacific Counseling, 2*(2), 133–146.

Jennings, L., & Skovholt, T. M. (1999). The cognitive, emotional, and relational characteristics of master therapists. *Journal of Counseling Psychology, 46*(1), 3–11.

Jennings, L. Skovholt, T. M., Goh, M., & Lian, F. (2013). Master therapists: Explorations of expertise. In M. H. Rønnestad & T. M. Skovholt (Eds.), *The developing practitioner*. New York, NY: Routledge.

Jennings, L., Sovereign, A., Bottorff, N., Mussell, M. P., & Vye, C. (2005). Nine ethical values of master therapists. *Journal of Mental Health Counseling, 27*(1), 32–47.

Lambert, M. J. & Barley, D. E. (2001). Research summary on the therapeutic relationship and psychotherapy outcome. *Psychotherapy: Theory, Research, Practice, Training, 38*(4), 357-361.

Kogan, M. J. (2000). Internationalizing psychology's curriculum. *Monitor on Psychology, 31*(9), 53.

Kwon, K., & Kim, C. (2007). Analysis of the characteristics of Korean master group counselors. *Korean Journal of Counseling, 8*(3), 979–1010.

Leong, R. T. L., & Ponterotto, J. G. (2003). A proposal for internationalizing counseling psychology in the United States: Rationales, recommendations, and challenges. *The Counseling Psychologist, 31*, 381–395.

Lisle, L. (1987). *Portrait of an artist: A biography of Georgia O'Keeffe*. Albuquerque, NM: University of New Mexico Press.

Marsella, A. (1998). Toward a "global-community psychology": Meeting the needs of a changing world. *American Psychologist, 53*, 1282–1291.

Martin, J., Slemon, A. G., Hiebert, B., Hallberg, E. T., & Cummings, A. L. (1989). Conceptualizations of novice and experienced counselors. *Journal of Counseling Psychology, 36*, 395–400.

Menigat, D. J. (2007). Exploring expert counselors spiritual development and how it contributes to their counseling work. *Dissertation Abstracts International: Section B. Humanities and Social Sciences, 68*(7-A), 2830.

Miller, S. D., Hubble, M. A., & Duncan, B. L. (2007). Supershrinks: What's the secret of their success? *Psychotherapy Networkers, 31*(6), 26–35.

Mullenbach, M., & Skovholt, T. M. (2004). Emotional wellness and professional resiliency of master therapists. In T. M. Skovholt & L. Jennings (Eds.), *Master therapists: Exploring expertise in therapy and counseling* (pp. 77–106). Boston, MA: Allyn & Bacon

Neimeyer, G. J., Taylor, J. M., & Cox, D. R. (2012). On hope and possibility: Does continuing professional development contribute to ongoing professional competence? *Professional Psychology: Research & Practice, 43*(5), 476–486. doi:10.1037/a0029613

Neimeyer, G. J., Taylor, J. M., & Philip, D. (2010). Continuing education in psychology: Patterns of participation and perceived outcomes among mandated and nonmandated psychologists. *Professional Psychology: Research and Practice, 41*(5), 435–441.

Nissen-Lie, H. A., Rønnestad, M. H., Høglend, P. A., Havik, O. E., Solbakken, O. A., Stiles, T. C., & Monsen, J. T. (2015). Love yourself as a person, doubt yourself as a therapist? *Clinical Psychology and Psychotherapy, 22*, 317–327, doi:10.1002

Norcross, J. C. (2010). The therapeutic relationship. In B. L. Duncan, S. D. Miller, B. E. Wampold, & M. A. Hubble (Eds.), *The heart and soul of change: Delivering what works in therapy* (2nd ed.). Washington, DC: American Psychological Association.

Norcross, J. C. (Ed.). (2011). *Psychotherapy relationships that work: Evidence-based responsiveness.* New York, NY: Oxford University Press.

Orlinsky, D., Rønnestad, M., & Willutzi, U. (2004). Fifty years of psychotherapy process–outcome research: Continuity and change. In M. Lambert (Ed.), *Bergin and Garfield's handbook of psychotherapy and behavior change* (5th ed., pp. 307–389). New York, NY: Wiley.

Orlinsky, D. E., & Rønnestad, M. H. (2005). *How psychotherapists develop: A study of therapeutic work and professional growth.* Washington, DC: American Psychological Association.

Owen, J., & Lindley, L. D. (2010). Therapists cognitive complexity: Review of theoretical models and development of an integrated approach for training. *Training and Education in Professional Psychology, 4*, 128–137.

Řiháček, T., Kahancová, M., Jennings, L., Roubal, J., & Vybíral, Z. (2015). *Czech master therapists.* Unpublished manuscript.

Roffman, A. E. (2013). Rigor, imagination, humility and love: Systemic wisdom in psychotherapy practice. *Journal of Systemic Therapies, 33*(2), 1–15.

Rønnestad, M. H., & Orlinsky, D. E. (2005). Clinical implications: Training, supervision, and practice. In M. H. Rønnestad & D. E. Orlinsky (Eds.), *How psychotherapists develop: A study of therapeutic work and professional growth* (pp. 181–201). Washington, DC: American Psychological Association.

Rønnestad, M. H., & Skovholt, T. M. (Eds.). (2013). *The developing practitioner.* New York, NY: Routledge.

Schreiber, R., Crooks, D., & Noerager Stern, P. (1997). Qualitative meta-analysis. In J. M. Morse (Ed.), *Completing a qualitative project: Details and dialogue* (pp. 311–328). Thousand Oaks, CA: Sage.

Shy, J. D. (2008). Expert and novice practitioner use of the computer-based test interpretation for the self-directed search: A qualitative analysis. *Dissertation Abstracts International: Section A. Humanities and Social Sciences, 70*(2-A), 476.

Skovholt, T. M., Jennings, L., & Mullenbach, M. (2004). Portrait of the master therapist: The highly functioning self. In T. M. Skovholt & L. Jennings (Eds.), *Master therapists: Exploring expertise in therapy and counseling.* Boston, MA: Allyn & Bacon.

Skovholt, T. M., & Rønnestad, M. H. (1995). *The evolving professional self.* New York, NY: Wiley.

Skovholt, T. M., & Starkey, M. T. (2010). The three legs of the practitioner's learning stool: Practice, research/theory, and personal life. *Journal of Contemporary Psychotherapy, 40*(3), 125–130.

Smith, A. (2008). *Personal characteristics of master couple therapists.* Unpublished doctoral dissertation, University of Alberta, Edmonton, Alberta, Canada.

Sperry, L., & Carlson, J. (2014). *How master therapists work.* New York, NY: Routledge.

Sullivan, M. F., Skovholt, T. M., & Jennings, L. (2005). Master therapists' construction of the therapy relationship. *Journal of Mental Health Counseling, 27*(1), 48–70.

Timulak, L. (2009). Meta-analysis of qualitative studies: A tool for reviewing qualitative research findings in psychotherapy. *Psychotherapy Research, 19*(4–5), 591–600.

Trull, T., & Prinstein, M. (2012). *Clinical psychology.* Belmont, CA: Cengage.

Wampold, B. E., & Brown, G. S. (2005). Estimating variability in outcomes attributable to therapists: A naturalistic study of outcomes in managed care. *Journal of Consulting and Clinical Psychology, 73*(5), 914–923.

Wampold, B. E. & Imel, Z. E. (2015). *The great psychotherapy debate: The evidence for what makes psychotherapy work* (2nd ed.). New York, NY: Routledge.

Wong, B. (2013). Political meritocracy in Singapore: Lessons from the PAP government. In D. A. Bell & C. Li (Eds.), *The East Asian challenge for democracy: Political meritocracy in comparative perspective*. New York, NY: Cambridge University Press.

Zimmerman, B. J. (2006). Development and adaptation of expertise: The role of self-regulatory processes and beliefs. In K. A. Ericsson, N. Charness, P. J. Feltovich, & R. R. Hoffman (Eds.), *The Cambridge handbook of expertise and expert performance* (pp. 705–722). New York, NY: Cambridge University Press.

APPENDIX

The Cognitive, Emotional, and Relational Characteristics of Master Therapists

Len Jennings and Thomas M. Skovholt

We have permission to reprint Journal of Counseling Psychology article.

Journal of Counseling Psychology
1999, Vol. 46, No. 1, 3–11

0022-0167/99/$3.00

The Cognitive, Emotional, and Relational Characteristics of Master Therapists

Len Jennings
University of St. Thomas

Thomas M. Skovholt
University of Minnesota, Twin Cities

Cognitive, emotional, and relational characteristics among 10 peer-nominated master therapists were identified through qualitative research methods. Results suggest that master therapists (a) are voracious learners; (b) draw heavily on accumulated experiences; (c) value cognitive complexity and ambiguity; (d) are emotionally receptive; (e) are mentally healthy and mature and attend to their own emotional well-being; (f) are aware of how their emotional health impacts their work; (g) possess strong relationship skills; (h) believe in the working alliance; and (i) are experts at using their exceptional relational skills in therapy. These findings suggest that researchers studying therapist expertise may want to explore emotional and relational characteristics in addition to an almost exclusive focus on the therapist's cognitive attributes.

In the last few decades, the focus of many researchers has been on identifying the complex factors that go into effective psychotherapy. Factors explored include client variables, therapist variables, client–therapist personality matching, the therapeutic alliance, and "common factors" across various therapeutic modalities (Miller, 1993). In particular, the therapeutic alliance is considered to play a central role in producing effective psychotherapy outcomes (Beutler, Machado, & Neufeldt, 1994; Horvath & Symonds, 1991; Luborsky, McLellan, Woody, O'Brien, & Auerbach, 1985). Sexton and Whiston (1994) stated in the first line of their abstract that "the quality of the counseling relationship has consistently been found to have the most significant impact on successful client outcome" (p. 6).

Assuming that the personal characteristics of the therapist influence the quality of the therapeutic alliance, it may be useful to understand more fully the qualities effective therapists bring to their work. Even more helpful would be to identify the characteristics of master therapists, those considered the "best of the best" among mental health practitioners.

In reviewing the literature on therapist effectiveness, the majority of studies used neophyte therapists or even therapist trainees as subjects. The few investigations that did study experienced therapists revealed scant information on the personal characteristics of effective therapists. Wicas and Mahan (1966) found effective therapists to be more self-controlled and sympathetic toward others compared with less effective therapists. Jackson and Thompson (1971) reported that effective therapists held more positive attitudes toward themselves, clients, most people, and therapy than did ineffective therapists. Studying two therapists intensively, Ricks (1974) found major differences in the success of the two therapists treating disturbed adolescent boys and attributed these differences to therapist personality differences and the handling of countertransference reactions by the two therapists. In a classic study, Orlinksy and Howard (1975) used the data from 890 patient sessions and 470 therapist sessions to focus on subjective reports of therapists and clients about their experiences in therapy. Wiggins and Weslander's (1979) research revealed that highly effective therapists reported greater job satisfaction than did less effective therapists. Luborsky et al. (1985) found a significant relationship between patient outcomes and therapeutic alliance, and stated that "the major agent of effective psychotherapy is the personality of the therapist, particularly the ability to form a warm and supportive relationship" (p. 609). Although Luborsky et al. (1985) asserted that the personality of the therapist is critical in forming therapeutic alliances that make therapeutic successes possible, therapist effectiveness research has yielded only minimal information on what these therapeutic personality characteristics may be.

Even the few studies seeking to define characteristics of master therapists have revealed little. Harrington (1988) found that Diplomates of the American Board of Professional Psychology (defined as master therapists) scored similar to each other on 30 of 37 subscales of the Adjective Check List. With Diplomates sharing 30 descriptors, the results of this study served to cloud, not clarify, the definition of master therapists. Goldberg (1992) interviewed 12 psychiatrists recommended by colleagues as exceptional therapists. Goldberg found that, as a group, these therapists seemed to be sensitive, caring, and dedicated to their clients' welfare and their own personal and professional growth. They seemed pleased by their career choice and reported being helped by a competent mentor and rejuvenated professionally by mentoring others. Finally, Albert (1997) interviewed 12 psychiatrists nominated by their colleagues as expert clinicians and found that the therapists' flexibility,

Len Jennings, Graduate Department of Professional Psychology, University of St. Thomas; Thomas M. Skovholt, Counseling and Student Personnel Psychology Program, University of Minnesota, Twin Cities.

Correspondence concerning this article should be addressed to Len Jennings, Graduate Department of Professional Psychology, Mail MPL 451, 1000 La Salle Avenue, Minneapolis, Minnesota 55403.

sensitivity, ability to create a place of sanctuary for the client, and ability to create a therapeutic alliance were all important in providing effective psychotherapy.

Apart from therapist efficacy, another potential factor in being a master therapist relates to the knowledge and skill base of the therapist and the cognitive processes that help organize and access that knowledge base. Although the literature on therapist expertise is limited, interest has increased in this line of research. Hillerbrand (1989) defined the expert therapist as a person who

> is able to conceptualize clients, integrate factual information into performance, and recognize interpersonal processes. Expertise consists of the cognitive skills of comprehension and problem solving. That is, the ability to identify and understand incoming information and then cognitively process this information for the purpose of reaching a conclusion or solution. (p. 292)

Similar to expertise research in other domains, research on differences between expert and novice therapists suggests that expert therapists have more complex schemata and tend to notice more subtle features of problems than novice therapists (Martin, Slemon, Hiebert, Hallberg, & Cummings, 1989). This promising line of research is not without problems, however. For instance, many of the studies purporting to study therapist expertise use years of experience as the main criterion for judging expertise (Martin et al., 1989; Cummings, Hallberg, Martin, Slemon, & Hiebert, 1990; Kivlighan & Quigley, 1991). However, years of experience has not been found to clearly differentiate levels of expertise (Skovholt, Ronnestad, & Jennings, 1997).

In an attempt to define the term *master therapist* better, the present study focuses on the question, "What are the personal characteristics of master therapists?" More specifically, what are the characteristics of therapists considered outstanding by their professional colleagues? Despite the lack of a clear definition, the term master therapist is used frequently in the mental health lexicon to describe therapists considered to be "the best of the best" among fellow practitioners. Whereas much of psychotherapy research has focused on neophyte therapists (Goldberg, 1992), we believe that a considerable amount can be learned about potentially efficacious therapist characteristics by studying highly experienced, well-regarded therapists across various professional mental health disciplines.

Qualitative methodology was used in this study of master therapists. Many methodologists consider qualitative designs to be the most effective means for exploratory phases of investigation (Hoshmand, 1989; Patton, 1990). Because of the exploratory nature of the current study and the desire to gain a better understanding of a complex human construct (i.e., master therapists), qualitative interviews were chosen as the data-gathering method.

Method

Respondents

Of the 10 master therapists (7 women and 3 men) interviewed, there were 6 PhD psychologists, 3 master's-level social workers, and 1 psychiatrist. All held licenses in their respective fields; some held more than one license. The master therapists ranged in age from 50 to 72 years (M = 59 years, SD = 7.89 years). Their level of experience practicing psychotherapy ranged from 21 to 41 years (M = 29.50 years, SD = 6.62 years). The theoretical orientations of the master therapists were divided into four major camps: psychodynamic therapists (n = 4), family systems therapists (n = 2), integrative therapists (n = 2), and existential-humanistic therapists (n = 2). All of the master therapists were European American. All worked full time in private practice. Overall, their therapy practices included short- and long-term work, with both managed-care and "out-of-pocket" clients who paid fees within the fee structure of the community.

Procedure

In this qualitative study, a purposeful sampling strategy was used to identify master therapists. With purposeful sampling, exemplars of the concept being studied are identified (Patton, 1990). In the present study, well-regarded therapists in a major midwestern metropolitan area were asked to nominate colleagues whom they considered to be master therapists. This type of purposeful sampling is called "snowball sampling." With snowball sampling, "well-situated" people are asked to identify information-rich key informants. Individuals who are repeatedly named by a variety of informants constitute the core subject pool (Patton, 1990).

Reliance on the judgment of peers or colleagues is inherent in the snowball sampling method. Peer nomination techniques have been found to accurately assess personal and interpersonal characteristics for therapists and a wide variety of other subject groups (Cole & White, 1993; Hillerbrand & Claiborn, 1990; Luborsky et al., 1985; Serbin, Lyons, Marchessault, Schartzman, & Ledingham, 1987). For example, on the basis of their research, Luborsky et al. (1985) stated that "therapists are able to identify other potentially effective therapists and to discriminate them from those who are less effective" (p. 609). In the present study, the snowball sampling–peer nomination method continued until therapists ultimately chosen for the sample were distinguished from a larger pool of individuals who received only one or two nominations.

To begin the nomination procedure, three well-regarded practicing psychologists (two male, one female) with a mean of 31 years of therapy experience were chosen as key informants. These three initial key informants were chosen because of their: (a) involvement in the training of therapists; (b) long-standing involvement with the local mental health community; and (c) reputation for being well-regarded therapists. Two of the key informants worked at a major university counseling center and one worked in private practice.

Each key informant was asked to nominate three master therapists within the large metropolitan area of the sample group. Nomination of master therapists was based on the following criteria: (a) This person is considered to be a "master therapist"; (b) this person is most frequently thought of when referring a close family member or a dear friend to a therapist because the person is considered to be the "best of the best"; and (c) one would have full confidence in seeing this therapist for one's own personal therapy. Therefore, this therapist might be considered a "therapist's therapist."

Len Jennings telephoned each person nominated as a master therapist by one of the key informants. In the next step of sample selection, the nominated master therapist was asked to nominate three master therapists using the same criteria. Master therapists were not allowed to nominate themselves.

Patton (1990) recommended that the investigator conclude this sample-gathering method when a point of redundancy and saturation occurs, that is, when certain individuals are repeatedly nominated and few new names emerge. Eight repetitions of the nomination procedure were needed to reach a point of redundancy and saturation. When the nomination process was concluded, a total of 103 different therapists had been nominated as master therapists. Of the 103 therapists nominated, 66 therapists received one nomination, 12 received two nominations, 15 received three nominations, 3 received four nominations, 2 received six nominations, 2 received seven nominations, and the remaining 3 therapists received 10, 12, and 17 nominations, respectively.

A minimum of four nominations was chosen as the cutoff point for the sample group. This break point was chosen so that neither too many nor too few master therapists were interviewed. In choosing between breadth (brief interviews with many subjects) and depth (in-depth interviews with few subjects), we chose what we considered a sufficient number of participants to obtain an adequate balance between breadth and depth. The mean number of nominations for the $N = 10$ sample group was eight (range = 4–17). Overall, the 10 master therapists from the pool of 103 accounted for 36% of the total nominations (77 of 212).

An interview–follow-up design (a first interview set and a follow-up interview set) was selected in an attempt to achieve "validity through dialogue" (Skovholt & Ronnestad, 1995, p. 147). Guba (1978) stated that this methodological approach enhances validity: "Who is in a better position to judge whether the categories appropriately reflect their issues and concerns than the people themselves?" (pp. 56–57).

The principal investigating method was a semistructured interview questionnaire consisting of 16 open-ended questions (see Table 1). Initially, a list of questions was generated partly by Len Jennings drawn from topics illuminated by a literature review on therapist effectiveness (Goldberg, 1992; Harrington, 1988; Jackson & Thompson, 1971; Luborsky et al., 1985; Miller, 1993; Wicas & Mahan, 1966; Wicas & Weslander, 1979) and partly from a list of questions produced by a survey of cohorts from Len Jennings's counseling program. The questionnaire was designed to elicit information concerning the characteristics of master therapists. The counseling students were instructed to think of questions they would like to have answered by a master therapist. After an initial rating process for clarity and salience by three doctoral interns in counseling psychology, the questionnaire was revised. Next, Len Jennings conducted two pilot interviews with experienced therapists using the questionnaire. Then the interview questionnaire was modified once more by the researchers.

The first set of interviews were audiotaped and conducted at the respondent's practice site. Before each interview, Len Jennings explained the purpose of the study, and each respondent signed an informed consent form. Each interview proceeded through the 16 open-ended questions and averaged approximately 90 min in duration.

A necessary step before data analysis was to transcribe verbatim the audiotaped interviews. Because of an equipment malfunction, one of the audiotapes from the first round of interviews was deemed inaudible. The respondent agreed to be interviewed again, and another interview covering the same questions was conducted with that respondent. After the transcripts were completed, Len Jennings listened to each interview while reading the typed transcriptions to ensure the accuracy of the transcriptions.

Analysis of the data was based on inductive analysis (Patton, 1990), which starts with specific observations and builds toward general patterns. The data analysis consisted of organizing the smallest units of data (concepts) into meaningful and progressively broader themes, categories, and domains. The inductive analysis procedure used in this study was a collaborative process in which the researchers, a research assistant, and the master therapists themselves contributed to the analysis of the data. In the beginning stages of the analysis, the researchers and the research assistant identified the concepts and themes. The latter stages of analysis involved the master therapists and the researchers identifying themes and categories.

To begin the data analysis, Len Jennings and the research assistant analyzed each paragraph and wrote one or two words that best represented the concept for that paragraph. Next, each concept was written on one side of a note card with the corresponding supporting data, which was a quote from the respondent on the opposite side. A total of 1,043 concepts were generated from a paragraph by paragraph analysis of the 10 written transcripts. At this stage of analysis, Patton (1990) emphasized identification of important examples, themes, patterns, and natural variation in the data. The 1,043 concepts were then sorted by Len Jennings and the research assistant into many different groupings until themes and categories emerged. From this process, 40 preliminary themes were identified by the researchers and organized under four major categories.

Approximately 2 months after the first interviews were analyzed, a 60-min follow-up interview was conducted with each respondent. The follow-up interview focused on validating and refining prelimi-

Table 1
Interview Questions for Master Therapists

1. How are you different from when you started your career?
2. What distinguishes a good therapist from a great therapist?
3. What do you think are the characteristics of a master therapist?
4. To become a master therapist, does one need years of experience? Explain.
5. Given two equally experienced therapists, why does one become an expert whereas the other remains mediocre?
6. What is particularly "therapeutic" about you?
7. Is there one distinguishing aspect of your expertise?
8. How does your emotional health impact the therapy you do?
9. How does the person you are impact the therapy you do?
10. How do you know when you are doing a good job with a client?
11. Are you helpful with some clients and not others? Explain.
12. Can you estimate what percentage of your clients you have helped?
13. What is psychotherapy?
14. How does psychotherapy heal?
15. How much of psychotherapy is an art versus a science?
16. If there were a recipe for making a master therapist, what ingredients would you include?

nary results derived from an analysis of the first interview data. The follow-up interviews were also audiotaped. During this interview, respondents were asked to evaluate the accuracy of the preliminary data by indicating which themes and categories seemed to fit with their individual experience. Respondents were invited to comment regarding how the results did or did not reflect their experience. Finally, respondents were asked to add any information not yet addressed that they considered relevant in defining the term "master therapist." Quotes that best represented each theme were later transcribed.

On the basis of feedback obtained from respondents during the follow-up interviews, themes and categories were again modified. We included in the results only themes in which the majority of respondents (i.e., 8 of 10) agreed accurately represented their individual experiences, perceptions, and beliefs. Domains as the major organizer were then selected based on themes and categories. Twenty-six themes within eight categories were organized under the following three broad domains: cognitive, emotional, and relational. These domains represent major attribute areas of a master therapist. In the final data analysis by the researchers, the themes were incorporated within the text to describe the categories and another category emerged. The results presented here have nine categories under three domains.

Results

The findings are organized under three domains representing key attribute areas of master therapists: cognitive, emotional, and relational. Within each domain, there are three categories. Next, selected quotes from the respondents are offered as "raw data" to best illustrate both category and domain.

Cognitive Domain

Category 1: Master therapists are voracious learners. Continuous professional development seems to be a hallmark of the master therapist. When speaking about learning and knowing, many respondents used terms such as "hunger" or "thirst." Their voracious appetite for knowledge appears to be an intense source of development. One respondent said:

> I can't stay content in what I know. And I get embarrassed at how much I seek out other learning experiences. My family is forever kidding me about it. Because I do take classes, I still do . . . Oh, my joke is that when I die, they ought to put on my epitaph, "Now her question is answered," like the curiosity of what the death experience would be. So curiosity has been a big thing all my life.

Another respondent shared how a love for learning is a source of renewal:

> [I] go to workshops, give workshops, teach in consultation groups. All those kinds of things that take energy, take interest, take wanting to know more . . . I love getting together with people, reading and talking about what we're reading. Some people don't like that at all, and I just love it . . . It provides constant energy for one thing, and I think what happens in our field is that we can get tired and exhausted. But I think that's one of the things that keeps me feeling high energy, and [it creates] a lot of interest and love for what we do, and it's exciting.

Category 2: Accumulated experiences have become a major resource for master therapists. Over time, the respondents, with an average of 29.5 years of professional experience, have rich life and work experiences upon which they draw in their work. These experiences seem to have increased respondents' depth and competence as human beings and mental health practitioners. The benefits of experience were cited frequently during the interviews. For example, one respondent shared how a returning client noticed the development of character and expertise the respondent had gained over the years:

> I was really lucky just 2 years ago, a fellow whom I had seen 17 years ago called me and said that he wanted to come back into therapy . . . probably about 3 months into it, he said "Boy, you're really different." And I said, "You know what, I'd like to hear it." And it was wonderful. He said, "You've just got so much more of yourself, and there's so much more of you in the room, and I'm getting so much more out of this. You know, my sense of you back then was that you were going by the book." And I was, because that's all I knew how to go by.

Although respondents gained greatly from accumulated experience, most agreed that experience alone did not guarantee optimal professional development. Several respondents shared that it was a commitment and openness to learning from one's experiences that counted. One respondent stated:

> I don't think years of experience by itself does it . . . I might have the same year of experience 20 times. So [one] needs to put that together with good consultation and a good collegial system so that you actually are learning from what you're doing, [learning] more about yourself and about how you are impacting people.

Category 3: Master therapists value cognitive complexity and the ambiguity of the human condition. Respondents do not merely tolerate ambiguity and complexity, they seek it out. One respondent said it would be fun to be a meteorologist and deal with complex systems such as the weather. Another reads about chaos theory as a leisurely pursuit. When therapists are on the "cutting edge" of understanding human life, they are likely to encounter complexity and the unknown. The respondents seemed to welcome the complexity. For example, one respondent said:

> None of us ever arrive when we're in this business of working with people. . . There's always an AIDS, the thing around the corner. There's always that level of complexity. . . And the minute you start thinking things are simple, you better quit [psychotherapy]. That [reminds me of] my favorite quote, by the way: "If the brain was simple enough for us to understand it, we'd be too simple to understand it."

Similarly, respondents use complex and multiple criteria in judging therapy outcomes. Respondents recognize the difficulty of assessing a process as complex as psychotherapy. Like other therapists, respondents look for positive changes in clients' behaviors, cognitions, and feelings as evidence of efficacious therapeutic outcome. However, respondents shared a number of sophisticated and somewhat idiosyncratic methods for judging effective outcome. For example, one respondent said:

> On some levels, I don't think psychotherapy has an end point. I think that successful therapies have continued internally for clients. And I think I wouldn't have known it in the earlier years, but after having practiced so many years, I've had the opportunity to have people who knew me 15 years ago come back because of life circumstances or whatever, and quite clearly they have had an ongoing process with me even though we didn't meet for 15 years. So [psychotherapy] is in some ways a process that activates something internally for people, and I think therapy that truly ends on the last meeting day maybe wasn't psychotherapy.

Emotional Domain

Category 4: Master therapists appear to have emotional receptivity defined as being self-aware, reflective, nondefensive, and open to feedback. Respondents spoke of engaging in personal therapy, peer consultation, and supervision to obtain various sources of feedback to heighten their awareness of themselves and others. Respondents seem to be constantly striving to learn more about their work and themselves. For example, one respondent spoke of a need for continuous self-reflection and feedback:

> [I need to be] fully aware of myself and my own motivational system, what's moving me inside . . . So I get a chance to look at myself on the outside over and over and over again, through personal therapy, through lots of supervision, through ongoing consultation. That helps incredibly.

Their openness to feedback includes feedback from clients. One respondent shared a critical incident in which valuable feedback from a client was offered and received:

> My clients have taught me a lot. Early in my career, I saw a couple for a year, and what she complained about was his drinking. What he was basically saying was "I wouldn't be drinking if you didn't bug me so much." And I knew absolutely nothing about alcoholism at that point. They kind of faded out [of therapy], and I don't blame them when I look back on it because we didn't do much. A year later, she called me to make an appointment, came in, sat down, and said "I just want to tell you face-to-face how destructive you were to us." And that was one of the most powerful things that could have happened. I mean, I am forever grateful. It was incredibly hard to hear, but I had a sense that I had really done a lousy job and there was something about her being strong enough to come back. I was embarrassed. . . . It made a powerful impression. . . . I knew it was true and that I had a lot to learn. And I think that the other part was that I was incredibly impressed with the fact that she had the guts to do it. And I thought, you know, if she had the guts to do it, then I've got the guts to learn from it. . . . It colored my absolute commitment to learn about what I didn't know.

Category 5: Master therapists seem to be mentally healthy and mature individuals who attend to their own emotional well-being. As one indicator of emotional health, respondents strive to act congruently in their personal and professional lives. Many respondents described themselves as congruent, authentic, and honest. For example, one respondent said:

> My integrity or my believability rests on what I do in my work and what I do in my personal life. . . I don't go to work and come home and live a different life. . . I fully require in my personal life and in my professional life a kind of absolute, and in this sense it's rigid but absolute honesty. . . . It's not that you're making a dedication to the client, it's that you're making a dedication to a congruent life. . . . It's a life in which the inside and the outside match. It's when what people think you are, it's who you are.

As another indicator of emotional health, respondents seem to have a healthy perspective on their sense of importance. Respondents displayed a genuine sense of humility and were not self-centered or grandiose in presentation. They appeared to be comfortable with themselves and held a realistic perspective on their importance in the world. In short, respondents seemed to have struck a healthy balance between confidence and humility.

In addition, respondents attend to their well-being through personal therapy and other self-care practices. Respondents take preventive action to protect what they consider their most important therapeutic tool: themselves. They understand that maintaining their emotional well-being is an ongoing process and have found numerous ways to do so, such as with personal therapy, exercise, and the practice of spirituality. One respondent, wanting to be sure of "practicing what one preaches" concerning self-care, said:

> I exercise every day. I try to do what I encourage other folks to do. I have a strong support system. I have a lot of long-term good friends whom I meet with regularly, that I do things with. I have quiet time every day, where I have a chance just to be with myself. I eat well. I would feel really fraudulent to not do [these things]. . . . To not do it would not be good self-care, I think.

Category 6: Master therapists are aware of how their emotional health affects the quality of their work. Respondents are keenly aware of how their emotional health affects their work. One respondent offered a convincing argument for the saliency of the therapist's emotional health when observing the following:

> See, one of my firm beliefs is that the only way, the only hope we have of becoming good therapists is if we're willing to look at our own stuff. Because we can learn all the skills in the world and if we're in this long enough, we learn plenty of skills, but if we haven't gotten our own stuff cleared out of the way, we're going to be acting that out on our clients over and over and over again. . . . [There needs to be a] commitment to getting [our] own psychological shit out of the way, with whatever that's going to take. And the understanding that we have to be willing to do that all of our lives, because practically every hour that we see somebody, there's something hitting on our old stuff.

Relational Domain

Category 7: Master therapists possess strong relationship skills. In their families of origin, many respondents developed skills of listening, observing, and caring for the welfare of others. This may have given the respondents a 10- to 15-year head start on developing relational skills. For example, one respondent said:

> My father would always come to me for solace when he was upset with my mother. My mother would come to me when she was upset with him, and I was always trying to help both

of them. So maybe that created a need to be needed . . . to be there for people [was] well ingrained very early.

In addition, the respondents' own emotional wounds seemed to have increased their sensitivity and compassion to others. Respondents shared personal accounts of suffering and how their experiences increased their sensitivity to others. For example, one respondent said:

> I have been through a hard 5 years, during which time I sold my house, moved into another place, and had my last surviving sibling die of a brain tumor and my mother and an aunt die. So I was picking myself up and kind of holding onto myself for a while. And the interesting thing is, when I was in the most pain, I was a very good therapist. And it was like the bank robbers who sandpaper their skin so that they can really be sensitive to the movements of the machine they are trying to break open. . . . I think I was more sensitive to what my clients were doing.

During the interview process, respondents exuded warmth, respect, caring, and a genuine interest in people. Respondents seem to have highly developed social skills, which enabled them to relate well with others. Perhaps master therapists have a gift for helping clients feel special. One respondent described relationship skills this way:

> Well, I think I have a pretty natural capacity for empathy, which is the starting place for most relationships. The ability to put myself in the other person's shoes and to imagine that even if I haven't lived a life anything like theirs, I have the capacity to imagine what that would be. I am terribly responsible and reliable. I think I create an environment where people can visit pain and count on me to be there, both in terms of time and space, and be predictable . . . I think [empathy and predictability] create a safe environment. People bring in problems that are frightening and abhorrent to themselves and to most people in their lives. I try to create a situation where these problems are approachable, something that can kind of counteract the person's embarrassment or shame or whatever and be able to go on to address the problems. I think the empathy has the effect of helping someone be empathic to themselves.

Category 8: Master therapists believe that the foundation for therapeutic change is a strong working alliance. Although the respondents represented a variety of disciplines and theoretical orientations, all agreed on the necessity of establishing a strong working alliance. One respondent spoke of the relationship's importance:

> Therapy is a real partnership, as I view it. . . I think we generate an alliance that allows us to do what, without it, we could not otherwise do. . . That's where the healing is, in the use of the relationship.

Some spoke of the relationship as therapy itself. For example, one respondent explained:

> The core of psychotherapy to me is the development of that relationship and the connection, and so it's the development of a relationship . . . the purpose of which is to heal or help the other person. . . Psychotherapy is the relationship, as opposed to a technique that I do or whatever else. It's really about forming and working in the in-between.

Moreover, respondents firmly believe in their clients' ability to change, which may instill hope and strengthen the working alliance. Respondents have a deep respect for their clients' right to self-determination and believe that client change is possible. In fact, one respondent explained how change is inevitable:

> The very fact that they're sitting in this office means that they've got a push to make things better, and that's what you have to support all of the time. . . It's a part of the function of the human cell, if you want to get down to that [level]. . . Growth is part of life. So there will always be growth, just like change is a constant; there will always be change. The issue isn't whether there will be change, the issue is whether you can steer it a little bit, you know, help it go in one direction as opposed to another . . . help them choose what direction they want to go, and then help them make it go in that way.

Category 9: Master therapists appear to be experts at using their exceptional relationship skills in therapy. Not only do respondents provide safety and support, but they can also challenge clients when necessary. After establishing a relationship through warmth and safety, respondents seem to be able to address very difficult and painful client issues. Respondents seem to have a strength of character and a personal power that enables them to face tough issues and challenge clients when needed. For example, one respondent said:

> I think that part of the reason that I probably get good feedback has to do with both being supportive and challenging. . . I guess that I'm both gentle and strong, and I can be really soft and compassionate. But if need be, I can also be strong. I'm someone that [a client] can push against and I won't fold over.

Another common characteristic was that respondents expressed no fear of their clients' strong emotions. Respondents expressed their willingness to be with clients during very intense moments. One respondent explained that the therapist can be present with the client's pain only to the degree that the therapist has dealt with his or her own pain:

> If therapists are afraid of their own pain, they cannot stay with their clients in their pain, they'll cut them off. And what the client learns from that, because they pick up on your discomfort, is that there's something wrong with them for having that kind of pain. It's so important not to be afraid of someone's pain.

In addition, respondents seem to have become skilled at the art of timing, pacing, and "dosage" when working with clients. With years of experimenting and learning from mistakes and successes, respondents have a fine-tuned sense of judgment related to the timing and intensity of their interventions. One respondent gave an example of dosage:

> You trust that you won't overrespond or underrespond. You see, if [a client] had gotten mad at me, then I would have pulled back and done something else. Part of it is a gestalt concept of dosage. That you have to put out the right level of experiment. Because if it isn't enough, it is not going to get the adrenaline going and if it is too much, they get overwhelmed.

Discussion

Only a few researchers, such as Harrington (1988), Goldberg (1992), Skovholt and Ronnestad (1995), and Albert (1997), have sought to tap the wealth of knowledge and wisdom that seasoned, well-regarded practitioners possess. Similarly, we sought to identify and illuminate the characteristics of master therapists, those considered the "best of the best" among their professional colleagues.

On the basis of the current findings, it appears that becoming a master therapist is more than just an accumulation of time and experience. The master therapists in this sample seem to continuously capitalize on and proactively develop a number of characteristics in an effort to improve professionally. These master therapists appear to be voracious learners who are open to experience and nondefensive when receiving feedback from clients, colleagues, and others. The master therapists seem to use both experience and intelligence to increase their confidence and comfort when dealing with complexity and ambiguity. In addition, they appear to be quite reflective and self-aware and use these attributes to continue to learn and grow personally and professionally. These master therapists seem to possess emotional maturity and strength of character that come from years of active learning and living. Finally, the master therapists appear to be able to relate superbly with others, which one can assume often leads to a strong working alliance and positive therapeutic outcomes.

There is convergence between the results reported here and those of other research. For example, many of the themes embedded in the nine categories of the present research are similar to the stages and themes presented by Skovholt and Ronnestad (1995). Regarding the qualities which develop competence and expertise, there is strong agreement between the results reported here and other reports in the literature (Colton & Sparks-Langer, 1993; Neufeldt, Karno, & Nelson, 1996; Ronnestad & Skovholt, 1991, 1997; Schon, 1983, 1987; Skovholt & Ronnestad, 1995; Tremmel, 1993; Ward & House, 1998; Worthen & McNeill, 1996). A central tenet in this literature involves an embracing of complexity and reflecting on this complexity in order to grow professionally. The underlying concern here is how to use experience to increase competence and the move toward expertise. The alternative is "misuse of experience," where the practitioner is not impacted by it but just routinely repeats the same process over and over again.

Ward and House (1998) discussed the embracing of complexity in the education and supervision process when they described how professional growth for the practitioner in training comes through "experiencing increased levels of emotional and cognitive dissonance" (p. 23). They add that

> counselors are encouraged to reflect in the moment of action when situations do not present themselves as given, and clinical direction must be constructed from events that are puzzling, troubling, and uncertain (Schon, 1983). It is this recognition of discomfort in response to professional experiences that highlights the reflective learning process and . . . encourages supervisees to willingly explore dissonant counseling experiences. (p. 25)

This emphasis on facing complexity and working through it through reflection is central to the Uncertainty–Certainty Principle of Professional Development (Ronnestad & Skovholt, 1997). Here the supervisor's orientation is to always present a searching stance through the uncertainty while also presenting the certainty of specific techniques and ideas to the novice.

Regarding implications of the present study, we offer the following scenarios, posed as questions, for consideration. Could it be that some therapists have the cognitive ability to understand the dynamics of difficult cases but lack the relationship skills needed to establish a therapeutic alliance with their clients? Could it be that some therapists relate extremely well with their clients, but their own emotional needs interfere with their clients' work? Could it be that some emotionally healthy therapists do not have the cognitive wherewithal to understand the complexity of their clients' problems? On the basis of the present research findings, we propose the CER model of the master therapist: It is hypothesized here that those who go on to become master therapists have developed cognitive (C), emotional (E), and relational (R) domains to a very high level and have all three domains at their service when working with clients. The CER model of the master therapist consists of a blend of this three-legged expertise stool, which includes cognitive attributes (cognitive complexity and voracious appetite for learning), emotional attributes (emotional receptivity and maturity), and relational attributes (interpersonally gifted).

Three suggestions for future research are offered. First, although the therapist expertise research has offered a substantive contribution to the understanding of the cognitive processes of a therapist (Cummings et al., 1990; Hillerbrand & Claiborn, 1990; Kivlighan & Quigley, 1991; Martin et al., 1989), the present findings suggest that therapist expertise researchers expand the definition of expertise to include the emotional and relational domain of the therapist. Again, we suggest that expertise in psychotherapy is much more than a cognitive dimension. The cognitive domain is only one leg of the three-legged expertise stool. We believe that all three legs (i.e., cognitive, emotional, and relational) are needed for a solid base to perform as an expert in psychotherapy (Skovholt, Ronnestad, & Jennings, 1997).

Second, although the present research highlights a number of potentially desirable therapist characteristics, future researchers will want to explore whether master therapists actually achieve better results than other therapists on measures such as establishing a therapeutic alliance, reducing clients' symptoms, and satisfying clients.

Finally, it appears that many of the master therapist characteristics highlighted in this study are related to concepts such as Rogers's (1961) "fully functioning person," Maslow's (1970) "self-actualized" person, Skovholt and Ronnestad's (1995) senior therapist in the integrity stage of therapist development, and Erikson's (1963) ego integrity stage of human development. In the future, researchers may want to explore commonalities between master therapists and highly functioning individuals found in a variety of professional fields, that is, those who have acquired a high level of maturity and wisdom through their experiences. Our study may have tapped personal characteristics resulting from optimal human development, regardless of career field.

The results of this study should be interpreted in light of several limitations. As with any qualitative design, the findings are not generalizable beyond the context of this group because the sampling method focused on an information-rich versus representative participant pool (Patton, 1990). In addition, the sampling method may have excluded some outstanding therapists who are lesser known among their colleagues. Next, although attempts were made to minimize experimenter bias by using a collaborative data analysis between the researchers and the respondents, there was still subjectivity throughout the research process. Another limitation was the lack of diversity in the research sample. Although the sample was fairly representative of the northern state in which the study was conducted, future researchers would do well to incorporate the richness of a diverse participant pool.

If future research replicates our findings, then these characteristics of master therapists may serve as guideposts for therapists and therapist training programs seeking to promote optimal therapist development. For therapists, the results suggest attending to several areas of personal and professional development. Therapists are encouraged to seek out opportunities for continuous learning, feedback, and reflection. Therapists would do well to keep an open mind when dealing with complexity and ambiguity in their work. Therapists are encouraged to attend to their own emotional well-being, seek their own therapy when necessary, and continue to hone their relational skills. Training programs may want to consider elevating the saliency of the personal characteristics of prospective students to a level on par with the emphasis given to the candidate's cognitive abilities (e.g., Graduate Record Exam scores and grade point average). Moreover, training programs can strive to provide a learning environment to develop these desirable characteristics further in their trainees. Overall, the results of this study highlight the importance of developing the emotional domain, the relational domain, as well as the cognitive domain of the therapist.

References

Albert, G. (1997). What are the characteristics of effective psychotherapists? The experts speak. *Journal of Practical Psychology and Behavioral Health, 3,* 36–44.

Beutler, L. E., Machado, P. P., & Neufeldt, S. A. (1994). Therapist variables. In S. L. Garfield & A. E. Bergin (Eds.), *Handbook of psychotherapy and behavior change* (4th ed., pp. 229–268). New York: Wiley.

Cole, D. A., & White, K. (1993). Structure of peer impressions of children's competence: Validation of the peer nomination of multiple competencies. *Psychological Assessment, 5,* 449–456.

Colton, A. B., & Sparks-Langer, G. M. (1993). A conceptual framework to guide the development of teacher reflection and decision-making. *Journal of Teacher Education, 44,* 45–54.

Cummings, A. L., Hallberg, E. T., Martin, J., Slemon, A., & Hiebert, B. (1990). Implications of counselor conceptualizations for counselor education. *Counselor Education and Supervision, 30,* 120–134.

Erikson, E. (1963). *Childhood and society* (2nd ed.). New York: Norton.

Goldberg, C. (1992). *The seasoned psychotherapist.* New York: Norton.

Guba, E. G. (1978). Toward a methodology of naturalistic inquiry in educational evaluation. Los Angeles: University of California, Center for the Study of Evaluation.

Harrington, K. M. (1988). *Personal characteristics of diplomates defined as master therapists.* Unpublished doctoral dissertation, University of Minnesota.

Hillerbrand, E. (1989). Cognitive differences between expert and novices: Implications for group supervision. *Journal of Counseling and Development, 67,* 293–296.

Hillerbrand, E. T., & Claiborn, C. D. (1990). Examining reasoning skill differences between expert and novice counselors. *Journal of Counseling and Development, 68,* 684–691.

Horvath, A. O., & Symonds, B. D. (1991). Relation between working alliance and outcome in psychotherapy: A meta-analysis. *Journal of Counseling Psychology, 38,* 139–149.

Hoshmand, L. L. S. T. (1989). Alternate research paradigms: A review and teaching proposal. *Counseling Psychologist, 17,* 3–79.

Jackson, M., & Thompson, C. L. (1971). Effective counselor: Characteristics and attitudes. *Journal of Counseling Psychology, 18,* 249–254.

Kivlighan, D. M., & Quigley, S. T. (1991). Dimensions used by experienced and novice group therapists to conceptualize group process. *Journal of Counseling Psychology, 38,* 415–423.

Luborsky, L., McLellan, T. A., Woody, G. E., O'Brien, C. P., & Auerbach, A. (1985). Therapist success and its determinants. *Archive of General Psychiatry, 42,* 602–611.

Martin, J., Slemon, A. G., Hiebert, B., Hallberg, E. T., & Cummings, A. L. (1989). Conceptualizations of novice and experienced counselors. *Journal of Counseling Psychology, 36,* 395–400.

Maslow, A. (1970). *Motivation and personality.* New York: Harper & Row.

Miller, L. (1993). Who are the best psychotherapists? *Psychotherapy in Private Practice, 12,* 1–18.

Neufeldt, S. A., Karno, M. P., & Nelson, M. L. (1996). A qualitative study of experts' conceptualization of supervisee reflectivity. *Journal of Counseling Psychology, 43,* 3–9.

Orlinsky, D. E., & Howard, K. I. (1975). *Varieties of psychotherapeutic experience.* New York: Teachers College Press.

Patton, M. Q. (1990). *Qualitative evaluation and research methods* (2nd ed.). Newbury Park, CA: Sage.

Ricks, D. F. (1974). Supershrink: Methods of a therapist judged successful on the basis of adult outcomes of adolescent patients. In D. F. Ricks, M. Roff, & A. Thomas (Eds.), *Life history research in psychopathology.* Minneapolis: University of Minnesota Press.

Rogers, C. (1961). *On becoming a person.* Boston: Houghton Mifflin.

Ronnestad, M. H., & Skovholt, T. M. (1991). En modell for profesionell utvikling og stagnasjon hos tetapeuter og radgivere [A model of the professional development and stagnation of therapists and counselors]. *Tidsskirft for Norsh Psykologforening, 28,* 555–567.

Ronnestad, M. H., & Skovholt, T. M. (1997). Berufliche entwicklung und supervision von psychotherapeuten [Professional development and supervision of psychotherapists]. *Psychotherapeut, 42,* 299–306.

Schon, D. (1983). *The reflective practitioner: How professionals think in action.* New York: Basic Books.

Schon, D. A. (1987). *Educating the reflective practitioner: Toward a new design for teaching and learning in the professions.* San Francisco: Jossey-Bass.

Serbin, L. A., Lyons, J. A., Marchessault, K., Schartzman, A. E., & Ledingham, J. E. (1987). Observational validation of a peer nomination technique for identifying aggressive, withdrawn, and aggressive/withdrawn children. *Journal of Consulting and Clinical Psychology, 55,* 109–110.

Sexton, T. L., & Whiston, S. C. (1994). The status of the counseling relationship: An empirical review, theoretical implications, and research directions. *The Counseling Psychologist, 22,* 6–78.

Skovholt, T. M., & Ronnestad, M. H. (1995). *The evolving professional self.* Chichester, England: Wiley.

Skovholt, T. M., Ronnestad, M. H., & Jennings, L. (1997). In search of expertise in counseling, psychotherapy, and professional psychology. *Educational Psychology Review, 9,* 361–369.

Tremmel, R. (1993). Zen and the art of reflection practice in teacher education. *Harvard Educational Review, 63,* 434–458.

Ward, C. C., & House, R. M. (1998). Counseling supervision: A reflective model. *Counselor Education and Supervision, 38,* 23–33.

Wicas, E. A., & Mahan, T. W. (1966). Characteristics of counselors rated effective by supervisors and peers. *Counselor Education and Supervision, 6,* 50–56.

Wiggins, J. D., & Weslander, D. L. (1979). Personality characteristics of counselors rated as effective or ineffective. *Journal of Vocational Behavior, 15,* 175–185.

Worthen, V., & McNeill, B. W. (1996). A phenomenological investigation of "good" supervision events. *Journal of Counseling Psychology, 43,* 25–34.

Received October 20, 1997
Revision received September 4, 1998
Accepted September 8, 1998 ■

Acknowledgment

The journal office is located at the University of Maryland, College Park, and I wish to thank the Department of Psychology, which has been generous in its support of the journal's activities by providing space, bookkeeping assistance, computer and telephone facilities, and release time for my editorial work.

I am especially grateful to Marge Hyatt for her incredible organizational ability, dedication, patience, and humor in running the day-to-day operations of the journal. I am also grateful to Tim Butler, Deborah Farrell, Shelly Klein, Jody Bailey, Kathleen Sheedy, Katherine Givens, and the staff at the Journals Department of the American Psychological Association for their work in producing the journal.

Gail Hackett and Bruce Wampold have done a superb job as associate editors, providing thoughtful, insightful decisions about manuscripts. Charles D. Claiborn, Lenore Harmon, and Howard E. A. Tinsley have kindly served as action editors for the year 1997 for manuscripts submitted by the current editorial team.

The consulting editors have provided thorough, educational reviews that authors often cite as being helpful. In addition, the following people served as ad hoc reviewers for 1997, giving valuable feedback and new ideas to the review process:

Albert A. Agresti
Frank Baker
Ann W. Barich
John T. Behrens
Lois A. Benishek
Kathleen Bieschke
Sharon Bowman
Michael T. Brown
Paul C. Burnett
Angela M. Byars
Hardin L.K. Coleman
Madonna G. Constantine
Alexandra F. Corning
Rene V. Dawis
Robert J. DeRubeis
Changming Duan
Traci L. Edwardson
Timothy Elliott
Ruth E. Fassinger
Patricia Frazier
Miki Friedlander
Mary Alice Fukuyama
Itamar Gati
Beth R. Golden
Paul A. Gore
Bethany R. Hampton
Colleen Haney
Nancy E. Downing Hansen
Bruce W. Hartman
Laurie Heatherington
William T. Hoyt
Jeanmarie Keim
Richard T. Kinnier
Eric L. Kohatsu
Beverly A. Kopper
Thomas S. Krieshok
Douglas H. Lamb
Richard T. Lapan
Becky J. Liddle
Frederick G. Lopez
Margaretha S. Lucas
Anna Madill
David K. Marcus
Micah L. McCreary
Michael E. McCullough
Paul J. McCusker
Ellen Hawley McWhirter
Timothy P. Melchert
Marie L. Miville
Michael Mobley
Steven J. Morris
Susan L. Morrow
Helen Neville
Michael D. Newcomb
Donald R. Nicholas
L. W. Oliver
Raji Pannu
Michael J. Patton
Trent A. Petrie
M. Carole Pistole
Laurie E. Powers
Dale J. Prediger
Anne M. Regan
Peggy Rios
James B. Rounds
Linda J. Rubin
Roger Segalla
James N. Sells
Thomas L. Sexton
Victoria A. Shivy
Jane M. Simoni
Elizabeth A. Skowron
Cindy Juntunen Smith
Arnold R. Spokane
Anastassios Stalikas
Mark H. Stone
Barbara J. Thompson
Chalmer Thompson
Jay Wade
Elizabeth Nutt Williams
Carrie L. Winterowd
Everett L. Worthington

Name Index

Subject Index

www.ingramcontent.com/pod-product-compliance
Lightning Source LLC
LaVergne TN
LVHW011820200926
848484LV00005B/1260
* 9 7 8 0 1 9 0 2 2 2 5 0 5 *